CIMA

Paper E3

Enterprise Strategy

Study Text

CIMA PUBLISHING

WORKING TOGETHER FOR YOU

ELSEVIER

KAPLAN PUBLISHING

CIMA Publishing is an imprint of Elsevier
The Boulevard, Langford Lane, Kidlington, Oxford, OX5 1GB, UK
225 Wyman Street, Waltham, MA 02451, USA
Kaplan Publishing UK, Unit 2 The Business Centre, Molly Millars Lane, Wokingham, Berkshire
RG41 2QZ

Notice

British Library Cataloguing in Publication Data
A catalogue record for this book is available from the British Library

ISBN 978-0-85732-570-9

Printed and bound in Great Britain

12 13 14 10 9 8 7 6 5 4 3 2 1

Contents

Paper Introduction

Acknowledgements

Every effort has been made to contact the holders of copyright material, but if any here have been inadvertently overlooked the publishers will be pleased to make the necessary arrangements at the first opportunity.

How to Use the Materials

These Official CIMA learning materials brought to you by Elsevier/CIMA Publishing and Kaplan Publishing have been carefully designed to make your learning experience as easy as possible and to give you the best chances of success in your '*Enterprise Strategy'* exam.

The product range contains a number of features to help you in the study process. They include:

- a detailed explanation of all syllabus areas;
- extensive 'practical' materials;
- generous question practice, together with full solutions;
- an exam preparation section, including a suggested approach on how to tackle the pre-seen information, both before and during the exam.

This Study Text has been designed with the needs of home-study and distance-learning candidates in mind. Such students require very full coverage of the syllabus topics, and also the facility to undertake extensive question practice. However, the Study Text is also ideal for fully taught courses.

This main body of the text is divided into a number of chapters, each of which is organised on the following pattern:

- *Detailed learning outcomes* expected after your studies of the chapter are complete. You should assimilate these before beginning detailed work on the chapter, so that you can appreciate where your studies are leading.
- *Step-by-step topic coverage*. This is the heart of each chapter, containing detailed explanatory text supported where appropriate by worked examples and exercises. You should work carefully through this section, ensuring that you understand the material being explained and can tackle the examples and exercises successfully. Remember that in many cases knowledge is cumulative: if you fail to digest earlier material thoroughly, you may struggle to understand later chapters.

- *Activities*. Some chapters are illustrated by more practical elements, such as comments and questions designed to stimulate discussion.
- *Question practice*. The test of how well you have learned the material is your ability to tackle exam style questions. Make a serious attempt at producing your own answers, but at this stage do not be too concerned about attempting the questions in exam conditions. In particular, it is more important to absorb the material thoroughly by completing a full solution than to observe the time limits that would apply in the actual exam.
- *Solutions*. Avoid the temptation merely to 'audit' the solutions provided. It is an illusion to think that this provides the same benefits as you would gain from a serious attempt of your own. However, if you are struggling to get started on a question you should read the introductory guidance provided at the beginning of the solution, where provided, and then make your own attempt before referring back to the full solution.

Having worked through the chapters you are ready to begin your final preparations for the exam. The final three chapters of this Study Text provide you with the guidance you need. It includes the following features:

- How to use the pre-seen information and prepare for the exam.
- Guidance on how to tackle the exam itself.
- An exam standard set of pre-seen information, with detailed analysis and example requirements and answers.
- Revision questions. These are exam standard and should be tackled in exam conditions, especially as regards the time allocation.
- Solutions to the revision questions.
- A sample paper that you can attempt under exam conditions, along with the relevant answers.

You should plan to attempt the sample paper just before the date of the real exam. By this stage your revision should be complete and you should be able to attempt the sample paper within the time constraints of the real exam.

If you work conscientiously through the official CIMA Study Text according to the guidelines above you will be giving yourself an excellent chance of success in your exam. Good luck with your studies!

Icon Explanations

Definition – these sections explain important areas of knowledge which must be understood and reproduced in an exam environment.

Key Point – identifies topics which are key to success and are often examined.

Supplementary reading – indentifies a more detailed explanation of key terms, these sections will help to provide a deeper understanding of core areas. Reference to this text is vital when self studying.

Test Your Understanding – following key points and definitions are exercises which give the opportunity to assess the understanding of these core areas.

Illustration – to help develop an understanding of particular topics. The illustrative exercises are useful in preparing for the Test your understanding exercises.

Exclamation Mark – this symbol signifies a topic which can be more difficult to understand, when reviewing these areas care should be taken.

Study technique

Passing exams is partly a matter of intellectual ability, but however accomplished you are in that respect you can improve your chances significantly by the use of appropriate study and revision techniques. In this section we briefly outline some tips for effective study during the earlier stages of your approach to the exam. Later in the text we mention some techniques that you will find useful at the revision stage.

Planning

To begin with, formal planning is essential to get the best return from the time you spend studying. Estimate how much time in total you are going to need for each subject you are studying for at the Managerial Level. Remember that you need to allow time for revision as well as for initial study of the material. You may find it helpful to read "Pass First Time!" second edition by David R. Harris ISBN 978-1-85617-798-6. This book will provide you with proven study techniques. Chapter by chapter it covers the building blocks of successful learning and examination techniques. This is the ultimate guide to passing your CIMA exams, written by a past CIMA examiner and shows you how to earn all the marks you deserve, and explains how to avoid the most common pitfalls. You may also find "The E Word: Kaplan's Guide to Passing Exams" by Stuart Pedley-Smith ISBN: 978-0-85732-205-0 helpful. Stuart Pedley-Smith is a senior lecturer at Kaplan Financial and a qualified accountant specialising in financial management. His natural curiosity and wider interests have led him to look beyond the technical content of financial management to the processes and journey that we call education. He has become fascinated by the whole process of learning and the exam skills and techniques that contribute towards success in the classroom. This book is for anyone who has to sit an exam and wants to give themselves a better chance of passing. It is easy to read, written in a common sense style and full of anecdotes, facts, and practical tips. It also contains synopses of interviews with people involved in the learning and examining process.

With your study material before you, decide which chapters you are going to study each week, and which weeks you will devote to revision and final question practice.

Prepare a written schedule summarising the above and stick to it!

It is essential to know your syllabus. As your studies progress you will become more familiar with how long it takes to cover topics in sufficient depth. Your timetable may need to be adapted to allocate enough time for the whole syllabus.

Students are advised to refer to the notice of examinable legislation published regularly in CIMA's magazine (Financial Management), the students e-newsletter (Velocity) and on the CIMA website, to ensure they are up-to-date.

The amount of space allocated to a topic in the Study Text is not a very good guide as to how long it will take you. The syllabus weighting is the better guide as to how long you should spend on a syllabus topic.

Tips for effective studying

(1) Aim to find a quiet and undisturbed location for your study, and plan as far as possible to use the same period of time each day. Getting into a routine helps to avoid wasting time. Make sure that you have all the materials you need before you begin so as to minimise interruptions.

(2) Store all your materials in one place, so that you do not waste time searching for items around your accommodation. If you have to pack everything away after each study period, keep them in a box, or even a suitcase, which will not be disturbed until the next time.

(3) Limit distractions. To make the most effective use of your study periods you should be able to apply total concentration, so turn off all entertainment equipment, set your phones to message mode, and put up your 'do not disturb' sign.

(4) Your timetable will tell you which topic to study. However, before diving in and becoming engrossed in the finer points, make sure you have an overall picture of all the areas that need to be covered by the end of that session. After an hour, allow yourself a short break and move away from your Study Text. With experience, you will learn to assess the pace you need to work at.

(5) Work carefully through a chapter, making notes as you go. When you have covered a suitable amount of material, vary the pattern by attempting a practice question. When you have finished your attempt, make notes of any mistakes you made, or any areas that you failed to cover or covered more briefly.

(6) Make notes as you study, and discover the techniques that work best for you. Your notes may be in the form of lists, bullet points, diagrams, summaries, 'mind maps', or the written word, but remember that you will need to refer back to them at a later date, so they must be intelligible. If you are on a taught course, make sure you highlight any issues you would like to follow up with your lecturer.

(7) Organise your notes. Make sure that all your notes, calculations etc can be effectively filed and easily retrieved later.

Structure of subjects and learning outcomes

Each subject within the syllabus is divided into a number of broad syllabus topics. The topics contain one or more lead learning outcomes, related component learning outcomes and indicative knowledge content.

A learning outcome has two main purposes:

(a) To define the skill or ability that a well prepared candidate should be able to exhibit in the examination

(b) To demonstrate the approach likely to be taken in examination questions

The learning outcomes are part of a hierarchy of learning objectives. The verbs used at the beginning of each learning outcome relate to a specific learning objective e.g.

"Evaluate the proposed strategy to expand into the North American market."

The verb **'evaluate'** indicates a level five learning objective.

These verbs are outlined in the first chapter of the text.

PAPER E3
ENTERPRISE STRATEGY

Syllabus overview

Paper E3 continues the integration of skills across functions, but concentrates on developing the knowledge and skills used in designing and implementing strategy. Strategy is developed in a context, and understanding how the organisation's external environment and stakeholders affect strategy development is important. Context and the internal capabilities of the organisation shape the generation and evaluation of strategic options. Implementing strategy involves tools and techniques associated with change management. Finally, the paper requires the application of tools to assist in the evaluation of the performance implications of a given strategy.

Syllabus structure

The syllabus comprises the following topics and study weightings:

A	Interacting with the Competitive Environment	20%
B	Change Management	20%
C	Evaluation of Strategic Options	30%
D	Implementation of Strategic Plans	30%

Assessment strategy

There will be a written examination paper of three hours, plus 20 minutes of pre-examination question paper reading time. The examination paper will have the following sections:

Section A – 50 marks
A maximum of four compulsory questions, totalling fifty marks, all relating to a pre-seen case study and further new unseen case material provided within the examination.

(***Note***: The pre-seen case study is common to all three of the strategic level papers at each examination sitting i.e. Paper E3, P3 and F3).

Section B – 50 marks
Two questions, from a choice of three, each worth twenty five marks. Short scenarios will be given, to which some or all questions relate.

E3 – A. INTERACTING WITH THE COMPETITIVE ENVIRONMENT (20%)

Learning outcomes **On completion of their studies students should be able to:**		**Indicative syllabus content**
Lead	**Component**	
1. evaluate the key external factors affecting an organisation's strategy.	(a) evaluate the impact and influence of the external environment on an organisation and its strategy; (b) recommend approaches to business/government relations and to relations with civil society; (c) discuss the drivers of external demands for corporate social responsibility and the organisation's response; (d) recommend how to manage relationships with stakeholders; (e) recommend how to interact with suppliers and customers.	• Non-market strategy and forms of corporate political activity. [2] • External demands for responsible business practices and ways to respond to these. [3] • Stakeholder management (stakeholders to include government and regulatory agencies, non-governmental organisations and civil society, industry associations, customers and suppliers). [3] • The customer portfolio: Customer analysis and behaviour, including the marketing audit and customer profitability analysis as well as customer retention and loyalty. [13] • Strategic supply chain management. [13] • Implications of these interactions for Chartered Management Accountants and the management accounting system. [13]
2. evaluate the impact of information systems on an organisation.	(a) evaluate the impact of the internet on an organisation and its strategy; (b) evaluate the strategic and competitive impact of information systems.	• The impact of IT (including the internet) on an organisation (utilising frameworks such as Porter's Five Forces, the Value Chain). [11] • Competing through exploiting information (rather than technology), e.g. use of databases to identify potential customers or market segments, and the management of data (warehousing and mining). [12] • Contemporary developments in the commercial use of the internet (e.g. Web 2.0). [11]

E3 – B. CHANGE MANAGEMENT (20%)

Learning outcomes On completion of their studies students should be able to:		**Indicative syllabus content**
Lead	**Component**	
1. advise on important elements in the change process.	(a) discuss the concept of organisational change; (b) recommend techniques to manage resistance to change.	• External and internal change triggers (e.g. environmental factors, mergers and acquisitions, re organisation and rationalisation). [15] • Stage models of change. [16] • Problem identification as a precursor to change. [15] • Cultural processes of change i.e. change within the context of the whole firm. [15]
2. evaluate tools and methods for successfully implementing a change programme.	(a) evaluate approaches to managing change; (b) compare and contrast continuous and discontinuous change; (c) evaluate tools, techniques and strategies for managing the change process; (d) evaluate the role of leadership in managing the change process.	• The importance of managing critical periods of discontinuous change. [15] • Tools, techniques and models associated with organisational change. [16] • Approaches, styles and strategies of change management. [16] • Importance of adaptation and continuous change. [16] • Leading change. [16]
3. recommend change management processes in support of strategy implementation.	(a) evaluate the role of change management in the context of strategy implementation; (b) evaluate ethical issues and their resolution in the context of organisational change.	• Change management and its role in the successful implementation of strategy. [15], [16] • The advantages and disadvantages of different styles of management on the successful implementation of strategy. [16] • Group formation within organisation and its impact on change processes within organisations. [15] • Business ethics in general and the CIMA Code of Ethics for Professional Accountants (Parts A and B) in the context of implementation of strategic plans. [16]

E3 – C. EVALUATION OF STRATEGIC POSITION AND STRATEGIC OPTIONS (30%)

Learning outcomes On completion of their studies students should be able to:		**Indicative syllabus content**
Lead	**Component**	
1. evaluate the process of strategy development.	(a) evaluate the process of strategy formulation; (b) evaluate strategic options; (c) evaluate different organisational structures; (d) discuss the role and responsibilities of directors in the strategy development process.	• Mission statements and their use in orientating the organisation's strategy. [3] • The process of strategy formulation. [1] • The identification and evaluation of strategic options. [8] • Strategic options generation (e.g. using Ansoff's product/market matrix and Porter's generic strategies). [8] • Real Options as a tool for strategic analysis. ***Note:*** Complex numerical questions will not be set. [8] • Scenario planning and long range planning as tools in strategic decision-making. [7] • Game theoretic approaches to strategic planning and decision-making. ***Note:*** Complex numerical questions will not be set. [8] • Acquisition, divestment, rationalisation and relocations strategies and their place in the strategic plan. [8] • The relationship between strategy and organisational structure. [10] • The role and responsibilities of directors in making strategic decisions (including issues of due diligence, fiduciary responsibilities). [2]
2. evaluate tools and techniques used in strategy formulation.	(a) evaluate strategic analysis tools; (b) recommend appropriate changes to the product portfolio of an organisation to support the organisation's strategic goals; (c) produce an organisation's value chain; (d) discuss both qualitative and quantitative techniques in the support of the strategic decision making function.	• Audit of resources and the analysis of this for use in strategic decision-making. [6] • Forecasting and the various techniques used: trend analysis, system modelling, in-depth consultation with experts (Delphi method). [7] • Management of the product portfolio. [8] • Value chain analysis. [6] • Strategic decision-making processes. [8]

E3 – D. IMPLEMENTATION OF STRATEGIC PLANS AND PERFORMANCE EVALUATION (30%)

Learning outcomes On completion of their studies students should be able to:		**Indicative syllabus content**
Lead	**Component**	
1. evaluate the tools and processes of strategy implementation.	(a) recommend appropriate control measures; (b) evaluate alternative models of performance measurement; (c) recommend solutions to problems in performance measurement; (d) advise managers on the development of strategies for knowledge management and information systems that support the organisation's strategic requirements; (e) recommend changes to information systems appropriate to the organisation's strategic requirements.	• Alternative models of performance measurement (e.g. the balanced scorecard). [9] • Business unit performance and appraisal, including transfer pricing, reward systems and incentives. [10] • Project management: monitoring the implementation of plans. [14] • The implementation of lean systems across an organisation. [14] • Theories of control within organisations and types of organisational structure (e.g. matrix, divisional, network). [10] • Assessing strategic performance (i.e. the use and development of appropriate measures that are sensitive to industry characteristics and environmental factors). [10] • Non-financial measures and their interaction with financial ones. (***Note:*** candidates will be expected to use both qualitative and quantitative techniques). [9] • The purpose and contents of information systems strategies, and the need for strategy complementary to the corporate and individual business strategies. [11] • Critical success factors: links to performance indicators and corporate strategy, and their use as a basis for defining an organisation's information needs. [6]

MATHS TABLES AND FORMULAE

Present value table

Present value of $1, that is $(1 + r)^{-n}$ where r = interest rate; n = number of periods until payment or receipt.

Periods	Interest rates (r)									
(n)	1%	2%	3%	4%	5%	6%	7%	8%	9%	10%
1	0.990	0.980	0.971	0.962	0.952	0.943	0.935	0.926	0.917	0.909
2	0.980	0.961	0.943	0.925	0.907	0.890	0.873	0.857	0.842	0.826
3	0.971	0.942	0.915	0.889	0.864	0.840	0.816	0.794	0.772	0.751
4	0.961	0.924	0.888	0.855	0.823	0.792	0.763	0.735	0.708	0.683
5	0.951	0.906	0.863	0.822	0.784	0.747	0.713	0.681	0.650	0.621
6	0.942	0.888	0.837	0.790	0.746	0.705	0.666	0.630	0.596	0.564
7	0.933	0.871	0.813	0.760	0.711	0.665	0.623	0.583	0.547	0.513
8	0.923	0.853	0.789	0.731	0.677	0.627	0.582	0.540	0.502	0.467
9	0.914	0.837	0.766	0.703	0.645	0.592	0.544	0.500	0.460	0.424
10	0.905	0.820	0.744	0.676	0.614	0.558	0.508	0.463	0.422	0.386
11	0.896	0.804	0.722	0.650	0.585	0.527	0.475	0.429	0.388	0.350
12	0.887	0.788	0.701	0.625	0.557	0.497	0.444	0.397	0.356	0.319
13	0.879	0.773	0.681	0.601	0.530	0.469	0.415	0.368	0.326	0.290
14	0.870	0.758	0.661	0.577	0.505	0.442	0.388	0.340	0.299	0.263
15	0.861	0.743	0.642	0.555	0.481	0.417	0.362	0.315	0.275	0.239
16	0.853	0.728	0.623	0.534	0.458	0.394	0.339	0.292	0.252	0.218
17	0.844	0.714	0.605	0.513	0.436	0.371	0.317	0.270	0.231	0.198
18	0.836	0.700	0.587	0.494	0.416	0.350	0.296	0.250	0.212	0.180
19	0.828	0.686	0.570	0.475	0.396	0.331	0.277	0.232	0.194	0.164
20	0.820	0.673	0.554	0.456	0.377	0.312	0.258	0.215	0.178	0.149

Periods	Interest rates (r)									
(n)	11%	12%	13%	14%	15%	16%	17%	18%	19%	20%
1	0.901	0.893	0.885	0.877	0.870	0.862	0.855	0.847	0.840	0.833
2	0.812	0.797	0.783	0.769	0.756	0.743	0.731	0.718	0.706	0.694
3	0.731	0.712	0.693	0.675	0.658	0.641	0.624	0.609	0.593	0.579
4	0.659	0.636	0.613	0.592	0.572	0.552	0.534	0.516	0.499	0.482
5	0.593	0.567	0.543	0.519	0.497	0.476	0.456	0.437	0.419	0.402
6	0.535	0.507	0.480	0.456	0.432	0.410	0.390	0.370	0.352	0.335
7	0.482	0.452	0.425	0.400	0.376	0.354	0.333	0.314	0.296	0.279
8	0.434	0.404	0.376	0.351	0.327	0.305	0.285	0.266	0.249	0.233
9	0.391	0.361	0.333	0.308	0.284	0.263	0.243	0.225	0.209	0.194
10	0.352	0.322	0.295	0.270	0.247	0.227	0.208	0.191	0.176	0.162
11	0.317	0.287	0.261	0.237	0.215	0.195	0.178	0.162	0.148	0.135
12	0.286	0.257	0.231	0.208	0.187	0.168	0.152	0.137	0.124	0.112
13	0.258	0.229	0.204	0.182	0.163	0.145	0.130	0.116	0.104	0.093
14	0.232	0.205	0.181	0.160	0.141	0.125	0.111	0.099	0.088	0.078
15	0.209	0.183	0.160	0.140	0.123	0.108	0.095	0.084	0.079	0.065
16	0.188	0.163	0.141	0.123	0.107	0.093	0.081	0.071	0.062	0.054
17	0.170	0.146	0.125	0.108	0.093	0.080	0.069	0.060	0.052	0.045
18	0.153	0.130	0.111	0.095	0.081	0.069	0.059	0.051	0.044	0.038
19	0.138	0.116	0.098	0.083	0.070	0.060	0.051	0.043	0.037	0.031
20	0.124	0.104	0.087	0.073	0.061	0.051	0.043	0.037	0.031	0.026

Cumulative present value of $1 per annum, Receivable or Payable at the end of each year for *n* years $\frac{1-(1+r)^{-n}}{r}$

Periods (*n*)	Interest rates (*r*) 1%	2%	3%	4%	5%	6%	7%	8%	9%	10%
1	0.990	0.980	0.971	0.962	0.952	0.943	0.935	0.926	0.917	0.909
2	1.970	1.942	1.913	1.886	1.859	1.833	1.808	1.783	1.759	1.736
3	2.941	2.884	2.829	2.775	2.723	2.673	2.624	2.577	2.531	2.487
4	3.902	3.808	3.717	3.630	3.546	3.465	3.387	3.312	3.240	3.170
5	4.853	4.713	4.580	4.452	4.329	4.212	4.100	3.993	3.890	3.791
6	5.795	5.601	5.417	5.242	5.076	4.917	4.767	4.623	4.486	4.355
7	6.728	6.472	6.230	6.002	5.786	5.582	5.389	5.206	5.033	4.868
8	7.652	7.325	7.020	6.733	6.463	6.210	5.971	5.747	5.535	5.335
9	8.566	8.162	7.786	7.435	7.108	6.802	6.515	6.247	5.995	5.759
10	9.471	8.983	8.530	8.111	7.722	7.360	7.024	6.710	6.418	6.145
11	10.368	9.787	9.253	8.760	8.306	7.887	7.499	7.139	6.805	6.495
12	11.255	10.575	9.954	9.385	8.863	8.384	7.943	7.536	7.161	6.814
13	12.134	11.348	10.635	9.986	9.394	8.853	8.358	7.904	7.487	7.103
14	13.004	12.106	11.296	10.563	9.899	9.295	8.745	8.244	7.786	7.367
15	13.865	12.849	11.938	11.118	10.380	9.712	9.108	8.559	8.061	7.606
16	14.718	13.578	12.561	11.652	10.838	10.106	9.447	8.851	8.313	7.824
17	15.562	14.292	13.166	12.166	11.274	10.477	9.763	9.122	8.544	8.022
18	16.398	14.992	13.754	12.659	11.690	10.828	10.059	9.372	8.756	8.201
19	17.226	15.679	14.324	13.134	12.085	11.158	10.336	9.604	8.950	8.365
20	18.046	16.351	14.878	13.590	12.462	11.470	10.594	9.818	9.129	8.514

Periods (*n*)	Interest rates (*r*) 11%	12%	13%	14%	15%	16%	17%	18%	19%	20%
1	0.901	0.893	0.885	0.877	0.870	0.862	0.855	0.847	0.840	0.833
2	1.713	1.690	1.668	1.647	1.626	1.605	1.585	1.566	1.547	1.528
3	2.444	2.402	2.361	2.322	2.283	2.246	2.210	2.174	2.140	2.106
4	3.102	3.037	2.974	2.914	2.855	2.798	2.743	2.690	2.639	2.589
5	3.696	3.605	3.517	3.433	3.352	3.274	3.199	3.127	3.058	2.991
6	4.231	4.111	3.998	3.889	3.784	3.685	3.589	3.498	3.410	3.326
7	4.712	4.564	4.423	4.288	4.160	4.039	3.922	3.812	3.706	3.605
8	5.146	4.968	4.799	4.639	4.487	4.344	4.207	4.078	3.954	3.837
9	5.537	5.328	5.132	4.946	4.772	4.607	4.451	4.303	4.163	4.031
10	5.889	5.650	5.426	5.216	5.019	4.833	4.659	4.494	4.339	4.192
11	6.207	5.938	5.687	5.453	5.234	5.029	4.836	4.656	4.486	4.327
12	6.492	6.194	5.918	5.660	5.421	5.197	4.988	7.793	4.611	4.439
13	6.750	6.424	6.122	5.842	5.583	5.342	5.118	4.910	4.715	4.533
14	6.982	6.628	6.302	6.002	5.724	5.468	5.229	5.008	4.802	4.611
15	7.191	6.811	6.462	6.142	5.847	5.575	5.324	5.092	4.876	4.675
16	7.379	6.974	6.604	6.265	5.954	5.668	5.405	5.162	4.938	4.730
17	7.549	7.120	6.729	6.373	6.047	5.749	5.475	5.222	4.990	4.775
18	7.702	7.250	6.840	6.467	6.128	5.818	5.534	5.273	5.033	4.812
19	7.839	7.366	6.938	6.550	6.198	5.877	5.584	5.316	5.070	4.843
20	7.963	7.469	7.025	6.623	6.259	5.929	5.628	5.353	5.101	4.870

FORMULAE

Annuity

Present value of an annuity of $1 per annum, receivable or payable for *n* years, commencing in one year, discounted at *r*% per annum:

$$PV = \frac{1}{r}\left[1 - \frac{1}{[1+r]^n}\right]$$

Perpetuity

Present value of $1 per annum, payable or receivable in perpetuity, commencing in one year, discounted at *r*% per annum:

$$PV = \frac{1}{r}$$

chapter

2

The process of strategy formulation

Chapter learning objectives

Lead	Component
C1. Evaluate the process of strategy development	(a) Evaluate the process of strategy formulation. (d) Discuss the role and responsibilities of directors in the strategy development process.

Indicative syllabus content

- The process of strategy formation.
- The role and responsibility of directors in making strategic decisions (including issues of due diligence, fiduciary responsibilities).

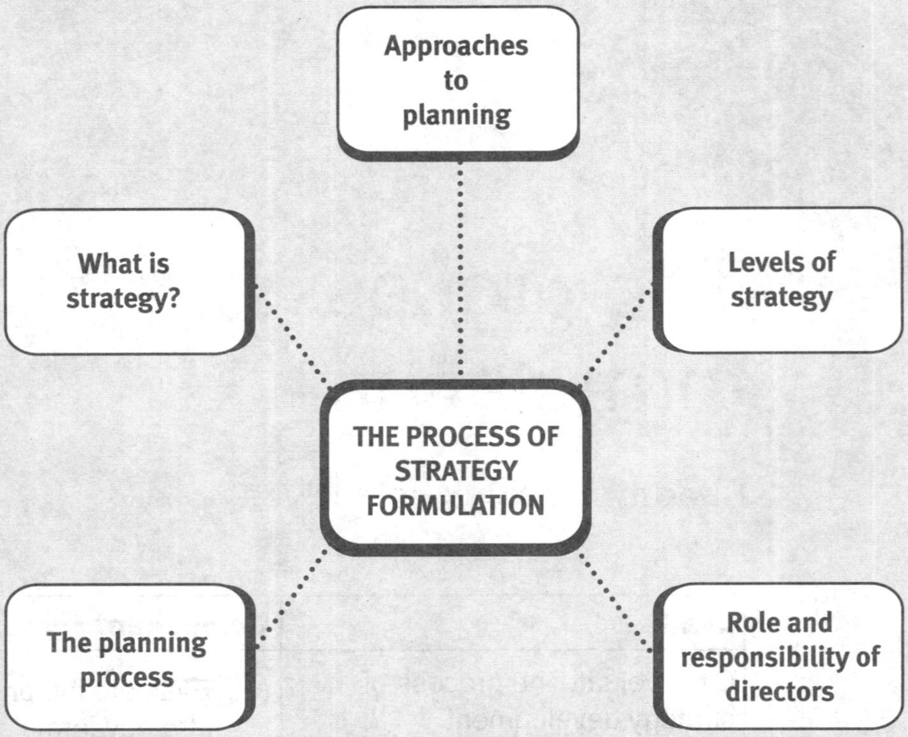

1 Introduction

In this chapter we look at the process of strategy formulation and the role of directors within that process. In the exam you may have to **evaluate** this process so it is vital that you understand the different possible approaches and their relative strengths and weaknesses.

2 What is strategy?

A definition of strategy – provided by Johnson, Scholes and Whittington

'Strategy is the direction and scope of an organisation over the **long term**: which **achieves advantage** for the organisation through its **configuration of resources** within a **changing environment**, to meet the needs of markets and to **fulfil stakeholder expectations**.'

Essentially strategy involves setting the future plans of the organisation, but it requires a comprehensive understanding of the organisation's resources (such as cash, assets and employees), it's environment (such as markets, political and economic issues, customers and competitors) and exactly what the organisation's stakeholders (anyone with an interest in the business, such as shareholders, staff, customers, government, etc) expect of the company.

Another definition is:

'The core of a company's strategy concerns its markets and its products and is about choosing:

(1) **where** to compete – which business segments.

(2) **how** to compete – on what basis shall we compete.'

'A means to achieve a **sustainable competitive advantage'**.

The characteristics of strategic decisions

In their book 'Exploring Corporate Strategy', Johnson, Scholes and Whittington outline the characteristics of strategic decisions. They discuss the following areas:

- Strategic decisions are likely to be affected by the scope of an organisation's activities, because the scope concerns the way the management conceives the organisation's boundaries. It is to do with what they want the organisation to be like and be about.
- Strategy involves the matching of the activities of an organisation to its environment.
- Strategy must also match the activities of an organisation to its resource capability. It is not just about being aware of the environmental threats and opportunities but about matching the organisational resources to these threats and opportunities.
- Strategies need to be considered in terms of the extent to which resources can be obtained, allocated and controlled to develop a strategy for the future.
- Operational decisions will be affected by strategic decisions because they will set off waves of lesser decisions.
- As well as the environmental forces and the resource availability, the strategy of an organisation will be affected by the expectations and values of those who have power within and around the organisation.
- Strategic decisions are apt to affect the long-term direction of the organisation.

In his book 'Competitive Strategy', Michael Porter put it this way:

'The essence of formulating competitive strategy is relating a company to its environment.'

3 The strategic planning process

There are a number of useful diagrams to summarise the strategic planning process.

For instance, this is the **rational model:**

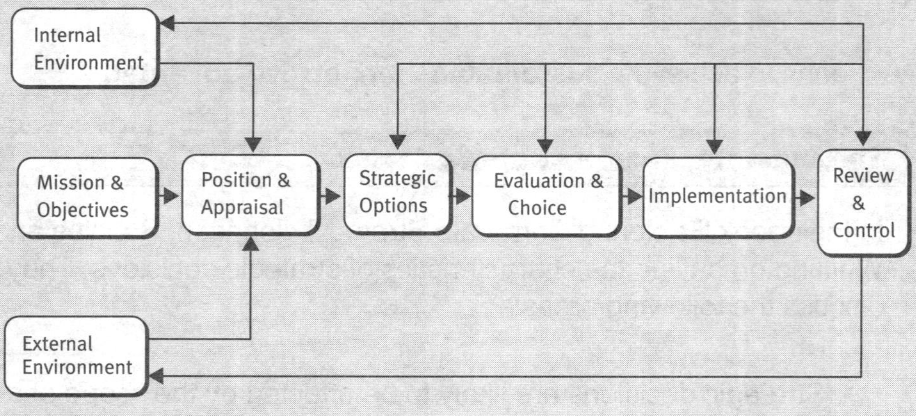

Johnson, Scholes and Whittington took the above stages and grouped them into three main stages:

Strategic analysis

- External analysis to identify opportunities and threats
- Internal analysis to identify strengths and weaknesses
- Stakeholder analysis to identify key objectives and to assess power and interest of different groups
- Gap analysis to identify the difference between desired and expected performance.

↓

Strategic choice

- Strategies are required to 'close the gap'
- Competitive strategy – for each business unit
- Directions for growth – which markets/products should be invested in
- Whether expansion should be achieved by organic growth, acquisition or some form of joint arrangement.

↓

Strategic implementation

- Formulation of detailed plans and budgets
- Target setting for KPIs
- Monitoring and control.

e.g

Illustration 1

A full-price airline in considering setting up a 'no-frills', low-fare subsidiary. The strategic planning process would include the following elements:

Strategic analysis: Competitor action, oil price forecasts, passenger volume forecasts, availability of cheap landing rights, public concern for environmental damage, effect on the main brand.

Strategic choices: Which routes to launch? Set up a subsidiary from scratch or buy an existing low-cost airline? Which planes to use? Which onboard services to offer?

Strategic implementation: How autonomous should the new airline be? How should new staff be recruited and trained? Acquisition of aircraft and obtaining of landing slots.

4 Approaches to planning – rational and emergent strategies

(1) The rational (or traditional) approach

The rational model requires a logical, step-by-step approach. It involves the careful and deliberate formulation, evaluation and selection of strategies for the purpose of preparing a cohesive long-term course of action to attain objectives.

The rational model requires users to follow a set series of stages as shown in the diagram above.

For example, applying a formal rational approach to the analysis/choice/implementation framework of Johnson, Scholes and Whittington, would see:

- strategic analysis being completed before strategic choice, and
- strategic choice being finished before detailed plans for implementation are formulated
- only then would the strategy actually be implemented.

This version of the model is often referred to as the 'three-legged model'.

The first two stages would probably be undertaken once a year in a major planning exercise.

In some versions of the traditional model, 'mission and objectives' come first followed by 'external analysis', 'internal analysis' and 'corporate appraisal'. In others the 'external' and 'internal' analysis stages are followed by 'corporate appraisal' and only then does the business attempt to formulate a mission and objectives.

This rational approach to strategy is often criticised because it ignores the fact that humans are rarely logical and rational and also, short-term changes in the environment often prevent long-term goals being reached and necessitate alterations to the plan.

(2) **The emergent approach**

This approach suggests the strategy tends to emerge rather than be as a result of a logical formal process. It is evolving, continuous and incremental.

A strategy may be tried and developed as it is implemented. If it fails a different approach will be taken. It is likely to be more short term than the traditional process. To attempt to rely on emergent strategies in the longer term requires a culture of innovation where new ideas are readily forthcoming.

In effect the timing, order and distinctions between analysis, choice and implementation become blurred in emergent approaches. For this reason the analysis/choice/implementation approach is sometimes shown as a triangle rather than a straight line.

Problems with deliberate long-term planning

Setting corporate objectives

A criticism frequently levelled at the practice of spelling out corporate objectives is that the exercise descends into the formulation of empty platitudes that offer no positive directional indicators for decision-making. It is too simplistic to suggest that the problem arises from poor planning. It is frequently the case that contradictory objectives are implied by the firm’s long-run strategy and the conflicting interests of key stakeholders – maximising profit for the shareholders may involve employee redundancy as a consequence of restructuring.

Dealing with conflicting stakeholder needs will be discussed in more detail in chapter 3.

The difficulties of forecasting accurately

There are difficult problems associated with trying to accurately forecast for the long term:

- The fact that it is a long-term period.
- The complexity of the environment that needs to be forecast.
- The rapidity and novelty of environmental change.
- The interrelationships between the environmental variables involved.
- The limitations of the data available.
- The amount and complexity of the calculations involved.

Several studies have shown that assessing the likelihood of future events is one of the hardest things that executives are asked to do, and most are not particularly good at it. However, this is only half the problem; even if strategists guess what is going to happen, they still have to devise effective responses and implement them effectively. Writers such as Hannan argue that this is virtually impossible in all but the most stable markets, and argue that good management at least gives a firm a chance to change as things develop, while a long-term strategy might develop the company in inappropriate ways.

Short-term pressures

The pressures on management are for short-term results and ostensibly strategy is concerned with the long term, e.g. 'What should we be doing now to help us reach the position we want to be in, in five years' time?'. Often it is difficult to motivate managers by setting long-term expectations when short-term problems can consume the whole working day. This is particularly true if senior managers are prone to changing their long-term strategy frequently, which may sound contradictory but is in fact rather common.

Rigidity

Operational managers are frequently reluctant to specify their planning assumptions because the situations that their plans are designed to meet may change so rapidly that they can be made to look foolish. Even if a plan is reasonably accurate, the situation might change for reasons other than those forecast. Executives are often held prisoner by the rigidity of the planning process, because plans have to be set out in detail long before the period to which they apply.

The rigidity of the long-term plan, particularly in regard to the rationing and scheduling of resources, may also place the company in a position where it is unable to react to short-term unforeseen opportunities, or serious short-term crisis.

Stifling initiative

If adherence to the strategy becomes all-important, it discounts flair and creativity. Operational managers can generate enthusiasm or dampen down potential trouble spots, and quick action may be required to avert trouble or improve a situation by actions outside the strategy. If operational managers then have to defend their actions against criticisms of acting 'outside the plan', irrespective of the resultant benefits, they are likely to become apathetic and indifferent.

The cost

The strategic planning process can be costly, involving the use of specialists, sometimes a specialist department, and taking up management time. The process generates its own bureaucracy and associated paper or electronic data flow. Personal authorities are, to a greater or lesser extent, replaced by written guidelines.

A plan adds unwarranted comfort

Such writers as Ralph Stacey argue that the main reason that long range plans are popular is that they give security to executives, and allow the deployment of a range of instruments that managers feel comfortable about – budgeting, long-term cash flows, investment appraisal and so on. Consequently the firm is frequently surprised when the real world stubbornly refuses to behave in the way that planners have predicted, and the strategies developed by their techniques have become irrelevant. For Stacey good management is about coping with things that are unexpected and poorly understood, and less about preparing for some anticipated but seldom-realised future.

Why start now?

A general attitude particularly shown by managers in small, growing companies is that they have managed quite successfully in the past without formalised strategic planning systems. So why start now?

Management distrust of techniques

The strategic planning process involves the use of management accounting techniques, not least forecasting, modelling, cost analysis and operational research. This can produce adverse reactions for two reasons. Firstly, senior management may distrust 'laboratory techniques untested in their range of activity', and secondly, they might distrust the recommendations of younger specialist people who are, 'on balance heavy on academic learning but light on practical experience'. It is worth pointing out that it is not only managers in post that distrust many techniques used in long-range strategic management; there are many academics that greatly distrust these models.

The clash of personal and corporate loyalties

The adoption of corporate strategy requires a tacit acceptance by everyone that the interests of departments, activities and individuals are subordinate to the corporate interests. Department managers are required to consider the contribution to corporate profits or the reduction in corporate costs of any decision. They should not allow their decisions to be limited by departmental parameters. It is only natural that managers should seek personal advancement. As a company is the primary vehicle by which this can be achieved, a split of loyalty may occur. A problem of strategic planning is identifying those areas where there may be a clash of interests and loyalties, and in assessing where an individual has allowed vested interests to dominate decisions.

Empirical evidence

If long-range strategy really were as effective as its supporters claim, then it should be possible to produce evidence to demonstrate that companies that adopt a long-range view and planning techniques consistently outperform those that do not. Unfortunately, the result of a large number of studies is inconclusive, with some studies finding some evidence, but many finding none at all. Scott Armstrong's exhaustive review of all the evidence suggested that planning might give a small advantage in some manufacturing environments only, but other writers, Henry Mintzberg in particular, have been extremely critical of the theory and practice on planning.

The problems that strategic planners try to solve are real – adaptation, positioning and resource use, etc are major problems that must be resolved in some way. Thinking about these problems, and taking the most appropriate action, is the best that a firm can hope to achieve. Some firms may be able to do these things through a planning process better than they would have done without one. For other firms the opposite will be the case.

Incrementalism and freewheeling opportunism

Incrementalism (Lindblom)

Lindblom did not believe in the rational model of decision-making as he suggested that in the real world it was not used, citing the following reasons:

- Strategic managers do not evaluate all the possible options open to them but choose between relatively few alternatives.
- It does not normally involve an autonomous strategic planning team that impartially sifts alternative options before choosing the best solution.

- Strategy-making tends to involve small-scale extensions of past policy – 'incrementals' rather than radical shifts following a comprehensive search.

Lindblom believed that strategy-making involving small-scale extensions of past practices would be more successful as it was likely to be more acceptable since consultation, compromise and accommodation were built into the process. He believed that comprehensive rational planning was impossible and likely to result in disaster if actively pursued.

Freewheeling opportunism

Freewheeling opportunists do not like planning. They prefer to see and take opportunities as they arise.

Intellectually, this is justified by saying that planning takes too much time and is too constraining. It is probable that the approach is adopted more for psychological reasons – some people simply do not like planning.

Often such people are entrepreneurs who enjoy taking risks and the excitement of setting up new ventures. However, once the ventures are up and running, the owners lose interest in the day-to-day repetitive administration needed to run a business.

Test your understanding 1

HAA plc is an computer games company that operates in country F. It is planning to expand abroad, into the European market. To support this, HAA has undertaken a detailed review of its existing operations and the European market. This has been used to produce a three-year budget and operational plan for its proposed European operations.

The European electronics market has always been seen as a difficult market for new entrants. This is due to the fast-moving, innovative nature of the companies currently operating there. HAA has a high spend on research and development and its directors feel that the company is well placed to compete with European games manufacturers.

Required:

Evaluate HAA's current approach to strategic planning and suggest more appropriate alternatives.

5 Approaches to planning: accounting-led, market-led or competence-based

While each aspect of strategic analysis is important, firms may prioritise the perspectives in different ways:

(1) **The traditional 'accounting-led' approach**

The accounting-led approach starts by looking at stakeholders and their objectives (e.g. increase EPS by 5% per annum). The emphasis is then on formulating plans to achieve these objectives.

Objectives are very important but this approach is often flawed in so far as objectives are often set in isolation from market considerations and are thus unrealistic.

However, this approach can be particularly useful for not-for-profit organisations where a discussion of mission and objectives is often key.

(2) **The 'market-led' or 'positioning' approach**

The more modern 'positioning' approach starts with an analysis of markets and competitors' actions before objectives are set and strategies developed.

The essence of strategic planning is then to ensure that the firm has a good 'fit' with its environment. If markets are expected to change, then the firm needs to change too. The idea is to be able to predict changes sufficiently far in advance to control change rather than always having to react to it.

The main problem with the positioning approach lies in predicting the future. Some markets are so volatile that it is impossible to estimate further ahead than the immediate short term.

(3) **The 'resource-based' or 'competence-led' approach**

Many firms who have found anticipating the environment to be difficult have switched to a competence or resource-based approach, where the emphasis of strategy is to look at what the firm is good at – its core competences.

Ideally these correlate to the areas that the firm has to be good at in order to succeed in its chosen markets (critical success factors or CSFs) and are also difficult for competitors to copy.

Test your understanding 2

GYU is a large company which manufactures mobile phone handsets. This is an extremely competitive market and GYU has recently been struggling to keep up with other companies in its sector. This is due to the fast-paced nature of the market. New handsets with increasingly complex features are constantly being launched by competitors and the directors of GYU are concerned that the range of handsets manufactured by the company are beginning to look dated.

This has caused a sharp fall in GYU's cash balances and in response, for the first time in its history, GYU has had to cut its dividend. The fall, which was around 10%, was met with an angry response by shareholders and GYU's share price has fallen significantly since the announcement.

While GYU's position appears weak, it is still seen as a market leader in the production of mobile handset software. While the reviews of its handsets are no longer entirely favourable, most customers agree that the software on the mobile phones is significantly superior to that produced by any of GYU's competitors.

Required:

Explain the three different types of approaches to strategy that GYU could use and discuss which you feel is the most appropriate.

6 Levels of strategy

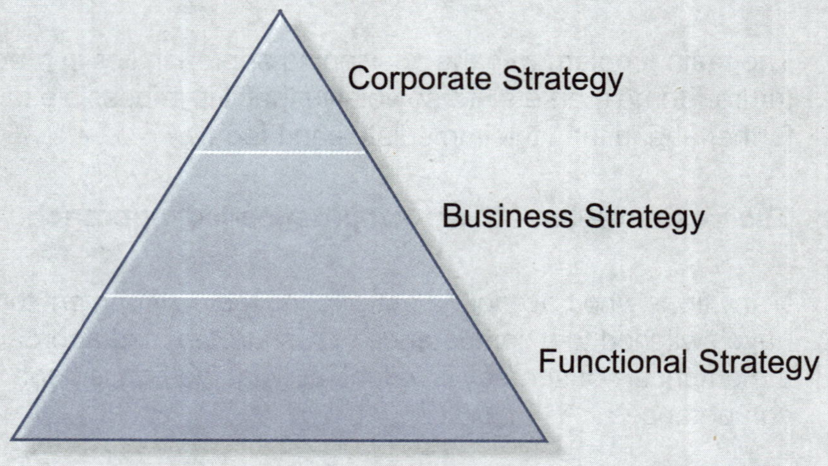

Corporate or Strategic level (which)

It raises the question of **which businesses shall we be in?**

This may involve consideration of acquisition and diversification and will see an organisation being in more than one business.

Corporate strategy is concerned with:

- entering new industries
- leaving existing industries.

Business or management level (how)

Having selected a market, the organisation must develop a plan to be successful in that market. The aim is to compete successfully in the individual markets that the company chooses to operate in.

Business strategy is concerned with how to:

- achieve advantage over competitors
- avoid competitive disadvantage.

Corporate strategy affects the organisation as a whole while business strategy will focus upon **strategic business units (SBUs)**. An SBU will be a unit within an organisation for which there is an external market for products distinct from other units.

Functional or operational level (day to day)

This is concerned with how the component parts of the organisation in terms of resources, people and processes are pulled together to form a strategic architecture which will effectively deliver the overall strategic direction.

Operational strategy is concerned with:

- human resource strategy
- marketing strategy
- information systems and technology strategy
- operations strategy.

These could be unique to the SBU and benefit from being individually focused or the corporate unit may seek to centralise them and so benefit from synergy.

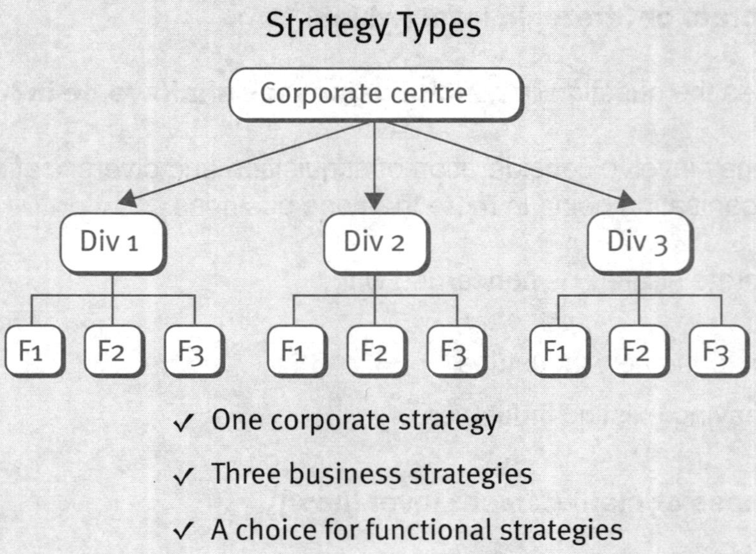

Remember that all three levels are linked. A corporate or business level strategy is only going to succeed if it is supported by appropriate operational strategies.

For instance, a hotel chain may have a high level strategy of 'excellence in customer care', but the success or failure of this will depend on the staff who clean the rooms and cook the meals, etc.

It is worth mentioning that *formulating* the strategy is the easy part. Actually *implementing* it is the difficult part. Premiership football clubs in the UK will all have strategies in place to win their league. Only one will actually do so!

e.g

Illustration 2

Gap is an international clothing retailer. Classification of different levels of planning could be as follows.

Strategic

- Should another range of shops be established to target a different segment of the market? (Gap opened Banana Republic, a more up-market chain to do just that.)
- Should the company raise more share capital to enable the expansion?

Business

- What markets should the new range of shops open in?
- How often should inventories be changed?
- What prices should be charged in the new stores?

Operational

- How will suitable premises be found and fitted out for the new range of shops?
- Which staff should we hire for the new stores?
- Which IT systems need to be installed in the stores?

Whichever approach is chosen, remember that many different types of organisation will need a strategy. This will include companies (large and small), unincorporated businesses, multinational organisations, not-for-profit organisations such as charities, schools and hospitals, etc.

Essentially – anywhere that is likely to have a management accountant is likely to need a strategy. Remember that the exam itself will be based on any of these organisations. Be prepared for a wide range of scenarios!

7 The role and responsibilities of directors

The responsibilities of directors

Directors have a fiduciary duty to shareholders. This means they have been placed in a position of trust and must act in good faith to further the interests of their company, rather than their own interests. They also have a duty to exercise care and skill.

In most discussions the "interests of the company" and those of the shareholders are seen as one and the same. Thus directors should put shareholders' interests first in any and all strategic planning decisions.

This raises a number of key issues that are developed throughout the E3 syllabus:

- How can we ensure that **shareholders'** interests are prioritised? In some respects this is the main theme of corporate governance, discussed later in this chapter.
- What about the interests of other **stakeholder** groups? Stakeholder analysis and the related issues of ethics and corporate social responsibility (CSR) are covered in chapter 2.
- How should the performance of companies, divisions and managers be **measured** to ensure congruence with the objective of maximising shareholder value? Performance measurement is developed in chapters 9 and 10.

Directors' duties in the UK

The complete range of directors' duties and responsibilities varies from one country to another and are usually derived from a mixture of common law, stock exchange regulations, statute and governance regulations.

In the UK, for example, the Companies Act 2006 codifies seven duties:

- the duty to act within powers
- the duty to promote the success of the company
- the duty to exercise independent judgment
- the duty to exercise reasonable care, skill and diligence
- the duty to avoid conflicts of interest and of duties
- the duty not to accept benefits from third parties
- the duty to declare interest in proposed transactions or arrangements.

Company or shareholders?

Directors' duties under company law (as opposed to specific duties under other statutes such as those relating to health and safety or the environment) are owed to the company, rather than directly to an individual shareholder or group of shareholders.

Breaches of those duties can (subject to certain exceptions) be enforced only by the company, not by its shareholders. However, while in most cases shareholders will have the same interests as the company, there can be conflicts if the company, through its directors, is proposing to act in a way which benefits some shareholders to the detriment of others or, indeed, which is seen to benefit the directors. In such circumstances the affected shareholders may be able to take action themselves.

As a general rule, directors should ensure they act fairly towards all shareholders although this will not necessarily mean exact equality of treatment.

Wider stakeholder concerns

Within the second duty listed above – "to promote the success of the company", the Act highlights that directors must have regard (among other things) to certain specific matters, i.e.:

- the likely consequence of any decision in the long term
- the interests of the company's employees
- the need to foster the company's business relationships with suppliers, customers and others

- the impact of the company's operations on the community and the environment
- the desirability of the company maintaining a reputation for high standards of business conduct
- the need to act fairly as between the members of the company.

This is not intended to be an exhaustive list of factors (so matters such as financial profitability and value to shareholders clearly continue to be relevant), but does highlight the need to consider wider stakeholder concerns.

8 Corporate governance

In the Cadbury Report (1992) governance is defined as "the system by which companies are directed and controlled".

This definition has subsequently been expanded to "the system by which companies are directed and controlled in the interests of shareholders and other stakeholders". This expanded definition highlights the agency issues involved and wider concerns over social responsibility.

Purpose and objectives of corporate governance

When talking about governance we make a distinction between purposes and objectives:

- The main purpose of governance is to monitor those parties within the company who control the resources owned by investors.
- The main objective of governance is to contribute to improved performance and accountability in creating long-term shareholder value.

CORPORATE GOVERNANCE

PURPOSES

Primary:

Monitor those parties within a company who control the resources owned by investors.

Supporting:

- Ensure there is a suitable balance of power on the board of directors.
- Ensure executive directors are remunerated fairly.
- Make the board of directors responsible for monitoring and managing risk.
- Ensure the external auditors remain independent and free from the influence of the company.
- Address other issues, e.g. business ethics, corporate social responsibility (CSR), and protection of 'whistleblowers'.

OBJECTIVES

Primary:

Contribute to improved corporate performance and accountability in creating long-term shareholder value.

Supporting:

- Control the controllers by increasing the amount of reporting and disclosure to all stakeholders.
- Increase level of confidence and transparency in company activities for all investors (existing and potential) and thus promote growth.
- Ensure that the company is run in a legal and ethical manner.
- Build in control at the top that will 'cascade' down the organisation.

Further detail on governance

The Board of Directors is responsible for the governance of their companies. This is where strategy is set.

Relevant aims of corporate governance (for E3):

- to increase the **disclosure** to stakeholders in general
- to ensure that companies are **run on ethical grounds** and do not operate illegally
- to provide **increased confidence** in the company for existing and potential investors and thus promote investment in companies and subsequent economic growth
- to increase **transparency** at the board level of operations.

Corporate governance seeks to improve the confidence of stakeholders in the companies that operate within an environment. Better confidence sees improved investment by stakeholder groups.

Key ideas

The latest edition of the code of corporate governance came into force for accounting periods starting on or after 29 June 2010.

The principles of the UK Corporate Governance Code relate to the following areas:

- leadership
- effectiveness
- accountability
- remuneration
- relations with shareholders.

Leadership

- Every company should be **headed by an effective board** which is collectively responsible for the long-term success of the company.
- There should be a **clear division of responsibility** between running the board (the role of the chairman) and running the company's business (the role of the CEO). These two roles should not be held by one individual.
- **Boards should include non-executive directors**, who should constructively challenge and help develop proposals on strategies.
- The Chairman of the Board has the responsibility of achieving a **culture of openness and debate** and ensuring that adequate time is given to discussions.

Effectiveness

- The board and its committees should have an **appropriate balance of skills**, **experience**, independence and knowledge.
- There should be a **formal, rigorous and transparent procedure for the appointment of new directors** to the board.

Accountability

- The board should **present a balanced and understandable assessment** of the company's position and prospects.
- Directors must **publish a statement of their responsibility** for preparing the accounts.
- The board should **conduct a review of the effectiveness of the risk management and internal controls** in the organisation at least annually.

Remuneration

- There should be a **formal and transparent procedure for developing policy on executive remuneration** and for fixing the remuneration packages of individual directors. No director should be involved in deciding his or her own remuneration.
- Executive rewards are to be subject to the recommendations of a **remuneration committee.**

Relations with shareholders

- The board as a whole has a responsibility for ensuring that a satisfactory dialogue with shareholders takes place.
- The board should use the AGM to communicate with investors and to **encourage their participation.**

The implications of governance for strategy

The results of the increasing focus on governance issues are as follows:

- Increasing power of governance bodies.
- Increasing shareholder power, ensuring that companies are run with shareholders' interests prioritised.
- Greater pressure on boards to formulate strategy and be seen to control the businesses concerned.
- Greater scrutiny of quoted businesses, resulting in more short-termism.
- Greater emphasis on risk assessments, so directors may feel pressured to undertake lower-risk (and hence lower-return) projects.
- Greater scrutiny of mergers and acquisitions in particular.

Test your understanding 3 – ADF

ADF is a large national firm that retails clothes direct to the public through a chain of 250 high-street stores in country F.

ADF's executive directors are all employees who have worked their way up through the company. Half of the board is made up of non–executive directors.

The Chairman of the board is a retired director of a major electrical retailer. All of the other non–executive directors are personal friends of his and were appointed on his recommendation.

Only one member of the board is female. All the directors are from country F and between the ages of 45 and 55.

ADF does have a small internal audit department but this is understaffed. The Head of Internal Audit has stated several times that the work undertaken on ADF's stores is minimal and that a number of stores have never been visited by internal audit.

ADF is concerned that its current market is saturated and is looking to expand abroad into neighbouring countries, though the Chairman has expressed concern over this as he feels it is too risky.

Required:

Identify the key weaknesses in ADF's corporate governance. Explain what strategic effect these will have on the company.

9 The role of the management accountant

It is important to appreciate the role of management accountants within the process of developing strategy. Normally this will involve providing information to aid in strategic planning and decision–making.

Strategic management accounting

Strategic management accounting is a 'form of management accounting in which emphasis is placed on information which relates to factors **external** to the entity, as well as non-financial information and internally generated information'.

CIMA Official Terminology

This indicates some key differences between **strategic** and **traditional** management accountants.

External focus

Traditional management accountants tend to focus on internal company issues. This is because their role is, amongst other things, to:

- aid in the creation of operational strategies for the business
- safeguard company assets – both tangible and intangible
- measure and report both financial and non–financial performance to managers
- ensure efficient use of assets and resources.

Strategic management accountants must provide information to help managers make key strategic decisions. This requires a stronger external focus – especially regarding the behaviour of competitors, customers and suppliers. This information will be vital to allow the business to understand the market it is operating in, which is a fundamental part of strategic planning.

Forward-looking

A large part of a traditional management accountant's role is to do with the measurement of historic performance of a business and its divisions.

Strategic management accountants need to be more forward-looking. This is because they will be analysing strategies that the business will employ in the future, rather than looking back at past performance.

Information provided by strategic management accountants

The information provided by strategic management accountants will include:

- **competitor analysis** – identification of competitors and detailed analysis of their activities
- **customer profitability** – which customers are the most important?
- **pricing decision** – forecasting of customer behaviour as well as competitor responses may help the business to decide on product pricing
- **portfolio analysis** – identification of key products and the strategies that should be adopted for each
- **corporate decision support** – this could include helping managers to decide whether or not to launch new products or enter/leave new markets.

A comparison of the information produced by strategic and traditional management accountants may be useful:

Traditional management accountants:	**Strategic management accountants:**
Cost structure	Competitor cost structure
Product costs	Competitor product costs
Market share	Relative market share
Profitability	Relative profitability
Price margins	Competitor price margins

Value of strategic management information

The information produced by strategic management accountants will help the business in a number of ways, including:

- more effective strategic planning
- increased awareness of the business and its environment
- increased control over business performance
- better decision–making

Strategic planning for not-for-profit organisations

Strategic planning

Most of the organisations in exam questions will be profit-seeking companies. However, some may involve charities, councils, schools, hospitals and other organisations where profit is not the main objective. With such an 'NFP' a discussion of objectives is likely to be problematic for the following reasons:

- It is more likely to have multiple objectives. A large teaching hospital may want to give the best quality care and treat as many patients as possible and train new doctors and research new techniques. Conflict is inevitable.

  This is not just an issue for NFPs, profit-seeking organisations also have multiple stakeholders with conflicting demands.

- It will be more difficult to measure objectives. How can one measure whether a school is educating pupils well? Performance in exams? Percentage going on to university? Percentage getting jobs? Percentage staying out of prison once they leave?

- There may be a more equal balance of power between stakeholders. In a company, the shareholders hold ultimate power. If they do not use it, the directors generally get their way. In a school, the balance of power may be more even (or even undefined) between parents, governors, the headmaster and the local education authority.
- The people receiving the service are not necessarily those paying for it. The government and local NHS trusts determine a hospital's funding, not the patients. Consequently there may be pressure to perform well in national league tables at the expense of other objectives.

In spite of these problems, NFPs are still likely to need strategies. In the UK, for example, many public sector organisations have to produce strategic plans for between one and five years ahead as this is a government requirement.

One of the reasons for this is that the public sector is required to hit certain targets and key performance indicators (KPIs), which are set by central government. In a company these targets and KPIs are used to ensure that the business is competitive. For a public sector organisation, they are used by the government to exert control over the activities of the organisation and to ensure that the government's funding is being used appropriately.

For more detail on KPIs, see chapter 6.

The 3Es

Public sector organisations and charities often have difficulty in using traditional private-sector-based approaches to objective setting since they do not make a profit by which their success or failure can be measured. One way to address this problem is to use the following approach.

The 'three **E**s approach' of the Audit Commission:

- **Effectiveness** looks at the outputs (the goal approach). The 'goal approach' looks at the ultimate objectives of the organisation, i.e. it looks at output measures. For example, for an NHS hospital, have the waiting lists been reduced? Have mortality rates gone down? How many patients have been treated?

- **Efficiency** looks at the link between outputs and inputs (the internal processes approach). The 'internal processes approach' looks at how well inputs have been used to achieve outputs – it is a measure of efficiency. For example, what was the average cost per patient treated? What was the average spend per bed over the period? What was the bed occupancy rate that this achieved?
- **Economy** looks solely at the level of inputs, e.g. did the hospital spend more or less on drugs this year? Or on nurses' wages?

The best picture of the success of an organisation is obtained by using all of the above approaches and by examining both financial and non-financial issues. Think about effectiveness meaning 'doing the right things' and efficiency 'about doing things right'.

10 Summary

By the end of this chapter, you should be able to discuss:

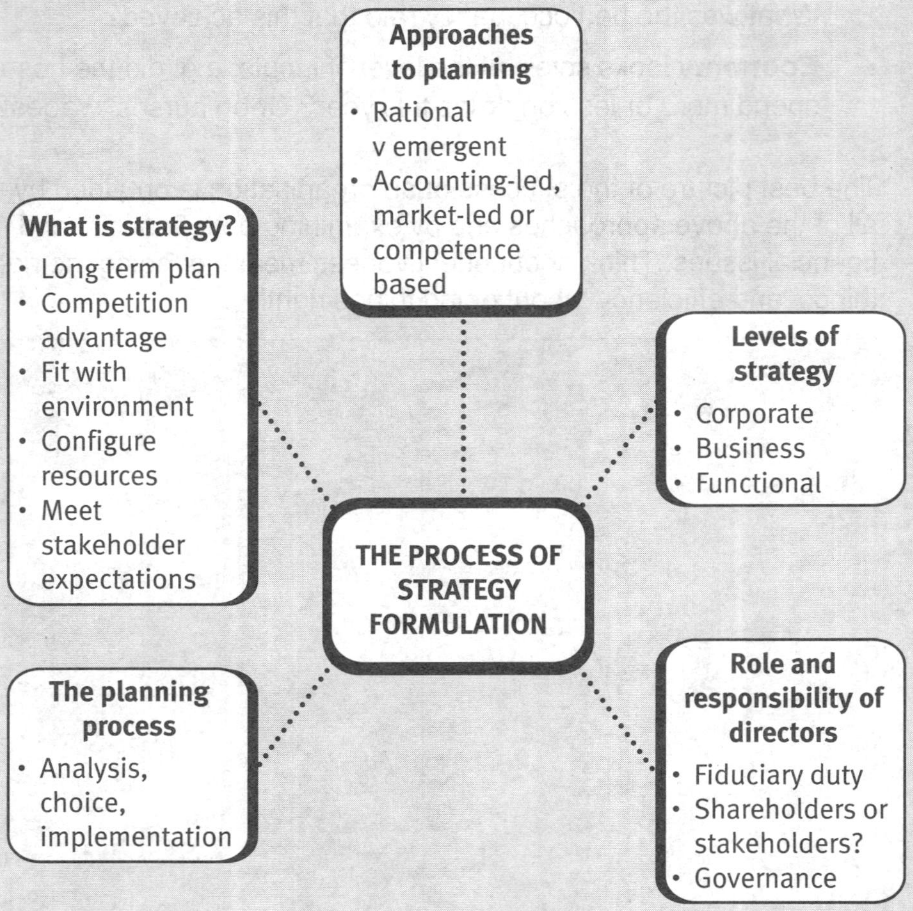

Test your understanding answers

Test your understanding 1

Current approach to strategy

HAA is currently using the rational model to develop its strategies. This involves taking a logical, step-by-step approach. HAA has clearly done this by undertaking such detailed planning, including strategic analysis of the market and the production of detailed operating plans.

The key advantage of such an approach to HAA is the level of understanding it will give them in the new market. They are currently not used to operating in the European market, so the initial strategic analysis they have performed will be invaluable. It will give them a picture of the their own capabilities as well as the European market they will be entering.

However, the European market is fast-moving, both due to its nature (high-tech) and the level of innovation by competitors. HAA will have to be prepared to quickly change its approach to deal with unexpected developments in the market. If the company produces a detailed operational plan, this may stifle the innovation that is required.

In addition, given the lack of experience that HAA has in the European market, any detailed forecasts it produces may prove to be unreliable. This may cause it to make inaccurate decisions based on flawed market predictions.

Alternative approaches to strategy for HAA

HAA could adopt the **emergent model.** While this would still involve some initial formal planning, these plans would merely be a starting point for the European operations. They will be continuously reviewed and updated as the games market changes, improving HAA's chances of success in the fast–moving market.

Alternatively HAA could choose the **freewheeling opportunism** approach to strategy. This would involve not producing a formal strategy – instead merely taking advantage of opportunities as they arise. The more rapidly the market evolves, the more applicable this approach may be, although it is considered too high risk for many managers.

Test your understanding 2

There are three main approaches to strategic planning that GYU could take.

Traditional or 'accounting-led'

This would involve GYU examining its key stakeholders and developing objectives that will meet their needs. The two key stakeholders in the scenario are GYU's customers and shareholders. The shareholders are clearly upset with the reduction in their dividend and will expect GYU to reverse this in coming years. The customers will be looking for handsets with more features and that are less 'dated'.

Unfortunately, while these are important objectives, they may be difficult for GYU to accomplish in the short term. Given the poor level of its finances, it may struggle to either increase dividends or invest enough in research and development to update its product line.

Market-led

This will involve the examination of GYU's competitors and market. Doing so should help GYU to ensure that it is competitive in what is a very fast-paced market.

While this appears to have been a weakness of GYU's to date (given the fact that it seems to have fallen so far behind many of its competitors), it may be inherently difficult in the mobile phone handset market. As the market is changing so rapidly, it may be difficult for GYU to accurately predict future trends and create appropriate strategies.

Resource-based

This involves GYU focusing its business strategies on areas that it is good at. For GYU its key area of skill is in the production of mobile handset software. It is acknowledged to be the market leader in this area and it appears to be very important to customers. Any future strategies should therefore be based around leveraging this area of skill.

For example, if it feels unable to produce handsets that are competitive, GYU could consider focusing on producing software which could then be licensed on other manufacturer's handsets. If this is a big enough market, this could help GYU to turn its business around.

Conclusion

Based on the information provided, the resource–based approach is likely to be best for GYU.

Test your understanding 3 – ADF

Weaknesses include:

Lack of diversity of the board of directors

Most of the directors in ADF are older men from country F. There is only one woman on the board.

Having a diverse board can ensure that the company has a wide range of experience to draw on when making decisions.

For example, ADF wants to expand abroad. By having directors from other countries or with experience of these foreign markets, the company would be far better placed to achieve this growth.

Lack of independence of non–executive directors

All the non–executive directors are linked to the Chairman. This makes it unlikely that they will act impartially. They are likely to vote along with the Chairman.

This could lead them to reject acceptable projects, such as the proposed foreign expansion, merely because the Chairman disapproves.

Weak internal audit

The fact that the directors allow ADF to have such an inadequate internal audit function indicates an alarming lack of control. If they are unable to rely fully on the accounts produced, they may find it difficult to implement sensible strategies in the future.

Overall

The ultimate goal of corporate governance is to provide investors with increased confidence in the company and increase the transparency of the board's decisions.

Should investors feel that ADF has poor corporate governance, it can damage ADF's reputation with investors. This may harm its share price and make it harder for the company to raise much needed finance in the future – which is likely to be important if it is planning overseas expansion.

chapter

3

Mission, objectives and stakeholders

Chapter learning objectives

Lead	Component
A1. Evaluate the key external factors affecting an organisation's strategy	(b) Recommend approaches to business/government relations and to relations with civil society (c) Discuss the drivers of external demands for corporate social responsibility and the organisation's response (d) Recommend how to manage relationships with stakeholders

Indicative syllabus content

- Non–market strategy and forms of corporate political activity.
- External demands for responsible business practices and ways to respond to these.
- Stakeholder management (stakeholders to include government and regulatory agencies, non–governmental organisations and civil society, industry associations, customers and suppliers).
- Mission statements and their use in orientating the organisation's strategy.

1 Mission

A mission statement is a 'published statement, apparently the entity's fundamental objective(s). This may or may not summarise the true mission of the entity.'

An organisation's mission is its 'fundamental objective(s)... expressed in general terms.'

CIMA Official Terminology

Essentially, the mission statement is a statement in writing that should describe the basic purpose of an organisation, that is, what it is trying to accomplish.

It outlines the broad direction that an organisation will follow and summarises the reasoning and values that underlie that organisation.

There are a number of fundamental questions that an organisation will need to address in its search for purpose. According to Drucker, these are:

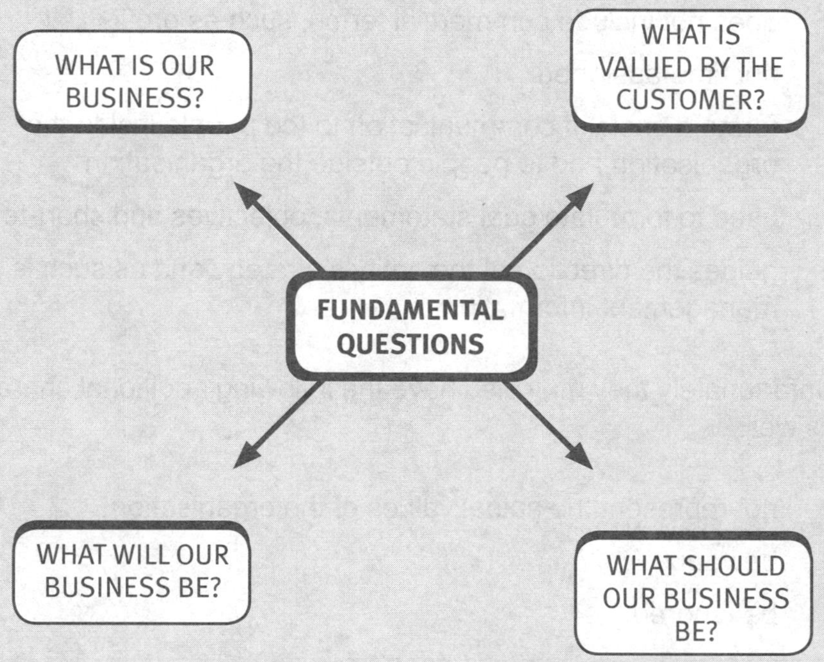

e.g

Examples of missions

'To produce cars and trucks that people will want to buy, will enjoy driving and will want to buy again'

(Chrysler)

'Our Mission is:

- To refresh the world in mind, body and spirit.
- To inspire moments of optimism through our brands and actions.
- To create value and make a difference everywhere we engage.'

(Coca Cola)

Characteristics of mission statements

Mission statements will have some or all of the following characteristics:

- usually a brief statement of no more than a page in length
- very general statement of entity culture
- states the aims (or purposes) of the organisation
- states the business areas in which the organisation intends to operate
- open-ended (not stated in quantifiable terms)

- does not include commercial terms, such as profit
- not time-assigned
- forms a basis of communication to the people inside the organisation and to people outside the organisation
- used to formulate goal statements, objectives and short-term targets
- guides the direction of the entity's strategy and as such is part of management information.

Unfortunately they may also have the following additional characteristics as well:

- not represent the actual values of the organisation
- be vague
- be ignored.

Mission statements fulfil a number of purposes:

- to communicate to all the stakeholder groups. It has been described as the 'reason for being'
- to help develop a desired corporate culture by communicating core values
- to assist in strategic planning.

In the exam you could be asked to consider mission statements and their use in orientating the organisation's strategy, probably within the wider context of evaluating the process of strategy formulation.

To do this you will need to consider whether the mission statement as given aids or hinders the planning process.

This is particularly relevant as the whole process of mission setting has been criticised heavily as some feel that it is a waste of scarce resources and does not produce significant benefits that outweigh the costs.

In addition, the CIMA official definition stated at the beginning of this section could be interpreted as evidence that mission statements are often merely for public consumption and only reflect what the organisation wants the public to believe its intentions are.

The process of writing a mission statement

Mission statements are normally drafted by the senior managers or directors of the organisation, as they are uniquely positioned to understand the needs and aims of the business at a high level.

Usually the first step in creating a mission statement is to analyse the stakeholders of the organisation – customers, shareholders and employees (amongst others). More detail on this stage can be found in section 3.

The directors of the company should identify the needs and aims of these stakeholders. They can then attempt to create a mission statement that reflects these aims and that shows how the organisation wants to relate to the stakeholders.

A draft mission statement can then be written and distributed to key stakeholders for review. Any feedback can be built into the final mission statement, which can then be published and widely distributed to as many interested parties as possible.

The life span of a mission statement

There are no set rules on how long a mission statement will be appropriate for an organisation. It should be reviewed periodically to ensure it still reflects the company's environment.

If the market or key stakeholders have changed since the mission statement was written, then it may no longer be appropriate.

e.g

Illustration 1 – Yahoo

Yahoo – an internet search based company – had a mission statement in the early 2000s which identified that it wanted to be 'the most essential global internet service for consumers and businesses'.

However, by 2007 Yahoo was beginning to struggle due to the rise of major competitors such as Google, whose mission statement was 'to organise the world's information and make it universally accessible and useful.' Yahoo felt that its existing mission statement did not show stakeholders how it was different to these rivals.

It therefore made its mission statement more specific, changing it to reflect that it wanted to 'connect people to their passions, their communities and the world's knowledge'.

This attempted to show the difference between the two companies. Yahoo wished to position itself in the entertainment market, rather than merely providing information like Google.

Test your understanding 1

The mission statement of C plc is "to provide our customers with a top quality product at a fair price".

Required:

Evaluate the usefulness of this mission statement.

2 Objectives

A mission is an open-ended statement of the firm's purpose and strategy. Objectives are more specific and seek to translate the mission into a series of mileposts for the organisation to follow.

To be useful for motivation, evaluation and control purposes, objectives should be SMART:

- **S**pecific – clear statement, easy to understand
- **M**easurable – to enable control and communication down the organisation
- **A**ttainable – it is pointless setting unachievable objectives
- **R**elevant – appropriate to the mission and stakeholders
- **T**imed – have a time period for achievement.

Key issues

In the same way that an organisation's overall strategic plans need to be translated into a hierarchy of lower level tactical and operational plans, there will be a hierarchy of objectives where the mission statement is translated into detailed strategic, tactical and operational objectives and targets.

Typical issues this gives rise to are as follows:

- Objectives drive action, so it is important that goal congruence is achieved and the agreed objectives do drive the desired strategy.
- It can be difficult (although necessary) to prioritise multiple, often conflicting objectives.

- This made more complex when some objectives are hard to quantify (e.g. environmental impact).
- There will be a mixture of financial and non-financial objectives.
- There is always the danger of short-termism.
- Objectives will vary across stakeholder groups and a strategy may satisfy some groups but not others.

Test your understanding 2

JAA plc is a publisher of both fiction and non–fiction books, a market in which it faces significant competition.

It has recently published a new mission statement:

'JAA will continue to grow and innovate as an organisation, while acting in a socially responsible way.'

For a future meeting of the Board of Directors, the Marketing Director has been asked to prepare a presentation to discuss this in more detail. She has asked you to help her by suggesting objectives that could be used to help the company achieve its missions of 'growth' and 'innovation'.

The Marketing Director has suggested that the only objective for 'social responsibility' will be the happiness of the workforce.

Required:

Identify two possible objectives each for growth and innovation for JAA, as requested by the Marketing Director.

Comment on her proposed objective for social responsibility and suggest and justify an alternative.

Not-for-profit organisation (NPO) objectives

While we often look at organisations that seek to make a profit, there are many organisations for whom this is not the primary objective. These include:

- government departments and agencies
- trade unions
- schools
- charities (e.g. Oxfam, Red Cross)
- mutual associations (e.g. building societies)

Rather than seeking to make a profit, these organisations will try to satisfy particular needs of their members or the sections of society they have been set up to benefit.

Illustration – the Chartered Institute of Management Accountants

The objectives of the Institute are (amongst other things):

- 'To promote and develop the science of Management Accountancy and to foster and maintain investigations into and research into the best means and methods of developing and applying such science...'
- '...by means of examination and other methods of assessment to test the skill and knowledge of persons desiring to enter the profession.'

The services provided by many of these organisations are limited only by the funds they have available. This means they normally aim to:

- raise as much money as possible
- spend this money as effectively as possible on the target group (with the minimum of administration costs).

Setting formal objectives can be difficult for NPOs. This is often due to the wide range of possible stakeholders as well as the fact the stakeholders who provide the funds may be different to the stakeholders who benefit from the NPO's activities (e.g. a charity). This gives much more power to the providers of finance and their objectives may not be the same as the NPO's.

3 Stakeholders

Mission and objectives need to be developed with two sets of interests in mind:

(1) the interests of those who have to carry them out e.g. managers and staff

(2) the interests of those who focus on the outcome e.g. shareholders, customers, suppliers, etc.

Together these groups are known as stakeholders – the **individuals and groups who have an interest in the organisation** and as such may wish to influence its mission, objectives and strategy.

Given the range of interests in organisations, it is not surprising to find that the mission may take several months of negotiation before it is finalised. The key aspect is that the organisation must take the stakeholders into account when formulating the mission and objectives of the company. The problem is that stakeholder objectives often conflict and so an order of priority is required based upon relative power and interest.

The mission-setting process can be a useful basis for getting the stakeholder groups to communicate their ideas and then be able to appreciate other viewpoints.

Stakeholder power analysis

This can be broken down into five steps:

(1) Identify the **key** stakeholders.

(2) Establish their **interests and claims** on the organisation, especially as new strategic initiatives are likely to be developed.

(3) Determine the **degree of power** that each group holds through its ability to force or influence change as new strategies are developed.

(4) Consider **how to divert trouble** before it starts, possibly by negotiating with key groups in advance.

(5) Develop a **mission, objectives and strategy**, possibly prioritising to minimise power clashes. This may involve negotiation amongst the various groups of stakeholders.

Stakeholder groups and possible power sources

A large company, for example, could have a wide range of different stakeholders:

Stakeholders		Objectives
Internal	• Managers • Employees	Career development, pay, security, enjoyable jobs
External	• Government • Pressure groups	Compliance with the law, tax Protecting the environment (amongst others)
Connected	• Shareholders • Customers • Financiers • Suppliers	Profit, share price and dividends Low prices, quality Interest payments, security High prices, assured demand

Examples of conflict are:

- shareholders want higher profits, employees want better pay and working conditions
- customers want 24/7 service, employees want 9 to 5 jobs, 5 days a week
- customers want high quality and low prices, shareholders want high profits
- suppliers want prompt payment, lenders want overdraft limits adhered to.

Different groups will have different influence – each case will need to be treated in context.

Typically, stakeholder power can come from a number of sources:

- **Positional power:** This arises because of an individual's position in the organisational hierarchy and is reflected in their formal authority and reputation. Directors, for example, will usually be powerful because of their rank in the organisation.
- **Resource power:** This arises because an individual can control, obtain or create resources or other items of value. For instance, a unionised workforce will be powerful as they control the key labour resource in the business.

- **System power:** This arises because a stakeholder has high visibility or political access and relevance to a particular situation. A director who is closely connected to a major shareholder is likely to have significant power within the organisation.
- **Expert power:** This arises where an individual has information, knowledge or expertise that is important to the organisation. Skilled employees, for example, will normally have more power than unskilled employees as they have skills that are important to the business and they are harder to replace.
- **Personal power:** This arises because an individual has good communication skills and reputation and (usually) is well liked within the organisation. A popular director is likely to have more power in an organisation, as staff will be willing to follow his or her instructions.

The more power and interest, the greater the involvement in setting the mission and strategy.

Porter's view on the influence of government

The influence of government on an industry

Porter identifies seven ways in which a government can affect the structure of an industry.

- Capacity expansion. The government can take actions to encourage firms or an industry as a whole to increase or cut capacity. Examples include capital allowances to encourage investment in equipment; regional incentives to encourage firms to locate new capacity in a particular area, and incentives to attract investment from overseas firms. The government is also (directly or indirectly) a supplier of infrastructure such as roads and railways, and this may influence expansion in a particular area.
- Demand. The government is a major customer of business in all areas of life and can influence demand by buying more or less. It can also influence demand by legislative measures. The tax system for cars is a good example: a change in the tax relief available for different engine sizes has a direct effect on the car manufacturers' product and the relative numbers of each type produced. Regulations and controls in an industry will affect the growth and profits of the industry, for example minimum product quality standards.
- Divestment and exit. A firm may wish to sell off a business to a foreign competitor or close it down, but the government might prevent this action because it is not in the public interest (there could be examples in health, defence, transport, education, agriculture and so on).

- Emerging industries may be controlled by the government. For instance, governments may control numbers of licences to create networks for next-generation mobile phones.
- Entry barriers. Government policy may restrict investment or competition or make it harder by use of quotas and tariffs for overseas firms. This kind of protectionism is generally frowned upon by the World Trade Organisation, but there may be political and economic circumstances in which it becomes necessary.
- Competition policy. Governments might devise policies which are deliberately intended to keep an industry fragmented, preventing one or two producers from having too much market share.
- New product adoption. Governments regulate the adoption of new products (e.g. new drugs) in some industries. They may go so far as to ban the use of a new product if it is not considered safe (a new form of transport, say). Policies may influence the rate of adoption of new products, e.g. the UK government intends to 'switch off' the analogue television networks by the year 2012, effectively forcing users to buy digital, cable or satellite services.

Actors (Braithwaite and Drahos)

It is worth mentioning Braithwaite and Drahos to consider the full range of 'actors' who may have an influence on the way an organisation conducts its business.

- **Organisations of states**: Organisations formed by groups of states that meet and employ staff to explore common agendas (e.g. the WTO, the EU).
- **States**: Organised political communities with governments and geographical boundaries recognised by international law (e.g. Sweden).
- **Organisations formed by firms** and/or business organisations with common agendas, such as Chambers of Commerce.
- **Corporations**: Organisations formed by actors who invest in them as commercial vehicles (e.g. Ford, British Telecom).
- **Non-Governmental Organisations (NGOs):** Organisations (excluding business organisations) that explore common agendas. They can be international (e.g. Consumers International) or national (e.g. British Standards Institute).

- **Mass publics**: Large audiences of citizens who express together a common concern about an issue.
- **Knowledge based (epistemic) communities**: These consist of state, business and NGO representatives who meet sporadically and share a common discourse based on shared knowledge – sometimes technical knowledge requiring professional training; CIMA is an example.

The last three groups may be collectively termed **civil society.** Civil society includes, among others, non-government organisations; people's organisations; civic clubs; trade unions; gender, cultural, and religious groups; charities; social and sports clubs; co-operatives; environmental groups; professional associations; academic and policy institutions; consumers/consumer organisations and the media.

4 Mendelow's power/interest matrix

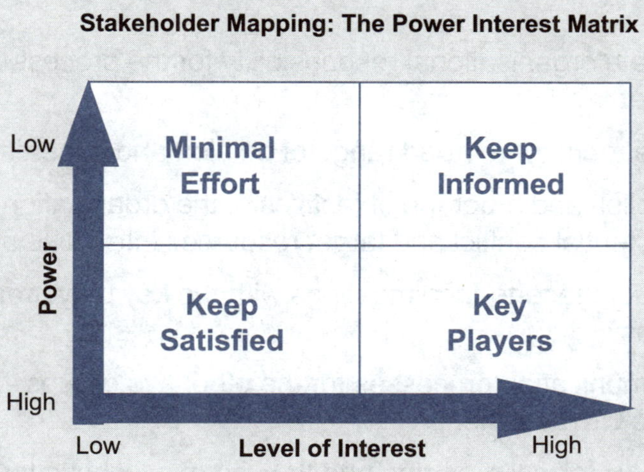

- **Minimal effort**

  Their lack of interest and power makes these stakeholders open to influence. They are more likely than others to accept what they are told and follow instructions.

- **Keep informed**

  These stakeholders are interested in the strategy but lack the power to do anything. Management needs to convince opponents to the strategy that the plans are justified; otherwise they will try to gain power by joining with parties with high power but low interest.

- **Keep satisfied**

  The key here is to keep these stakeholders satisfied to avoid them gaining interest and moving to the "key players" box. This could involve reassuring them of the outcomes of the strategy well in advance.

- **Key players**

  These stakeholders are the major drivers of change and could stop management plans if not satisfied. Their participation in the planning process is vital. Management, therefore, needs to communicate plans to them and then discuss implementation issues.

Managing the relationship with stakeholder groups

Powerful stakeholder groups must have confidence in the management team of the organisation. The organisation should ensure therefore that adequate management systems are in place. Some suggestions:

- Allocate organisational responsibility for the process along with a budget.
- Use a team for a broad range of opinion and expertise.
- Establish and order the objectives of the organisation. Identify the areas for potential conflict and target resources into those areas.
- Frequent face-to-face meetings with the key player and keep satisfied groups.
- Communication processes for the other two groups – possibly via public Q&A sessions.
- Periodic formal reporting and the use of a website for 'frequently asked questions'.

It is worth remembering that this is complicated by the fact that individuals may be part of more than one stakeholder group at any point in time. For example, factory workers can also be members of the local community or even elected local government officials. This can mean that there are conflicts between their interests and objectives regarding a particular decision that the company is about to make.

Tackling questions on stakeholders

Be careful when answering a question on stakeholders – it will **not always require you to use Mendelow's matrix.** In the March 2011 exam, a question was asked about how to handle stakeholder's conflicting objectives. Many candidates saw the word 'stakeholder' and immediately wrote about Mendelow's matrix – even though this is clearly inappropriate (see 'Resolving competing stakeholder objectives' below).

When answering a question that **does** ask you to analyse or allocate different shareholders into the various categories in Mendelow's matrix, it is important to explain your answer. For each stakeholder explain **why** you think it has high or low power and **why** you think it has high or low interest in the scenario. Then explain what the approach to that stakeholder should therefore be.

You may not always choose the same category as the model answer, but as long as you have reasonably justified your answer, you should still score well.

Remember that few, if any, marks will be available for explaining the model itself and unless specifically requested to do so (which is highly unlikely) drawing the matrix will merely waste time.

Test your understanding 3

AYL operates the only public hospital within a small city in country U. All of its income is provided by the central government. However, due to a recent economic downturn, the central government is urgently looking for ways to save money. It has therefore decided to significantly cut AYL's budget for the coming period.

The management of AYL have therefore been looking at ways of reducing their expenditure while attempting to minimise the impact on the services provided to the public. They are planning to freeze pay for the semi-skilled nurses working at the hospital.

This has prompted significant opposition from nurses. Nurses are not heavily unionised, but the remaining staff members in the hospital, such as doctors, are all members of the same union. No plans have emerged for cuts to their numbers.

Required:

Identify the key stakeholders that the managers will need to consider. Using Mendelow's matrix, suggest what approach the managers of AYL should take in relation to each one.

Note: You are NOT required to draw Mendelow's matrix.

Resolving competing stakeholder objectives

Cyert and March suggest four ways to resolve conflicting stakeholder objectives.

- **Satisficing** involves negotiations between key stakeholders to arrive at an acceptable compromise.
- **Sequential attention** is when management focus on stakeholder needs in turn. For example, staff may receive a pay rise with the clear implication that it will not be their 'turn' again for a few years and so they should not expect any further increases.
- **Side payments** are where a stakeholder's primary objectives cannot be met so they are compensated in some other way. For example, a local community may object to a new factory being built on a site that will cause pollution, noise and extra traffic. The firm concerned may continue to build the factory but try to appease the community by also building local sports facilities.
- **Exercise of power** is when a deadlock is resolved by a senior figure forcing through a decision simply based on the power they possess.

Non-market strategy and corporate political activity

Why is non-market strategy important?

Competitive advantage is often viewed as a function of market matters – products, customers, market share and the like. But, increasingly, competitive advantage can be built or lost outside of markets.

A firm maintains relationships with its customers, suppliers and competitors (the "market environment") but also with governments, regulators, non-government organisations (NGOs), the media and society at large – whether it wants to or not.

So there are huge opportunities for companies here, but also immense dangers for those focused purely on the market side. Anyone can be affected by non-market forces and in very consequential ways.

Example

In the 1990s Chiquita Brands sourced most of their bananas from Latin America; Europe was their biggest market. Meanwhile the European Union changed its banana policies to favour non-Latin American suppliers.

- Chiquita missed this non-market event and suffered as a result.
- Dole, on the other hand, one of the largest producers of fresh fruit and vegetables, was tracking the workings of the EU Commission, diversified its suppliers and improved its business as a result.

The increasing importance of non-market strategy

In many markets it is becoming increasingly difficult to achieve a sustainable competitive advantage:

- It is harder to come up with products that are different enough to protect market share.
- "Excellence" is a 30-year-old concept.
- Most companies have "squeezed" costs to maximise profits.

Non-market matters, such as reputation, the ability to work with NGOs, the capability to foresee relevant government actions and even to shape policy – these are the factors that can make a difference, even though many firms have no clear strategy in this respect.

Clearly in order to ensure that they are aware of these issues, a company would have to undertake detailed environmental analysis. This could be accomplished using models such as PEST and Porter's Five Forces, which will be covered in chapter 5.

Business/government relations

Businesses can try to influence government policies in a number of ways.

- By employing lobbyists, who will put their case to ministers and civil servants and try to obtain their support.
- By giving MPs and retired senior civil servants non-executive directorships, in the hope that they will take an interest in legislation that affects the business and will exercise their influence.
- By influencing public opinion, and hence the legislative agenda, using advertising or other means of marketing communications.

Depending on the political regime and the country in question another method may be to make donations to party funds. Obviously this is open to question as it could be seen as a form of bribery.

It is usually in the interest of a government to consult with the business sector when it is forming new policies, both to widen its perspective and so that it can defend its actions politically. In most developed countries there is a strong business lobby consisting of individual companies and business-related organisations.

In the UK, for example, the business lobby consists of protagonists such as the following:

- The Confederation of British Industry (CBI), representing the entire private business sector.
- The Federation of Small Businesses (FSB) and local Chambers of Commerce.
- The Institute of Directors (IOD).
- Several thousand trade associations and employers' organisations, representing particular industries and sectors.

Very large companies are likely to be in frequent contact with government departments and parliament on an individual basis and many have distinct departments for government liaison. Such departments will monitor and advise on political and governmental developments, make regular contacts with politicians and senior civil servants, organise representation and undertake lobbying operations in London, Brussels, Washington, Geneva and so on, often assisted by non-executive directors and consultants.

5 External demands for responsible business practices

Corporate social responsibility

In the modern world, it is seen as being increasingly important to consider how organisations manage their business processes to have an overall positive impact on society.

It is worth noting that corporate social responsibility (CSR) is distinct from ethics. Business ethics comprise principles and standards that govern behaviour in the world of business.

CSR, however, refers to a **firm's obligation to maximise its positive impacts upon stakeholders while minimising the negative effects**.

The extent to which the organisation fulfils the economic, legal, ethical and charitable responsibilities placed on it by its stakeholders will determine to what extent it is seen as having good CSR.

The problem is that there is no one definition or theory of CSR.

Consider the following points. Is it ethical to:

- Experiment on animals?
- Drill for oil?
- Build roads through countryside?
- Pay high salaries to senior executives?

Different individuals will have different views on each of these issues.

As far as possible, managers have to take account of a range of differing viewpoints when deciding on their strategies. In addition, there is always the need to balance a company's responsibility to society with its responsibility to earn financial returns for its investors.

Arguments against CSR

It can be argued that companies should not pursue corporate social responsibility. Milton Friedman argues that:

'The business of business is business.'

This means that the primary purpose of a business is to try and earn a profit. In a company, for instance, the managers have been employed in order to earn the owners of the business a return on their investment.

As such, it is a manager's duty to act in a way that maximises shareholder wealth, while conforming to all relevant laws and customs. If a manager does anything that is not directly related to wealth maximisation, he is failing in his responsibilities to the owners and therefore acting unethically.

For example, it can be argued that it is not right for a manager to donate any company funds to charity. The manager should instead work to maximise the return to the owner. If the owner wishes to make donations to charity, he can do so out of his earnings from the business.

In addition, it can be argued that maximising the wealth of business owners is, in itself, socially responsible. This is because:

- Increased returns will lead to increased tax payments made to the state. These can then be passed on to 'worthy causes'.
- A high proportion of company shares are owned by pension funds. This means that any gains will go to help provide pensions to individuals who may well be disadvantaged.

Other arguments

Don't forget that there may also be practical reasons why a business chooses not to pursue CSR. These can include:

- Increased cost of sourcing materials from ethical sources (e.g. Fairtrade products or free-range eggs).
- Having to turn away business from customers considered to be unethical (e.g. an 'ethical' bank may choose not to invest in a company that manufactures weapons).
- The management time that can be taken up by CSR planning and implementation.

Arguments for CSR

Not everyone agrees with Friedman's statements. There are a number of reasons why many businesses feel that CSR is a vital part of their strategy. These include:

- A key part of running a successful business is the ability to offer customers and consumers what they need. One of those needs is often a requirement for socially responsible behaviour from the organisation.

  Basically, **having good CSR can attract customers**! This can be because good CSR tends to enhance a company's reputation and therefore its brand. It can also be used a basis for differentiation in the market place – given the choice, many customers will prefer to trade with a company they feel is ethical.

- Good CSR is likely to involve good working conditions for employees, allowing the business to **attract a higher calibre of staff**.
- Avoiding discrimination against workers is likely to give the company **access to a wider human resource base**.

- Avoiding pollution will tend to save companies in the long run – many governments are now **fining or increasing taxes of more polluting businesses**.
- Sponsorship and charitable donations are tax deductible, improve staff morale and can be seen as a **form of advertising**.

Ultimately, having good CSR can **increase the financial value of the business**. Remember that the value of the business will be the present value of its perceived future cash flows discounted at its risk-adjusted cost of capital.

- Good CSR will reduce the risk of adverse environmental reactions against the company. Anything that reduces risk should lower the risk adjusted cost of capital, increasing the value of the company.
- A socially responsible business will be allowed to operate for longer in society. This will mean that there will be more years of cash flows in the future. This would also increase the value of the company.

Ethical stances

Johnson, Scholes and Whittington define ethical stance as:

'The extent to which an organisation will exceed its minimum obligations to stakeholders.'

There are four possible ethical stances:

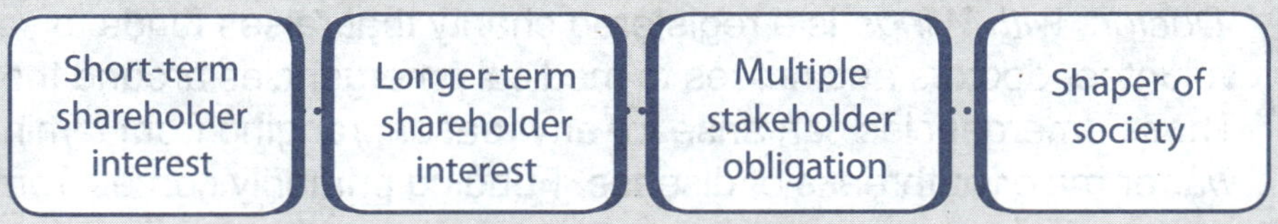

Short-term shareholder interest (STSI)

This ethical stance has a short-term focus in that it aims to maximise profits in the financial year. Organisations with this ethical stance believe that it is the role of governments to set the legal minimum standard, and anything delivered above this would be to the detriment of their taxpayers.

Longer-term shareholder interest (LTSI)

This ethical stance takes broadly the same approach as the short-term shareholder interest except that it takes a longer-term view. Hence it may be appropriate to incur additional cost now so as to achieve higher returns in the future. An example could be a public service donating some funds to a charity in the belief that it will save the taxpayer the costs associated with providing the entire service should the charity cease to work. Hence this ethical stance is aware of other stakeholders and their impact on long-term profit or cost.

Multiple stakeholder obligation (MSO)

This ethical stance accepts that the organisation exists for more than simply making a profit, or providing services at a minimal cost to taxpayers. It takes the view that all organisations have a role to play in society and so they must take account of all the stakeholders' interests. Hence they explicitly involve other stakeholders, and believe that they have a purpose beyond the financial.

Shaper of society

This ethical stance is ideologically driven and sees its vision as being the focus for all its actions. Financial and other stakeholders' interests are secondary to the overriding purpose of the organisation.

Test your understanding 4

'*Doctors with Wings*' is a registered charity that raises funds to send volunteer doctors and nurses to medical emergencies around the world. Those emergencies can arise for any reason, ranging from famine to war or major outbreaks of disease. Funding primarily comes from government agencies and corporate donations, although the charity seeks donations from the public, as well as medicines and other supplies from manufacturers. The majority of volunteers are recruited, often with the support of teaching hospitals, immediately after qualification. These new doctors are often persuaded to donate their time to the charity during presentations made by volunteer doctors who have just returned from a medical emergency.

Bryson, in his 1995 book, *Strategic Planning for Public and Non-profit Organisations*, makes the following statement:

'I would argue that if an organisation has time to do only one thing when it comes to strategic planning, that one thing ought to be a stakeholder analysis.'

Required:

(a) Critically discuss the components and process of such an analysis and the benefits that 'Doctors with Wings' would gain from the exercise.

(10 marks)

(b) Evaluate the principal stakeholders in the organisation and analyse the nature of the influence and importance that they hold in their relationship with the charity.

(15 marks)

(Total: 25 marks)

Sustainability

One concept that is also becoming increasingly important is sustainability.

Sustainability is the use of resources in such a way that they do not compromise the needs of future generations. It also involves not polluting the environment at a rate faster than they can be absorbed.

There are many examples of this. For example, some logging companies plant a tree for every one they fell.

Other companies try to make their products easy to recycle, helping to ensure that materials are reused rather than wasted. The computer manufacturer Apple has used this as part of its marketing approach for some years.(http://www.apple.com/recycling/)

The reason that sustainability is so important for many businesses is that acting in a sustainable manner not only helps look after the environment and the wider community, but it strengthens the business and helps ensure its long-term survival.

The difficulty for many businesses is that many companies focus on short term gains, rather than the long-term sustainability of the business and its environment. This is often evident in businesses that offer senior managers bonuses based on short-term or annual performance.

Incorporating ethics into strategy

CIMA itself has been heavily involved in identifying and discussing the implications of sustainability for the business. To this end, in 2010 they published a research article discussing this.

The article came to six key conclusions:

- Strong ethical principles that go beyond upholding the law can add great value to a brand, whereas failure to do the right thing can cause social, economic and environmental damage, undermining a company's long–term prospects in the process.
- Once they have adopted an ethical approach, companies will often find there are bottom-line benefits from demonstrating high ethical standards.
- The ethical tone comes from the top.
- High-quality management information on social, environmental and ethical performance is vital for monitoring the environmental and social impacts of a company and for compiling connected reports showing how effective its governance arrangements are.
- Corporate communications and reporting on sustainability need to do more than just pay lip service to the green agenda. They need to provide hard evidence of the positive impact on society, the environment and the strategic returns for the business, and how any negative effects are being addressed.
- Management accountants have a particular ethical responsibility to promote an ethics-based culture that doesn't permit practises such as bribery.

The full report can be found here:

http://www.cimaglobal.com/Thought-leadership/Research-topics/Sustainability/incorporating-ethics-into-strategy.

Further CIMA information on sustainability

In December 2010, CIMA collaborated with the AICPA and CICA in a report entitled 'Evolution of corporate sustainability practices'.

Some key issues that this report raised include:

General

Business sustainability is about ensuring that organisations implement strategies that contribute to long–term success. Organisations that act in a sustainable manner not only help to maintain the well–being of the planet and people, they also create businesses that will survive and thrive in the long run.

The accounting profession can play an important role in this. Accountants can serve as leading agents for change by applying their skills and competencies to develop sustainability strategies, facilitate effective implementation, accurate measurement and credible business reporting.

Why do businesses have sustainability plans?

According to research conducted by CIMA, the key reasons include:

- **Compliance** – the need to comply with laws and regulations.
- **Reputational risk** – companies are concerned with how stakeholders will view them if they fail to act in a sustainable manner.
- **Cost-cutting and efficiency** – acting in a sustainable manner (for example becoming more energy-efficient) can help to reduce business expenditure. This is especially valuable for smaller companies.

Ten elements of organisational sustainability

The following areas are considered crucial to the successful embedding of sustainability within an organisation. It is worth noting that the accounting function will be useful in a number of these areas.

Strategy and oversight

- Board and senior management commitment.
- Understanding and analysing the key sustainability drivers for the organisation.
- Integrating the key sustainability drivers into the organisation's strategy.

Execution and alignment

- Ensuring that sustainability is the responsibility of everyone within the organisation (not just a specific department).
- Breaking down the sustainability targets and objectives for the organisation as a whole into targets and objectives which are meaningful for individual subsidiaries, divisions and departments.
- Processes that enable sustainability issues to be taken into account clearly and consistently in day-to-day decision-making.
- Extensive and effective sustainability training.

Performance and reporting

- Including sustainability targets and objectives in performance appraisal.
- Champions to promote sustainability and celebrate success.
- Monitoring and reporting sustainability performance.

The full report can be found here:

http://www.cimaglobal.com/Documents/
Thought_leadership_docs/CIMA_AICPA_CICA sustainability_report.pdf

6 CIMA's code of ethics

Introduction

CIMA's code of ethics is an 81-page document that offers guidance on how to recognise and respond to tricky ethical situations. You are only expected to be aware of the main concepts in the code in the exam. The code is structured as follows:

- Part A: fundamental principles and general application of the code
- Part B: professional accountants in business
- Part C: professional accountants in public practice.

The full content of the code can be found at:

http://www.cimaglobal.com/Professional-ethics/

However, the E3 syllabus only examines parts A and B of the code.

Section 100.1 of part A states that professional accountants should "act in the public interest" and therefore "responsibility is not exclusively to satisfy the needs of an individual client or employer".

The code provides a conceptual framework with guidance on fundamental ethical principles:

- Integrity
- Objectivity
- Professional competence and due care
- Confidentiality
- Professional behaviour

Fundamental ethical principles

Integrity

Integrity implies fair dealing and truthfulness.

Members are also required not to be associated with any form of communication or report where the information is considered to be:

- materially false or to contain misleading statements
- provided recklessly
- incomplete such that the report or communication becomes misleading by this omission.

Objectivity

Accountants need to ensure that their business/professional judgement is not compromised because of bias or conflict of interest.

However, there are many situations where objectivity can be compromised, so a full list cannot be provided. Accountants are warned to always ensure that their objectivity is intact in any business/professional relationship.

Professional competence and due care

There are two main considerations under this heading:

(1) Accountants are required to have the necessary professional knowledge and skill to carry out work for clients.

(2) Accountants must follow applicable technical and professional standards when providing professional services.

Appropriate levels of professional competence must first be attained and then maintained. Maintenance implies keeping up to date with business and professional developments, and in many institutes completion of an annual return confirming that continued professional development (CPD) requirements have been met.

Where provision of a professional service has inherent limitations (e.g. reliance on client information) then the client must be made aware of this.

Confidentiality

The principle of confidentiality implies two key considerations for accountants:

(1) Information obtained in a business relationship is not disclosed outside the firm unless there is a proper and specific authority or unless there is a professional right or duty to disclose.

(2) Confidential information acquired during the provision of professional services is not used to personal advantage.

The need to maintain confidentiality is normally extended to cover the accountants' social environment, information about prospective clients and employers, and where business relationships have terminated. Basically there must always be a reason for disclosure before confidential information is provided to a third party.

The main reasons for disclosure are when:

(1) it is permitted by law and authorised by the client

(2) it is required by law, e.g. during legal proceedings or disclosing information regarding infringements of law

(3) there is professional duty or right to disclose (when not barred by law), e.g. provision of information to the professional institute or compliance with ethical requirements.

Ethical considerations on disclosure

The accountant needs to consider the extent to which third parties may be adversely affected by any disclosure.

The amount of uncertainty inherent in the situation may affect the extent of disclosure – more uncertainty may mean disclosure is limited or not made at all.

The accountant needs to ensure that disclosure is made to the correct person or persons.

Professional behaviour

Accountants must comply with all relevant laws and regulations.

There is also a test whereby actions suggested by a third party which would bring discredit to the profession should also be avoided.

An accountant is required to treat all people contacted in a professional capacity with courtesy and consideration. Similarly, any marketing activities should not bring the profession into disrepute.

Test your understanding 5

Explain why each of the following actions appears to be in conflict with fundamental ethical principles.

(1) An advertisement for a firm of accountants states that their audit services are cheaper and more comprehensive than a rival firm.

(2) An accountant prepares a set of accounts prior to undertaking the audit of those accounts.

(3) A director discusses an impending share issue with colleagues at a golf club dinner.

(4) The finance director attempts to complete the company's taxation computation following the acquisition of some foreign subsidiaries.

(5) A financial accountant confirms that a report on his company is correct, even though the report omits to mention some important liabilities.

(6) You believe your colleague has asked you to include what you believe to be misleading information in your forecast

(7) Your analysis of a strategic proposal suggests that profitability will be improved by making 30 people redundant.

(8) You can outsource your manufacturing to a country where labour costs are much lower.

(9) Your country is allowed, legally, to dump its waste into a river. This will kill all aquatic life along a 50-mile stretch.

Resolving ethical conflicts

The code is clear that the professional accountant should respond to an ethical conflict. Inaction or silence may well be a further breach of the code.

Ethical conflicts can be resolved as follows:

(1) Gather all relevant facts.

(2) Establish ethical issues involved.

(3) Refer to relevant fundamental principles.

(4) Follow established internal procedures.

(5) Investigate alternative courses of action.

(6) Consult with appropriate persons within the firm.

(7) Obtain advice from professional institutes.

(8) If the matter is still unresolved, consider withdrawing from the engagement team / assignment / role.

Test your understanding 6

Explain your response to the following ethical threats.

(1) Your employer asks you to suggest to a junior manager that they will receive a large bonus for working overtime on a project to hide liabilities from the financial statements.

(2) In selecting employees for a new division, you are advised to unfairly discriminate against one section of the workforce.

(3) You have been asked to prepare the management accounts for a subsidiary located in South America in accordance with specific requirements of that jurisdiction. In response to your comment that you do not understand the accounting requirements of that jurisdiction, your supervisor states 'no problem, no one will notice a few thousand dollars' error anyway'.

Ethical threats and safeguards

Ethical threat	Safeguard
Conflict between requirements of the employer and the fundamental principles For example, acting contrary to laws or regulations or against professional or technical standards.	• Obtaining advice from the employer, professional organisation or professional advisor • The employer providing a formal dispute resolution process • Legal advice
Preparation and reporting on information Accountants need to prepare/ report on information fairly, objectively and honestly. However, the accountant may be pressurised to provide misleading information.	• Consultation with superiors in the employing company • Consultation with those charged with governance • Consultation with the relevant professional body
Having sufficient expertise Accountants need to be honest in stating their level of expertise – and not mislead employers by implying they have more expertise than they actually possess. Threats that may result in lack of expertise include time pressure to carry out duties, being provided with inadequate information or having insufficient experience.	• Obtaining additional advice/training • Negotiating more time for duties • Obtaining assistance from someone with relevant expertise

Financial interests Situations where an accountant or close family member has financial interests in the employing company. Examples include the accountant being paid a bonus based on the financial statement results which he is preparing, or holding share options in the company.	• Remuneration being determined by other members of management • Disclosure of relevant interests to those charged with governance • Consultation with superiors or relevant professional body
Inducements – receiving offers Refers to incentives being offered to encourage unethical behaviour. Inducements may include gifts, hospitality, preferential treatment or inappropriate appeals to loyalty. Objectivity and/or confidentiality may be threatened by such inducements.	• Do not accept the inducement! • Inform relevant third parties such as senior management and professional association (normally after taking legal advice)
Inducements – giving offers Refers to accountants being pressurised to provide inducements to junior members of staff to influence a decision or obtain confidential information.	• Do not offer the inducement! If necessary, follow the conflict resolution process outlined in the next section
Confidential information Accountants should keep information about their employing company confidential unless there is a right or obligation to disclose, or they have received authorisation from the client. However, the accountant may be under pressure to disclose this information as a result of compliance with legal processes such as anti-money laundering/terrorism – in this situation there is a conflict between confidentiality and the need for disclosure.	• Disclose information in compliance with relevant statutory requirements, e.g. money laundering regulations

Whistleblowing Situations where the accountant needs to consider disclosing information, where ethical rules have been broken by the client.	Follow the disclosure provisions of the employer, e.g. report to those responsible for governance. Otherwise disclosure should be based on assessment of: legal obligations, whether members of the public will be adversely affected, gravity of the matter, likelihood of repetition, reliability of the information, reasons why employer does not want to disclose.

Answering ethics questions in the exam

The examiner has stated that students are unlikely to see ethical issues that have clear solutions in the exam. Ethical issues are complex and therefore there may not be a 'right' answer as to how to resolve them.

The examiner's approach will usually be to:

(1) Produce a scenario.

(2) Ask how it fits with the CIMA Code of Ethics.

(3) What action(s) the Code suggests that a CIMA member could take?

(4) What safeguards does the Code suggest could handle such a dilemma?

(5) Therefore – what recommendation(s) would you make for action in these circumstances, and why?

Test your understanding 7

Router plc, a mining company, has said in its mission statement that it will 'endeavour to make the maximum possible profit for its shareholders while recognising its wider responsibility to society'.

Router plc has an opportunity to mine for gold in a remote and sparsely populated area. The mining process proposed in this instance would remove all vegetation from the land concerned. After mining has finished, there will remain substantial lakes of poisonous water which will remain toxic for a hundred years.

The mining process is profitable, given the current high world value of gold. However, if the company were to reinstate the mined land, the process would be extremely unprofitable. The company has received permission from the government to carry out the mining. The few local residents are opposed to the mining.

Required:

(a) Discuss the extent to which Router's mission statement is contradictory. **(5 marks)**

(b) Advise Router how it could deal with strategies that present a conflict of objectives. **(6 marks)**

(c) Discuss the ethical issues surrounding the decision to mine for gold. **(6 marks)**

(Total: 17 marks)

7 Summary

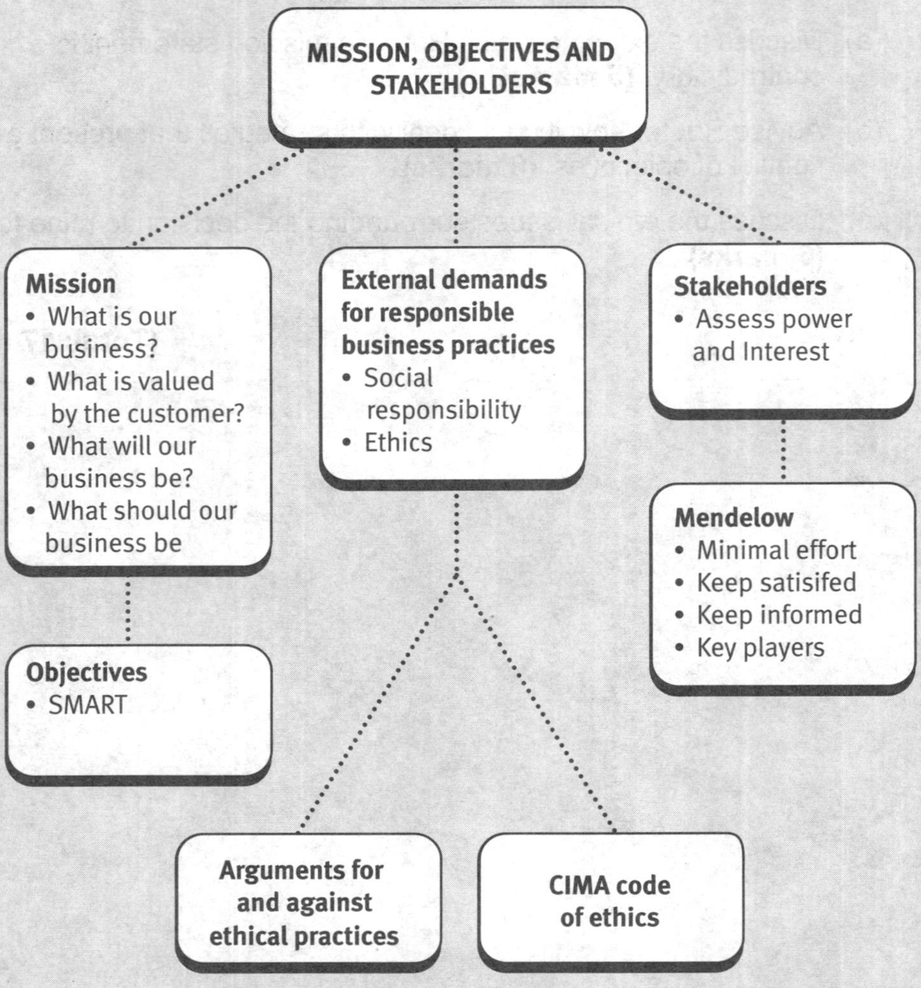

MISSION, OBJECTIVES AND STAKEHOLDERS
Mission
• What is our business?
• What is valued by the customer?
• What will our business be?
• What should our business be
Objectives
• SMART
External demands for responsible business practices
• Social responsibility
• Ethics
Arguments for and against ethical practices
CIMA code of ethics
Stakeholders
• Assess power and Interest
Mendelow
• Minimal effort
• Keep satisifed
• Keep informed
• Key players

Test your understanding answers

Test your understanding 1

This can be criticised as a mission statement for a number of reasons.

- It does not state the business areas in which the company intends to operate. As such it would not be useful to assess a strategy of market development, for example.
- It does not give a reason for the company's existence. In particular, the statement fails to give any indication why the company will be better than its competitors in what it does.
- It appears to focus on customer requirements only, and has nothing to say about other stakeholder groups, particularly employees and shareholders. It does not actually define who its customers are or who it wants its customers to be.
- It is dull. Short mission statements should be inspiring.
- It communicates nothing about the firm's values to employees.
- The terms 'top quality' and 'fair price' are unclear in their meaning. It is not clear what is meant by 'quality', nor what 'fair' is in terms of price. Assuming that it will be expensive to achieve top quality, how high might a fair price be? Does it mean fair to the customer or fair to the shareholders? Taken at face value there is a danger the company could make a loss!

In defence of the statement it does highlight the need to meet customer expectations in order to be successful.

On balance, however, the mission statement will fail to inspire employees, determine culture or assist strategic planning.

Test your understanding 2

Possible objectives for JAA could include:

Growth

JAA could set itself an objective to increase its **sales volume** – either in terms of the additional number of books it wishes to sell, or in terms of the percentage increase it wishes to see compared to its current sales volume.

The company could also consider setting itself an objective relating to its **market share.** As it operates in a highly competitive market, JAA may wish to set itself an objective to achieve a set percentage share of the total market for fiction and non–fiction books.

Innovation

To achieve this objective, JAA could set itself objectives relating to the **number of new books launched** each year. By bringing more new books to market than its competitors, it may be able to increase its market share and put pressure on other publishers.

JAA could also set objectives relating to the **number of new ways of selling its products** that it utilises. This could involve selling its books online, as electronic downloads or through tablet computers and electronic readers.

Marketing director's suggestion

The marketing director has suggested that the happiness of employees could be used as the sole objective for social responsibility. While it is correct that an employer who has good social responsibility should see an increase in staff happiness, this will not make a good objective on its own.

Firstly, social responsibility extends beyond how the company treats its employees. To get a full picture, the company needs to examine how its actions are impacting on other stakeholders and the wider environment.

In addition, employee happiness in itself is not directly measurable, meaning it cannot be a good objective. The marketing director needs to be more specific. For example, she could measure the staff turnover to get an indication of how staff feel about the company.

Test your understanding 3

Nurses

Given the proposals to cut or freeze their pay in the coming period, nurses will have **high interest** in the proposals.

However, they are not unionised. This would tend to indicate a **lower level of power** as they lack a clear ability to co-ordinate strike action and could be relatively easy to replace due to their relatively low level of skill.

Under Mendelow's matrix, nurses should therefore be **kept informed**. The management of AYL need to try and convince them of the need for the pay freeze in order for the hospital to continue to function. This may, however, be difficult to do. This may lead to the nurses attempting to gain power by unionising and joining with the other workers in AYL, or alternatively lobbying the government.

Patients

If the proposed pay cuts are implemented, patients are unlikely to see a significant change in their level of care. This will give them a **low level of interest**.

In addition, while patients may collectively have an influence on the elected national government, there is no indication that patients have any kind of organisation, indicating a **low level of power**.

Mendelow's matrix would therefore suggest that the managers of AYL should adopt a **minimal effort** approach with regards to patients in this area. They are likely to accept what the management tell them as long as it does not affect their level of care. Should it do so, they may become more interested.

Other members of hospital staff

As it stands, there is no evidence that any other types of hospital staff will be affected by the pay cuts. Given the fact that the nurses are not part of the main union that represents the other members of staff, it is likely that they will have **low interest**.

However, should they choose to take an interest, the remaining members of staff will probably have **high power**. They are unionised and include key members of staff (skilled doctors). This means that any strike action could be extremely damaging to the hospital.

As such, the managers of AYL should adopt an approach of **keeping them satisfied**. By reassuring other workers that their circumstances are not affected by the cuts, AYL may be able to prevent them taking an active interest in the proposals.

Central government

The government ultimately controls the budget for the hospital. This gives it **high power**.

In addition, it is currently looking for ways to reduce its expenditure, so it has **high interest** in the success of AYL's proposals.

AYL have no choice but to adopt a **key players** approach. They need to fully communicate their plans to the central government and ensure they are happy with the proposals. If the central government recommends changes to the proposed cuts, AYL's managers would be wise to accept them.

Test your understanding 4

(a) Stakeholders can be defined as people and organisations who have a say in what the organisation is to do, what resources the organisation can have and what is to be achieved. They are affected by, and feel they have a right to benefit from, or be pleased by, what the organisation does.

Beneficiaries can be considered as both intended beneficiaries and collateral beneficiaries who will benefit indirectly from the success of the organisation or the service it provides.

The process of stakeholder analysis would best be served by a brainstorming process using a focus group drawn from within the company. Stakeholders should be categorised as internal or external to the organisation. It should be remembered that stakeholder groups are not mutually exclusive and there will be overlap between them.

The stages of the process should be:

- identify stakeholders
- identify their interests, values and concerns
- identify sources of stakeholder power
- identify what claims they can make on the organisation
- rank the most important stakeholders from the organisation's perspective in terms of their ability to influence the organisation
- map the relationship between the stakeholder groups
- identify the resulting strategic challenges.

When looking to determine the stakeholder values, these could be considered in terms of what they want the organisation to do for them, what the organisation actually does for them, and how well they judge the organisation's efforts. The organisation should also consider how it is informed of stakeholder perception of its performance. It is important to consider why the stakeholders choose to come to this particular organisation - do they have a choice? Some organisations talk of holding particular values, but do not actually live them in practice. It is important to distinguish between the desired, spoken and lived values. For instance, a public transport service may well have a desired value of no delays for passengers. The spoken values, espoused in terms of targets set, will relate to a lesser performance level. The lived values may well be at an even lower level.

Having determined the stakeholders' value systems there should be an assessment of the power they can exercise on the organisation. Power can arise by virtue of:

- possession of expertise
- control of or access to resources
- control of or access to information
- preparedness to fight
- charisma or referent power
- networks.

All stakeholders will have an element of power in their dealings with an organisation to a greater or lesser extent. The power that a stakeholder can bring to bear in dealing with the organisation should be carefully considered since this can affect the way an organisation chooses to deal with that particular stakeholder or stakeholder group. The greater their power the more influential they become.

The importance of stakeholders at any point in time will depend upon their interest in the strategic initiatives being planned at the time. If the initiative ties in with their values and concerns then they must be considered important in the next stage of analysis. Alternatively where a stakeholder may have limited, or little interest in the successful completion of an initiative, they will need to be convinced of the importance for the organisation as a whole.

Once stakeholders have been classified in terms of their importance and influence they can be ranked in terms of the way the organisation must deal with them, if strategies are to be successfully implemented.

The organisation will need to develop excellent working relationships with those stakeholders who have both high degrees of influence and high importance. They are potential partners in the planning and implementation of any initiatives.

Those stakeholders who have high degrees of influence, and can affect the initiative's outcomes, but are of limited importance at this point in time, are a source of risk requiring careful monitoring and management. They must be consulted and kept informed.

Stakeholders who are highly important, but of low power to influence, should be kept informed, but can do little to affect the outcome of the strategic initiative.

Stakeholders of both low influence and low importance will require limited monitoring and evaluation but are, at this time, of low priority.

Having conducted this type of stakeholder analysis Doctors with Wings will benefit from a clearer idea of the way forward in implementing any strategy it proposes. Strategic initiatives will invariably involve change management and without the support of the stakeholders are unlikely to succeed. By developing a better knowledge of stakeholders, their power and their value system, it will be far easier for the organisation to make decisions on how it should deal with the different groups as it introduces any new strategy.

More informed decisions are needed when the organisation comes to answer the following questions:

– Should it deal with stakeholders directly or indirectly?
– Should it take the offensive or deal defensively with resistance?
– Should it accommodate, negotiate, manipulate or resist stakeholder claims?
– Should it operate with a combination of these approaches or select a single course of action?

(b) The list of stakeholders includes:

Government funding agencies

Government agencies would expect to see value for money and the good name of the host country promoted. It is unlikely that a government would want to be associated with the funding of a charity which played an active part in a medical emergency arising from a conflict in which that government had an active, or vested, interest. Depending on the proportion of funding they provide, their power could be quite considerable. They also have network power in that they can influence other foreign governments and supranational funding agencies such as UNESCO to assist the charity or, if not impressed, to damage its interests.

Corporate donors

These have similar interests to government agencies in that they would want to see transparent and cost effective operations, gaining reputational capital by association. It is unlikely that they would want to be seen to be supporting one side in areas of conflict if they had interests in the region. Their power would again depend on the size of the donation they made to the organisation. It should be remembered that the donation might not be purely financial in that they might offer transport and other facilities in the affected area and would gain additional reputational capital from so doing.

Medical companies that donate

Aside from philanthropic interests, medical companies would want to improve their reputational capital by being seen to do the right thing. Power would again depend on the size of the contribution to the costs of the organisation but, additionally, in particular medical emergencies they may well provide power in terms of pharmaceutical expertise to the doctors.

Public donors

The interest of public donors is philanthropic – they would wish to have a satisfied feeling from having done the right thing. Power is not limited to resource manipulation in the size of the donation made, but would also involve their ability to raise the profile of the charity where word of mouth marketing is important.

Doctors and nurses donating time after qualifying for the first time

The interest of the donors is both philanthropic from a desire to give something back, but also to gain good-quality post-qualification experience. There will also be an element of self-esteem in taking an interest in the charity. Their power is high being based on their expertise and preparedness to do the work.

Doctors and nurses returning from medical emergency

The interest is again philanthropic, and there is also a desire to increase reputational capital. Their power is high both in terms of expertise and charisma or referent power.

Teaching hospitals facilitating doctors donating time

The interest is primarily based on reputational capital in that those they have trained are seen to be "doing the right thing". Their power is relatively high in terms of referent power.

Staff working at Doctors with Wings

The interest is primarily to do with self-esteem and, bearing in mind the likely salary, somewhat philanthropic. Their power is primarily resource-based in that they provide their services and time for relatively low rewards.

Other similar charities

Other charities will be interested in the performance of Doctors with Wings from the perspective of both competition for resource from donors, but also quite possibly as collaborators when some emergencies reach the proportions that, unfortunately, attract a lot of interest.

Beneficiaries, and victims of medical emergencies

The interests of the beneficiaries will be purely self-serving in that they will want prompt and effective treatment and relief. Their power is virtually non-existent.

Test your understanding 5

(1) Potential conflict with professional behaviour – audit services observe the same standards, therefore implying that a rival has lower standards suggests that a firm is not complying with professional standards.

(2) The accountant is likely to lose objectivity because errors in the accounts made during preparation may not be identified when those accounts are reviewed.

(3) As the information is likely to be confidential, discussing it in a public place is inappropriate.

(4) The accountant needs to ensure that knowledge of the foreign country's taxation regime is understood prior to completing the return, otherwise there is the possibility that the appropriate professional skill will not be available.

(5) There is an issue of integrity. The accountant should not allow the report to be released because it is known that the report is incorrect.

(6) This is an issue of integrity. Accountants must not be associated with any form of communication or report that they know to be either materially false or misleading.

(7) The reduction of the number of staff in an organisation in order to increase profit is not necessarily unethical. For example, if the business has an unnecessarily high number of employees, reducing this number may be appropriate. However, the accountant would need to ensure that the analysis was accurate, as it will impact on individual's livelihoods. If there is any uncertainty in the results, they may need to consider whether it should be disclosed. In addition, the accountant will need to be aware of the implications and should ensure that the decision-makers are made aware of the potential ethical considerations.

(8) Again, this is an operational decision. There are ethical concerns over the loss of current staff which the accountant should make the decision-maker aware of along with the potential adverse impact on the reputation of the company.

(9) Ethics involves avoiding negative impacts on the environment that the company operates in. Even though legal, the decision to dump pollution into a river is unethical due to the impact on marine life. Should an accountant be complicit in such an action, it is likely to bring the profession into disrepute.

Test your understanding 6

Threat 1

- Do not offer the inducement!
- If necessary, follow the conflict resolution process of the employer.
- Consider the impact of the financial statements being misrepresented.

Threat 2

- Obtaining advice from the employer, professional organisation or professional advisor.
- The employer providing a formal dispute resolution process.
- Legal advice.

Threat 3

- Obtaining additional advice/training.
- Negotiating more time for duties.
- Obtaining assistance from someone with relevant expertise.

Test your understanding 7

(a) **Conflicting mission statement**

The mission statement that Router plc has published states that the firm aims to make the 'maximum possible profit'. It is quite common for objectives of this kind to be included in mission statements.

In addition, the 'wider responsibilities to society' are recognised. This company objective is difficult to measure and there will be instances where this conflicts with the maximisation of profit. The gold-mining project provides a perfect example of this. It is expected to be profitable, but also result in the loss of vegetation and the creation of poisonous lakes for the one hundred years.

While the business could attempt to repair the local environment, doing so would make the mine unprofitable, leading to a loss of value to Router's shareholders.

However, it could be argued that in the long run, being socially responsible could increase the wealth of Router's shareholders. Router needs the government to grant it licences in order to mine for gold and shareholders to continue investing in it. If it develops a reputation as a 'dirty' firm, both stakeholders may change their minds. This would cause a loss of profits and a drop in the share price. This would of course mean a fall in shareholder wealth.

(b) **Dealing with conflicting objectives**

As identified above, Router's objectives may conflict with each other. Methods of dealing with this include:

(1) **Establish a hierarchy of objectives:** Prioritise objectives and score alternative projects against them. For Router, it may need to decide which is more important – its wider social responsibilities or its desire to maximise profits.

(2) **Satisficing:** Router could try to give each stakeholder group something of what it wants. In this case, it could proceed with the mine and then provide some small amount of environmental restitution so that some of the damage is repaired.

(3) **Sequential attention:** This involves giving each stakeholder group's interests consideration over time, though not necessarily for every project. The effect is to keep them on board. In this case the mine could be abandoned because the environmental costs are too great. However, the next project, with less environmental damage, will be adopted. Shareholders and environmentalists will both feel that something has been achieved.

(4) **Side payments:** These are compensatory payments to keep stakeholders content. Perhaps good quality housing could be provided for the labour force which could be left after the works had finished. This could be pointed to as some compensation for the environmental damage and population displacement.

(c) **The principal ethical issues in mining are:**

(1) **The use of non-renewable resources:** The mining operation results in non-replaceable resources being extracted from the mine. This deprives both the present owners and future generations of the resources. Adequate compensation should be provided to the current owners and the resources extracted should not be wasted out of consideration for future generations.

(2) **The use of power in negotiations:** In the negotiations it is important that the profit motive does not lead to Router acting improperly and exploiting the present owner of the mining rights. Where the country is poor this is a particular concern.

(3) **The environmental damage:** Poisoning the land for a hundred years is clearly not a socially acceptable outcome. Router has an ethical duty to minimise the effect of this pollution by developing a plan to deal with the problem. This should be seen as the minimum the company should do.

(4) **Impacts on the life of local residents:** While they may benefit from the economic boost the mine provides to the region, it is likely that the pollution will also affect them. While there may only be a small number of local residents, this does not give Router the right to ignore their needs. They should explain the steps the company is going to take to minimise the effect on their local environment.

(5) **Safety of procedures:** Mining is an industry noted for its poor safety record. Router must ensure that strict safety guidelines are in place and that they are followed by the workforce. It should ensure these conform to best practises in its industry – even if this is more than the legal requirements in the country of operation.

chapter

4

Environmental analysis

Chapter learning objectives

Lead	Component
A1. Evaluate the key external factors affecting an organisation's strategy	(a) Evaluate the impact and influence of the external environment on an organisation and its strategy

Indicative syllabus content

- The customer portfolio: Customer analysis and behaviour, including the marketing audit and customer profitability analysis as well as customer retention and loyalty.

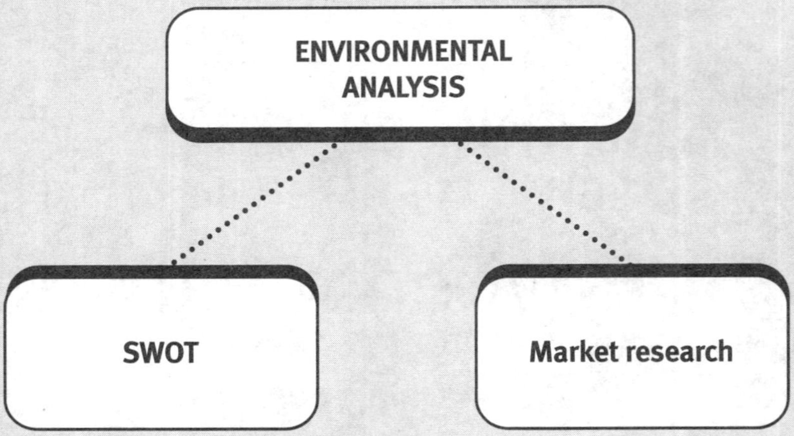

1 Environmental analysis

Organisations are strongly affected by their environment – essentially the world around them.

Part of the strategic planning process requires an analysis of the environment that the organisation operates within. Management should try to understand the past and the potential for the future and its possible impact upon the organisation. It should be remembered that all organisations are different and that modern environments are turbulent by nature and subject to ongoing change.

In order to make it easier to analyse the environment, it is sometimes broken down into two parts – the **internal** and **external** environments.

Internal environmental analysis will look for the **strengths and weaknesses** of the organisation.

External environmental analysis will look for the **opportunities and threats** that the organisation needs to be aware of.

There are a variety of tools and techniques to assist this environmental research which can also be used for general strategic planning purposes. Those for external analysis will be covered in chapter 5, while the models for internal analysis will be covered in chapter 6.

Environments have degrees of uncertainty attached to them which makes the task more difficult. Understanding them will involve research by skilled teams with appropriate budgets and the use of a variety of analytical skills.

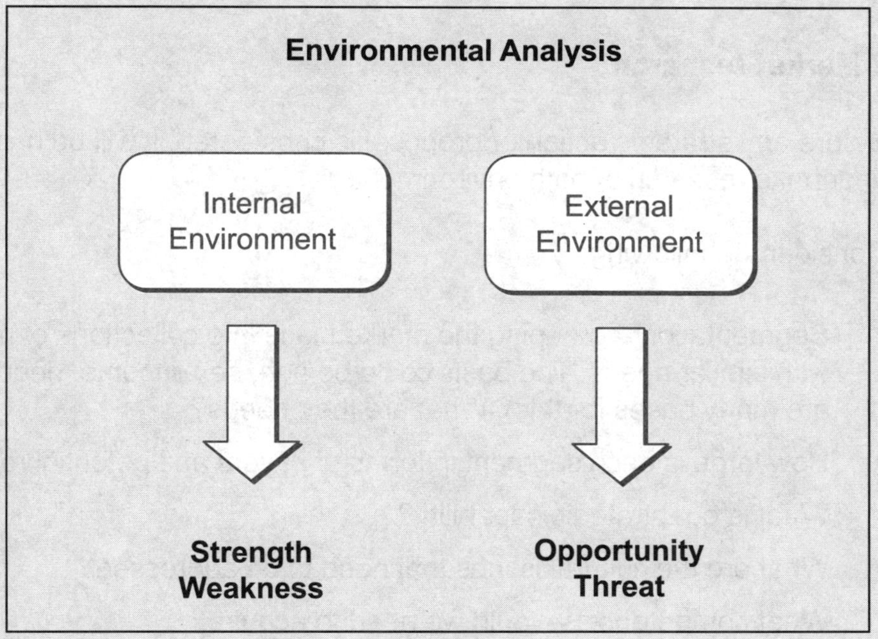

Resource Based (Internal)

S	W
• The things we are doing well • The things we are doing that the competition are not • Major successes	• The things we are doing badly (need to correct or improve) • The things we are not doing but should be • Major failures
O	**T**
• Events or changes in the external environment that can be exploited • Things likely to go well in the future	• Events or changes in the external environment we need to protect ourselves from or defend ourselves against • Things likely to go badly in the future

Position Based (External)

The internal and external appraisals of SWOT analysis will be brought together and it is likely that alternative strategies will emerge.

2 Market research

Before any strategic action or proposal is considered, it will be necessary to undertake research of both environments.

Consider the following:

- Segmentation – grouping the marketplace into collections of buyers with similar needs. The basis could be age, sex, income, needs... (there are many bases for this). What are their needs?
- How large is each segment in terms of buyers and potential revenues?
- What is our strategic capability?
- What are the cultural issues that need to be addressed?
- What competencies would we need to acquire?
- What are the consumer and customer needs now? What have they been in the past and how do we expect them to change in the future?
- How and when do they buy? How sophisticated is the demand?
- Who are the competition and what are they currently offering? Full competitor analysis needed.
- Environmental analysis perhaps using PEST or Porter's five forces as a starting position.
- Where are we in the life cycle? Innovation of product or process?

Approach

Secondary research undertaken first. Using material that is already available is cheaper though it has the downside of having been prepared for other purposes. The emphasis or assumptions used originally may therefore render the data misleading or useless.

Primary research should be undertaken after secondary has isolated key areas where accurate data is going to be needed. This approach is more time-consuming and costly and needs to be used sparingly. Organisations should ensure they have the HR and IT skills to be able to undertake this level of analysis.

Data collection

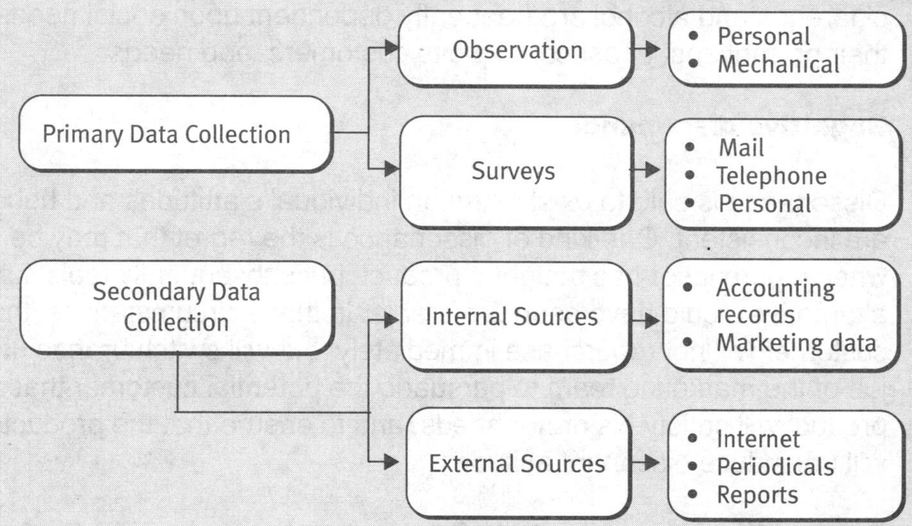

Customer analysis and behaviour – consumer markets

Customer behaviour

It is critical in consumer markets to understand **why** buyers purchase an organisation's goods or services. This will enable an organisation to identify critical success factors (CSFs) in markets, see if they have the required core competences to meet those CSFs and , hence, to determine an appropriate strategy.

Traditional views of marketing tend to assume that people purchase according to the value-for-money that they obtain. The customer considers the functional efficiency of the alternative products, and arrives at a decision by comparing this with the price. This set of beliefs is demonstrably inadequate in explaining consumer behaviour.

Maslow's hierarchy of needs

Remember that Maslow developed a hierarchy of needs to explain human motivation and behaviour. His 'need hierarchy' is as follows:

- physiological needs
- safety needs
- social needs
- status/ego needs
- self-fulfilment needs.

Products and services could be considered against this hierarchy. For example, insurance and banking are involved with safety needs; cigarettes and alcohol are frequently dependent upon social needs in their promotions; a fast car exploits customers' ego needs.

Cognitive dissonance

Dissonance is said to exist when an individual's attitudes and behaviour are inconsistent. One kind of dissonance is the regret that may be felt when a purchaser has bought a product, but subsequently feels that an alternative would have been preferable. In these circumstances, that customer will not repurchase immediately, but will switch brands. It is the job of the marketing team to persuade the potential customer that the product will satisfy his or her needs, and to ensure that the product itself will not induce dissonant attitudes.

Personality and product choice

Products, and their brand names, tend to acquire attributes in the mind of the potential customer; indeed, this is one of the primary functions of branding. When considering goods or services for a purchase, customers will invariably select those that have an image consistent with their own personality and aspirations.

Influence of other people

When people make purchase decisions, they reflect the values of their social and cultural environment. Often the form of products and services for sale has been determined by that environment. Among the more obvious influences are those of family and of reference groups.

The family is often important in engendering brand purchasing habits in grocery lines, although it also has a far broader influence in forming tastes in its younger members.

Customer analysis – consumer segmentation

Psychological

Consumers can be divided into groups sharing common psychological characteristics. One group may be described as security-oriented, another as ego-centred and so on. These categories are useful in the creation of advertising messages.

A recent trend is to combine psychological and socio-demographic characteristics to give a more complete profile of customer groups. Appropriately called lifestyle segmentation by one of the companies originating the method, this kind of segmentation uses individuals to represent groups that form a significant proportion of the consumer market. These individuals are defined in terms of sex, age, income, job, product preferences, social attitudes and political views.

Purchasing characteristics

Customers may be segmented by the volume they buy (heavy user, medium user, light user, non user). They may be segmented by the outlet type they use, or by the pack size bought. These variables, and many others, are useful in planning production and distribution and in developing promotion policy.

Demographic

Customers are defined in terms of age, sex, socio-economic class, country of origin, or family status. The most widely used forms of demographic segmentation in the UK are the socio-economic classification based on class (A, B, C1, C2 , D and E) and the life cycle model (Bachelor, Newly married couple, Full nest 1, Full nest 2, Full nest 3, Empty nest 1, Empty nest 2).

Geographic

Markets are frequently split into regions for sales and distribution purposes. Many consumer goods manufacturers break down sales by television advertising regions.

Benefit

Customers have different expectations of a product. Some people buy detergents for whiteness, others want economy, and yet others stain removal.

It can be seen that, within the same product class, different brands offer different perceived benefits. An understanding of customers' benefits sought enables the manufacturer to create a range of products each aimed precisely at a particular benefit.

Customer analysis and behaviour – industrial markets

Customer behaviour

Here are the main features of industrial buyers:

Motivation

An industrial buyer is motivated to satisfy the needs of the organisation rather than his or her individual needs. Often, purchases are repeat orders when the stock of items has fallen below a certain level and thus the buying motive is clear, i.e. avoiding nil stocks. With significant one-off purchases, the motivation will be the achievement of the organisation's goals or targets. Thus a profit target may mean the buyer placing an emphasis on cost minimisation. A growth target expressed in terms of sales motivates a purchase that will promote that goal.

The influence of the individual or group

An industrial purchase may be made by an individual or group. The individual or group is buying on behalf of the organisation but the buying decision may be influenced by the behavioural complexion of the individual or group responsible. The behavioural complexion will be influenced by the same influences on consumer buyers already discussed.

General organisational influences

Each organisation will have its own procedures and decision-making processes when purchases are made. Large centrally controlled organisations will often have centralised purchasing through a purchasing department. The purchase decisions will tend to be formal with established purchasing procedures. In small organisations there will not be a purchasing department. Purchasing decisions will tend to be made on a personal basis by persons who have other functions as well in the organisation. Personal relationships between the supplier and the buyer will often be very important.

Reciprocal buying

A feature in many industrial markets is the purchase of goods by organisation A from organisation B only on condition that organisation B purchases from organisation A.

Purchasing procedures

An industrial buyer appraises a potential purchase in a more formal way than a consumer buyer. Written quotations, written tenders and legal contracts with performance specifications may be involved. The form of payment may be more involved and may include negotiations on credit terms, leasing or barter arrangements.

Size of purchases

Purchases by an industrial buyer will tend to be on a much larger scale.

Derived demand

Demand for industrial products is generally derived from consumer demands. For example, when consumers demand more motor cars, the demand for steel, glass, components and so on will increase in the industrial sector. Industrial strategists have to know what markets the demand for their products is derived from, and monitor this market as well as their own. This may sound obvious, but when the firm is selling through intermediaries, or in overseas markets, there may be very little contact with users and end-users.

When industrialists predict a downturn in consumer markets, they will often cut back on production in the short run. This, of course, has the effect of lowering demand in the consumer markets through its effect on employment and wages, and is part of the trade cycle process discussed earlier.

Customer analysis – Industrial segmentation

- **Geographic:** The basis for sales-force organisation.
- **Purchasing characteristics:** The classification of customer companies by their average order size, the frequency with which they order, etc.
- **Benefit:** Industrial purchasers have different benefit expectations from consumers. They may be oriented towards reliability, durability, versatility, safety, serviceability, or ease of operation. They are always concerned with value for money.
- **Company type:** Industrial customers can be segmented according to the type of business they are, i.e. what they offer for sale. The range of products and services used in an industry will not vary too much from one company to another. A manufacturer considering marketing to a particular type of company would be well advised to list all potential customers in that area of business.

- **Company size:** It is frequently useful to analyse marketing opportunities in terms of company size. A company supplying canteen foods would investigate size in terms of numbers of employees. Processed parts suppliers are interested in production rate, and cutting lubricants suppliers would segment by numbers of machine tools.

3 Summary

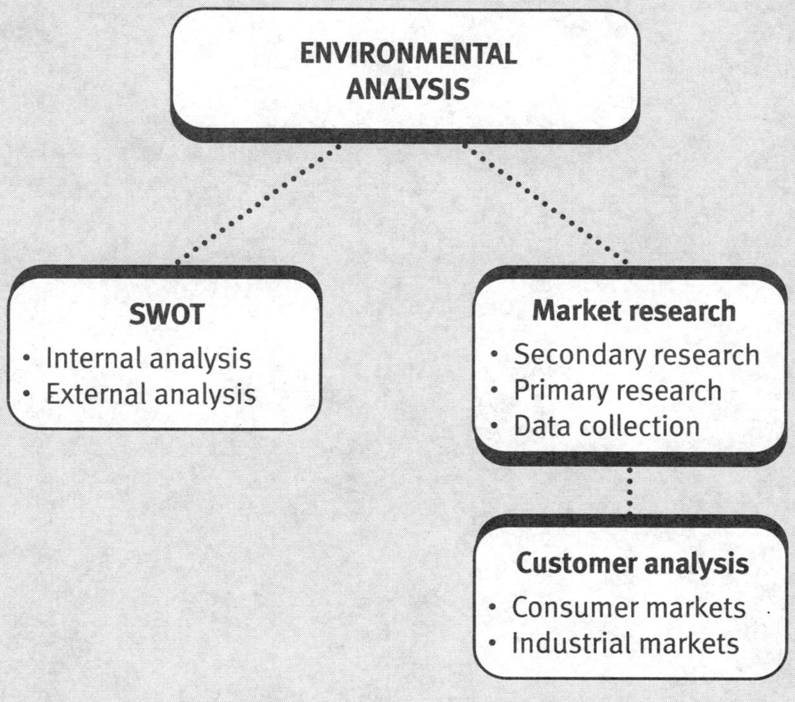
ENVIRONMENTAL ANALYSIS
SWOT
• Internal analysis
• External analysis
Market research
• Secondary research
• Primary research
• Data collection
Customer analysis
• Consumer markets
• Industrial markets

chapter

5

External environment

Chapter learning objectives

Lead	Component
A1. Evaluate the key external factors affecting an organisation's strategy	(a) Evaluate the impact and influence of the external environment on an organisation and its strategy
C1. Evaluate the process of strategy development	(b) Evaluate strategic options
C2. Evaluate the tools and techniques used in strategy formulation	(a) Evaluate strategic planning tools

Indicative syllabus content

- Evaluate strategic analysis tools.

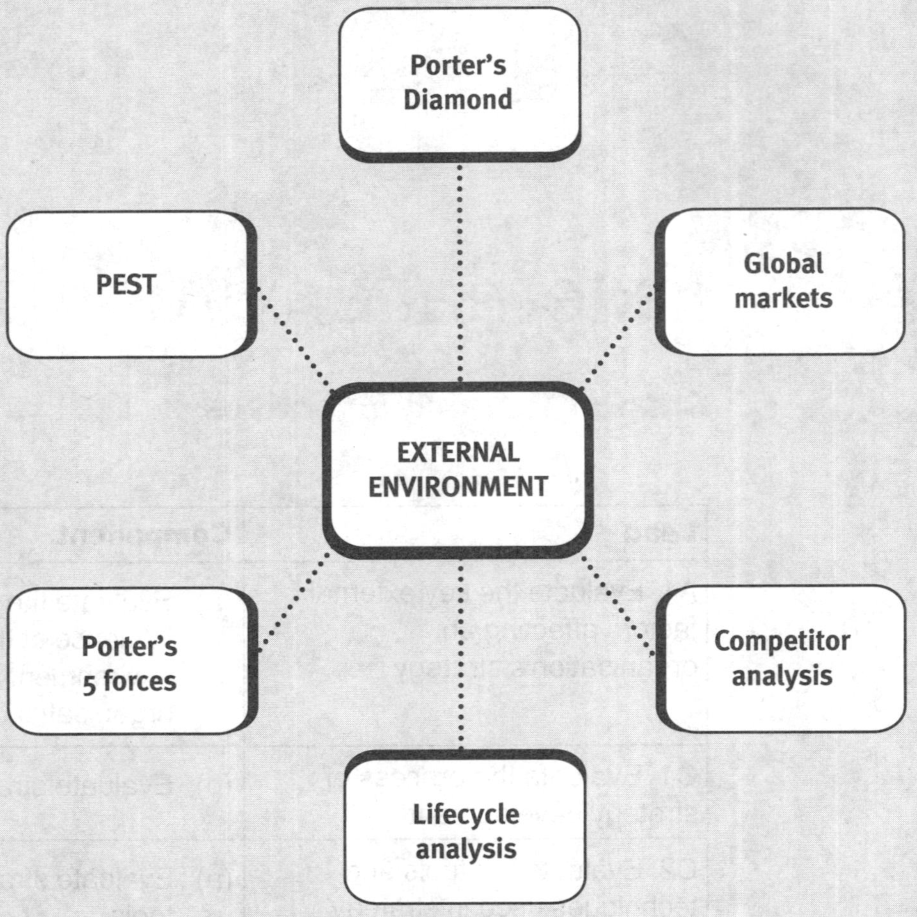

1 Introduction and the CIMA verb hierarchy

As stated in earlier chapters, a key aspect of strategy development lies in **positioning** an organisation within its external environment.

Within paper E2, Enterprise Management (previously P5 Integrated Management), you met a range of models for analysing the external environment, including PEST, Porter's 5 Forces, competitor analysis and Porter's diamond. These models are still needed for E3 for two reasons:

- Firstly they may be useful to analyse the preseen information that will form the basis of the Section A question in the E3 exam.
- Secondly the tools are still relevant to E3 exam questions except that E3 requirements will focus on higher level verbs in the CIMA verb hierarchy.

In E2 (P5) you were expected to use the models to "**discuss**" the nature of environments. In E3 you will be asked to **"evaluate"** the impact of the external environment, **"evaluate"** strategic options and **"evaluate"** strategic analysis tools.

Previous syllabus examiners often commented that they would set a level 5 requirement (e.g. "evaluate") but get a level 2 response (e.g. "describe") from students. To ensure you target your answer at the level required you need to consider the following:

(1) Use the models to identify relevant issues.

(2) Assess how significant the issue is and why.

(3) Try to see the bigger picture and consider what the organisation should now do.

e.g

Illustration

Superbooky owns a chain of betting shops in major cities and is considering the option of buying a rival chain. The betting industry is characterised by the following:

- Local authorities limit the number of betting shops they allow within their area through a licensing system.
- There is an ongoing debate in government over allowing more super-casinos, such as those seen in Las Vegas, for example.
- The main industry growth area is online betting.

Evaluate the strategy.

Solution

Note: this solution illustrates a possible thought process rather than detailing what you would write in the exam.

Step 1 – identify relevant issues ("what?")

Hopefully common sense would identify the licensing system as a barrier to entry for traditional betting shops. Alternatively a consideration of PEST (political factors) and/or Porter's 5 forces (threat of new entrants) would get to the same point. Following a similar process you should also have decided to discuss the growth of online betting.

Step 2 – further analysis ("so what?")

The licensing system is a major barrier to entry as it is impossible for rivals to open new shops without such permission and the number of licences is usually limited. This means there is a low threat of entry so the profits of incumbent operators in a particular area should be less risky. On the other hand it makes it difficult for all firms to expand to new areas, making the option of growth by acquisition more attractive.

The high growth in online betting is due to increasing access to the Internet. The main difference with traditional betting shops is precisely the much lower barriers to entry – it is relatively easy for new operators to set up a website and start trading. While there are some barriers to overcome such as website security and establishing a recognised brand name through marketing, this still much easier, quicker and cheaper than opening shops. However, it also means that competitive rivalry for online betting is likely to intensify.

Step 3 – recommendations ("what now?")

The proposal is for expansion within traditional betting shops. You could argue that the market for traditional shops is likely to decline in the future as people switch to online and perhaps Superbooky should consider expanding into Internet betting. However, traditional shops are less risky than online, where the lack of barriers will give rise to increasing competition.

If Superbooky does want to expand in traditional operations then the acquisition looks attractive as the alternative of organic growth is limited by the licensing system. Further analysis here could involve looking at exactly where the rival's shops are and whether the territories overlap.

2 PEST analysis

Exam focus

- Analyses the general macro-environment, identifying key drivers of change and hence sources of risk.
- Particularly good at identifying whether a market is growing/declining and why.
- Can also be used to generate ideas for a position analysis – identifying opportunities and threats.

Model

P Political (including legal)

E Economic

S Social

T Technological

Also known as PESTLE, SLEPT, Le Pest & co.

Look for factors on local, industry, national and global levels, both now and in the future.

Political	Social
• Change of government • New laws • Political union • War • Tax • Global political moves	• Demography • Culture & lifestyle • Education • Income • Consumerism
Economic	**Technological**
• Interest rates • Exchange rates • Inflation • Unemployment • Balance of payments • Business cycle	• Rate of development & transfer • Innovation • Obsolescence • Changing cost base

3 Porter's Five Forces analysis

Exam focus

- Just because an industry is large and/or growing, high profits do not necessarily follow. The five forces determine profit potential, both for the industry as a whole and for individual firms/SBUs.
- Strong collective forces give low profitability overall.
- An individual firm can earn better margins than competitors if it can deal more effectively with key forces.
- The model can also be useful to generate ideas for a position analysis – especially threats.

Model

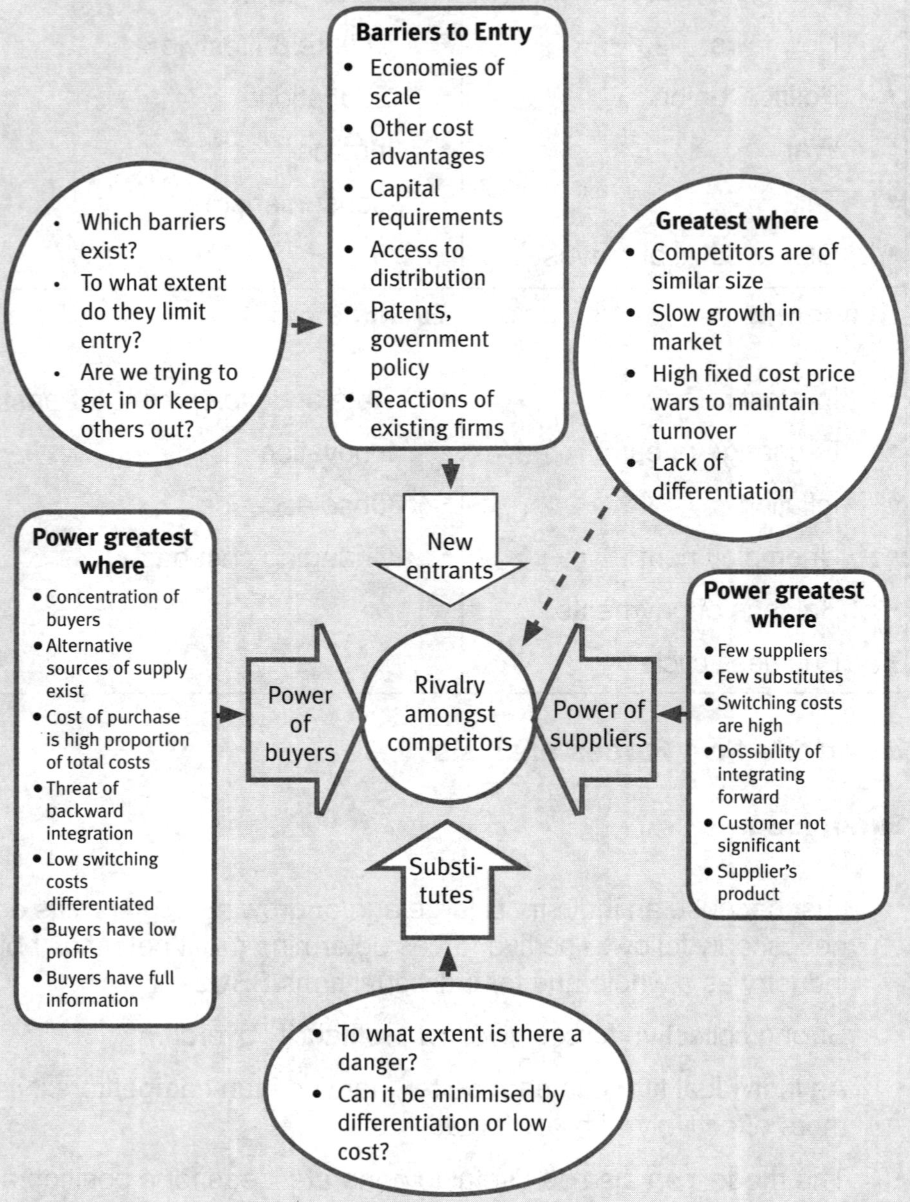
Barriers to Entry
• Economies of scale
• Other cost advantages
• Capital requirements
• Access to distribution
• Patents, government policy
• Reactions of existing firms
• Which barriers exist?
• To what extent do they limit entry?
• Are we trying to get in or keep others out?
Greatest where
• Competitors are of similar size
• Slow growth in market
• High fixed cost price wars to maintain turnover
• Lack of differentiation
New entrants
Power greatest where
• Concentration of buyers
• Alternative sources of supply exist
• Cost of purchase is high proportion of total costs
• Threat of backward integration
• Low switching costs differentiated
• Buyers have low profits
• Buyers have full information
Power of buyers
Rivalry amongst competitors
Power of suppliers
Power greatest where
• Few suppliers
• Few substitutes
• Switching costs are high
• Possibility of integrating forward
• Customer not significant
• Supplier's product
Substi-tutes
• To what extent is there a danger?
• Can it be minimised by differentiation or low cost?

Explanation of Porter's 5 Forces

(1) **Threat of new entrants**

This will depend upon the extent to which there are **barriers to entry**.

Establish:

- which barriers exist
- the extent to which they are likely to prevent entry
- the organisation's position – is it trying to prevent or attempt entry?

Economies of scale

The scale of operation allows economies of scale to be reaped which new entrants may not be able to match, e.g. UK supermarkets with bulk purchasing, the computer industry and the steel industry.

Capital requirement for entry

This could be high for capital intensive industries such as chemicals, power and mining but low for high-street retailers who would be able to lease premises. Pharmaceutical industry has large R&D costs and long lead times.

Access to distribution channels

For decades brewing firms have invested in bars and pubs which has guaranteed distribution of their product and made it difficult for competitors to break into the marketplace. Effectively the new entrant is prevented from reaching the customer.

Cost advantages independent of size

Access to cheaper labour or raw materials. Well-established companies know the market well and have the confidence of the major buyers along with the established architecture which serves the market.

Expected retaliation

If you expect a competitor to retaliate on your entry then this may act as a deterrent to enter the market – they may enter a price war and drive down margins in response to your entry.

Legislation

Legal conditions may exist for entry, e.g. licences and personal guarantees, telecommunications and financial services.

Differentiation

Branding and/or high quality may create customer loyalty and inelastic demand for their product, which may take longer to break down for the new entrant.

Switching costs

Customers may have to invest in the trading relationship via contractual arrangements or an investment in IT. To switch supplier would entail substantial costs and therefore the new entrant would have a challenge on their hands.

(2) **Bargaining power of buyers**

This is likely to be high when there is a concentration of buyers, particularly if the volume purchases of the buyers are high, e.g. grocery retailing.

This is likely to be further accentuated when the selling industry comprises a large number of small firms and the product is standard with little or no switching costs involved.

(3) **Bargaining power of suppliers**

Close linkages to the preceding section. Supplier power is likely to be high when:

- the input is important to the buying company
- the supplier industry is dominated by a few suppliers who have secure market positions and are not subject to competitive pressure
- supplier products are branded or involve switching costs
- supplier customers are highly fragmented with little buying power.

(4) **Threat of substitutes**

Substitutes can render products obsolete and can be direct or indirect. They can be based on actual products or uses, e.g. a Rover or a SAAB; a car or a bicycle.

There can also be substitution based on income or even doing without, e.g. new furniture or a holiday; giving up smoking.

The availability of substitutes can place a limit on price and change the basis of the product. Consideration must be given to the ease with which consumers can switch to substitutes along with the perceived value that consumer groups would place on the products. At the same time, evaluation of potential actions to build customer loyalty should be undertaken. For example, advertising to build brand image.

(5) **Competitive rivalry**

Some markets are more competitive than others. In highly competitive markets companies regularly monitor competitors. It can be intense or remote and tends to depend upon historical development.

Factors affecting level of rivalry:

- The extent to which competitors are in balance – roughly equal-sized firms in terms of market share or finances – often leads to highly competitive marketplaces.
- Stage of the life cycle. During market growth stages all companies grow naturally, whilst in mature markets growth can only be obtained at the expense of someone else.
- High storage costs may lead to cost-cutting to improve turnover which in turn increases the rivalry.
- Extra capacity comes in large increments which means price cutting may follow to fill capacity.
- Difficulty in differentiating products leaves the basis for competition on price or augmented product.
- High exit barriers mean that some companies must stay in the market.

Conclusion

A desirable circumstance would be a situation where there are weak suppliers and buyers, few substitutes with high barriers to entry and little rivalry.

Criticisms of Porter's 5 Forces model

Over the last three decades business has focused on one fundamental idea – the pursuit of sustainable competitive advantage. While the idea of competition is not new, Michael Porter expanded the concept from competing with rivals to incorporating the struggle for power between the firm and five competitive forces. Porter argued that each of these forces can reduce overall industry profitability and the individual firm's share of that profit – their 'profit potential' – because they can influence prices, costs and the level of investment required.

Not everyone agrees with Porter – some would argue that the idea of satisfying customer needs should not be abandoned in favour of a view that sees customers either as direct competitors or as means to the firm's end. Customers are not objects whose reason for being is to be fought over by competitors seeking 'sustainable competitive advantage'. Porter's model might thus distract managers from seeing customers as potential partners.

Other limitations include the following:

Limitations in the use of the 5 Forces model

Dynamic industries

- May find little benefit from industry analysis
- By the time the analysis has been done, the industry has moved on
- Focus more on risk management and competences

Outside-in vs. inside-out

- 5 Forces is of great help to strategic planning but is difficult to apply for competence based businesses (strategic management) – e.g. hi-tech/innovative companies.

Role of government

- Some analysts add this as a 6th force (e.g. Ryanair have sued the EU for allowing airlines such as Air France and Lufthansa to receive government subsidies allowing them to cut the price of European flights).

Collaboration

- Model assumes businesses operate independently against each other and ignores collaborative benefits (e.g. joint ventures, alliances etc)

NFP

- 5 Forces focuses on industry profitability → not a main objective of NFPs.
- Also any business not pursuing a profit objective may not find it useful.

Test your understanding 1

Hawk Leathers Ltd ("Hawk") is a company based in the UK that employs around 60 people in the manufacture and sale of leather jackets, jeans, one- and two-piece suits and gloves. These are aimed primarily at motorcyclists, although a few items are sold as fashion garments.

Hawk sells 65% of its output to large retail chains such as Motorcycle City and Carnells, exports 25% to the USA and Japan, and sells the remaining 10% to individuals who contact the company directly. The latter group of customers specify their requirements for a made-to-measure suit (they are often professional racers whose suits must be approved by the authorities, such as the Auto Cycle Union). The large retailers insist on low margins and are very slow to settle their debts.

There are around a dozen companies in the UK who make similar products to Hawk, plus very many other companies who compete with much lower prices and inferior quality. Hawk's typical selling price for a one-piece suit is £1,000, whereas the low quality rivals' suits retail at around £400. As Hawk say in their literature "if you hit the tarmac, there's no substitute for a second skin from Hawk". Synthetic materials are waterproof, unlike leather, but do not currently offer sufficient protection in an accident.

Sales of leathers in the UK are growing rapidly, mainly due to a resurgence of biking from more mature riders of large, powerful machines. Such riders are often wealthy and have family and financial commitments. Currently Hawk, and its rivals for quality leathers are finding it hard to keep up with demand. However, government policy and EU emissions controls are likely to limit motorcycle performance, and some experts predict that these regulations will cause sales of large motorcycles to level off.

Whilst supplies of leather from Asia, Scandinavia and the UK are plentiful, a key problem is recruiting and training machinists to stitch and line the garments. Hawk has been able to invest in modern machinery to help production but the process is still labour intensive. Hawk has found that the expertise, reputation and skilled labour needed to succeed in the industry takes years to build up.

Although the industry is fairly traditional, there are some new developments such as a website for individual customers to browse and specify requirements, and new colours such as metallics for leathers, and a small but growing demand from non-bikers who are interested in 'recreational' and 'club wear' items.

Required:

(a) Analyse the issues facing Hawk's industry using a PEST analysis.

(b) Using Porter's 5 forces, evaluate the strength of each competitive pressure facing Hawk.

Use the information above and aim for one or two points under each heading.

4 Industry life cycle analysis

Product life cycle

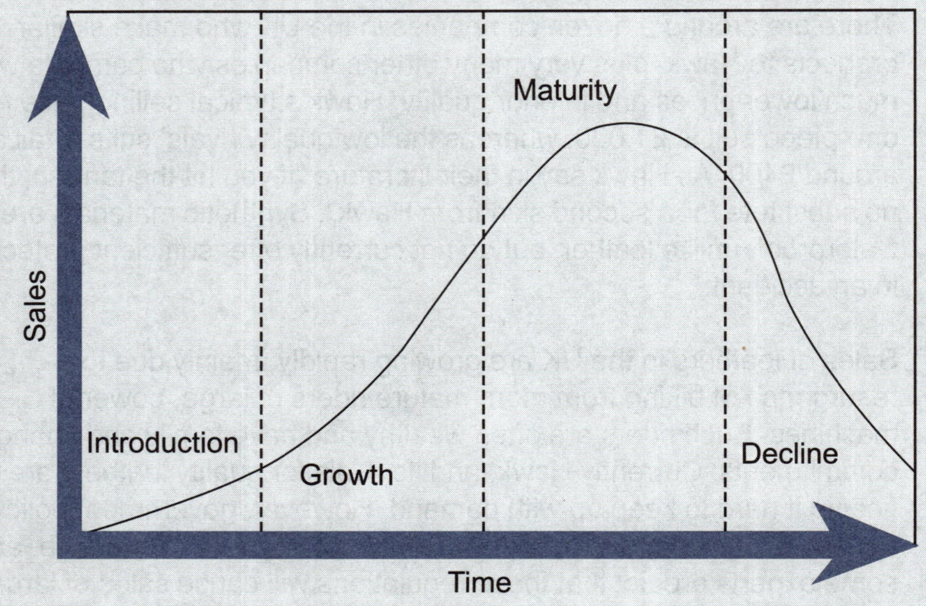

Products and industries are thought to have a finite life which goes through stages. SBUs should be considered in this light to ensure that an adequate balance exists.

It can be used to predict competitive conditions and identify key issues for management in corporate appraisals and strategic choices.

Introduction stage

The product is new to the market at this stage. Key points are:

- it will be purchased by 'innovators'
- high launch and marketing costs are likely
- production volumes will be low and product cost will be high
- buyers are unsophisticated
- competition is little if any.

Price elasticity of demand will influence the pricing strategy.

- **Price skimming** is appropriate when the product is known to have a price-inelastic demand.
- **Penetration pricing** is appropriate where the demand is thought to be price-elastic and when gaining market share is seen as more important than fast recovery of development costs.

'Pioneer companies', who are the first to the market with a particular product, are usually forced to sell the concept. These early promotions will help competitor companies who enter later with 'me too' versions of the product concept.

Early entry is risky as heavy requirement for cash and product idea may fail BUT early entry allows the prospect of establishing market share and developing first mover advantage.

Growth stage

During this stage the market grows rapidly. Key points are:

- sales for the market as a whole increase
- new competitors, attracted by the prospects, enter to challenge the 'pioneer'
- new segments may be developed
- demand becomes more sophisticated
- competition levels increase.

The market becomes profitable and cash flows increase to recover the initial investment in development and launch costs.

There are many new consumers with no preference who they buy from.

It will become more difficult in later stages to persuade people to switch from their existing brand. It is important to build a brand during this stage if possible to ease the traumas at the later stages via defensive strategy.

Prices often fall due to economies of scale and increasing competitive pressure, and evidence of differentiation will become apparent, e.g. branding develops.

Maturity stage

During this stage market growth slows or even halts. Key points are:

- fully sophisticated demand
- high levels of competition
- price becomes more sensitive
- demand reaches saturation. The only way to increase market share is to gain business from competitors or from 'late adopters' or 'laggards'
- it would be desirable to have a high market share at this stage or to have successfully developed a niche
- large market share changes can be difficult to achieve at this stage and most companies would concentrate on defensive strategies to protect their current position and compete hard for the new customers coming into the marketplace
- over time the company must be vigilant to detect and anticipate changes in the market and be ready to undertake product or market modifications with a view to lengthening the life.

Decline

During this stage the number of customers falls. Key points are:

- competition reduces as players leave
- price falls to attract business as sophisticated customers expect cheap prices
- slow 'harvesting' must be balanced with straight divestment
- investment kept to a minimum to take up any market share that may be left by departing competitors
- there may be profitable niches remaining after industrial death.

Considerations

- Offer a range of products at various stages of the life cycle – mature products will fund the development of new products
- competencies need to change – at the early stages, creativity and innovation are key whilst at later stages efficiencies and low costs become important

- life cycles are difficult to predict, can change quickly and will vary from one product to another. Turning points are very hard to predict
- management anticipation of decline can cause decline! Reduction in investment and advertising can cause the appropriate market response
- SWOT varies across the life cycle
- strategies will need to change as the organisation progresses through the life cycle.

Consider

The market for calculators started with scientists and engineers and then moved to business before moving to higher education students. Finally the market moved to include schoolchildren, which proved to be the largest segment of all. A pioneer wishing to stay the course would experience radical change as they move from the organisational markets to the mass consumer version.

Summary of industry life cycle

	Intro	Growth	Maturity	Decline
Sales	Low	Rapidly rising	Peak	Declining
Costs per customer	High cost	Average	Low	Low
Profits	Negative	Rising	High	Falling
Customers	Innovators	Early adopters	Middle majority	Laggards
Competitors	Few	Growing number	Stable number beginning to decline	Declining number
Objectives	Create product awareness & trial	Maximise market share	Maximise profit whilst defending market share	Reduce expenditure & 'milk the brand'

Strategies

Product	Offer basic product	Offer product extensions, service & warranty	Diversify brands & models	Phase out weak items
Price	Cost plus	Price penetration	Price matching	Price cutting
Promotion	Build product awareness amongst early adopters & dealers	Build awareness & interest in mass market	Stress brand differences & benefits	Reduce to level to maintain hard core loyals
Place	Limited	Growing	Maximum	Limited

Test your understanding 2

You have recently been appointed to the European strategy steering group at PTP Electronics, the holding company for a number of subsidiary companies making household name consumer electronic products. Four products were discussed at the recent meeting. All appear to be profitable, and some large retail outlets sell the whole range of PTP products in their stores.

- Recordable DVD players – the market has been expanding very quickly since its launch four years ago and PTP has a very small share compared to Sony and Panasonic.
- Traditional DVD players – sales are levelling off as people switch to Blu-Ray players and downloading movies over the Internet. PTP's brands have been a market leader since the late 1990s.
- Conventional CRT colour television monitors – demand for CRT TVs is declining as customers and manufacturers turn to newer technologies. PTP has recently built a new factory in Holland to produce plasma and LCD televisions (see below). Consequently it has not pushed sales of conventional TVs, but has a small share of the CCTV market.
- Plasma and LCD televisions – although expensive, PTP sees these as a huge future market with the increase in digital broadcasting. It is the market leader in this field although sales in volume terms are not rising as fast as had been hoped. Launch was five years ago.

Required:

(a) Use the product lifecycle model to **identify and comment** on the lifecycle position of each product type, with reasons.

(b) **Evaluate** the balance of PTP's product portfolio as a whole. **Advise** PTP's directors of one idea that you feel may help improve the portfolio balance.

5 Competitor analysis (competitor intelligence)

This can be defined as a set of activities which examines the comparative position of competing enterprises within a given strategic sector. It seeks to:

- provide an understanding of the company's competitive advantage/disadvantage relative to its competitor's positions
- help generate insights into competitors strategies - past, present and potential
- give an informed basis for developing future strategies to sustain/establish advantages over competitors.

Grant highlights three purposes:

- to forecast competitors' future strategies and decisions
- to predict competitors' likely reactions to a firm's strategic initiatives
- to determine how competitor **behaviour** can be influenced to make it more favourable for the organisation.

A framework for competitor analysis

Step 1: identify competitors

- **Brand competitors** sell similar products to the same customers we serve, e.g. Coke and Pepsi.
- **Industry competitors** sell similar products but in different segments, e.g. BA and Singapore Airlines.
- **Form competitors** sell products that satisfy the same need as ours though technically very different, e.g. speedboat and sports car.
- **Generic competitors** compete for the same income, e.g. home improvements and golf clubs.

Step 2: analyse competitors

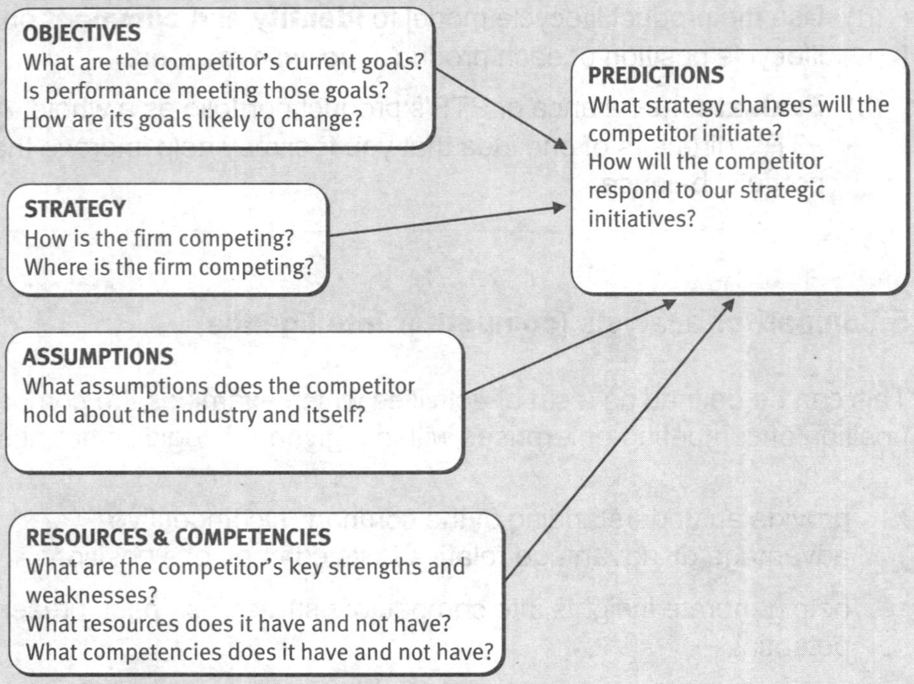

Step 3: develop competitor response profiles

- **Laid back:** Does not respond;
- **Selective:** Reacts to attack in only selected markets;
- **Tiger:** Always responds aggressively;
- **Stochastic:** No predictable pattern exists.

6 The nature of global competition

Why enter foreign markets?

- **Pressure** from shareholders to increase their return on capital employed
- **saturated** domestic markets making home expansion difficult
- **opportunities** as emerging markets arise with increases in economic income and spending power
- **trade barriers coming down** enabling competitors to compete in our domestic markets as well as increasing the opportunities for our company overseas.

Risks arising

- **Marketing mix adaptations** are needed and questions must be addressed as to how these modifications should be made and when. Consideration must be given to the cultural implications and the potential costs involved.
- **Cultures vary** more dramatically when national boundaries are traversed and cultural environment needs full evaluation.
- **Varying cost structures** will exist from one country to another as will **factor quality** – there may not be sufficient skilled labour and management to enable a global strategy.
- **Different competitive levels** will exist in different markets and the level of competition will need to be determined.
- **Exchange rate volatility** requires the deployment of control systems to protect the company.
- **Different economic situations** will alter the demand for the product and the availability of factors of production.
- **Political involvement** as governments will seek to be involved in decisions. Careful planning will be needed to ensure that no conflict arises or, if likely, the allocation of responsibility to a suitably qualified individual.
- **Political situation** should be considered with regard to war, terrorism and government stability. What are the risks to our personnel and our organisation?
- **Entry requirements?** What do we have to do to get in? Is it legal and ethical?

Benefits of entering global markets

- **Economies of scale** are possible as research and development can now be spread over wider production volumes. Bulk-buying discounts may be available as the volume of our purchases and our reputation increases.
- **Management opportunity** is increased and this may prove motivational to certain types of managers whilst at the same time allowing those managers to experience a wider range of cultural situations.
- This in turn allows the **challenge to the traditional home cultural** perspective. Items can be viewed from a different perspective with cultural benchmarks being developed.
- **Cheaper sources of raw materials** and labour may allow the development of a competitive advantage which could be sustainable for a period of time.

- **Market development** as the emerging markets bring a whole new range of consumers who will be embarking on their 'first buy' and so may not be as 'fussy' as consumers in a saturated market.
- **Risk reduction** via portfolio spread will arise when different markets are combined into a portfolio.
- **Political sponsorship** will be possible as national governments, keen to boost or maintain home employment, offer attractive packages to global companies to invest in that country.
- **Political power** becomes possible as the company grows in size and is seen to be contributing to wealth creation as opposed to exploitation of the nation concerned.

7 Competitive advantage of nations – Porter's Diamond

Porter's questions were:

(1) Why do certain nations house so many successful international firms?

(2) How do they sustain superior performance in a global marketplace?

(3) What are the implications for government policy and strategy?

The study suggests reasons why some nations are more competitive than others and why some industries within nations are more competitive than others.

Porter's Diamond

The competitive advantage of nations

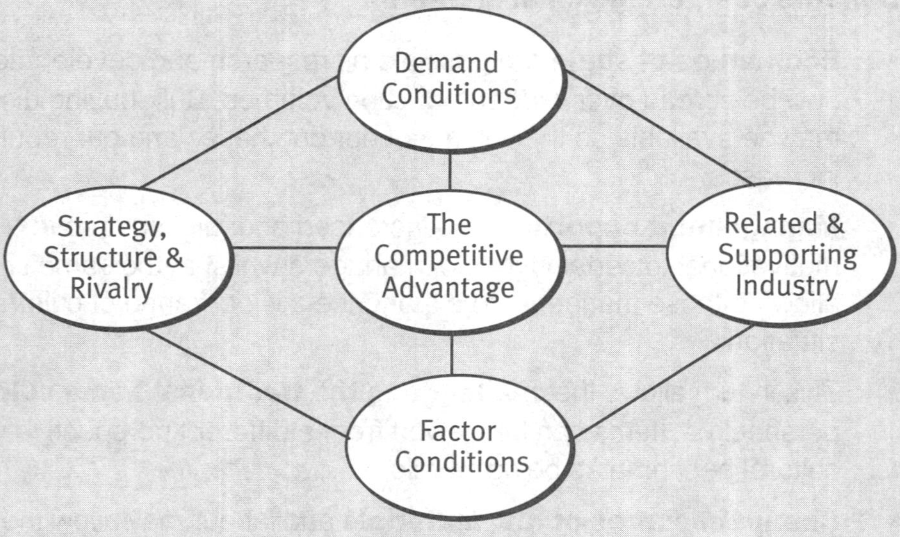

Factor conditions – supply side

A supply of production factors that convey advantage. They provide initial advantage which is then subsequently built upon to develop more advanced factors. Basic factors are unsustainable as they are easily copied (unskilled labour) whilst advanced factors can convey the advantage as they are less easy to emulate (scientific expertise).

They include human, physical, knowledge, capital and infrastructure, for example:

- linguistic ability of the Swiss has provided advantage in the banking industry
- financial expertise within the UK.

You can use the national identity as the basis for a brand, e.g. New Zealand lamb.

Demand conditions – demand side

Sophisticated home demand can lead to the company developing significant advantages in the global marketplace. Fussy consumers set high standards for products whilst past experience of the product's progress through the life cycle in the home market can provide valuable input to new strategic initiatives.

- Japanese customers have high expectations of their electrical products, which forces producers to provide a technically superior product for the global marketplace. They are so used to dealing with sophisticated customers that when they come across unsophisticated markets, they excel way beyond the competition.
- Nokia – a Finnish Telecoms company.

Related and supporting industry – the value chain and system

Advantage conveyed by the availability of superior supplier industries, e.g. Italy has a substantial leatherwear industry which is supported by leather-working plants and top fashion and design companies.

Strategy, structure and rivalry – the competition element

Different nations have different approaches to business in terms of structure and the intensity of rivalry that can take place. If a company is used to dealing with strong competition then it will have experience of rivals' attacks and so will be better able to fight them off.

Domestic rivalry can keep the organisations 'lean and mean' so that when they go out into the global marketplace they can compete more successfully with the less capable foreign competition, e.g. Nokia and Finland's approach to the regulation of telecoms.

Governments can promote this rivalry via policy.

Other events

Porter points out that countries can produce world-class firms due to two further factors:

- **The role of government** – subsidies, legislation and education can all impact on the other four elements of the diamond to the benefit of the industrial base of the country.
- **The role of chance events** – wars, civil unrest, chance discoveries and others can also change the four elements of the diamond unpredictably.

Cultural empathy

The key to success for the international firm lies with researching and understanding each country's culture and proactively building cultural empathy with a view to establishing a long-term market position.

Cultural empathy is achieved in a number of ways:

- acquire in-company knowledge and experience
- continuous market research
- visit foreign country and customers
- hire local personnel
- use distributors/agents
- joint ventures and strategic alliances
- build language skills.

Research – the important factor

Research is critical before entering a foreign market. Then on a regular basis, more research is needed as well as the setting up of systems to ensure that it is continually updated and monitored.

What should they research? Some suggestions:

- customer and consumer needs
- the environment
- satisfaction surveys and the value chain
- competitor identification and analysis
- position review.

Market entry decisions

Decision criteria

The decision as to which countries and markets are to be entered first will be based upon a number of important factors:

- **The potential size of the market** – is the market for the product in the country likely to be significant? This will, in turn, be determined by the following:
- **Economic factors** – are income levels adequate to ensure that significant numbers of people are likely to be able to afford the product?
- **Cultural and linguistic factors** – is the culture of the country likely to favour acceptance of the product to be offered?
- **Political factors** – what are the factors which may limit entry to markets in the host country?
- **Technological factors** – are levels of technology adequate to support provision of the product in the host market and are technological standards compatible?
- **The means of entry** – acquisition, alliance/joint venture or organic growth.

A business will initially choose to enter markets in those countries where the above conditions are most favourable. This involves considering the attractiveness of the markets and the barriers to entry that may exist. Strong position audit is needed to assess our company's strategic capability in these new segments.

At the same time decisions must be made as to the extent of ethical variation that an organisation is prepared to involve itself in.

Criticisms of Porter's Diamond model

The following criticisms are made of Porter's Diamond model:

- Porter developed the model by looking at ten developed countries. The model thus only really applies to developed economies.
- Porter argues that inbound-FDI does not increase domestic competition significantly because domestic firms lack the capability to defend their own markets and face a process of market-share erosion and decline. However, there seems to be little empirical evidence to support that claim.
- The Porter model does not adequately address the role of MNCs. There seems to be ample evidence that the diamond is influenced by factors outside the home country.
- Porter's analysis focused on manufacturers, banks and management consultancy firms. Some have questioned its relevance to service-based companies such as McDonalds.
- Porter's focus is on the domestic country rather than which foreign markets have been targeted. A careful choice of target is essential to ensure that the firm has the competences required for success.
- Not all firms from a given country are successful, suggesting that corporate management is more important than geographical location.

Test your understanding 3

Australia has a long-established wine industry, but in the 1970s it decided to expand exports to Europe and the USA, since growth was becoming limited in domestic markets.

Australian producers had benefitted from strong domestic demand, and had produced excellent results by cultivating grape varieties imported from Europe, combined with innovative techniques such as cool fermentation in stainless steel containers. Producers had achieved success in a wide range of wines including red, white, sparkling, dry and sweet.

Although many producers started out as independent small businesses, major listed groups such as Penfolds had consolidated many of these small producers into well-known labels.

Required:

(a) Discuss two reasons why Australian wine producers decided to enter foreign markets, and two risks arising.

(b) By giving one example of each element, use Porter's Diamond to evaluate the degree of competitive advantage achieved by the Australian wine industry.

Test your understanding 4

PD – international issues and Porter's diamond

PD has traded very successfully in its domestic country for many years. It has built up its reputation for quality and reliability as a result of supplying products which are specifically designed to meet the needs of its customers.

PD's directors are now considering launching the company's products in other parts of the world, but they have no experience of trading internationally. The managing director has heard of Porter's Diamond theory of the competitive advantage of nations. He has turned to you as the management accountant to provide some advice on whether Porter's theory can be applied to assist PD in its international development, and the factors which should be considered before developing internationally.

Required:

Advise PD's board of directors of the factors which it should consider before launching the company's products internationally.

Your advice should include an assessment of how Porter's Diamond theory can be applied to assist the company in determining whether or not it should develop internationally.

(25 marks)

(May 2001)

8 Summary

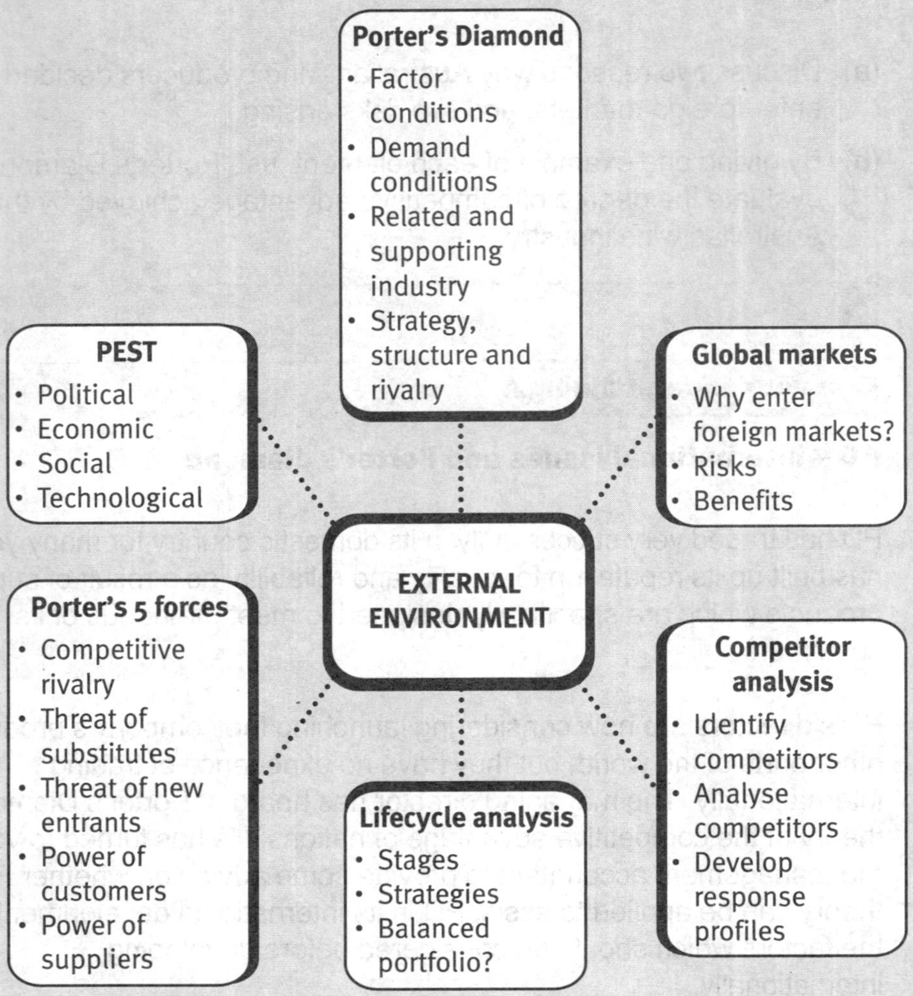
Porter's Diamond
• Factor conditions
• Demand conditions
• Related and supporting industry
• Strategy, structure and rivalry
PEST
• Political
• Economic
• Social
• Technological
Global markets
• Why enter foreign markets?
• Risks
• Benefits
EXTERNAL ENVIRONMENT
Porter's 5 forces
• Competitive rivalry
• Threat of substitutes
• Threat of new entrants
• Power of customers
• Power of suppliers
Competitor analysis
• Identify competitors
• Analyse competitors
• Develop response profiles
Lifecycle analysis
• Stages
• Strategies
• Balanced portfolio?

Test your understanding answers

Test your understanding 1

PEST analysis

Political factors

Approval from the ACU is vital for Hawk's racing suits. Whilst this will require regular inspections, it is important for credibility amongst customers. It may be seen as an endorsement of quality for the entire range (the so-called "halo effect").

Government/EU regulation that could damage motorcycle sales is an issue for the whole industry. If there is a clamp down it might seriously threaten sales. Hawk might consider setting up a lobby group with other manufacturers.

Economic factors

The recession in the UK economy (and foreign markets) is likely to result in lower disposable incomes for what is often a luxury purchase. Hawk may well find a major dip in sales as the recession continues.

The weakening pound is making exports to the USA and Europe easier, but is increasing the import costs of leather. There is little Hawk can do about that, so it is likely to seek new global markets such as the BRIC economies (Brazil, Russia, India and China).

Social factors

There has been a growth in demand from mature riders ("born-again bikers"). Have companies such as Hawk done any research to assess the life of this trend? How effective is Hawk's marketing at reaching this potentially important market segment?

More emphasis on safety of riders who often have family; this is a boost for the industry and Hawk's customers are likely to be responsible bikers.

Technological factors

Relevant issues include website ordering and metallic paints but neither of these is especially important. However, Hawk and others should be aware of new ideas that could help with their processes.

Porter's five forces

Threat of new entrants

The threat of new entrants is reasonably high from overseas rivals but is limited by existing entry barriers. These include recruiting skilled staff, close associations with racing teams, established relationships with major retailers and brand reputation.

Bargaining power of customers

The power of customers depends on which customers are being considered. For individual customers it is low because they will be loyal to the brand and are not buying in bulk.

However, for the large retailers there is higher power that arises from the volumes purchased. Retail chains will exercise this power in terms of designs, lead times, prices paid and credit period taken. Hawk need to meet these needs or risk losing major customers to existing/new competition.

It will also be high for the professional racing teams. Having Hawk's products associated with top class racing teams is imperative to maintain the quality of its brand in the marketplace. Suits must be made to a high quality and exactly to customer specification/compliance with the Auto Cycle Union's requirements.

Bargaining power of suppliers

The power of suppliers is generally low, because leather and machinery are readily available. (Note: It may be that supply of leather of the required quality for professional suits is limited, in which case the power would be higher.)

However, supplies of skilled labour are limited and Hawk may find it has to pay high wages.

Threat of substitutes

Hawk believes that the threat from substitutes is low and states that only leather can offer the required degree of abrasion resistance. Clearly this must be kept under review as newer fabrics and technologies may change this perception.

The threat of substitute products/fabrics may be higher in the fashion lines, although this does not yet constitute a major proportion of Hawk's turnover.

Competitive rivalry

Rivalry is considered to be low. Those "rivals" that offer cheap leathers are not really rivals at all, because serious bikers will not contemplate such offerings.

Furthermore, sales are rising so quickly that all players are working at near capacity without the need to take customers from one another.

Summary

The key risk areas for Hawk do not come from within the industry as, with the exception of the power of larger retailers, competitive forces are low. However, there are major issues that impact the industry as a whole in respect of the current economic climate and government policy.

(**Tutorial note:** each point within the models has been explained and assessed for its importance. Finally key points must be highlighted in order to then formulate or appraise strategy.)

Test your understanding 2

(**Tutorial note:** it is relatively straightforward to classify the individual products / SBUs but make sure you justify your choice. The higher skills element is in looking at the bigger picture to evaluate the overall portfolio balance.)

The market for recordable DVD recorders is still expanding and hence is in the growth phase. PTP really must try to boost its presence in this crucial market area (see below), or risk being left behind by rivals.

Sales of conventional DVD players are static, indicating a market that is mature and possibly saturated. This is a problem given PTP's historical dependence on this product stream. The risk is that profits will soon decline or disappear if retailers lose interest in this product group.

The market for conventional CRT televisions is in decline, suggesting that PTP should focus instead on LCD and plasma televisions – the growth area. However, the niche in CCTV products may have a longer-term future, depending on the degree of competition.

Despite being a market leader, PTP's sales of LCD and plasma televisions are only rising modestly suggesting that the industry (or at least PTP's products) are still in late introduction or early growth stages. PTP believes that this segment is going to be huge, so will need to invest heavily in marketing and product development to ensure it can capitalise on the high growth when it arises.

Overall portfolio evaluation

The balance of a portfolio can be assessed against a range of criteria including cash flow, growth, risk and investment required. This can be achieved to some extent by having products at different stages throughout the lifecycle. While PTP has products at different stages within the lifecycle, the main problems with its portfolio are:

- CRT TVs are facing decline but PTP does not have any new products in the development stage to replace them.
- The overall portfolio may require a net investment of cash in the future. Conventional DVD players may be strong cash generators but both recordable DVD players and LCD and Plasma TVs require investment to benefit from future growth.

Suggestions for re-balancing the portfolio include:

- Invest to develop Blu-Ray players and recorders. PTP might offer a guaranteed trade-in value for old units if customers purchase a new Blu-Ray DVD.
- Switch production away from the old factory to the new one in Holland, perhaps selling the old site and using the proceeds for an acquisition of a home entertainment-focused business.

Test your understanding 3

Why enter export markets?

Australian producers would have been under pressure to increase profits since some are effectively listed companies. Furthermore, it is likely that domestic markets had become saturated. There must be a limited consumption in Australia, therefore producers' attention would turn to export volumes. They would have spotted an opportunity to target growth markets in the UK and Europe.

Likely risks

One risk would have been culture and tradition. For example, wine drinking in the UK was far less common than it is today, and the risk would have been non-acceptance by a UK market.

Equally, the French are very protective of their own wines and reluctant to stock those from other countries. National bias would be a major barrier to overcome in some wine-drinking countries.

Another risk would be financial – namely exchange rate fluctuations and costs involved in transporting a product that is over 85% water for thousands of miles.

Porter's Diamond

Factor conditions would include the availability of land, the favourable climate, and the skill of Australian winemakers (so impressive that they have exported their talents back to European producers – the so-called "flying winemakers"). These would combine to give a strong advantage to Australia, because few rival countries possess such a favourable mix.

Demand conditions are also strong; Australia has an alcohol tolerant culture, and domestic consumers would have set high standards. However, this would also apply to countries such as France, so this factor may have given Australia a medium-level advantage overall.

Related and supporting industries will be strong since Australia is a modern, developed industrial nation. This will confer a medium-level advantage compared to Western-European countries and the USA, but a strong one compared to, say, Chile. Australian firms may also have had an advantage as they could have invested in newer technologies while rivals in France would have been committed to traditional methods.

Strategy structure and rivalry would be favourable, since there is a properly developed stock market, and reasonably intense local rivalry. This would give a strong advantage compared to developing economies such as Argentina and Bulgaria. It would also give a strong advantage compared to countries with old-fashioned rules about wine, such as France (these rules often prevent true competition).

Test your understanding 4

PD – international issues and Porter's diamond

Approach

The movement overseas would be a classic example of a **market development strategy** (Ansoff). You would need to brainstorm and then attempt to link points and put a plan together. In the small amount of time that you have, you would want to address the 'big hitters'. I started with the environments and took it from there.

External (Le Pest & co. & PROSAC)

Which markets are we considering? What are the sizes of the segments? For each:

- Political environment – type & stability? Is it likely to change?
- Laws – how do they differ? What must we satisfy? What are the implications for advertising, product characteristics and promotion?
- Economy – inflation, unemployment, growth, income levels. What price will we set our product at?
- Social attitudes – cultures, languages – for both consumer and customer.
- Technological issues – state of development, availability of technology.
- Competition – identify and apply full competitor analysis to key players (PROSAC).

Consider the arrival of new stakeholders and their relative power/interest.

Internal

- **Objectives** – ordered and prioritised for the new venture. What do you want it to do?
- **Strategic capability** – full position review to identify the current **competencies** and resources. Full consideration will need to be given to the threshold competencies for entry into the new markets. The more markets that are proposed, the more difficult it will become. Resources will be spread and different threshold competencies will exist for each marketplace. The required resources and competencies will need to be identified and any deficiencies will need to be considered. A brief mention of value creation and the value chain may improve the debate.
- How will the operational strategies need to **change** – what changes need to be made to the marketing mix, changes in HR base? What about the IT needs?
- What changes will need to be made to the **performance** measurement mix? Any changes to the reward schemes for key staff?

So all of this would need to be put into an action plan for the company.

Any entry to a foreign market needs **research and analysis** in the first instance. So consider:

- How much are you prepared to spend on this process?
- Who will be involved in the process? – In-house or subcontract?
- What size team? – Remember the range of opinion and expertise but too many in the team slows the process. Think of efficiency and effectiveness.
- What will the sources of information be? What is the balance between internal and external sources? How reliable are they? When were they checked? By whom?
- High profile key executive support needed to add credibility to the research.
- Don't forget to use benchmarks – learn from others' mistakes as well as their successes.
- Means of entry? New company or joint venture/alliance. Acquisition or organic entry? Franchise or licence?

There are so many factors that could be mentioned. Look at your list and plan how to present and combine some of the points. Think about which point you would start with.

Porter's Diamond theory

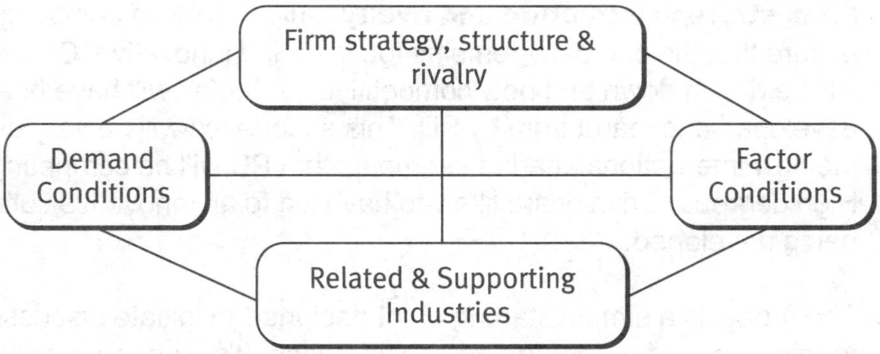

The model is designed to deal with the competitive advantage of nations. It essentially looks to see if there are any issues that could be used to form a sustainable competitive advantage overseas. PD has traded successfully in its home marketplace and so hopefully there may be issues which could be taken to a new market overseas.

Demand conditions – sophisticated customers at home will cause suppliers to focus onto quality and continually innovate. If you are used to fussy customers at home, then internationally you should have a good idea of user needs. Overseas customers may prove to be less sophisticated and so prove to be easier to market to. For PD, they will need to think about the product attributes that will be required and those that will win business. Sophisticated demand is likely to have provided PD with threshold competencies that would prove core in another marketplace. PD will need to understand how the new demand is likely to differ from the old. Research becomes of paramount importance. High levels of competition ensure that the company remains focused and innovative.

Factor conditions – the availability of factors of production. Land, labour capital and entrepreneurship. Does the home market of PD convey some unique advantages? Education, finance availability, land and resource availability. High degrees of regulation ensure that the company is experienced in change and bureaucracy. This can convey advantage or avoid disadvantage.

Related and support industries – is there a value chain created within a country context? Do suppliers add value to your product? PD has a reputation for quality and innovation and the quality will only come if there is quality being put in at the front end. A national attribute becomes very difficult to attack as the competitor will not have that attribute. It can thus form the basis of competitive advantage. The question then becomes 'Can PD forge a national identity for their product?'

Firm, strategy, structure and rivalry – high levels of competition ensure that the company remains focused and innovative. Cost levels will be driven down and new competitive strategies will have been developed and learnt from by PD. This experience will be very useful in the new international market segments that PD will be competing in. High degrees of rivalry are likely to have led to an innovative culture being developed.

The model is a simple starting point designed to initiate discussion and to raise issues for debate and consideration. It's a cheap, easily deployed model that most managers will have seen before. It will thus meet with minimal resistance and should act as the catalyst by which PD can ask itself the question 'On what basis and why will we succeed in our chosen overseas market?'

The model will not provide all of the answers but will go some way to starting the debate and identifying the research requirements. The model will provide insights as to where it will be possible to utilise a nationalistic attribute in the competitive advantage proposition.

chapter

6

Internal environment

Chapter learning objectives

Lead	Component
C1. Evaluate the process of strategy development	(b) Evaluate strategic options
C2. Evaluate strategic planning tools	(a) Evaluate strategic planning tools
	(c) Produce an organisation's value chain

Indicative syllabus content

- Audit of resources and the analysis of this for use in strategic decision-making.
- Value-chain analysis.

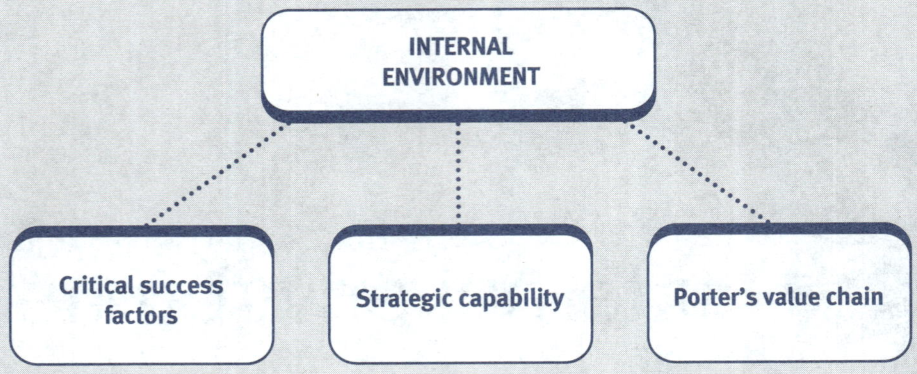

1 Introduction

When formulating strategy, the analyst will need to consider the strategic capability, i.e. the resources and competencies that will enable an organisation to apply a strategy.

This is particularly important where a resource-based approach to strategy is being followed:

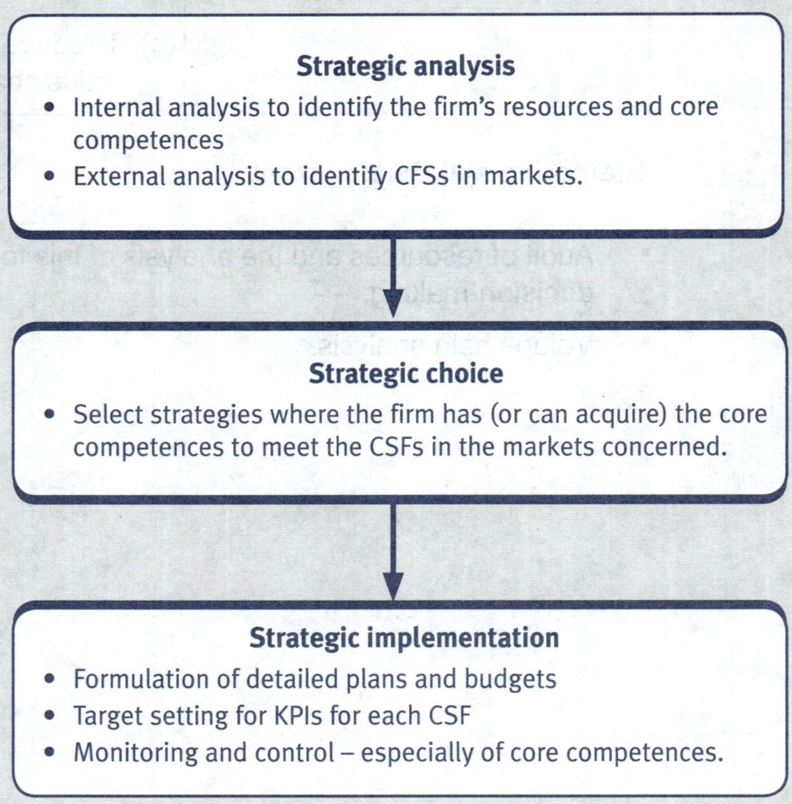

2 Critical success factors

Critical success factors (CSFs) are the limited number of areas in which results, if they are satisfactory, will ensure successful competitive performance for the business.

They are the vital areas where 'things must go right' and where the business must outperform its competitors.

It is important, therefore, that any assessment of resources, competences, strengths and weaknesses is done by reference to what we have to be good at.

For example, having the highest quality in the industry may be admirable but it misses the point if the market is driven by price wars and customers are only willing to pay low prices.

Examples of CSFs for major industries include:

- in the automobile industry – styling, an efficient dealer network, vehicle performance and fuel efficiency
- in the food manufacturing industry – new product development, good distribution channels, health aspects (e.g. low fat)
- in the supermarket industry – having the right product mix, competitive pricing.

Measured targets for CSFs are called key performance indicators (KPIs).

Test your understanding 1

What might a parcel delivery service such as DHL identify as two of its main critical success factors?

e.g

Illustration 1 – Critical success factors

The following is an example of CSFs developed for a shipping terminal.

Critical success factor	Indicator	Mechanism for measurement
Health and safety	• Accident record • Number of industrial injuries	• Factory inspector's report • Accidents reported
Customer satisfaction	• Complaints • Insurance claims • Losses of stock	• Complaints register • Correspondence • Internal audit
Maintenance of premises	• Repair costs	• Inspection
Efficient use of staff	• Time standards for loading and unloading	• Training schedules • Direct inspection

Test your understanding 2

Using the CSFs previously identified for a parcel delivery company such as DHL, explain how the company might measure their performance.

Sources of CSFs

Rockart claims that there are four sources for CSFs:

(1) The industry that the business is in – each has CSFs that are relevant to any company within it.

For example, the car industry must have as one of its CSFs 'compliance with pollution requirements regarding exhaust gases'.

(2) The company itself and its situation within the industry – e.g. its competitive strategy and its geographic location.

For example, a firm that has decided to compete on the basis of quality could have CSFs relating to identifying and delivering key product features that are valued by customers.

(3) The wider environment – e.g. the economy, the political factors and consumer trends in the country or countries that the organisation operates in.

For example, in a time of oil shortages 'energy supply availability' could be a critical success factor.

(4) Temporal organisational factors – these are areas of company activity that are unusually causing concern because they are unacceptable and need attention.

For example, a company with liquidity problems may place "short term cash management" as a CSF to ensure survival.

3 Strategic capability

Strategic capability refers to the organisation's ability to perform at a sufficient level to achieve the objectives and satisfy the mission. In most instances this will be a constraining factor.

The key question is, "What is the organisation capable of achieving strategically?"

Many of the issues of strategic management are related to changing strategic capability to fit with the changing environment. The principle aim will be to stretch the abilities to give the organisation a **sustainable competitive advantage** (which is the main purpose behind most of Porter's models). A competitive advantage is something that an organisation has that gives people reason to buy or use its services.

Organisations will need to understand the basis of their competitive advantage, how it may change and ensure that they remove the competitive disadvantages that may exist.

This involves understanding the resources and competencies of an organisation.

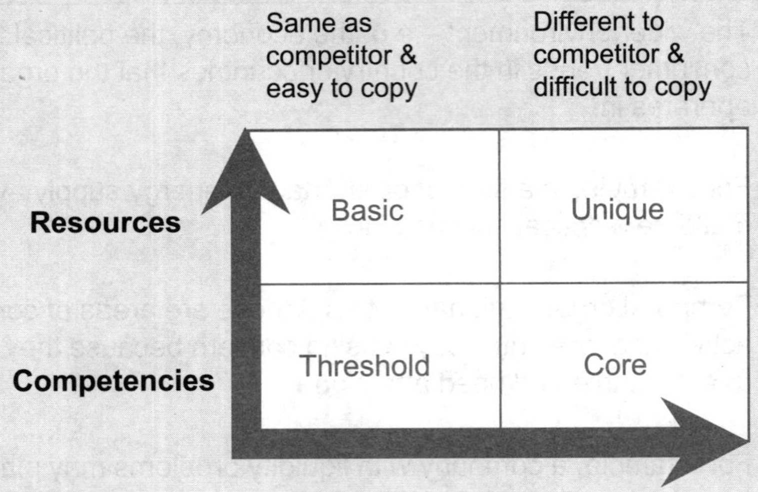

Resources

Resources are usually grouped under four headings:

- **physical or operational resources**
- **human resources**
- **financial resources**
- **intangibles.**

The key is to know what you have available to you and how this will help you in any strategic initiative. At the same time the organisation needs to know what it is lacking and how things may change in the future. Shortage of resources will often constrain strategic initiative.

Resources are needed to undertake a strategy. They will not ensure it ultimate success. For that, the resources will need to be combined together into competencies.

Competencies

Resources are combined together to achieve a competence. **Core competences** are things that you are able to do that are very difficult for your competitors to emulate. They form the basis for competitive advantage and they are referred to by **Johnson & Scholes** as '**the order winners**'.

Threshold competencies are those actions and processes that you must be good at just to be considered as a potential supplier to a customer. If these are not satisfied, you will not even get a chance to be considered by the buyer. These are '**the order qualifiers**'.

Over time the core competence will become threshold as:

- cultures adjust and expectations develop
- customers and consumers become more sophisticated in terms of their needs and expectations.

Thus organisations need to ensure that they are continually monitoring their marketplace to ensure that their core competencies are still valid and that all thresholds are duly satisfied.

'Remember, what is good today is not necessarily good tomorrow...'

e.g

Illustration 2 – Coca–Cola

The Coca-Cola Corporation has, for many years, maintained a very strong position in the soft drinks market. Consider its flagship product, Coca-Cola. This has largely survived competition from supermarkets' own-brand colas. There is no great secret in how to make a reasonable imitation (though purists would argue that the imitations are not as good) and the resources needed are not demanding. The own-label colas sell at much lower prices, so how has Coca-Cola managed to keep its dominant position?

It has been argued that physical resources are often less important. These are likely to form the **threshold competences**. Coca-Cola has bottling plants, access to suitable water, and a formulation for its drink. However, its competitors also have these things. They do not give Coca-Cola a competitive edge.

The reason Coca-Cola has managed to maintain its dominant position mainly lies in the non-physical or intangible resources, such as a very powerful brand. The **core competences** lie in managing the brand by producing memorable global advertising, global recognition, careful sponsorship and responding to customer requirements (diet/caffeine-free products).

4 Analysing strategic capability

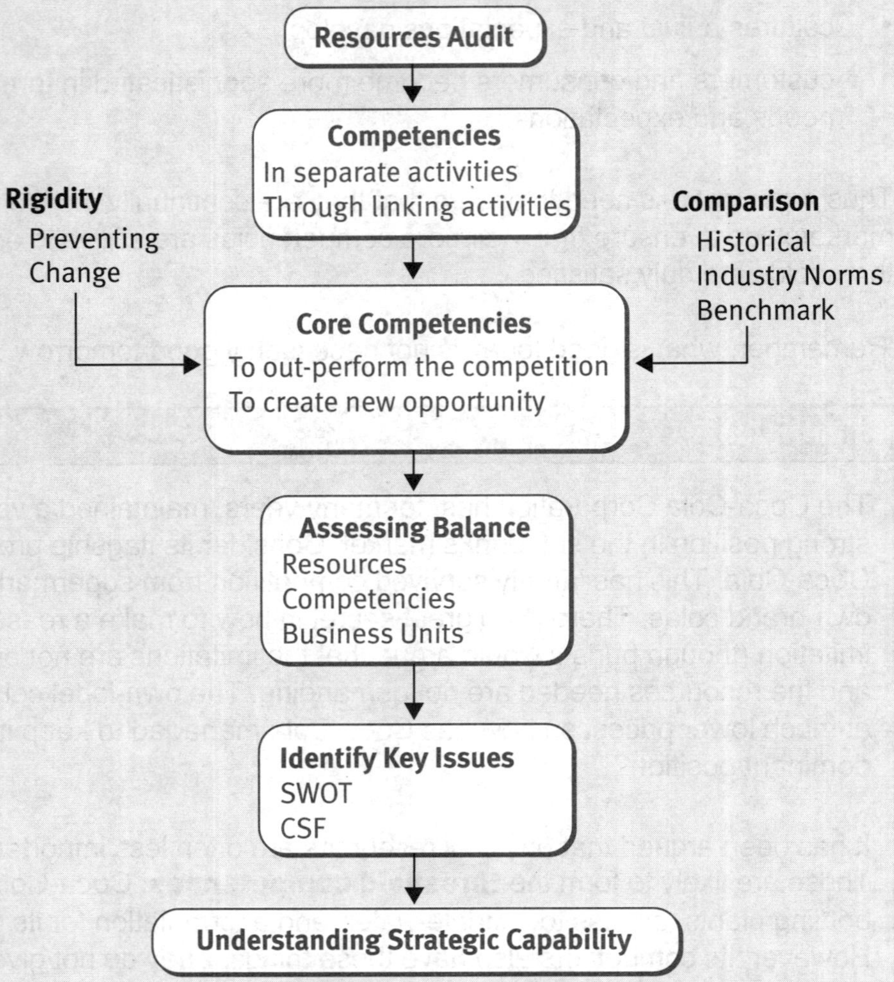

This involves understanding the resources and competencies of an organisation.

Resource audit

The resources audit identifies the resources that are available to an organisation and seeks to start the process of identifying competencies.

It attempts to assess the relative strength of the resource base – the quantity of resources available, the nature of those resources and the extent to which those resources are unique and difficult to imitate.

One model in particular may help managers undertaking a resource audit locate these key factors.

M's model

This model suggests that the items in a position audit can be categorised into factors beginning with 'M':

- **Manpower (human resources):** The human assets of the firm, their skills and morale.
- **Money:** The company's cash position, gearing, investment plans, short and long term finance, etc.
- **Management:** The quality, expertise and experience of the top team. Is the firm well managed and does is have the skills and vision needed to progress?
- **Machinery:** The physical assets of the business, their flexibility, relative costs and the quality of what they produce.
- **Markets:** The products and the markets the company currently operates in. The quality and position of the products.
- **Materials:** The relationship between the company and its suppliers. Cost, quality and future availability of materials.
- **Methods:** The processes adopted by the business – outsourcing, JIT, etc.
- **Management information:** Quality and timeliness of information provided to managers. Will impact on quality of decisions made.
- **Make-up:** The culture and structure of the organisation. Also, branding and other intangibles.

This is not an exhaustive list to memorise. Instead it is a memory aid to help the resource auditor to identify all the key resources that are central to a business' success.

Competencies

The audit should include all resources and competencies which can be accessed, not just legally owned. Some strategically important resources may exist such as a network of contacts or customers or maybe via a strategic alliance/joint venture.

The **competence audit** analyses how resources are being deployed to create competence and the processes through which these competencies may be linked. The key to success is usually found at this level. Porter's value chain analysis is very useful at this point as is the development into the value system concept.

Core competencies are identified along with threshold competencies at **identification and evaluation stage**. The aim is to identify the basis with which the organisation aims to out-perform the competition.

Competencies need to be **assessed** and so a basis for comparison is required. This often involves looking at historical data, industry norms and benchmarking exercises, which are usually undertaken by specialist teams.

These areas usually relate to separate SBUs and consideration must be given to the **balance** that may exist. Are the competencies unique to the SBU or the corporation? Are there any dependant linkages? Portfolio analysis with the help of BCG analysis assists here.

The final stage identifies the key issues for consideration in strategy formulation – **the critical success factors**. These need to be subject to due consideration to identify any resource constraints or any basis for developing advantage or developing barriers to entry.

5 Porter's Value Chain

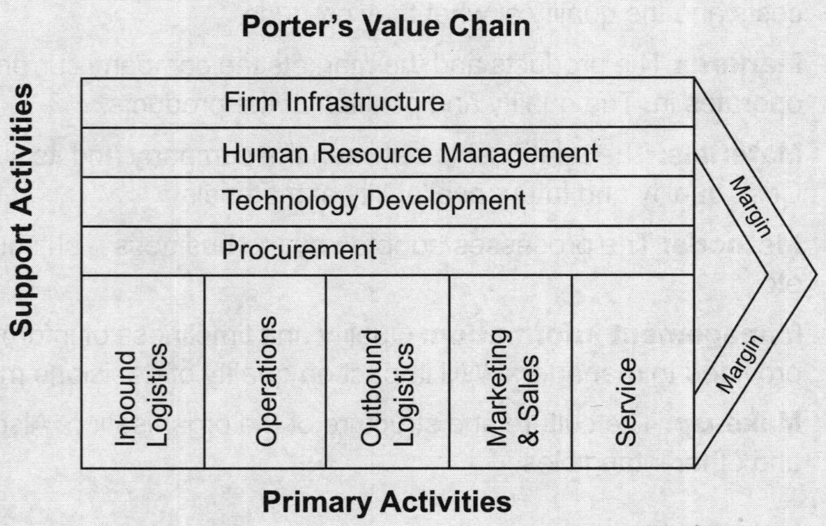

This is a means by which the activities within and around the organisation are identified and then related to the assessment of competitive strength.

Resources are of no value unless they are deployed into activities that are organised into routines and systems. These should then ensure that products are produced which are valued by customers and consumers. Porter argued that an understanding of strategic capability must start with an identification of the separate value-adding activities.

Primary activities

These activities are involved in the physical creation of the product, its transfer to the buyer and any after-sales service. Porter divided them into five categories:

(1) **Inbound logistics** are activities concerned with receiving, storing and distributing the inputs to the product. They include materials handling, stock control and transport.

(2) **Operations** transform these various inputs into the final product – machining, packing, assembling, testing and control equipment.

(3) **Outbound logistics** relate to collecting, storing and distributing the product to buyers.

(4) **Marketing and sales** provide the means whereby consumers and customers are made aware of the product and transfer is facilitated. This would include sales administration, advertising, selling and so on.

(5) **Service** relates to those activities which enhance or maintain the value of a product such as installation, repair, training and after-sales service.

Support activities

Each of the primary activities are linked to support activities and these can be divided into four areas:

(1) **Procurement** refers to the processes for acquiring the various resource inputs to the primary activities – not the resources themselves. As such it occurs throughout the organisation.

(2) **Technology development** – all value activities have a technological content, even if it is just 'know how'. IT can affect product design or process and the way that materials and labour are dealt with.

(3) **Human resource management,** which involves all areas of the business and is involved in recruiting, managing, training, developing and rewarding people within the organisation.

(4) **Infrastructure** refers to the systems of planning, finance, quality control, information management, etc. All are crucially important to an organisation's performance in primary activities. It also consists of the structures and routines that sustain the culture of the organisation.

Generally

The primary and secondary activities are designed to help create the organisation's margin by taking inputs and using them to produce outputs with greater value.

The value chain can be used to:

- give managers a deeper understanding of precisely what their organisation does
- identify the key processes within the business that add value to the end customer – strategies can then be created to enhance and protect these, and
- identify the processes that do not add value to the customer. These could then be eliminated, saving the organisation time and money.

The value system

Looks at linking the value chains of suppliers and customers to that of the organisation.

Can add value by:

- Enhancing the supply – e.g. organic food for ready meals.
- Controlling of the retail process – e.g. car dealerships.
- Linking it all together to give advantage – Porter's diamond.

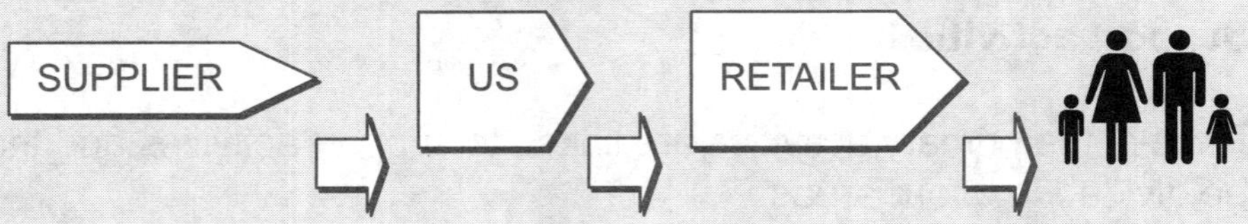

e.g

Illustration 3 – The Value Chain

Marks and Spencer plc compete in, amongst other areas, the food and grocery market. They have configured their value chain in order to offer customers a differentiated service.

	IL	O	OL	M/S	S
FI	Central control of operations & credit services				
TD		Recipe research	Electronic point of sale	Customer research and testing	Itemised billing
HRD	Recruitment of mature staff	Client care training	Flexible staff to help with enquiries and packing		
P	Own label products	Prime retail positions		Adverts in quality press and poster sites	
	Dedicated refrigerated transport	In-store food halls Modern store design Dairy cabinets	Collect by car service	No price discounts	No quibble refunds

Lidl also operates in the food and grocery market, but their value chain supports a cost–leadership approach.

Minimum head office costs				
Use of casual staff	De-skilled store ops	Dismissal for check-out error		
Branded and own-brand generics	Low-cost sites			Use of concessions
Bulk warehousing	Limited product range Price points Basic store design	Customers encouraged to use boxes Packing benches	Promotion of low prices Store manager decides stock	Nil

Criticisms of Porter's Value Chain

Proponents suggest that the value chain model has many benefits, including:

- It provides a generic framework to analyse both the behaviour of costs as well as the existing and potential sources of differentiation.
- Activities that are not adding value can be identified and addressed – for example, improved so they do add value or outsourced if this is not possible.
- It emphasises the importance of (re)grouping functions into activities to produce, market, deliver and support products, to think about relationships between activities and to link the value chain to the understanding of an organisation's competitive position.
- It makes it clear that an organisation is multifaceted and that its underlying activities need to be analysed to understand its overall competitive position.
- It is an attempt to overcome the limitations of portfolio planning in multidivisional organisations. Rather than assuming that SBUs should act independently, Porter used his Value Chain analysis to identify synergies or shared activities between them and to provide a tool to focus on the whole rather than on the parts.

The main criticisms of Porter's Value Chain model are as follows:

- It is more suited to a manufacturing environment and can be difficult to apply to a service provider
- The Value Chain model was intended as a quantitative analysis. However, this is time consuming since it often requires recalibrating the accounting system to allocate costs to individual activities.

The value shop

The value shop is an alternative representation of a value chain for a professional services firm which was developed in 1998 by Stabell and Fjelstad.

A value shop is considered to be a workshop which mobilises resources to solve specific problems. This may involve repeating a generic set of activities until a satisfactory solution is reached. The shop model applies to many organisations, particularly those whose main purpose is to identify and exploit specific opportunities like designing a bespoke product.

The model has the same support activities as Porter's Value Chain but the primary activities are described differently. In the value shop they are:

- problem finding and acquisition
- problem solving
- choosing among solutions
- execution and control/evaluation.

The management in the value shop organisation therefore focuses on areas such as the assessment of problems and opportunities, the mobilisation of resources, project management, the delivery of solutions, the measurement of outcomes and also learning.

The value shop primary activities are arranged in a circle showing that they are cyclical, with an organisation often moving back and forth to develop or reject theories before reaching a conclusion.

Test your understanding 3

Bowland Carpets Ltd is a major producer of carpets within the UK. The company was taken over by its present parent company, Universal Carpet Inc., in 20X3. Universal Carpet is a giant, vertically-integrated carpet manufacturing and retailing business, based within the USA but with interests all over the world.

Bowland Carpets operates within the UK in various market segments, including the high-value contract and industrial carpeting area – hotels and office blocks, etc. – and in the domestic (household) market. Within the latter the choice is reasonably wide, ranging from luxury carpets down to the cheaper products. Industrial and contract carpets contribute 25% of Bowland Carpets' total annual turnover, which is currently $80 million. Up until 15 years ago the turnover of the company was growing at 8% per annum, but since 20X2 sales revenue has dropped by 5% per annum in real terms.

Bowland Carpets has traditionally been known as a producer of high-quality carpets, but at competitive prices. It has a powerful brand name, and it has been able to protect this by producing the cheaper, lower-quality products under a secondary brand name. It has also maintained a good relationship with the many carpet distributors throughout the UK, particularly the mainstream retail organisations.

The recent decline in carpet sales revenue, partly recession induced, has worried the US parent company. It has recognised that the increasing concentration within the European carpet manufacturing sector has led to aggressive competition within a low-growth industry. It does not believe that overseas sales growth by Bowland Carpets is an attractive proposition as this would compete with other Universal Carpet companies. It does, however, consider that vertical integration into retailing (as already practised within the USA) is a serious option. This would give the UK company increased control over its sales and reduce its exposure to competition. The president of the parent company has asked Jeremy Smiles, managing director of Bowland Carpets, to address this issue and provide guidance to the US board of directors. Funding does not appear to be a major issue at this time as the parent company has large cash reserves on its balance sheet.

Required:

Acting in the capacity of Jeremy Smiles, you are required to outline the various issues which might be of significance for the management of the parent company. Your answer should cover the following:

(a) To what extent do the distinctive competences of Bowland Carpets conform with the key success factors required for the proposed strategy change?

(10 marks)

(b) In an external environmental analysis concerning the proposed strategy shift what are likely to be the key external influences which could impact upon the Bowland Carpets decision?

(15 marks)

(Total: 25 marks)

Test your understanding 4

Application of the value chain to university processes

A university which derives most of its funds from the government provides undergraduate courses (leading to bachelor's degrees) and post-graduate courses (leading to master's degrees). Some of its funds come from contributions from student fees, consultancy work and research. In recent years the university has placed emphasis on recruiting lecturers who have achieved success in delivering good academic research. This has led to the university improving its reputation within its national academic community, and applications from prospective students for its courses have increased.

The university has good student support facilities in respect of a library which is well stocked with books and journals and up-to-date IT equipment. It also has a gymnasium and comprehensive sports facilities. Courses at the university are administered by well-qualified and trained non-teaching staff who provide non-academic (that is, not learning-related) support to the lecturers and students.

The university has had no difficulty in filling its courses to the level permitted by the government, but has experienced an increase in the number of students who have withdrawn from the first year of their courses after only a few months. An increasing number of students are also transferring from their three-year undergraduate courses to other courses within the university but many have left and gone to different universities. This increasing trend of student withdrawal is having a detrimental effect on the university's income as the government pays only for students who complete a full year of study.

You are the university's management accountant and have been asked by the Vice-Chancellor (who is the Chief Executive of the university) to review the withdrawal rate of students from the university's courses.

(Candidates do not require any knowledge of university admission and withdrawal processes to answer this question.)

Required:

Apply Value Chain analysis to the university's activities, and advise the Vice-Chancellor how this analysis will help to determine why the rate of student withdrawal is increasing.

(25 marks)

(November 2001)

6 Summary

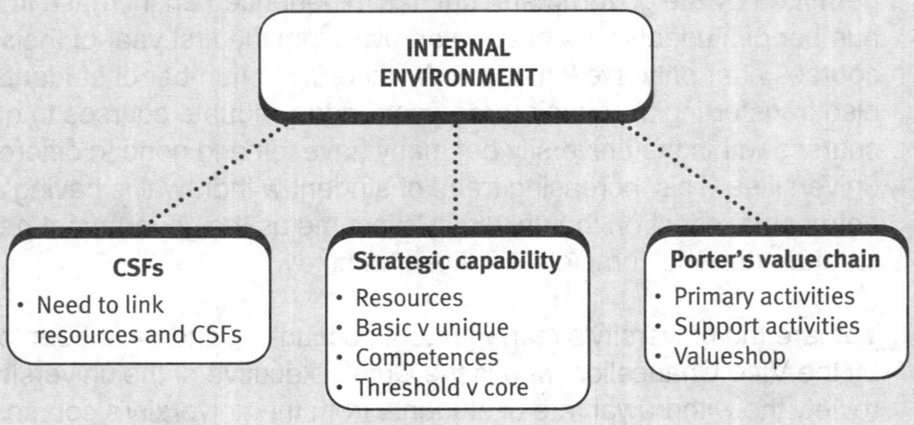
INTERNAL ENVIRONMENT
CSFs
• Need to link resources and CSFs
Strategic capability
• Resources
• Basic v unique
• Competences
• Threshold v core
Porter's value chain
• Primary activities
• Support activities
• Valueshop

Test your understanding answers

Test your understanding 1

The two main critical success factors would probably be:

- speedy collection from customers after their request for a parcel to be delivered
- rapid and reliable delivery.

Test your understanding 2

Their performance can be measured by establishing key performance indicators for each CSF and measuring actual achievements against them. For example:

- Collection from customers within three hours of receiving the order for orders received before 2.30p.m. on a working day.
- Next-day delivery for 100% of parcels to destinations within the UK.
- Delivery within two days for 100% of parcels to destinations within Europe.

Test your understanding 3

Key answer tips

Part (a) of the question can be split into three parts – what are Bowland's existing competencies, what are the key success factors needed in retailing, and do these two things match up. So a good approach would be to split your time evenly between all three elements

For part (b) an external analysis is normally a combination of both the PESTEL and 5 Forces models, but with only 15 marks available (and working on the basis of two marks per well-explained point) you do not have to cover every element. So if, for example, you can't determine any relevant 'Technical' issues then just leave this factor out.

(a) An organisation's **distinctive competences** are those things which an organisation does particularly well. They include the organisation's unique resources and capabilities as well as its strengths and its ability to overcome weaknesses. These competences can include aspects such as budgetary control, a strong technology base, a culture conducive to change and marketing skills.

Key success factors are those requirements which it is essential to have if one is to survive and prosper in a chosen industry/environment. These can include areas such as good service networks, up-to-date marketing intelligence and tight cost controls where margins are small.

It is not guaranteed that the distinctive competences and the key success factors are always in alignment. A company moving into the retail sector may have an excellent product research and development capability, but this alone will not help if it has no concept of service, or poorly sited retail outlets. It is critical to ensure that what the company excels at is what is needed to be successful in that particular area.

The **strengths of Bowland Carpets** include **strong brand names** which maintain integrity within the different market segments where the company operates. The company has a **balanced portfolio of customers** and the **range of products is equally balanced**, ensuring that any sectoral decline can be compensated for by growth in other markets. Other strengths which the company currently has include a **good relationship with distributors and strong support from a powerful parent company**. Some of its distinctive competences, such as a strong brand and a reasonable range of products, are critical in the proposed new environment, as will be the financial support of the parent company. However, there are some aspects which are cause for concern in the proposed new business environment.

The strength in the contract and industrial carpet segment will not be affected by the proposed vertical integration – sales tend to be through a direct sales force. The strong **relationship with distributors** will however be **jeopardised by the opening up of retail outlets**. Other retail chains will be unwilling to permit a rival to operate so freely, and therefore there will be a reluctance to stock Bowland's carpets. Unless Bowland Carpets can obtain wide retail market coverage to compensate for this potential problem, sales revenue will be adversely affected.

The **cost of developing extensive market coverage** will be enormous and whether it is in high-street outlets or specialist out-of-town centres the investment may be greater than the parent company has budgeted for. The company also has **no expertise in site appraisal and selection**. Although the newly structured value chain will generate greater control there is an associated **lack of flexibility** along with an **increase in the fixed cost base** of the business.

Another key success factor is the **need for expertise in retailing**. It may be that the UK company can import this from the USA but the culture of marketing household durables may not be transferable internationally. Bowland Carpets as the domestic company has no experience in this field.

A critical factor in successful retailing is the ability to provide a **comprehensive range of products**. Does Bowland Carpets have one? It is unlikely that the competitive carpet manufacturers will provide such a supply to one of their rivals.

It would, therefore, appear that there is no close conformity between the distinctive competences of Bowland Carpets and the key success factors required in the carpet retailing sector.

(b) The **external environment** scan is an essential prerequisite prior to selecting a strategic option. It enables the company to identify and understand the key external and uncontrollable influences which will have an impact upon the company's strategy. The environment is increasingly turbulent and often hostile. Without this knowledge and appreciation the strategist will be operating in a minefield. The acquisition of the external information is obtained by scanning the environment continuously and monitoring key indicators, which should enable the company to position itself appropriately with respect to the external environment and the competition. The external scan should be structured around a SLEPT framework covering the following environments – social, legal, economic, political and technological. In addition it is also important to assess potential competitive reactions as part of the scanning process.

The environmental scan will influence the decision as to whether Bowland Carpets should concentrate on the UK or seek diversification elsewhere, either in products or markets. Possible factors are as follows:

– **Social issues**: Trends towards increasing car-centred shopping (superstores and out-of-town sites) or movements back to city-centre shopping: trends in fashion and furnishing - will carpets become a fashion item and result in greater replacement sales? Other factors of importance to Bowland include the rate of growth or decline in populations and changes in the age distribution of the population. In the UK there will be an increasing proportion of the national population over retirement age. In developing countries there are very large numbers of young people. Rising standards of living lead to increased demand for certain types of goods. This is why developing countries are attractive to markets.

– **Legal issues**: Laws in the UK differ from the US. They come from common law, parliamentary legislation and government regulations derived from it, and obligations under EU membership and other treaties. Legal factors that can influence decisions include aspects of employment law, e.g. minimum wage, laws to protect consumers and tax legislation. The monopoly/competition issues in this case are likely to be insignificant.

– **Economic issues**: An increased concentration for Bowland Carpets within the UK economy will depend upon future economic prospects, taxation policy (sales tax) and interest rates, income distribution and unemployment (influencing site location), trade barriers (cheap imports from Third World suppliers, or even low-cost tufted carpets from countries such as Belgium).

– **Political issues**: Government policy affects the whole economy and governments are responsible for enforcing and creating a stable framework in which business can be done. The quality of government policy is important in providing physical infrastructure, (e.g. transport), social infrastructure, (e.g. education) and market infrastructure, (e.g. planning and site development – town centre or out-of-town developments).

– **Technological issues**: Is retailing technology evolutionary or revolutionary? Will it be costly or labour saving? Will inventory control be facilitated – so saving costs? Technology contributes to overall economic growth. It can increase total output with gains in productivity, reduced costs and new types of product. It influences the way in which markets are identified - database systems make it much easier to analyse the marketplace. Information technology encourages de-layering of organisational hierarchies and better communications.

– **Competitive issues**: It will be necessary to assess the likely responses of both carpet distributors and carpet manufacturers to the proposed incursion by Bowland Carpets. Will the reactions be benign or will they be aggressive?

Test your understanding 4

Application of the value chain to university process

Approach

A specialist value chain question that would warrant a brief introduction and possibly a diagram. Don't go mad with the diagrams that do not 'add value' that much. Value chain analysis (VCA) is a method of reviewing all the activities of an organisation and how they interact with each other. Key linkages are identified and areas that create value are focused upon. VCA is not restricted to just the organisation but also the suppliers and customers.

In this question we will have to address the issue of university suppliers of resources:

- students
- staff
- premises
- facilities

And customers/consumers:

- degree holders
- employers
- society.

The starting point is to identify the objectives for the university in this context. There appear to be three particular issues.

- Students dropping out in the first year.
- Students transferring to another university or just leaving.
- Students swapping courses within the university.

The idea is to look at the primary and support activities to establish why these problems may be arising.

Primary activities

Inbound logistics	Operations	Outbound logistics	Marketing & sales	Service
• Student supply • Staff supply • Facilities supply • Course selections	• Course • Lecturing • Research • Library • IT access • Premises	• Skills base • Employer view • Graduate view	• Marketing mix structure • USP/CA? • Promotions • Research? • Price elasticity	• Support functions • Admin. functions • Social aspects • Post-qualification career assistance

Secondary activities

Procurement	Technology	HRM	Infrastructure
• Food & drink • Accommodation • Building work • Support staff • Books • Students & staff	• Availability • Content • Training • Change	• Staff selection processes • Staff turnover rates • Appraisal processes • Admin. staff processes	• Culture • Layout • Org. Structure • Faculties • Planning systems • Control systems (FFWD & FBK)

These are some of the things that should be looked at within this context. Processes need to be viewed at first hand and discussed to see how the 'chain' links up. All that needs to happen for the chain to fail is for one link to break.

How will it help?

This model is twenty years' old and designed for application in the private sector but it does have its uses here. The model acts as a **simple starting point** to focus management attention onto the issues. It is not designed to provide an answer, rather to get the 'ball rolling' for management in trying to identify where the problems lie. Managers will have seen it before and be vaguely familiar with it so there will be less resistance. Solutions to these kinds of problems come from reasoned debate from informed people.

VCA will start management thinking where they can add value. They will consider how they differ from the competition and on what basis they will attract staff and students in the future. It will force them to identify the order winners or '**core competencies**'.

At the same time, the process will identify the **threshold competencies**, or order qualifiers, that are needed. Failure to satisfy threshold competencies will lead to consumer dissatisfaction. This would lead to the student problems evident in this case so it looks like VCA would be useful here in spotting those threshold competencies that are not being satisfied. Universities are age-old organisations and are not well known for embracing change. It is possible that this university may be suffering from competence slip – that is the situation that arises when a past core competence becomes threshold as a result of increasing consumer sophistication. That means, as the consumer gains more experience of the product, they become more expectant of the service offered. The VCA will force management to consider the issues of **competitive advantage and disadvantage**.

The analysis will see research into student, employer and staff perceptions whilst at the same time may see the application of benchmarking techniques. This would compare a similar institution with ours to see where any issues may exist. So VCA:

- Is the starting point for discussion.
- Gets people from all areas of the business talking – team perspective so a range of opinion and expertise.
- Starts or improves communication, and feedback and forward are encouraged.
- Step-by-step analysis allows the competencies to be analysed.

chapter

7

Position and gap analysis

Chapter learning objectives

Lead	Component
C1. Evaluate the process of strategy development	(b) Evaluate strategic options
C2. Evaluate strategic planning tools	(a) Evaluate strategic planning tools (d) Discuss both qualitative and quantitative techniques in the support of the strategic decision-making function

Indicative syllabus content

- Forecasting and the various techniques used: trend analysis, system modelling, in-depth consultation with experts (Delphi method).
- Scenario planning and long-range planning as tools in strategic decision-making.

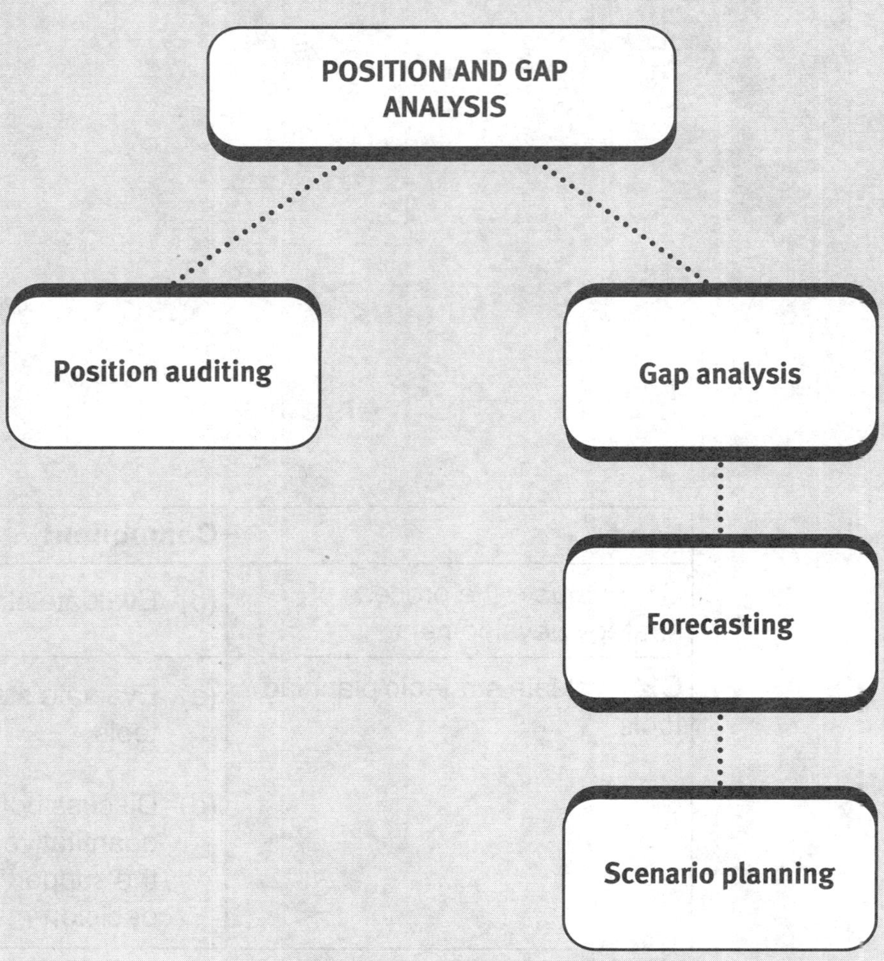

1 Position auditing (SWOT)

The purpose of the position audit is to act as the starting point for the corporate appraisal of an organisation. This is an essential part of the strategic management process as it raises the question – **'Where are we now?'**.

If an organisation is unsure of its current position then it will be very difficult to plot a successful strategy. It establishes the starting point for the process of strategic choice.

It requires an analysis of both environments of an organisation as well as the stakeholders, mission and objectives.

There are several well-known tools that are available to assist in this process, one of which is the **'SWOT' analysis**. This will identify the strengths, weaknesses, opportunities and threats as they relate to a particular organisation and usually involves a listing of points.

Key points

- SWOT analysis is a tool to assist the position audit process. It is not the only tool: e.g. the competitor analysis framework works well in this context and can provide a useful framework to analyse a company.
- Position auditing asks the question 'Where are we now?' and is viewed by many as being the starting point for the process of strategic choice.
- The audit will usually be undertaken by a team with a preset budget, objectives listing and support functions.
- The management accountant will be involved with delivering and monitoring the information flows into the process.

The position audit would seek to identify:

- **Threats focusing on weakness:** This would usually have top priority and the company should seek to identify and consider possible solutions. This requires a defensive response of some kind and may well necessitate rapid change.
- **Threats focusing on strength:** this requires a review of the supposed strength to ensure that it is still as strong as previously thought. Remember what is good today, may not be so tomorrow.
- **Opportunity focusing on strength:** this gives the organisation the chance to develop strategic advantage in the marketplace. Check the research and assess the strengths again.
- **Opportunity focusing on weakness:** this will require management to make a decision as to whether to change and pursue the opportunity or, alternatively, ignore the prospect and ensure resources are not wasted in this area in future. Usually substantial change will be required if the company is going to pursue the opportunity. Check that the company's internal competencies will allow them to exploit the opportunity.

The review should initially seek to identify what would happen if the organisation chose to do nothing. Remember this is always a strategic option!

The exercise is designed to allow the following:

- identification of the **current issues** relating to the organisation concerned
- analysis and identification of the relevant **problems** facing the organisation
- consideration of the **strategic capability** of the company and its history.

An approach

There are many, many ways that a position audit can be approached. Essentially you should have one in mind that you would be able to use as a basis for analysing a situation. Here is a starter...

- **o**rganisation – structure and type
- **m**anagement and governance – board and senior management
- **f**inancial review – the ratios compared and trends reviewed
- **s**trategy – what is it and the process of derivation?
- **e**xternal environment – PEST, etc.
- **c**ulture and change – all strategy involves change
- **m**arketing – the marketing mix
- **h**uman resource – how significant is HR?
- **i**nformation strategy/management
- **o**bjectives – ordering? Conflict? Stakeholders?
- **m**iscellaneous – taxation, societal and international issues?

2 Gap analysis

The comparison between an entity's ultimate objective and the expected performance from projects, both planned and under way, identifying means by which any identified difference or gap might be filled.

CIMA official terminology

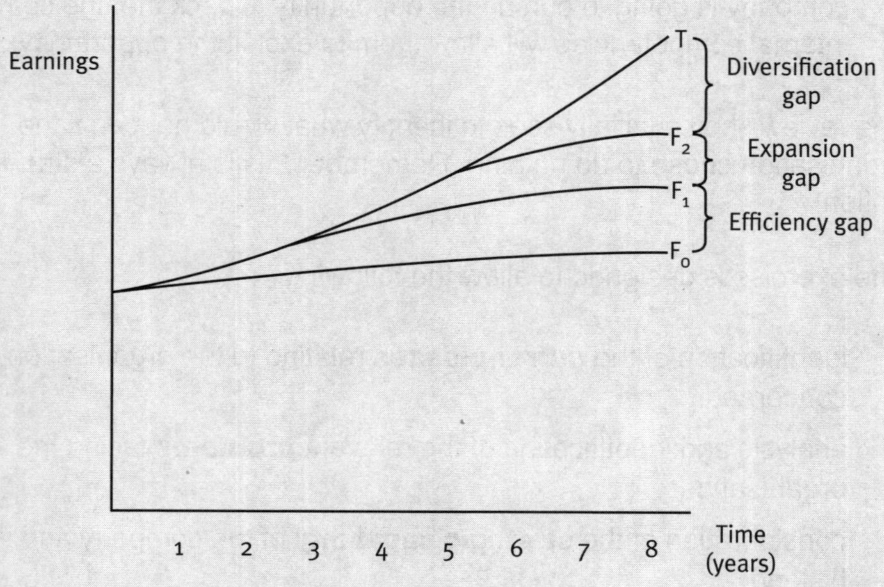

(1) The firm sets its key strategic objective for some time in the future (T), such as achieving a certain level of sales in five years time.

(2) The firm then forecasts its likely performance from current operations (F_0), after efficiency savings have been made (F_1) and after new strategic initiatives (F_2). (Note: These are often separated out as there is a greater degree of uncertainty associated with new initiatives.)

(3) Identify any remaining 'gap'. New strategies will be needed to close this gap.

Closing the gap

These strategies will include:

Efficiency drive – cost savings and actions to improve the output for a given set of inputs. This is usually the easier of the two approaches and so should be undertaken first.

Effectiveness drive – linked in with Ansoff (more detail in this model can be found in chapter 8).

- Market penetration strategies
- development strategies – either market or product. Different scenarios will direct the selection
- diversification as the last.

A plan is what you want to happen whilst a forecast is what you predict will happen given the current context and assumptions. The whole approach of gap analysis is based upon the feed forward control concept, i.e. the comparison of plan with forecast.

The aim is to identify deviance before the problems of missed targets arise so enabling corrective action to take place in advance. The strategy is too important to leave to reactive control systems. A proactive approach is needed and this will see the need for a significant spend on the forecasting systems. Spend will normally include expenditure on:

- the team
- IT
- data sourcing and audit
- scenario planning
- time to facilitate the action
- uncertainty evaluation techniques such as 'what if' analysis, high-low forecasting and simulation exercises.

The problems – the whole concept revolves around dealing with uncertainty in the environment. Recent times have seen the business environment becoming increasingly uncertain. This increasing amount of uncertainty makes the predictive capabilities of systems less effective. The predictive process works to an extent if the environmental context can be identified. The uncertainty that exists brings with it new unexpected parameters that can render the whole process a costly waste of time. This has been held as a reason for the abandonment of gap analysis.

The other issue is that in recent years there has been an increasing number of powerful stakeholder groups emerging with the knock-on effect being that there is a greater range of often conflicting objectives. Gap analysis does not entertain the multiplicity of objectives with conflict and compromise running through the whole system.

Does it have any benefits?

The answer is yes!

(1) The approach acts as a simple starting point to initiate further debate and consideration.

(2) It is easy to understand and as such acts as an effective communication device.

(3) It highlights the need to keep an eye on the long-term time horizon and draws attention away from the short-term focus.

(4) It provides some basic options that may be considered for closing the gap.

(5) If it is held as a tool to assist and not as the solution provider, the approach still has a place in most planning systems within organisations.

(6) It allows the questioning of the realism of the objective – if there is a gap, it may be that the objective is unrealistic given the strategic capability of the organisation. This may lead to a reappraisal of the objectives and the generation of more realistic versions.

(7) Stable environments will still provide a basis for effective gap analysis

3 Forecasting

Statistical models

The statistical approach to forecasting is concerned with the projection of time series. Time series analysis involves the identification of short- and long-term trends in previous data and the application of these patterns for projections.

Where there are numerous short- and long-term factors at work, forecasting becomes very difficult. If the series of data being analysed is very regular, some simple procedure such as exponential smoothing may be sufficient. On the other hand, more complex patterns may require techniques of regression analysis, risk analysis and multiple regression.

Trend analysis is a particularly useful tool for companies who have to forecast demand that is influenced by seasonal fluctuations, or where demand is strongly influenced by the business cycle, but in reality many of the techniques are very crude, and cannot predict with adequate certainty.

System modelling

Many large firms seek to develop sophisticated programmes to model economic systems, market competition and so on.

The difficulty lies in identifying all the variables and defining how they relate to each other.

A number of software products are available to help with this. Most large accounting packages will include forecasting facilities, and Enterprise Resource Management (ERM) software generally includes facilities to model business processes.

Intuitive forecasting methods

What distinguishes intuitive techniques is the relative emphasis they place on judgement, and the value of such techniques lies not in their statistical sophistication but in the method of systematising expert knowledge.

Intuitive forecasting techniques include the use of think tanks, Delphi methods, scenario planning, brainstorming and derived demand analysis.

Intuitive forecasting methods

Think tank

A think tank comprises a group of experts who are encouraged, in a relatively unstructured atmosphere, to speculate about future developments in particular areas and to identify possible courses of action. The essential features of a think tank are:

- the relative independence of its members, enabling unpopular, unacceptable or novel ideas to be broached
- the relative absence of positional authority in the group, which enables free discussion and argument to take place
- the group nature of the activity that not only makes possible the sharing of knowledge and views, but also encourages a consensus view or preferred scenario.

Think tanks are used by large organisations, including government, and may cross the line between forecasting and planning. However, the organisations that directly employ, or fund, them, are careful to emphasise that their think-tank proposals do not necessarily constitute company or government policy.

Think tanks are useful for generating ideas and assessing their feasibility, as well as providing an opportunity to test out reactions to ideas prior to organisational commitment.

The Delphi technique

Delphi seeks to avoid the group pressures to conformity that are inherent in the think tank method. It does this by individually, systematically and sequentially interrogating a panel of experts.

- Members do not meet, and questioning is conducted by formal questionnaires.
- Where the experts are speculating about the future, they are asked for subjective probabilities about their predictions.
- A central authority evaluates the responses and feeds these back to the experts who are then interrogated in a new round of questions

The system is based on the premise that knowledge and ideas possessed by some but not all of the experts can be identified and shared and this forms the basis for subsequent interrogations.

Brainstorming

This is a method of generating ideas. There are different approaches but a popular one is for a number of people (no fewer than six, no more than fifteen) drawn from all levels of management and expertise to meet and propose answers to an initial single question posed by the session leader.

- Each person proposes something, no matter how absurd.
- No one is allowed to criticise or ridicule another person's idea.
- One idea provokes another, and so on.
- All ideas are listed and none rejected at this initial stage.
- Rationality is not particularly important, but what is essential is that a wide range of ideas emerges and in the ensuing discussion that these ideas are picked up, developed, combined and reshaped.
- Only after the session are ideas evaluated and screened against rational criteria for practicality.

Brainstorming provides a forum for the interchange of ideas without erecting the normal cultural, behavioural and psychological barriers that so often inhibit the expression of ideas.

Derived demand

Derived demand exists for a commodity, component or good because of its contribution to the manufacture of another product.

For example, the demands for the chromium, copper and rubber used in the manufacture of many different products, including cars, are derived demands.

The forecasting technique involves analysing some aspects of economic activity so that the level of other aspects can be deduced and projected. The principle is simple, but the practice is complex and costly.

Take the example of chrome matched with car manufacture. In order to forecast the demand for cars (thus chrome) the forecaster will be faced with the mammoth task of analysing an enormous number of influences and correlated factors.

Due to its cost and complexity the technique has a very restricted use.

Foresight

The value of strong brands, loyal customers, etc has diminished over time as the business environment has become more dynamic. Whereas once a company could rely on these things to bring them future success, they are increasingly unable to do so. Organisations must therefore develop vision and foresight.

For organisations, foresight means not only predicting the future but developing an understanding of all the potential changes, which if managed properly could produce many new opportunities.

By carrying out techniques to develop foresight, management try to shape the future, rather than 'wait' for it to happen and become a victim of changes they are unable to adapt to. The concept is crucial in the global commercial environment, where technological changes for example, or non-traditional competition can erode a company's dominant position overnight.

In their book 'Research Foresight: Creating the future', John Irvine and Ben Martin give the advantages of foresight as the 5Cs:

- **Communication** – bringing together groups of people and providing a structure in which they can communicate.
- **Concentration** – on the longer term.
- **Coordination** – enabling different groups to harmonise their future R&D activities.
- **Consensus** – creating a measure of agreement on future directions and research priorities.
- **Commitment** – to the results among those who will be responsible for translating them into research advances, technological developments and innovations for the benefit of society.

Techniques to improve an organisation's foresight include:

- **Scenario planning** – see below.
- **Visioning** – involves management developing a 'mental image' of the organisation in the future. This should be realistic, attractive and better than the company's current state. Management can then devise ways to reach this future ideal.
- **The Delphi method** – see above.
- **Morphological analysis** – the systematic investigation of all the components of large-scale problems. A matrix is used to identify new, reasonable combinations of these components that could result in plausible new outcomes.
- **Relevance trees** – start with a clear goal, which is traced back through the trends and events on which it depends so that the organisation can determine what needs to change or be developed for the desired outcome to be achieved.
- **Issues analysis** – issues arise through the convergence of trends and events. Potentially significant issues should be analysed in terms of probability and impact (i.e. risk).
- **Opportunity mapping** – identifying gaps in the current environment in order to reveal new business opportunities.
- **Cross impact analysis** – involves recording events on a matrix and at each matrix intersection analysing how the event in the row could affect the likelihood of occurrence of the event in the column.
- **Role-playing** – a group of people are given a description of a hypothetical future situation and are told to behave as they believe they would if that situation were true.

4 Scenario planning

Competence slip and organisational failure have been linked to the notion that management have failed to grasp the way that society is moving and have not conceptualised a possible future marketplace. It has been suggested that managers need a picture or scenario of where the world may be in a few years' time.

For example, how would an accountancy training college meet its objectives under the following circumstances:

(1) a merger between three accountancy bodies
(2) wide demand for computer-based training
(3) changes to immigration laws leading to a reduction in the number of overseas students.

The steps involved in scenario planning

Scenario planning involves the following steps:

(1) Identify high-impact, high-uncertainty factors in the environment.

Relevant factors and driving forces could be identified through a strategic analysis framework such as a PEST analysis. Once identified, factors need to be ranked according to importance and uncertainty.

For example, in the oil industry there may be a need to form a view of the business environment up to twenty-five years ahead and issues such as crude oil availability, price and economic conditions are critical.

(2) For each factor, identify different possible futures.

For example, oil companies would consider possible political uncertainty in oil-producing countries and the attitudes of future governments to climate change, pollution and energy policy.

Precision is not possible but developing a view of the future against which to evaluate and evolve strategies is important.

At 3M, for example, the general manager of each business unit is required annually to describe what his or her industry will look like in fifteen years.

(3) Cluster together different factors to identify various consistent future scenarios.

For example, two key factors may have been identified as:

(a) the threat of new entrants

(b) new legislation that may reduce the potential for profit.

Clearly, if new legislation is passed that reduces industry profit potential, then the likelihood of new entrants will fall.

This process usually results in between seven and nine mini-scenarios.

(4) 'Writing the scenario' – for the most important scenarios (usually limited to three), build a detailed analysis to identify and assess future implications.

As part of this, planners typically develop a set of optimistic, pessimistic and most likely assumptions about the impact of key variables on the company's future strategy.

The result of this detailed scenario construction should include:

– financial implications – anticipated net profits, cash flow and net working capital for each of three versions of the future
– strategic implications – possible opportunities and risks
– the probability of occurrence, usually based on past experience.

(5) For each scenario, identify and assess possible courses of action for the firm.

For example, Shell was the only major oil company to have prepared for the shock of the 1970s oil crisis through scenario planning and was able to respond faster than its competitors.

Some strategies make sense whatever the outcome, usually because they capitalise on or develop key strengths of the firm. For example, the firm concerned may have a global brand name and could seek to strengthen it by increasing its advertising spend in the short term.

However, in many cases, new resources and competences may be required for existing strategies to succeed. Alternatively, entirely new strategies may be required.

(6) Monitor reality to see which scenario is unfolding.

(7) Revise ("redeploy") scenarios and strategic options as appropriate.

Construction of scenarios

These need to be well thought out if they are to be effective. Hence the following should be considered:

- use a team for a range of opinions and expertise
- identify time-frame, markets, products and budget
- stakeholder analysis – who will be the most influential in the future?
- trend analysis and uncertainty identification
- building of initial scenarios
- consider organisational learning implications
- identify research needs and develop quantitative models.

As mentioned above, Shell makes use of scenario planning extensively in order to predict future changes in the energy industry so that it can attempt to prepare for them.

You can find some excellent examples of this on their website:

http://www.shell.com/home/content/aboutshell/our_strategy/shell_global_scenarios.

How useful is scenario planning?

The downside

- Costly and inaccurate – uses up substantial resources and time
- tendency for cultural distortion and for people to get carried away
- the risk of the self-fulfilling prophecy, i.e. thinking about the scenario may be the cause of it
- many scenarios considered will not actually occur.

The upside

- Focuses management attention on the future and possibilities
- encourages creative thinking
- can be used to justify a decision
- encourages communication via the participation process
- can identify the sources of uncertainty
- encourages companies to consider fundamental changes in the external environment.

Test your understanding 1

A book publisher has identified the following high-impact and high-uncertainty factors in its environment:

Factor	**Possible futures**
Development of e-books	• Rapid • Slow
Consumer attitudes to e-books	• Good substitute • Poor substitute
Cost of paper	• Rising • Stable

Suggest two plausible scenarios the publisher should analyse in more detail and suggest a possible strategy to deal with each.

Test your understanding 2

UHJ is a multinational company, based in Europe, which manufactures aircraft components. This is a fast–moving, dynamic market with a large number of innovative competitors attempting to take UHJ's market share.

UHJ recently expanded into the North American market and set up a new division with two factories on the west coast. Since this expansion, however, the North American market has been hit by a significant economic downturn. This downturn has continued for the last year and analysts are uncertain of how far and when it will recover.

This has led to a large reduction in orders for aircraft components and has meant that the North American division of UHJ is now barely breaking even. Its future profitability for the next few years depends on a large order from a North American airline, VTH. VTH will announce a decision on this order next month.

UHJ has recently been approached with an offer by one of its rivals to buy the factories for what UHJ considers to be a fair price. UHJ wishes to avoid closing the factories as it feels that the closure costs and redundancy payouts that would be required would be extremely high.

Required:

Advise UHJ on how scenario planning could help it to make a decision on the future of the North American division.

Test your understanding 3

Qualispecs has a reputation for quality, traditional products. It has a group of optician shops, both rented and owned, from which it sells its spectacles. Recently it has suffered intense competition and eroding customer loyalty, but a new chief executive has joined from one of its major rivals, Fastglass.

Fastglass is capturing Qualispecs' market through a partnership with a high-street shopping group. These shops install mini-labs in which prescriptions for spectacles are dispensed within an hour. Some competitors have successfully experimented with designer frames and sunglasses. Others have reduced costs through new computer-aided production methods.

Qualispecs has continued to operate as it always has, letting the product 'speak for itself' and failing to utilise advances in technology. Although production costs remain high, Qualispecs is financially secure and has large cash reserves. Fortunately the country's most popular sports star recently received a prestigious international award wearing a pair of Qualispecs' spectacles.

The new Chief Executive has established as a priority the need for improved financial performance. Following a review she discovers that:

(a) targets are set centrally and shops report monthly. Site profitability varies enormously, and fixed costs are high in shopping malls

(b) shops exercise no control over job roles, working conditions, and pay rates

(c) individual staff pay is increased annually according to a predetermined pay scale. Everyone also receives a small one-off payment based on group financial performance.

Market analysts predict a slowdown in the national economy but feel that consumer spending will continue to increase, particularly among 18- to 30-year-olds.

Required:

(a) Produce a corporate appraisal of Qualispecs, taking account of internal and external factors, and discuss the key strategic challenges facing the company.

(16 marks)

(b) Corporate appraisal offers a 'snapshot' of the present. In order to focus on the future there is a need to develop realistic policies and programmes. Recommend, with reasons, strategies from your appraisal that would enable Qualispecs to build on its past success.

(9 marks)

(Total: 25 marks)

Test your understanding 4

Chelsea is a large civil engineering company which carries out various building contracts within both its home and overseas markets. Its main area of work, particularly overseas, is in road construction. The company has a strong financial track record and successfully survived a major recession within its home market about ten years ago.

Economic circumstances in overseas markets

During the last three years, the overseas markets in which Chelsea has been carrying out building contracts have suffered a serious economic recession. Business confidence in these markets has been seriously weakened over this period. One country which has been adversely affected is Eastlandia. Chelsea has been engaged in carrying out contract work in Eastlandia for several years. Government action in Eastlandia to protect its ailing economy has also had an adverse impact on foreign contractors such as Chelsea operating within this country.

The concern felt by Chelsea's directors regarding the economic situation in Eastlandia has been increased as a result of recent events involving a large development company called Derby, which Chelsea has worked with in the past. Derby, which is wholly owned by Eastlandian shareholders, had previously received Eastlandian government backing. However, it has recently been allowed to go into receivership without any further government support. The government announced that partial repayment of debts owed by the development company to local investors would take priority over those it owed to foreign investors. The result of this is that foreign investors are unlikely to see any recovery of their loans.

The serious economic situation in Eastlandia has threatened to result in an economic recession. There has been a constant negative effect on related industries within the country, such as steel, building materials and transport. Another major concern for Chelsea's directors is the constant threat posed by currency fluctuations and the possibility of the Eastlandian government being forced into currency devaluation.

Work in progress

Currently Chelsea is engaged in the construction of a major road linking two parts of a new Eastlandian city, bypassing the central congested area. Chelsea is engaged as a subcontractor to a major Eastlandian development company – a different company from Derby, which went into receivership recently. Chelsea accepted the contract after estimating that it would provide a high net present value. At the time that the investment appraisal was undertaken, the expected currency exchange rate between Eastlands (Eastlandia's currency) and £ sterling (Chelsea's home currency) was 7.26 to the £ in the current year and 7.54 to the £ in the next year. In fact the current exchange rate is 7.74 to the £ and the forward rate in 12 months' time is quoted at 8.56 to the £.

As far as Chelsea's overall business is concerned, the contract represents about 10% of total turnover for the company. The contract commenced three months ago and Chelsea is to be paid in Eastlands. Progress payments for the work done to date have been delayed without any explanation. The contract is about 15% complete and is expected to be completed in 21 months, which is 3 months later than planned. This will result in penalty payments being incurred by Chelsea.

The directors of Chelsea have expressed to the contract manager for the road development in Eastlandia their concern regarding the need to undertake remedial work on what has been completed so far. This has resulted from use of faulty materials obtained from an Eastlandian supplier. The remedial work has already consumed the total amount of the financial contingency which was allowed for in the contract estimates.

Strategic information and market size

Chelsea uses external databases to establish the levels of its own share of the market and overall patterns of market growth and development. In addition, the management accounting department of the company provides internal information on market share and growth and internal capacity to meet its future contractual demands. Over the last two years there has been a general decline in market opportunities but Chelsea has managed to increase its overall market share. This has been achieved because of its strong reputation for using good quality materials and applying high standards of workmanship.

One of the major criticisms being made in Eastlandia is the poor quality of the civil engineering projects which have been completed quickly There have been reports of numerous site casualties amongst the site workers during the construction process. Some buildings have partially collapsed after construction has been completed and there have been instances where roads have started to break up shortly after they have opened. This has caused civilian casualties with some fatalities and resulted in noisy public protest in Eastlandia about the lack of attention to safety in civil engineering and building work.

Chelsea is well regarded by the Eastlandian government. It has taken a long time for the directors of Chelsea to build the company's reputation and gain recognition in Eastlandia for its workmanship.

Possible future development

The Eastlandian government has invited Chelsea's directors to tender for other civil engineering work. Chelsea has taken up the invitation and if the company were successful in all its tenders, the total commitment in Eastlandia would represent about 40% of its order book.

In recognition of the importance of the Eastlandian market and in order to reduce the potential losses from developers who engage their services becoming insolvent, the directors of Chelsea have proposed that a strategic alliance be formed. It is proposed that this alliance will be established with an Eastlandian civil engineering contractor who, it is hoped, will have an insight into the financial integrity of potential customers. The alliance partners would be able to give clear advice as to which of these Eastlandian customers would be suitable for the establishment of contractual arrangements.

Required:

Produce a SWOT analysis for Chelsea and identify factors that should be considered in order to reduce the potential impact posed by threats.

(May 2000 – adapted)

5 Summary

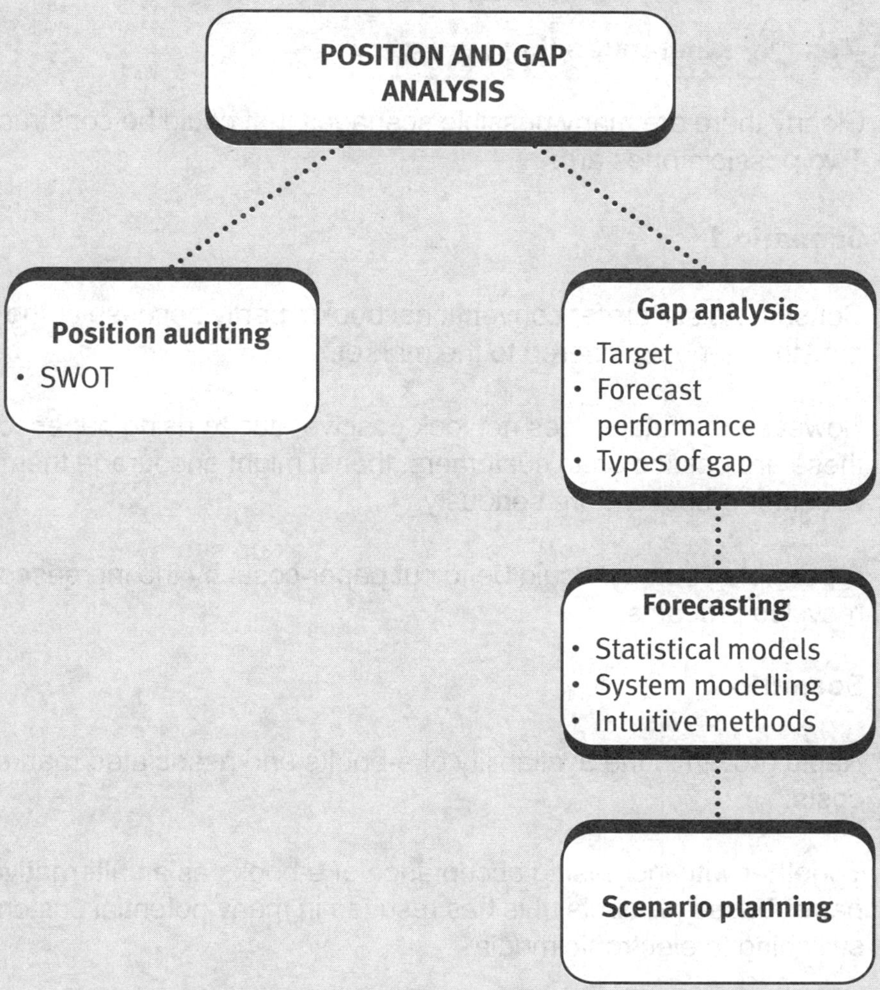
POSITION AND GAP ANALYSIS
Position auditing
• SWOT
Gap analysis
• Target
• Forecast performance
• Types of gap
Forecasting
• Statistical models
• System modelling
• Intuitive methods
Scenario planning

Test your understanding answers

Test your understanding 1

Clearly there are many possible scenarios that could be constructed. Two possible ones are:

Scenario 1

Consumers still prefer conventional books, partly because of the limited growth in e-books offered to the market.

However, the future does not look positive, due to rising paper costs. If these are passed on to customers, then it might encourage them to consider e-books more seriously.

A possible strategy would be to cut paper costs by the increased use of recycled products.

Scenario 2

Rapid growth in the availability of e-books and associated marketing costs.

Together with increasing acceptance of e-books as an alternative to paper-based products, this has resulted in many potential customers switching to electronic media.

A possible strategy would be to develop ranges of titles aimed at older customers, who will (presumably) be slower to accept e-books. Alternatively holiday novels could be targeted as many customers will prefer paperbacks when lazing by the pool.

Test your understanding 2

UHJ is faced with a dynamic and rapidly changing environment in the North American market. Scenario planning is the detailed and credible analysis of how the business environment might develop in the future, based on various environmental influences and drivers for change. The target for this analysis should be areas where the organisation considers there to be a high degree of uncertainty or opportunity.

Scenario planning would therefore enable UHJ to calculate and examine various possible strategic outcomes.

For example, UHJ would be able to examine the possible impact of the economic downturn lasting for several years, or alternatively beginning to reverse immediately. It could also compare combinations of events, such as:

- the sale of the division, followed by an economic recovery, but the loss of the VTH order
- the retention of the division, followed by a continuation of the economic downturn, along with the acquisition of the VTH order

and so on.

This approach will have two key benefits:

(1) It will help the directors of UHJ to see 'worst-case' scenarios. Should the North American economy suffer a prolonged downturn and the division lose the VTH order, there could be a significant impact on the division, along with the rest of the company. This may help the directors to decide how much of a risk maintaining the North American division is and whether it would be best to sell immediately.

(2) Scenario planning will also help the directors to anticipate potential problems with, or opportunities from, the North American division. For example, if UHJ waits to sell the division and the VTH order is lost, the price it achieves from the sale may well be much lower than is currently on offer. Alternatively, the market may recover in the near future and the sale of the division now may compromise UHJ's future growth prospects.

Test your understanding 3

Key answer tips

You are required to undertake a corporate appraisal for Qualispecs and use this to suggest suitable strategies for the company. It is vital that you use the information given to you in the scenario for this question, which is highly practical in nature. You do not need to perform a detailed analysis of the company using models such as PEST, Porter's Five Forces and so on. In part (b) an alternative to Ansoff's matrix would be the use of a TOWS matrix, which involves a process of conversion, matching and remedy. This involves converting threats into opportunities and weaknesses into strengths by building on the SWOT analysis. In practice one would probably consider the strategies suggested by Ansoff's matrix and the techniques implied by the TOWS matrix in order to produce a strategy.

(a) **Corporate appraisal**

A corporate appraisal is an overview of an organisation's current position. It leads on from the internal and external analysis undertaken as part of the business planning process.

As the company works towards achieving its objectives, the corporate appraisal is a summary of the company's:

- strengths within the organisation relative to competitors
- weaknesses within the organisation relative to competitors
- opportunities available from the external environment
- threats from the external environment.

The company must develop a strategy which:

- capitalises on the strengths
- overcomes or mitigates the impact of weaknesses
- takes suitable opportunities
- overcomes or mitigates the threats.

In the case of Qualispecs:

Strengths

– Reputation for quality.

  Quality is a major reason why people buy products, and continuing to build on this reputation will ensure customers continue to buy Qualispecs's products.

– Financially secure/large cash reserves.

  Qualispecs does not need to rush into the implementation of new strategies. It can take its time to ensure strategies chosen are appropriate for the business and implemented effectively. They also have funds to invest in new ventures without having to raise external funds.

– Backing of a famous sports star.

  This helps to improve the image of Qualispecs's products which in turn should result in higher sales, particularly amongst the younger market that might be influenced by the sports star.

– New chief executive.

  The group has a new chief executive who has joined from a rival, Fastglass. Fastglass has been a successful and innovative company and the chief executive may be able to bring new ideas and provide a fresh approach.

– Established group with many stores.

  The group has a good basic infrastructure including many stores and experienced staff. This allows them to implement new strategies quickly and easily.

Weaknesses

– Slower dispensing of spectacles.

  Customer service is worse than competitors in this respect and may be a reason for the reducing customer loyalty.

– Less trendy products than competitors.

  Some competitors have successfully sold designer frames. These are likely to be stylish and trendy compared to Qualispecs' traditional products. Qualispecs may need to update products more often with the latest designs.

– Smaller product range than competitors.

  Some competitors have a wider product range than Qualispecs. This provides more choice, which may attract customers, and also gives competitors the opportunity to on-sell products, i.e. selling prescription sunglasses at the same time as standard spectacles.

– Older production methods causing higher costs.

  This will either cause prices to be higher than competitors or margins to be less. In either case competitors have a distinct advantage.

– Varying performance around the group.

  Little action is being taken to improve performance of poorly performing stores causing varying performance around the group. This indicates a weakness in internal control systems and perhaps also in development and training programmes.

– Little autonomy for shops.

  Without autonomy there is little a shop manager can do to improve local operations. In London, for instance, pay may need to be higher to attract the right staff. With no local control over pay levels, shop managers may find it hard to employ good staff and hence improve their business.

  This lack of autonomy may also be demotivating to managers. Responsibility was one of the major factors outlined by Hertzberg in his motivation theory as a way to motivate staff.

– No incentive to improve for staff.

The use of group-based bonuses means that people cannot be rewarded for good individual performance. Individuals have little incentive to improve therefore.

Opportunities

Note: Opportunities should be in relation to the market as a whole. They therefore need to be available to all competitors in the market.

– To adopt new technologies to reduce costs (see earlier)
– to stock a wide range of up-to-date products (see earlier)
– consumer spending will continue to increase.

Despite a slowdown in the economy, consumer spending is likely to increase, suggesting an increasing market size in the future. There is therefore further opportunity for all competitors to increase sales.

– Targeting 18- to 30-year-olds.

The 18- to 30-year-old age group offers a particular opportunity since its spending is likely to increase especially quickly. There is therefore an opportunity to understand this group's needs and to target it specifically.

– Develop a partnership with a high-street shopping group.

Fastglass has already done this successfully and Qualispecs could follow suit. There are likely to be limited suitable partners so Qualispecs must act quickly before other firms make arrangements with the best partners.

Threats

– Intense competition/eroding customer loyalty.

Existing competitors are adopting new strategies with great success (e.g. Fastglass developed joint ventures). This has resulted in Qualispecs' customers moving to competitors, thus reducing profits. This is likely to be a continued threat to Qualispecs, who needs to respond.

– Downturn in the economy.

In the long term, if the downturn continues it will affect all industries and consumer spending will be likely to fall as people become more defensive in their spending habits.

Key strategic challenges

In summary the key strategic challenges are to:

– Improve the current lack of clear generic strategy ('stuck in the middle').

According to Michael Porter's generic strategies, Qualispecs appears to have neither a cost leader differentiation nor a focus on any particular niche. While traditionally quality has been their focus, new innovations from competitors have eroded its position as the highest quality spectacle retailer. In the long run it will find it hard to compete effectively if it does not rectify this.

Note: When asked to discuss current or future strategies Porter's generic strategies is always a good model to use. It is common in the exam to present failing companies (like Qualispecs) and you usually find such companies are 'stuck in the middle' and need to clarify their generic strategy in order to compete.

– Be more innovative in product and market development.

Competitors have successfully developed new strategies while Qualispecs has done very little. This has seen it lose business to competitors. To be successful in the future it needs to update its product range regularly and be more innovative in developing new strategies (e.g. joint ventures).

– Improve performance on a divisional basis by updating internal policies and procedures.

Current policies and procedures are demotivating staff and causing varying divisional performance.

(b) **Strategies to move the business forward**

Generic strategy

Given the key strength of Qualispecs, a reputation for quality spectacles, and their current weakness in the cost of products produced, it would appear logical for Qualispecs to refocus activities on quality by producing very high quality spectacles (modern design, hard wearing, up-to-date features) with a high-quality service (fast dispensing, knowledgeable staff).

Ansoff's matrix

A useful model to develop business strategies is Ansoff's matrix. Business strategies can be examined in all four boxes of this matrix for their suitability to the business compared to the corporate appraisal.

	PRODUCT: *Current*	PRODUCT: *New*
MARKET: *Current*	Market penetration Consolidate Divest	Product development
MARKET: *New*	Market development	Diversification – Related – Unrelated

Current product/current market

Qualispecs would benefit from consolidating its current strengths and refocusing on quality. It should invest in new technology in order to reduce costs which will allow it to be competitive. This also capitalises on its significant cash reserves.

It needs to improve its internal processes to ensure that staff are motivated through a good incentive scheme, quality training and by being given autonomy. This will capitalise on its skilled workforce and overcome the weakness in the way it is managed.

Current market/new products

Product development is a vital new strategy for Qualispecs to follow. Its competitors have been successful in doing this. One aspect of providing a high quality service is being able to offer a wide range of products to meet varying customer needs. Qualispecs may need to invest more in research and development and implement new product development programmes.

New market/current products

A joint-venture strategy with a retailer who competes based on quality (e.g. Marks and Spencer) would both build on the reputation of Qualispecs and also introduce it to a new group of customers who will buy its products through association with the retail group. The retail group may also have outlets in other parts of the country (or even internationally) which would allow Qualispecs to expand its markets.

Diversification

There appears to be no need at present to diversify. The disadvantages of operating in new markets with new products (e.g. lack of experience and reputation) outweigh any possible advantages.

Test your understanding 4

Strengths

- Strong financial track record
- life longer than ten years so well established
- good reputation in international marketplace
- increased market share despite market decline
- involved in many overseas markets so experienced
- resourced and competent
- good relationship with Eastlandian government built up over many years
- relationship with other stakeholders likely to be good also.

Weaknesses

- Exposed to construction industry
- exposed to Eastlandian government action
- venture partner – local company D – now failed
- unlikely to recover C's funding
- currency exposure and controls needed
- 10% of turnover on one contract
- financial contingency in contract seems inadequate
- general quality and project management problems evident
- committed to Eastlandia and so exit barrier exists.

Opportunities

- Recovery of funds from supplier of defective materials
- further projects may arise as competitors in Eastlandia appear to be poor in terms of competencies
- preferred status may be conveyed upon C by Easlandia government
- venture partner – culturally aware and acceptable to a range of stakeholders. Risk therefore reduces.

Threats

- Multinational – pressure groups
- reputation may suffer in future
- overseas markets have suffered recession
- Eastlandia economic situation – recession likely?
- 'knock on' effects within the economy
- threat of devaluation
- exchange rate movement – 7.26 to 8.56 = 18% loss in value
- progress payments delayed
- project late so penalty payments likely
- local customers may go bust and bad debt recovery may prove difficult as C is external to the Eastlandia culture
- high PEST risk = higher cost of capital = lower EVA.

Impact reduction

- Risk reduction – look for business in other countries
- harvest the Eastlandian projects
- look to improve the project management process for future projects via a post-completion audit of the current project in Eastlandia. Recruit a suitably qualified team to undertake the investigation
- control system review to attempt to improve collection of progress payments
- foreign exchange controls – forward exchange contracts
- local currency loans and other financial sources to be sought
- recruit senior staff from Eastlandia and have an Eastlandian in charge of the project as director. Give this individual the appropriate status relevant for the local culture
- full corporate analysis of any proposed customers
- look for guarantees from the Eastlandian government for dubious customer proposals
- lobby for local grants and assistance – especially with regard to the local supplier who provided the poor-quality materials
- full investigation of local partner and detailed legal agreement which clearly identifies the commitments of both sides in the JV
- this contract should detail when the arrangement will end, and how profits (and losses) should be shared
- ensure that a high-profile PR department is operational with great emphasis on social responsibility in general. Emphasise how they can help Eastlandia. Recruit a 'diplomat' to the board
- full research programmes and forecasting systems with regard to the future economic and political issues arising in Eastlandia – an early warning system.

chapter

8

Strategic choice

Chapter learning objectives

Lead	Component
C1. Evaluate the process of strategy development	(b) Evaluate strategic options
C2. Evaluate strategic planning tools	(a) Evaluate strategic planning tools (b) Recommend appropriate changes to the product portfolio of an organisation to support the organisation's strategic goals

Indicative syllabus content

- The identification and evaluation of strategic options
- Strategic options generation (e.g. using Ansoff's product/market matrix and Porter's generic strategies)
- Real options as a tool for strategic analysis. Note: Complex numerical questions will not be set
- Game theoretic approaches to strategic planning and decision-making. Note: Complex numerical questions will not be set
- Acquisition, divestment, rationalisation and relocation strategies and their place in the strategic plan
- Management of the product portfolio
- Strategic decision–making processes

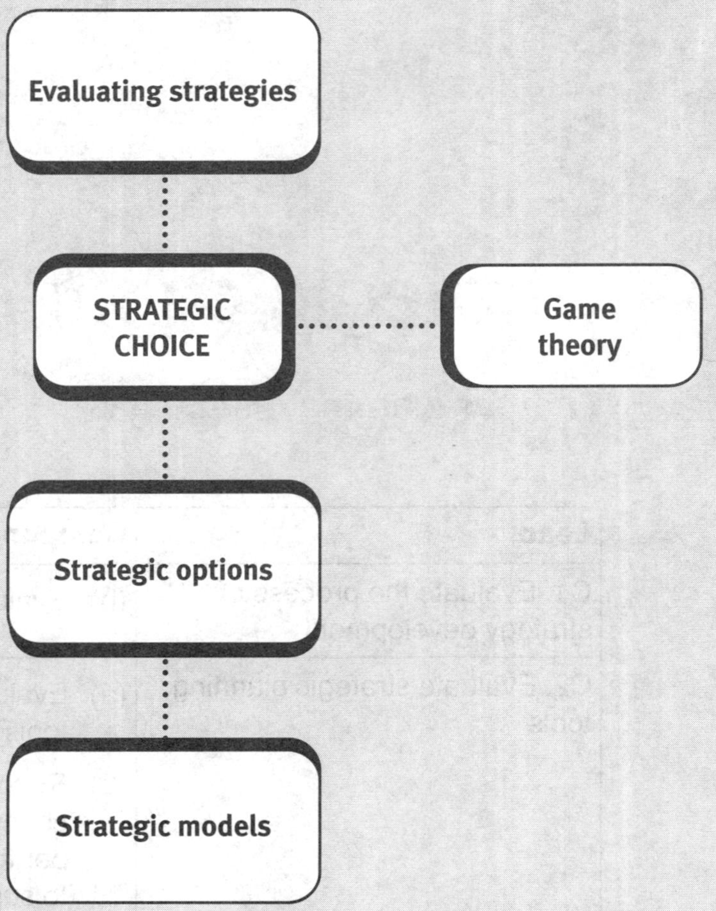

1 Strategic analysis and choice

Once the position has been identified, the organisation will be aware of the environments and the current strategic capability of the organisation. So the questions is "What should we do now to enable us to have the best chance of achieving our objectives?" In other words, which strategy should we follow?

There are many ways to achieve the end result! There is no one strategy that should be deployed in any given circumstance, rather a range of possible strategies that could be used singly or jointly.

This is known as **equifinality** – as such strategic choice involves the selection of a course of action by a management team, which is likely to be the result of lengthy discussion and formalised process. This would be most likely in larger organisations with a wider range of stakeholders. It could be the result of a deliberate steering along a predefined path or the strategy may just evolve as the company develops – the emergent strategy principle, which reflects the more reactive nature of some strategic determination.

2 Key decisions to make

As part of strategic choice there are three key levels of strategy to consider:

(1) **Where to compete?**

Which markets / products / SBUs should be part of our portfolio?

(2) **How to compete?**

For each SBU, what should be the basis of our competitive advantage?

(3) **Which investment vehicle to use?**

Suppose an attractive new market has been identified. Should the organisation enter the market via organic growth, acquisition or some form of joint expansion method, such as franchising?

3 The strategic models

There are several models that you must be familiar with.

- Porter – generic strategies – looks at competitive strategy
- Ansoff – product/market matrix – directions for growth
- BCG – growth/share matrix.

You must ensure that you can draw the relevant diagram and explain the basics of each model. However, the key will be to apply them in a scenario.

Benefits

- These models provide a useful starting point for the discursive process as they initiate discussion amongst the management teams.
- They are well-known and as such have credibility. This results in their easy application with minimal resistance.
- They generate options that can be used in the debate and allow comparison.
- They can in some instances be linked to each other to enhance the analysis.
- They can be used simply or be developed into more complicated applications.

Limitations

- They are simplistic – most are two-by-two models.
- Given their prominence in management education, undue emphasis tends to be placed upon them and there is a tendency at times to think that the models will provide a solution.
- They are dated and were produced when environments were very different. They tend to suggest that strategic choice is a straightforward process.
- They serve as a good basis for analysis, but are not perfect and do not apply to every situation.

4 Porter's Generic Strategies

Porter suggests that competitive advantage arises from the selection of a generic strategy which best fits the organisation's environment and then organising value-adding activities to support the chosen strategy.

		Competitive	**Stance**
Strategic scope	Broad scope Targets whole market	Cost leadership	Differentiation
	Narrow scope Targets one segment	Focus	

Cost leadership – being the lowest-cost producer.

Differentiation – creating a customer perception that the product is superior to that of competitors so that a premium can be charged, i.e. that it is different.

Focus – utilising either of the above in a narrow profile of market segments, sometimes called niching.

Porter argues that organisations need to address two key questions:

- Should the strategy be one of differentiation or cost leadership?
- Should the scope be wide or narrow?

He argues that organisations can run the risk of trying to satisfy all and end up being 'stuck in the middle'. This seems to suggest that Porter was advocating that organisations need to make a basic competitive decision early on in the strategic determination process.

Cost leadership strategy

Based upon a business organising itself to be the lowest-cost producer.

Potential benefits are:

- business can earn higher profits by charging the same price as competitors or even moving to undercut where demand is elastic
- lets company build defence against price wars
- allows price penetration entry strategy into new markets
- enhances barriers to entry
- develops new market segments.

Value chain analysis is central to identifying where cost savings can be made at various stages in the value chain. Attainment depends upon arranging value chain activities so as to:

- reduce costs by copying rather than originating designs, using cheaper materials and other cheaper resources, producing products with 'no frills', reducing labour costs and increasing labour productivity
- achieving economies of scale by high-volume sales allowing fixed costs to be spread over a wider production base
- use high-volume purchasing to obtain discounts for bulk purchase
- locating in areas where cost advantage exists or government aid is possible
- obtaining learning and experience curve benefits.

Differentiation strategy

This strategy is based upon the idea of persuading customers that a product is superior to that offered by the competition. Differentiation can be based on product features or creating/altering consumer perception. Differentiation can also be based upon **process as well as product**. It is usually used to justify a higher price.

Benefits:

- Products command a premium price so higher margins.
- Demand becomes less price elastic and so avoids costly competitor price wars.
- Life cycle extends as branding becomes possible – hence strengthening the barriers to entry.

Value chain analysis can identify the points at which these can be achieved by:

- creating products which are superior to competitors by virtue of design, technology, performance, etc. Marketing spend becomes important
- offering superior after-sales service by superior distribution, perhaps in prime locations
- creating brand strength
- augmenting the product, i.e. adding to it.
- packaging the product
- ensuring an innovative culture exists within the company.

Focus strategy

This strategy is aimed at a segment of the market rather than the whole market. A particular group of consumers are identified with similar needs, possibly based upon age, sex, lifestyle, income or geography and then the company will either differentiate or cost focus in that area.

Benefits:

- smaller segment and so smaller investment in marketing operations
- allows specialisation
- less competition
- entry is cheaper and easier.

Requires:

- reliable segment identification
- consumer/customer needs to be reliably identified – research becomes even more crucial
- segment to be sufficiently large to enable a return to be earned in the long run
- competition analysis – given the small market, the competition, if any, needs to be fully understood
- direct focus of product to consumer needs.

Niching can be done via specialisation by:

- location
- type of end user
- product or product line
- quality
- price
- size of customer
- product feature.

If done properly it can avoid confrontation and competition yet still be profitable. The attractiveness of the market niche is influenced by the following:

- the niche must be large enough in terms of potential buyers
- the niche must have growth potential and predictability
- the niche must be of negligible interest to major competitors
- the firm must have strategic capability to enable effective service of the niche.

e.g

Illustration 1 – Cost leadership

Casio Electronics Co. Ltd – Casio has sold over 1 billion pocket calculators. It follows an industry-wide cost leadership approach. Its calculators are certainly not inferior products, being able to perform over two hundred basic scientific functions. How does it do it? Consider its value chain:

- Operations – mass manufactured in China, which has cheaper labour and economies of scale.
- Operations – 'buttons', display and instructions manuals are multi–lingual – reducing the need to make calculators specific to one target country.
- Procurement – mass purchase/production of components.
- Outbound logistics – packaging is robust, yet allows a considerable number of calculators to be shipped at any time.

e.g

Illustration 2 – Differentiation

British Airways (BA) is a multinational passenger airline. It has adopted a differentiation approach by offering passengers a higher-quality experience than many of its rivals. This allows it to charge a premium for its flights compared to many other airlines. Again – examination of its value chain may help to explain how it achieves this:

- Procurement – prime landing slots are obtained at major airports around the world.
- Procurement – high-quality food and drink is sourced from suppliers.
- Operations – well-maintained, clean and comfortable aircraft are sourced.
- Operations – high numbers of attendants on each flight.
- Marketing – advertising based on quality of service provided.
- Human resources – training in customer care and the recruitment of high-quality staff.

e.g

Illustration 3 – Focus

Ferrari is an example of a company that focuses on a niche market in the automobile industry. It produces extremely high quality cars which command a high premium price. However, this means that Ferrari only has a very small percentage of the global car market, as the majority of consumers will be unable to afford its high sales prices.

This is a risk of the focus approach. The niche targeted may be small and fail to justify the company's attention. In addition the niche may shrink or disappear altogether over time as consumer tastes and fashions change.

Strategic approaches based on market position

Market leader

In many industries there is a dominant firm which is recognised to be the leading organisation. It typically has the largest market share and usually provides the benchmark for others in the industry.

Market challenger

This firm has a smaller market share, adopts an aggressive stance and seeks to attack other firms, which includes the leader. Marketing strategies tend to be confrontational and there is a continual search for new ideas. There is a tendency to look for 'first mover advantage' in the developing market place.

Market followers

These are less aggressive firms which tend to rely on other members of the industry to try things out and then 'follow' on after, either to pick up the pieces or follow the success of others. There is less risk and of course less potential for return. They forego the risk area of the search for first mover advantage in return for the safety of the follower.

'The strategy of product imitation rather than innovation' (T. Levitt).

Market nichers

Many industries have a series of small firms who specialise in parts of the market which are too limited in size and potential to be of any real interest to larger firms. The classic example that is always mentioned is Morgan sports cars, a UK company that hand-builds high quality cars for its customers. The nichers' success stems from their ability to build up specialist knowledge about a particular segment whilst being able to avoid the high costs of head-on fights with leaders and challengers.

5 Ansoff

The product/market growth framework

A commonly used model for analysing the possible strategic directions that an organisation can follow. Hence useful in areas of strategic choice:

		Products	
		Existing	*New*
Markets	Existing	Market penetration	Product development
	New	Market development	Diversification

Market penetration

Increasing market share in existing markets utilising existing products.

Market development

Entering new markets and segments using existing products.

Product development

Developing new products to serve existing markets.

Diversification

Developing new products to serve new markets.

When considering the use of each of these the company should consider:

- The potential reward.
- The potential risk.
- The remaining gap to meeting the company's objectives (from gap analysis).

Market penetration

The main aim is to increase market share using existing products within existing markets.

Approach

First attempt to stimulate **usage by existing customers:**

- new uses of advertising
- promotions, sponsorships
- quantity discounts.

Then attempt to attract **non-users** and **competitor customers** via:

- pricing
- promotion and advertising
- process redesign, e.g. Internet/e-commerce

Considered when:

- overall market is growing
- market not saturated
- competitors leaving or weak
- strong brand presence by your company with established reputation
- strong marketing capabilities exist within your company.

Market development

Aims to increase sales by taking the present product to new markets (or new segments). Entering new markets or segments may require the development of new competencies which serve the particular needs of customers in those segments, e.g. cultural awareness/linguistic skills.

Movement into overseas markets is often quoted as a good example as the organisation will need to build new competencies when entering international markets.

Approach

- Add **geographical** areas – regional and national
- add **demographic** areas – age and sex
- new **distribution** channels.

Key notes

- **Slight** product modifications may be needed
- advertising in different media and in different ways
- research – primary research at this point given significance of the investment
- company is structured to produce one product and high switching costs exist for transfer to other product types
- strong marketing ability is needed, usually coupled with established brand backing, e.g. Coca-Cola

Product development

Focuses on the development of new products for existing markets.

Offers the advantage of dealing with known customer/consumer bases.

May aim to:

- develop product features of a significant nature
- create different quality versions.

Company needs to be innovative and strong in the area of R&D and have an established, reliable marketing database.

Constant innovation allows for the developing sophistication of consumers and customers and ensures that any product-related competitive advantage is maintained.

Diversification

New products to new markets – the risky option?

Appropriate when existing markets are saturated or when products are reaching the end of their life cycle. It can spread risk by broadening the portfolio and lead to 'synergy-based benefits', allegedly.

This goes through periods of being in and out of favour and the debate is always continuing as to whether this is a good strategic option. Critics argue that it is madness to take resources away from known markets and products only to allocate them to businesses that the company essentially knows nothing about. This risk has to be compensated for by higher rewards, which may or may not exist.

Brand stretching ability is often seen as being the critical success factor for successful diversification – this is a possible discussion point. The new business and its strategy may well have 'teething problems' with its implementation and this may damage brand reputation, e.g. Virgin.

Reasons suggested:

- Objectives can no longer be met in known markets – possibly due to a change in the external environment.
- Company has excess cash and powerful shareholders;
- Possible to 'brand stretch' and benefit from past advertising and promotion in other SBUs.
- Diversification promises greater returns and can spread risk by removing the dependency on one product.
- Greater use of distribution systems and corporate resources such as research and development, market research, finance and HR leading to synergies.

e.g

Illustration 4 – Ansoff

- Kellogg's have repositioned their products through various advertising campaigns **(market penetration)**. For example, the 'have you forgotten how good they taste?' campaign was to remind adults, who buy cereals for their children, of the virtues of their product.
- Kwik Fit, a motor repair company, took the opportunity to cross sell insurance to customers on their database who had visited their outlets to have equipment fitted **(product development – 'piggybacking')**.
- Kaplan now sell their ACCA courses in Eastern Europe and Asia, amongst other countries, rather than just their traditional UK markets **(market development)**.
- Virgin, a multinational conglomerate, has expanded into a wide range of different activities, including airlines, trains, cosmetics, wedding wear and so on **(diversification)**.

Test your understanding 1

Esso is a successful oil company. It has run a 'pricewatch' campaign to ensure its fuels are priced at a similar level to supermarkets and other competitors. It has expanded its range of products available at Esso minimarkets to include groceries and household goods. It has signed agreements with China to sell fuels there and is contemplating acquisitions of engineering and textiles companies.

Required:

Categorise these actions using Ansoff's matrix. Explain your choices.

6 Diversification

Diversification can take **two** main forms:

Related diversification (concentric diversification)

- Growth into similar industries.
- Growth forward into the customer marketplace.
- Growth backward into the existing supply chain:
  - **Vertical backward** – a company seeks to operate in markets in which it currently obtains its resources, e.g. a supermarket producing some of the products it buys – the benefit would arise from greater control over resource supply.
  - **Vertical forward** – a company seeks to move into its customer base, e.g. a brewery establishing its own chain of pubs and off-licences.
  - **Horizontal** – involves a company entering into complementary or competing markets, e.g. Honda motorcycles and cars. (Not to be confused with horizontal integration, which refers to the acquisition of a competitor.)

Vertical integration

Taking over a supplier (backwards vertical integration) or customer (forwards vertical integration). Key issues relate to

- Cost.

  Is it cheaper to make a product in-house and avoid paying towards a supplier's profit margin or might the supplier have sufficient economies of scale for them to sell it cheaper than you can make it?

- Quality.

  Making a component in-house means you can tailor it to your own needs and use proprietary expertise... if you have the necessary resources and competences.

- Risk/flexibility.

  Outsourcing gives a firm the flexibility to switch suppliers and so exercise buyer power to drive down prices.

Vertical integration

Backward integration refers to developments into activities which are concerned with inputs to the company's present business, for example a company becoming a supplier of its own raw materials. Sometimes this form of integration is called "upstream" integration.

Forward integration refers to development into activities which are concerned with the company's outputs. For example, a company could set up its own distribution channels rather than relying on outside retailers. Sometimes this form of integration is called "downstream" integration.

Vertical integration can have important benefits and costs which need to be considered in any decision.

Benefits of integration

- Economies of combined operations, e.g. proximity, reduced handling.
- Economies of internal control and coordination, e.g. scheduling and coordinating operations should be better. Information about the market can be fed back to the production companies.
- Economies of avoiding the market, e.g. negotiation, packing, advertising costs are avoided.

- Tap into technology. Close knowledge of the upstream or downstream operations can give a company valuable strategic advantages. For example, computer manufacturers have instituted backwards integration into semi-conductor design and manufacturing to gain a better understanding of the technology and its potential.
- Safeguarding proprietary knowledge. If a firm makes components itself, it does not have to supply specifications to its suppliers; this information therefore stays confidential.
- Assured supply and demand. The firm will have first call on supplies in scarce periods and the greatest chance of having an outlet in periods of low demand. Fluctuations in supply and demand are not eliminated but can, perhaps, be better planned.
- Reduction in bargaining power of suppliers and customers. Two of Porter's forces on a firm are customer and supplier bargaining power. So if your suppliers are giving you a rough time, take them over or set up your own supply company. Similarly with distribution channels.
- Enhanced ability to differentiate. More of the product comes under your control so you have a greater ability to differentiate it. For example, a specialist chain of shops could be established with a distinctive brand image.
- Defend against "lock out". It may be necessary to defend against being cut off from access to suppliers or distributors. For example, if a competitor were buying up your suppliers you would have to acquire your own supplier to ensure continued supply of components.

Costs of integration

- Increased operating gearing. Vertical integration increases the proportion of the firm's costs which are fixed. For example, if the firm were to purchase from an outside source, all those costs would be variable. If the input is produced internally the firm has to bear all the fixed costs of production. Vertical integration increases business risk from this source.
- Reduced flexibility to change partners. If the in-house supplier or customer does not do well, then it is not easy to switch to outsiders. You will probably have to get rid of the in-house company first.

- Capital investment needs. Vertical integration will consume capital resources and must yield a return greater than, or equal to, the firm's opportunity cost of capital, adjusting for strategic considerations, for integration to be a good choice.
- Cut off from suppliers and customers. By integrating a firm may cut itself off from the flow of technology from its suppliers or market research information from its customers. For example, a firm will have to take responsibility for developing its own technology. Other potential suppliers may be reluctant to share their technology as they would be supplying it not only to a customer, but a customer who is also a competitor.
- Dulled incentives. The captive relationship between buyer and seller can quickly lead to inefficiencies. These can quickly spread through the group as too high cost products are passed through.
- Differing managerial requirements. Different businesses need different management skills. Because a company is a successful manufacturer, this does not mean that it can turn its hand to retailing with a reasonable chance of success. Many companies have found that they do best doing what they do best.

Horizontal diversification

Horizontal diversification refers to development into activities that are competitive with, or directly complementary to, a company's present activities. There are three cases.

(a) Competitive products. Taking over a competitor can have obvious benefits, leading eventually towards achieving a monopoly. Apart from active competition, a competitor may offer advantages such as completing geographical coverage.

(b) Complementary products. For example, a manufacturer of household vacuum cleaners could make commercial cleaners. A full product range can be presented to the market and there may well be benefits to be reaped from having many of the components common between the different ranges.

(c) By-products. For example, a butter manufacturer discovering increased demand for skimmed milk. Generally, income from by-products is a windfall: any you get is counted, at least initially, as a bonus.

Unrelated diversification (conglomerate diversification)

- Completely new areas with which the business shares no common ground
- more risk from going into unknown markets and products

- BUT could argue that you are spreading the risk by not remaining exposed in one area, e.g. Benetton
- taken when serious restrictions evident in existing markets and products or when growth opportunities appear in other areas
- possible economies of scale again
- greater spread of the overall portfolio risk
- opportunity for return exists and there is nothing else to do with the resources. The company may need to be seen as an 'aggressive' organisation and may embark on this course of action in order to appease powerful stakeholder groups.

7 Product Portfolio Theory – Boston Consulting Group (BCG)

Boston Consulting Group Growth / Share Matrix

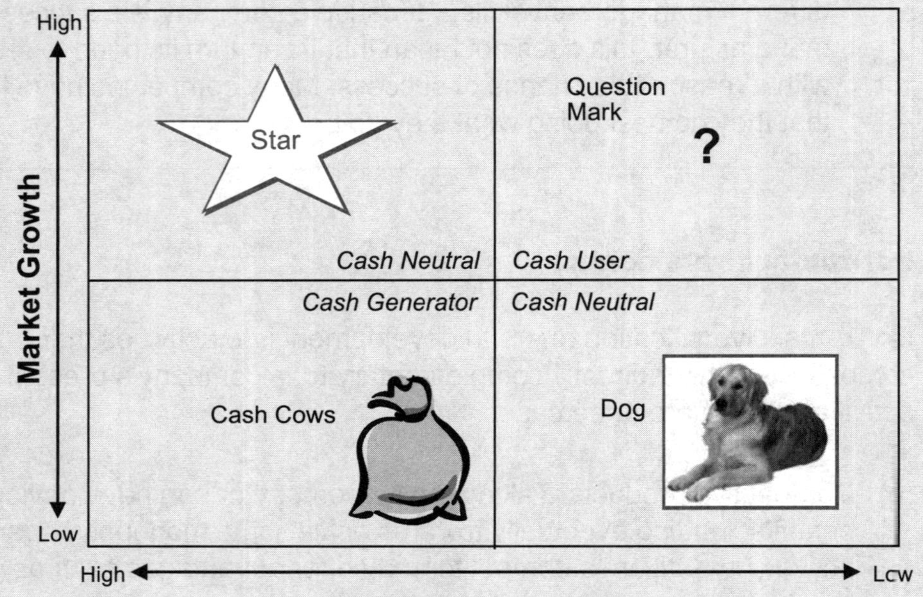

Developed originally to assist managers in identifying cash flow requirements of different businesses within the portfolio and to help to decide whether change in the mix of businesses is required. A broad portfolio indicates that a business has a presence in a wide range of products and market sectors – this may or may not be a good thing!

Four main steps:

(1) divide the company into SBUs

(2) allocate into the matrix

(3) assess the prospects of each SBU and compare against others in the matrix

(4) develop strategic objectives for each SBU.

Assessment covers:

Relative market share – the ratio of SBU market share to that of largest rival in the market sector. BCG suggests that market share gives a company cost advantages from economies of scale and learning effects. The dividing line is set at 1. A figure of 4 suggests that SBU share is four times greater than the nearest rival. A figure of 0.1 suggests that the SBU is 10% of the sector leader.

Market growth rate – represents the growth rate of the market sector concerned. High-growth industries offer a more favourable competitive environment and better long-term prospects than slow-growth industries. The dividing line is set at 10%.

SBUs are entered onto the matrix as dots with circles around the dots denoting the revenue relative to total corporate turnover. The bigger the circle, the more significant the unit.

Using the matrix

The model suggests that appropriate strategies would be:

- hold
- build
- harvest
- divest.

Cash cows – hold, build or harvest

- High market share in a low-growth market.
- Usually a cash generator and profitable.
- Often cost leaders as economies of scale usually earned. Likely that at one time the cash cow was a star and has now been subject to declining growth.
- Low growth implies a lack of opportunity and therefore the capital requirements are low. Fixed asset investment not required, hence cash surplus.
- Profits from this area can be used to support other products in their development stage. Therefore the balanced portfolio needs some of these.
- Defensive strategy often adopted to protect the position. This may involve reinvesting to protect position via the acquisition of new threshold competencies.

Stars – hold, divest or build

- High market share in high-growth areas – usually market leader
- offer attractive long-term prospects – may one day become a cash cow
- absorb large amounts of cash from investment needs as fixed asset investment required to sustain growth. Cash also required to beat off competitor attack strategies
- new areas and likely to be attacked – advertising required in both defensive and offensive style.

Question marks – build, harvest or divest

- Low market share in high-growth industries
- opportunity exists in these areas – a dilemma exists
- may need to invest heavily to secure market share
- potential to become a star if nurtured
- investment required – machines and expertise but degree of uncertainty as to exactly what is needed
- careful consideration required at corporate level
- sometimes known as the 'problem children' – they need to be caught early to ensure that they don't become 'problem adults'
- will usually absorb substantial management time and may not be successfully developed.

Dogs – build, harvest or divest

- Low market share in a low growth market
- to cultivate would require cost and substantial risk
- often divested – only question is then the speed of the divestment
- could be 'niched' and so turned into a success
- otherwise little in future prospects
- may require investment just to keep product in portfolio, especially if the company is offering a 'one stop shop' or is using the product as a 'loss leader'.

BCG recommendations

- Cash cow cash flows to be used to support stars and develop question marks
- cash cows to be defended
- weak, uncertain question marks should be divested to reduce demands on cash
- dogs should be divested, harvested or niched
- if portfolio is unbalanced, consider acquisitions and divestments
- harvesting reduces damage of sudden divestment but reduces the value at eventual disposal. A quick sale now may produce larger proceeds
- SBUs to have different growth targets and objectives and not be subject to the same strategic control systems.

Limitations

- Simplistic – only considers two variables
- connection between market share and cost savings is not strong – low-market share companies use low-share technology and can have lower production costs – e.g. Morgan cars
- cash cows do not always generate cash – Vauxhall motors would be a classic cash cow yet it requires substantial cash investment just to remain competitive – to defend itself!
- fail to consider value creation – the management of a diverse portfolio can create value by sharing competencies across SBUs, sharing resources to reap economies of scale or by achieving superior governance. BCG would divert investment away from the cash cows and dogs and fails to consider the benefit of offering the full range and the concept of 'loss leaders'.

Test your understanding 2 – BCG

GC is a conglomerate that comprises five strategic business units (SBUs), all operating as subsidiary companies. Information relating to each SBU (and the market leader or nearest competitor) is given in the following table:

Current market share

	GC %	**Market leader %**	**Nearest competitor %**	**Market growth expected by GC**
Building brick manufacturer (Declining profitability)	3	25		Small
Parcel carriage service (Long established, faces strong competition. Turnover and profitability over last three years have been stable but are expected to decline as competition strengthens)	1	6		Nil
Food manufacturer producing exclusively for household consumption (Long established with little new investment. High levels of turnover and profitability, which are being sustained)	25		5	Slowly declining
Painting and decorating contracting company (Established three years ago. Continuous capital injections from group over that period. Currently not making any profit)	0.025	0.5		Historically high but now forecast to slow down

Software development and supply company (Acquired two years ago. Market share expected to increase over next two years. Sustained investment from the group but profitability so far low)	10		8	Rapid

Required:

(a) Comment on GC's overall competitive position by applying the Boston Consulting Group growth/share matrix analysis to its portfolio of SBUs.

(8 marks)

(b) Discuss how GC should pursue the strategic development of its SBUs in order to add value to the overall conglomerate group.

(17 marks)

(Total: 25 marks)

(May 1998)

8 Acquisition

Acquisition may be more expensive than organic growth because the owners of the acquired company will need to be paid for the risks they have already taken. On the other hand, if the company goes for organic growth it must take the risks itself so there is a trade-off between cost and risk.

A company can gain synergy by bringing together complementary resources in their own business and that being acquired. Synergy is defined as **'the advantage to a firm gained by having existing resources which are compatible with new products or markets that the company is developing'.**

For example, sales synergy may be obtained through the use of common marketing facilities such as distribution channels. Investment synergy may result from the joint use of plant and machinery or raw materials.

An acquisition must add value in a way the shareholder cannot replicate in order to avoid the risks associated with diversified companies (see Ansoff).

Acquisition v organic growth

Advantages of acquisitions over organic growth

Acquisition has some significant advantages over internal growth.

- High-speed access to resources – this is particularly true of brands; an acquisition can provide a powerful brand name that could take years to establish through internal growth.
- Avoids barriers to entry – acquisition may be the only way to enter a market where the competitive structure would not admit a new member or the barriers to entry were too high.
- Less reaction from competitors – there is less likelihood of retaliation because an acquisition does not alter the capacity of the competitive arena.
- It can block a competitor – if Kingfisher's bid for Asda had been successful it would have denied Walmart its easy access to the UK.
- It can help restructure the operating environment – some mergers of car companies were used to reduce overcapacity.
- Relative price/earnings ratio – if the P/E ratio is significantly higher in the new industry than the present one, acquisition may not be possible because it would cause a dilution in earnings per share to the existing shareholders. But if the present company has a high P/E ratio it can boost earnings per share by issuing its own equity in settlement of the purchase price.
- Asset valuation – if the acquiring company believes the potential acquisition's assets are undervalued, it might undertake an asset-stripping operation.

Disadvantages of acquisitions growth

There are some disadvantages associated with this method of growth.

- Acquisition may be more costly than internal growth because the owners of the acquired company will have to be paid for the risk already taken. On the other hand, if the company decides on internal growth, it will have to bear the costs of the risk itself.
- There is bound to be a cultural mismatch between the organisations – a lack of 'fit' can be significant in knowledge-based companies, where the value of the business resides in individuals.

- Differences in managers' salaries – another example of cultural mismatch that illustrates how managers are valued in different countries.
- Disposal of assets – companies may be forced to dispose of assets they had before the acquisition. The alliance between British Airways and American Airlines was called off because the pair would have had to free up around 224 take-off and landing slots to other operators.
- Risk – of not knowing all there is to know about the business it seeks to buy.
- Reduction in return on capital employed – quite often an acquisition adds to sales and profit volume without adding to value creation.

9 Joint methods of expansion

Joint development methods

These include:

- Joint venture
- strategic alliances
- franchising
- licenses
- agents
- outsourcing.

In any joint arrangement key considerations are

- sharing of costs
- sharing of benefits
- sharing of risks
- ownership of resources
- control/decision making.

Joint development methods

Joint venture

A separate business entity whose shares are owned by two or more business entities. Assets are formally integrated and jointly owned.

A very useful approach for:

- sharing cost
- sharing risk
- sharing expertise.

Strategic alliance

A strategic alliance can be defined as a cooperative business activity, formed by two or more separate organisations for strategic purposes, that allocates ownership, operational responsibilities, financial risks, and rewards to each member, while preserving their separate identity/autonomy.

Alliances can allow participants to achieve critical mass, benefit from other participants' skills and can allow skill transfer between participants.

The technical difference between a strategic alliance and a joint venture is whether or not a new, independent business entity is formed.

A strategic alliance is often a preliminary step to a joint venture or an acquisition. A strategic alliance can take many forms, from a loose informal agreement to a formal joint venture.

Alliances include partnerships, joint ventures and contracting out services to outside suppliers.

Seven characteristics of a well-structured alliance have been identified.

- **Strategic synergy –** more strength when combined than they have independently.
- **Positioning opportunity –** at least one of the companies should be able to gain a leadership position (i.e. to sell a new product or service; to secure access to raw materials or technology).
- **Limited resource availability –** a potentially good partner will have strengths that complement weaknesses of the other partner. One of the partners could not do this alone.

- **Less risk** – forming the alliance reduces the risk of the venture.
- **Co-operative spirit** – both companies must want to do this and be willing to co-operate fully.
- **Clarity of purpose** – results, milestones, methods and resource commitments must be clearly understood.
- **Win-win** – the structure, risks, operations and rewards must be fairly apportioned among members.

Some organisations are trying to retain some of the innovation and flexibility that is characteristic of small companies by forming strategic alliances (closer working relationships) with other organisations. They also play an important role in global strategies, where the organisation lacks a key success factor for some markets.

Franchising

The purchase of the right to exploit a business brand in return for a capital sum and a share of profits or turnover.

- The franchisee pays the franchisor an initial capital sum and thereafter the franchisee pays the franchisor a share of profits or royalties.
- The franchisor provides marketing, research and development, advice and support.
- The franchisor normally provides the goods for resale.
- The franchisor imposes strict rules and control to protect its brand and reputation.
- The franchisee buys into a successful formula, so risk is much lower.
- The franchisor gains capital as the number of franchisees grows.
- The franchisor's head office can stay small as there is considerable delegation/decentralisation to the franchisees.

Licensing

The right to exploit an invention or resource in return for a share of proceeds. Differs from a franchise because there will be little central support.

Test your understanding 3

Which of licensing, joint venture, strategic alliance and franchising might be the most suitable for the following circumstances?

(1) A company has invented a uniquely good ice cream and wants to set up an international chain of strongly branded outlets.

(2) Oil companies are under political pressure to develop alternative, renewable energy sources.

(3) A beer manufacturer wants to move from their existing domestic market into international sales.

10 Divestment

May occur because:

- The SBU no longer fits with the existing group. The company may wish to focus on core competences.
- The SBU may be too small and not warrant the management attention given to it.
- Selling the SBU as a going concern may be a cheaper alternative to putting it into liquidation if redundancy and wind-up costs are considered.
- The parent company may need to improve its liquidity position.
- There may be a belief that the individual parts of the business are worth more than the whole when shares are selling at less than their potential value, e.g. ICI's demerger of its bio-sciences business, later called Zeneca.
- An MBO is one way a divestment can occur.

11 International growth

When deciding whether to expand abroad, a business has several possible strategies that it can adopt:

- **Exporting strategy** – the firm sells products made in its home country to buyers abroad. This often starts with the receipt of a chance order or perhaps poor sales at home force the business to export or collapse.

- **Overseas manufacture** – the firm may either manufacture its products in a foreign country and then either import them back to its home country or sell them abroad. Either way, the firm is involved in direct foreign investment because it is purchasing capital assets in another country. For example, Nissan Motors is a Japanese company, but operates plants to build its motor vehicles across the world, including North-East England.
- **Multinational** – these firms co-ordinate their value-adding activities across national boundaries. For example, a multinational car manufacturer will have engine plants in one country, car body plants in another and electrics in a third. Production capacity is often duplicated around the world.
- **Transnational** – these are 'nation-less' firms that have no 'home' country. Employees and facilities are treated identically, regardless of where they are in the world. The company may be listed on several national stock exchanges. This is often considered to be (currently) largely theoretical.

When deciding between which approach to take if expanding abroad, consideration should be given to the following points:

- **Exposure to risk** – both foreign exchange risk and political risk.
- **Need for capital investment** – this will be lower if an exporting strategy is used.
- **Customer relationships** – given the distance between the manufacturer and its foreign consumers, this can be hard to maintain in an exporting strategy.
- **Transportation costs** – manufacturing at a distance from your target market will increase the cost of getting the units to them.
- **Ethical issues** – if operating in countries with less developed labour laws, should the company take advantage of this to keep costs low?
- **Cultural issues** – managing operations in foreign countries can be difficult due to differences in language and customs. This can also make advertising and operational control difficult.

12 Evaluating strategies

Strategies need to have 'strategic fit' with their environment if they are to be effective. This 'fit' will be with both their internal and external environments and so the ability to assess viability relies very much on the reliability of the position audit.

Strategic options will be generated by various stakeholder groups and debate/discussion will need to follow to assess the viability of each option and make a final selection.

The final selection will be a function of the following:

(1) Relative stakeholder power and their personal characteristics
(2) information available and perceived reliability
(3) historical experience
(4) presentation of options – manner
(5) other corporate experiences
(6) expectations for the future
(7) objectives ordering and perceived ordering – there will be a significant political involvement at this stage.

Viability – a basic approach

According to Johnson, Scholes and Whittington, potential strategies can be evaluated against the following three criteria:

- **Suitability** is concerned with whether the strategy addresses the circumstances in which an organisation is operating – its strategic position.
- **Feasibility** is concerned with whether the strategy could be made to work in practice and as such looks at more detailed practicalities of strategic capability.
- **Acceptability** is concerned with the expected performance outcomes (such as return or risk) of a strategy and the extent to which these would be in line with the expectations of stakeholders.

This is a key model that is a regular feature in examinations – in particular in the 50-mark ‘A’ section. The ability to apply it is extremely important.

13 Suitability

Is the proposed strategy a suitable response to environmental events and trends. Do we have **strategic fit**? You should consider whether the proposed course of action fits with the existing position. Will it cause any problems elsewhere in the company?

(1) Will it take advantage of **opportunities**?

(2) Will it build on our **strengths**?

(3) How will new products fit with existing ones? Is the new **portfolio** balanced?

Use within Ansoff's matrix

A market development strategy would 'fit' where:

- Channels of distribution are available
- a business has a strong marketing presence
- products are superior to competitors
- an unsaturated markets exist
- spare production capacity exists
- economies of scale are possible.

A product development strategy would 'fit' where:

- brand reputation is high
- the brand is transportable
- strong research capabilities exist.

A market penetration strategy would 'fit' where:

- current markets are not saturated
- present customers will rebuy
- competitors are weak
- spare production capacity exists.

A consolidation strategy would 'fit' where:

- there is a lack of funding
- owners do not want to grow
- human resources not available
- any kind of restraining factor exists.

A diversification strategy would 'fit' where:

- there is a strong brand presence
- significant resources are available to enable the development of new competencies
- market research base is reliable and competent.

Example

Gucci sought growth in sales and so expanded into lower-priced goods and stretched its brand. It also pushed its products in department stores and duty-free channels. It let its name appear on many licensed products such as watches and perfumes.

Sales soared – they were very happy!

But they soon found that sales in their traditional high-priced, high-margin segment were plummeting as their traditional buyers became disillusioned by the fact that Gucci was now worn by many people thus removing the exclusivity of the product.

Their strategy was not suitable.

14 Feasibility

Can the necessary resources and competencies be obtained and the required changes be implemented? Any new strategy will require change of some kind and this is likely to meet resistance from some quarters. We will need to question whether the company concerned has the strategic capability to pursue the course of action concerned.

So the key questions revolve around:

(1) Resources – basic and unique.

(2) Competencies – threshold and core.

(3) Implementation issues with regard to dealing with strategic change.

Considerations should cover:

- Cultural change required and realism of change
- timescales
- potential resistance
- raw materials availability
- human resources availability
- distribution channel access

- marketing requirements
- IT requirements and skills
- finance:
  - How much is needed?
  - Where will it come from?
  - What options exist?
  - What will the impact be on our financial position and performance?

Don't forget the basic analysis relating to identifying the threshold and core competencies. Are there any sources of competitive advantage or disadvantage?

15 Acceptability

Any proposed strategy will need to be acceptable to the stakeholders of the organisation, both in terms of "returns" and risk.

All stakeholders will need to be considered relative to their power – the more powerful the stakeholder group, the greater the influence they will have and the more the strategist will have to consider their views.

Some areas for consideration:

- A new strategy usually involves some internal changes and due consideration will need to be given to the **staff** who may have to confront different work practices. Resistance is likely.
- **Financiers** often have required rates of return and liquidity positions.
- **Owners** may well have non-financial requirements of their investment. They may prefer to have less risk and accept a lower reward as the inevitable cost. They could require that all actions conform to their cultural expectations, e.g. Anita Roddick at the Body Shop.
- **Customers, consumers and suppliers** may also have required standards that must be met by the company.
- Local and national **governments** may have some concerns about any strategic proposals with regard to legality and political implications.
- Don't forget the **public** and their ability to form into 'pressure groups'. Ethical considerations may need to be included in the evaluation.

Evaluating "acceptability" will often involve quantitative analysis such as NPV calculations. However, it must be noted that conventional NPV analysis tends to undervalue projects with significant future flexibility. Real option theory, covered in more detail in the F3 paper, is an attempt to incorporate such flexibility into a "strategic NPV".

16 Evaluating strategies – the competitive advantage test

Tests of a winning strategy

The SFA approach is very useful but other considerations have been added which are worthy of note.

The first is referred to as the **competitive advantage test** and raises the questions:

- What is it?
- How long can it last?

The second question highlights that competitive advantage may not be sustainable, in other words does the **performance measurement** system show predicted improvement?

Thompson poses this strategic management principle:

'The more a strategy fits the enterprise's external and internal situation, builds sustainable competitive advantage and improves company performance, the more it qualifies as a winner.'

Strategy evaluation – the role of the management accountant

Making strategic decisions

Strategic options can be evaluated using the suitability, feasibility, acceptability framework.

The strategic management accountant will contribute to the acceptability and feasibility aspects in particular:

Aspect	Key concerns	Typical financial analysis
Acceptability	Returns to stakeholders	• Cash flow forecasts to ensure dividend growth requirements can be met • NPV analysis • ROCE • Valuation of real options • Shareholder value analysis • Economic value added • Cost/benefit analysis • Ratio analysis (e.g. dividend yield, growth)

	Risk	• Sensitivity • Break-even • Ratio analysis (e.g. gearing, dividend cover) • Expected values
Feasibility	Resources	• Cash flow forecast to identify funding needs • Budgeting resource requirements • Ability to raise finance needed • Working capital implications • Foreign exchange implications

Test your understanding 4

Blueberry is a quoted resort hotel chain based in Europe.

The industry

The hotel industry is a truly global business characterised by the following:

- Increasing competition.
- An increasing emphasis on customer service with higher standards being demanded.
- In particular the range of facilities, especially spas, is becoming more important as a differentiating factor.

Performance

- Blueberry offers services at the luxury end of the market only, based on a strong brand and prestigious hotels – although its reputation has become tarnished over the last five years due to variable customer satisfaction levels.
- Despite a reputation for having the most prestigious coastal resort hotels along the Mediterranean in 20X0, Blueberry was loss-making in the financial years 20X4/5 and 20X5/6.
- To some extent this situation has been turned around in 20X6/7 with an operating profit of €11 million. However, shareholders are putting the board under pressure to increase profits and dividends further.

- Management have responded to this by setting out an ambitious plan to upgrade hotel facilities throughout the company and move more upmarket. The bulk of the finance is planned to come from retained profits as Blueberry has historically kept its financial gearing low.

Acquisition opportunity

The management of Blueberry have been approached by the owner of 'The Villa d'Oeste', a luxury hotel on the shores of Lake Como in Italy, who is considering selling it. The hotel has an international reputation with world-class spa facilities and generates revenue throughout most of the year due to Lake Como's mild micro-climate. The asking price will be approximately €50m.

Required:

Outline the issues to be considered when assessing the acquisition.

17 Game theoretic approaches to strategic planning

A key aspect of strategic planning is anticipating the actions of competitors and acting accordingly. Game theory has been used to great effect in this matter.

Game theoretic approaches to strategic planning

Game theory

In many markets it is important to anticipate the actions of competitors as there is a high interdependency between firms – i.e. the results of my choice depend to some extent on your choices as well.

Game theory is concerned with the interrelationships between the competitive moves of a set of competitors and, as such, can be a useful tool to analyse and understand different scenarios.

Game theory has two key principles:

(1) Strategists can take a rational, informed view of what competitors are likely to do and formulate a suitable response.

(2) If a strategy exists that allows a competitor to dominate us, then the priority is to eliminate that strategy.

Despite the simplicity of these principles, game theory has become very complex.

Many of the bidders for third-generation mobile phone licences in the early 2000s and the governments auctioning those licences used game theory principles. In the UK this resulted in over a hundred rounds of bidding and revenue raised of £22 billion.

Example

The most famous example of game theory is the "Prisoner's dilemma" game. This can be applied to companies as follows:

Suppose there are two companies, A and B, who between them dominate a market. Both are considering whether to increase their marketing spend from its current low level.

- If just one firm decides to increase their spend, then it will see their returns increase.
- However, if both increase the spend then both end up with lower returns than at present.

These could be shown by the following pay-off table (figures = net profit).

		Competitor A	
		High spend	Low spend
Competitor B	High spend	A = 5 B = 5	A = 3 B = 10
	Low Spend	A = 10 B = 3	A = 7 B = 7

Viewed individually the dominant strategy for both firms is to invest heavily. Taking A's perspective:

- If B does not increase spending, then the best plan of action for A would have been to invest heavily.
- If B does increase spending, then the best plan of action for A would have been to invest heavily.

However, the end result ("equilibrium") is likely to be that both firms increase spending and thus end up worse off than if they had both kept their marketing spend at its current low level. Some degree of collusion to keep the spend low would benefit both parties.

Note: The original version of the prisoners' dilemma.

Suppose two men perpetrate a crime together and are later arrested by the police.

Unfortunately the police have insufficient evidence for a conviction, and, having separated both suspects, visit each of them to offer the chance of betraying their accomplice. Suppose the possible outcomes are as follows:

- If one testifies (defects from the other) for the prosecution against the other and the other remains silent (cooperates with the other), the betrayer goes free and the silent accomplice receives the full 10-year sentence.
- If both remain silent, both prisoners are sentenced to only six months in jail for a minor charge.
- If each betrays the other, each receives a five-year sentence.

Each prisoner must choose to betray the other or to remain silent. Each one is assured that the other would not know about the betrayal before the end of the investigation.

How should the prisoners act?

The unique equilibrium for this game is that rational choice leads the two players to both play defect, even though each player's individual reward would be greater if they both played cooperatively.

Application

A common application of this is to price wars. Price wars between two evenly matched competitors usually results in lower profits for all concerned and no change in market share. No one wins, except the customer.

18 Real options

When deciding on a strategic project, there are three possible 'real options' that a manager may wish to take into account.

- **Option to follow on**

  When choosing a project, many managers will make their choice on the basis of Net Present Value (NPV). Projects with a positive NPV will be accepted as they increase shareholder wealth. Negative NPV projects will be rejected.

  However, under options theory this may not always be the case. This is because a project with a negative NPV could provide the business with the opportunity to invest in other, more profitable projects in the future.

For example, an electronics company may find that designing, manufacturing and selling printers has a negative NPV due to the low prices that can be charged in this market. However, the investment will allow the company to sell a range of ink cartridges that have much higher profit margins and a larger positive NPV.

- **Option to abandon**

  If a project requires a large capital investment and has an uncertain outcome, the option to abandon may be valuable.

  For example, if a civil engineering company enters a fixed price contract to build a stadium, having an option to abandon the project will significantly reduce its risk. Should the costs spiral above the value of the contract, the company will be able to abandon the project and limit its losses.

- **Option to delay**

  The option to delay the beginning of a project can also be valuable to a business.

  A UK house-building company, for example, may have an option to build on a plot of land at any point over the next several years. Unfortunately, due to the current economic downturn, house prices have fallen sharply. The company can therefore delay the building of the homes until the market has recovered and house prices rise to a more acceptable level.

Generally these options will become more valuable as their duration increases and as the level of uncertainty in the project rises. Remember that you will not be asked for complex calculations in this area of the syllabus.

19 Summary

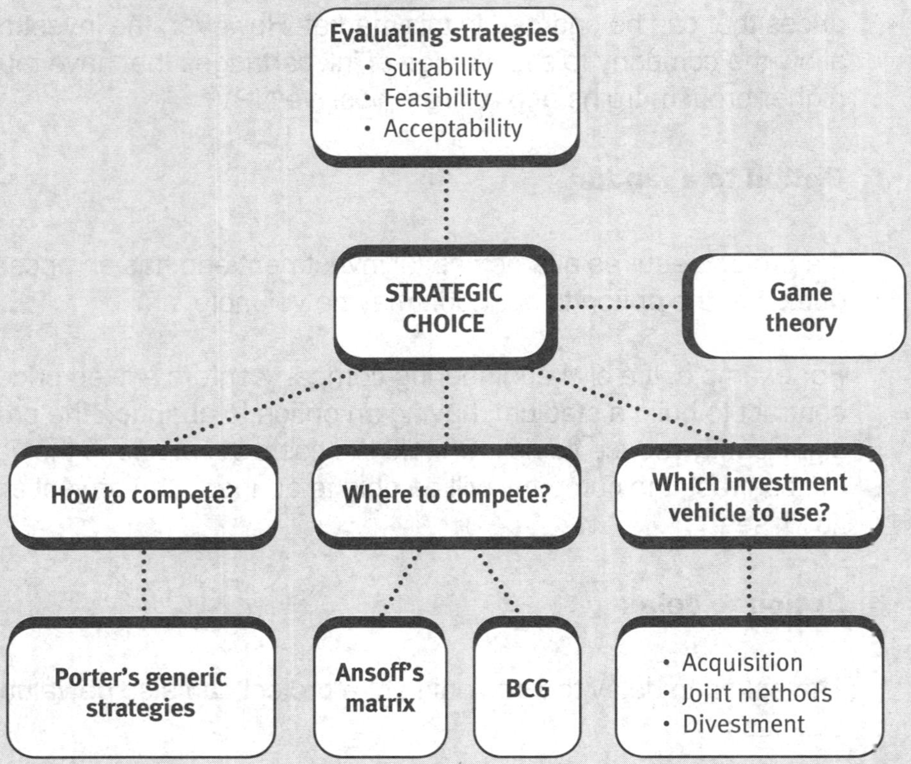
Evaluating strategies
• Suitability
• Feasibility
• Acceptability
STRATEGIC CHOICE
Game theory
How to compete?
Where to compete?
Which investment vehicle to use?
Porter's generic strategies
Ansoff's matrix
BCG
• Acquisition
• Joint methods
• Divestment

Test your understanding answers

Test your understanding 1

- **Pricewatch** – market penetration – building sales from existing customer base via lower prices (cost leadership).
- **Esso minimarkets** – product development – addressing customer bases who already use Esso outlets. Could also be categorised as market development if minimarkets are effectively acting as local ('corner') shops.
- **Distribution to China** – market development – taking existing products/technologies and selling them to a new market.
- **Acquisitions** – diversification – this involves Esso moving into completely new markets/industries.

Test your understanding 2 – BCG

Part (a)

- **Brick manufacturer** – dog
- **Parcel service** – dog
- **Food manufacturer** – cash cow, maybe dropping from star. Largely depends upon the current growth rate
- **Painting and decorating** – problem child. High growth at present but forecast to decline. Opportunity to turn this into a star
- **Software development company** – star

(May consider a diagram with SBUs located on the matrix.)

Representations in all sectors of the matrix with two dogs present. May need to question what to do with the problem child and the dogs. Dogs may need to be divested or harvested. Problem child needs management attention to stop it becoming a dog.

Food manufacturer (cash cow) will generate cash flows that can be used to fund the development of the star software company. Little need for strategic investment will see the cash surpluses rising.

Star will need investing in and penetration strategies will be appropriate. Branding strategies may be initiated with a view to future defence when star becomes the cash cow. Current cash cow will need defending.

SBUs will each need different business strategies as positions vary. Levels of competition and demand sophistication will vary across the SBU marketplaces and the research and information systems will become ever more important.

Part (b)

Considerations

Divest dogs – gets rid of the poor products quickly. But may not be poor performers! May be better to Harvest instead – slow decline leads to less damage elsewhere within the group in terms of bad publicity.

Niche dogs – a deliberate strategy to take the SBU into a specialist marketplace by aiming at a specific market segment and seek to earn high return from this focused approach.

Market development for dogs and problem children – aiming to expand market share and improve value via improved profitability.

Product development for the cash cow as a form of defensive strategy to extend the life cycle and the subsequent cash flows – but will the cash cow really be cash generative? Will it not need to reinvest to maintain threshold competence in the market place?

Market penetration for the star – the market is expanding with many new users and strategies should be aimed at building market share.

Aim to develop **synergy*** within the group:

- Possible **brand stretching** – taking the good reputation and respect from one brand name and attach it to other products in the form of either aggressive or defensive strategy, e.g. use a link from the food manufacturing to painting and decorating and/or software development.
- Possible sharing of **distribution channels** – there seems to be little scope for this given the diverse nature of the product portfolio.

- Possible use of **central resources** – scope here for central marketing function if a common linkage could be found (such as a brand). HR and IT functions offer scope for value added via cost savings on the functions.

McKinsey approach

- Manage investor relations
- turnaround strategies at SBU level
- outsourcing
- benchmarking
- cost reduction programmes
- manage structure of portfolio via acquisition, divestment and demerger
- consider and deploy value adding "group" activities such as brand stretching.

* The idea that combining certain operations/functions will produce a benefit in numerical terms that will be greater than the sum of the individual parts. The creation of 'excess value' from combination – what some refer to as '2 + 2 = 5'.

Test your understanding 3

(1) A franchise arrangement would work well here. There is more than just manufacturing involved – there is the whole retail offering, and entering into franchise agreements would be a quick, effective way of expanding.

(2) Unless the oil companies felt that, because of their size, there was no need for joint research, development, marketing and lobbying, a strategic alliance of some sort could be useful. Research costs and findings could be shared. Together they could bring powerful pressure to bear on governments to, for example, allow more generous time scales for implementation of the new technology. Alternatively, the new energy technology could be developed within a joint venture organisation.

(3) Almost certainly, this company would expand by licensing local brewing companies to make and distribute its product.

Test your understanding 4

Suitability

- The hotel market is becoming increasingly more competitive, so it might make more sense for Blueberry to try to diversify its activities more.
- Furthermore, the acquisition does not address Blueberry's underlying problems of inconsistent customer service levels.
- On the other hand, the Villa d'Oeste already has a world class spa facility and would fit well into Blueberry's current strategy of moving more 'upscale'.
- Also the goodwill attached to the Villa's reputation could enhance Blueberry's image, depending on branding decisions.

Feasibility

- Financing the acquisition could prove problematic:
- Debt finance: Historically the Board have chosen to keep Blueberry's financial gearing level relatively low. Blueberry's existing clientele of shareholders may thus resist any major increase in gearing.
- Equity finance: Given losses in two out of the last three years, Blueberry may struggle to raise the purchase price via a rights issue.

Acceptability

- Growth by acquisition is generally quicker than organic growth, thus satisfying institutional shareholders' desire to see growth in revenues and dividends.
- Further work is needed to assess whether the €50m asking price is acceptable.

- Buying another hotel should enable Blueberry to gain additional economies of scale with respect to insurance, staff costs such as pensions and purchasing economies on drinks. This should boost margins and profitability further.
- The new hotel would fit well into Blueberry's existing portfolio of hotels, for example, by having significant cash inflows throughout the year in contrast to Blueberry's highly seasonal business, thus reducing the overall level of risk.

Preliminary recommendations

- The opportunity to acquire the Villa d'Oeste should be rejected on the grounds that financing the acquisition would be problematic at present.
- Blueberry should instead focus on improving facilities and quality in existing hotels before looking to expand through acquisition.

chapter

9

The performance measurement mix

Chapter learning objectives

Lead	Component
D1. Evaluate the tools and processes of strategy implementation	(a) Recommend appropriate control measures (b) Evaluate alternative models of performance measurement (c) Recommend solutions to problems in performance measurement

Indicative syllabus content

- Alternative models of performance measurement (e.g. the balanced scorecard).
- Assessing strategic performance (i.e. the use and development of appropriate measures that are sensitive to industry characteristics and environmental factors).
- Non-financial measures and their interaction with financial ones. (Note: candidates will be expected to use both qualitative and quantitative techniques).
- The critical success factors: Links to performance indicators and corporate strategy, and their use as a basis for defining an organisation's information needs.

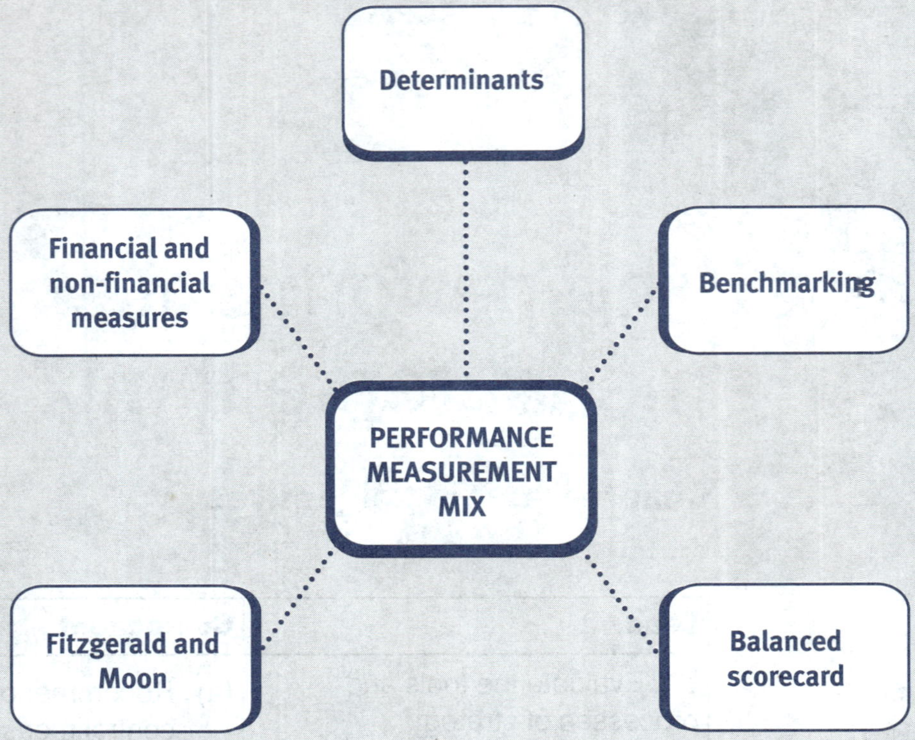

1 The performance measurement mix

An essential part of the strategic control process is the ability to measure output in terms of the objectives. This often proves more difficult than would first be imagined.

For example, is the measure of 'trains running on time' a good measure of a rail company's performance or 'school exam result league tables' a good measure of a school's abilities?

A bus company decided to measure the number of times that the buses ran on time. The driver's bonus was linked to this performance measure. The result was a disaster as buses sped through the city to keep in time, breaking speed limits as they went. The drivers soon identified that the most time-consuming part of the process was stopping to pick up passengers and so if there were too many passengers waiting at the stop, the bus would drive past in order to make up time. Clear suboptimality!

The challenge is to be able to design a measurement mix that can be used in the control process and not prove to be a burden and/or confusing.

Reasons for measuring performance

Neely (1998) explains the purpose of performance measurement by specifying the 'the four CPs of management':

- **Check position:** Measures allow the business to understand how well the business is performing at present. This is vital if the management is to detect problems and undertake remedial action.
- **Communicate position:** This ensures that stakeholders are aware of how the business is performing. This can include financial reporting and returns to regulators. This helps to build stakeholder support.
- **Confirm priorities:** Setting targets for particular key aspects of the business ensures that managers focus their time on these areas.
- **Compel progress:** Rewards can be linked to the achievement of these key performance measures.

Main principle

As outlined above, if something is important, then you should design a performance measure around that important issue. This will communicate new emphasis to all parties and will ultimately influence behaviour of staff, customers and consumers. Remember the phrases:

'If it is counted, it counts...'

'If it matters, measure it...'

Consider the linkage:

OBJECTIVES LISTING → CRITICAL SUCCESS FACTORS → PERFORMANCE MEASURES

Thus companies will need to develop measurement mixes to reflect their critical success factor listing. The mix will consider:

- Environment
- strategy
- business type.

Thus factors to consider would be:

- the objectives of the organisation
- the critical success factors of the processes. What are the value adding activities?

- the state of the environment, i.e. in terms of turbulence and unpredictability
- the strategy adopted
- the type of business with regards to service, manufacturing, multinational etc.
- the mix often forms the basis for the reward scheme for senior executives and consideration must be given to the issues of suboptimality and short-termist risks.

2 Determination of the measurement mix

(1) Identify the **objectives** of the process and order them in terms of priority.

(2) Identify the **critical success factors** of the operation as first seen.

(3) Perform a **position audit** to identify the current situation and identify any extra critical success factors.

(4) With a view of the critical success factors, develop a pilot measurement mix, perhaps containing a mixture of financial and non-financial elements. This is often referred to as a **'balanced scorecard'** approach.

(5) **Evaluate** the mix in terms of culture and change implications.

(6) **Deploy** and monitor.

The impact of change

The changing environment presents new risks and opportunities and these must be monitored and identified as early as possible. It is therefore likely that new measures will be added but consideration must also be given to keeping the mix as uncomplicated as possible and as such old unnecessary measures should be removed.

Notes:

- Too many measures lead to 'indicator overload'.
- If something is measured then the importance of that item is highlighted to staff and as such this is a communication exercise. Remember, if you change the mix, what are you telling people?
- At the same time, when you drop a measure from the mix, you will be communicating that it is no longer appropriate. You must ask yourself if that is what you want to achieve.

3 Financial and non-financial measures

Financial performance measures

These indicators concentrate on the profits made by a business and the assets used to generate those profits.

Typical indicators may include:

Sales margin (gross profit margin):

$$\frac{\text{Turnover} - \text{cost of sales}}{\text{Turnover}} \times 100\%$$

- this indicator focuses on the profitability of the business' trading account.

Net profit margin:

$$\frac{\text{Profit (before interest and tax)}}{\text{Turnover}} \times 100\%$$

- this indicator focuses on the profitability of the business in both its trading and its net operating expenses.

Return on capital employed:

$$\frac{\text{Profit (before interest and tax)}}{\text{Turnover}} \times 100\%$$

- ROCE measures the profitability of a business or division against the assets utilised in that business. (Capital employed is normally measured as shareholders funds + long–term debt).

Remember the principle of **controllability** when using these measures to assess divisional performance. The costs used in both cases should only be those that the division can directly control. Expenses such as head office costs would normally be excluded as it would be unfair to assess divisional managers on spending that they cannot alter.

Advantages of financial measures of performance

- Culturally expected
- focus on financial objectives
- comparable across companies
- cheap
- established framework for preparation in many cases
- tend to focus onto resource generation and so survival in the long term.

Disadvantages of financial measures of performance

- Inflation distortion
- leads to suboptimal and short-termist behaviour
- lack of comparability
- understood by the 'select few'
- subjectivity can exist in calculation, e.g. depreciation.

Non-financial performance measures

Businesses also need to focus on factors that actually cause profits to be earned – the non-financial measures.

For instance in an accountancy training business, sales and market share (financial issues) are caused by student pass rates, student satisfaction, class sizes, tutor quality, etc (non-financial issues). These non-financial issues will also need to be measured. If performance in these areas begins to fall, it will not be long before the financial measures deteriorate as well.

Advantages of non financial measures

- Wider view
- easier to calculate
- easy to understand (sometimes)
- not distorted by inflation
- can emphasise broad spectrum of management
- positive motivational implications.

Disadvantages of non financial measures

- Some can be difficult to calculate
- subjectivity exists in design, interpretation and calculation
- can lead to indicator overload
- costly
- culture clash implications
- constant change requires constant monitoring.

4 Fitzgerald and Moon

The building block model

Fitzgerald and Moon adopted a framework for the design and analysis of performance management systems. They based their analysis on three building blocks:

- **Dimensions**

  Dimensions are the goals for the business and suitable measures must be developed to measure each performance dimension. There are six dimensions in the building block model.

- **Standards**

  These are the measures used. To ensure success it is vital that employees view standards as achievable and fair and take ownership of them.

- **Rewards**

  To ensure that employees are motivated to meet standards, targets need to be clear and linked to controllable factors.

Dimensions

- **Financial performance**

  CSF: financial objectives.

- **Competitiveness**

  CSF: threat of loss of share.

- **Resource utilisation**

  CSF: scarce resources.

- **Quality issues**

  CSF: the threshold competency!

- **Innovation**

  CSF: the changing environment leads to shortening product life cycles.

- **Flexibility**

  CSF: the ability to respond to changing needs.

Financial performance and competitiveness were seen as the "results" and the others as "determinants" of success.

Fiztgerald and Moon suggested that these six dimensions could be used to generate the key performance measures that the business would need to monitor.

Test your understanding 1

Using the six dimensions of Fitzgerald and Moon suggest some measures (standards) for a national car dealership network.

5 The balanced scorecard

Presented by **Kaplan & Norton** in 1992 – 'Kaplan's cockpit'

'An approach to the provision of information to management to assist strategic policy formulation and achievement. It emphasises the need to provide the user with a set of information which addresses all relevant issues of performance in an objective and unbiased fashion. The information provided may include both financial and non-financial elements and cover areas such as profitability, customer satisfaction, internal efficiency and innovation'.

Its aim is to provide a broad range of both financial and non-financial measures designed to reflect the complexity and diversity of business circumstance.

It was a response to traditional performance measurement which had tended to focus on a narrow range of performance measures and helped adopt a short-term focus for management.

Kaplan likened running a business to flying a plane – airspeed, altitude, heading and fuel level are just a few of the pieces of information needed. Yet, in many businesses, managers have to rely on a narrow set of financial indicators to support their decision making – and this in an environment with many more complexities than a plane.

The balanced scorecard approach brings together a wide range of measures to give managers a broader perspective.

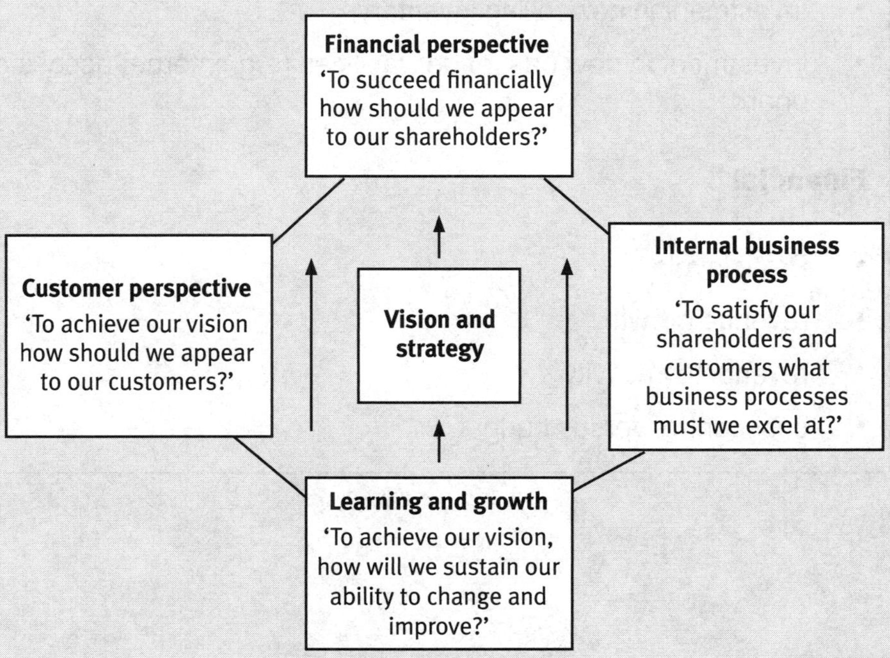

This is a powerful tool that assists in the running of an organisation. Gains in one area need to be considered with the losses that may arise in other areas and vice versa. Thus the manager's view is broadened and the tendency to concentrate on one measure is reduced, hopefully removed.

e.g

Illustration 1

For a train company, a balanced scorecard could include indicators such as:

Customers

- Percentage of trains running on time/cancelled
- percentage of trains running per hour between destinations
- cleanliness levels
- seat availability.

Internal

- Staff attendance rates
- number of training days per annum per staff member
- average time taken to process ticket enquiries
- percentage of trains in full working order.

Innovation and learning

- Investment in new rolling inventory
- investment in new passenger facilities (e.g. internet access on–board).

Financial

- Profit levels
- revenue growth
- revenue by activity
- cost control versus budget.

Strategy mapping

Strategy mapping – implementing the balanced scorecard more effectively

Strategy mapping was developed by Kaplan and Norton as an extension to the balanced scorecard and to make implementations of the scorecard more successful.

The steps involved are:

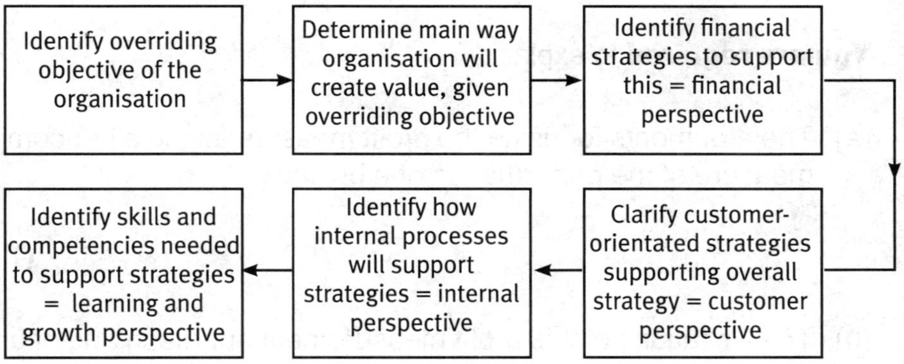

- At the head of the strategy map is the overriding objective of the organisation which describes how it creates value. This is then connected to the organisation's other objectives, categorised in terms of the four perspectives of the balanced scorecard, showing the cause-and-effect relationships between them.
- The strategy map helps organisations to clarify, describe and communicate the strategy and objectives, both within the organisation and to external stakeholders, by presenting the key relationships between the overall objective and the supporting strategy and objectives in one diagram.

Problems:

- Organisations have often found it difficult to translate the corporate vision into behaviour and actions which achieve the key corporate objectives.
- In practice many employees do not understand the organisation's strategy, and systems such as performance management and budgeting are not linked to the strategy.

Test your understanding 2

Suggest some goals and measures as part of a balanced scorecard for an electronic manufacturer.

Test your understanding 3

Recent articles have focused on summary information for running a business and on a 'balanced scorecard' approach, using a number of performance indicators.

You are required to explain:

(a) The arguments for using the profit measure as the all-encompassing measure of the performance of a business.

(7 marks)

(b) The limitations of this profit measurement approach and of undue dependence on the profit measure.

(9 marks)

(c) The problems of using a broad range of non-financial measures for the short- and long-term control of a business.

(9 marks)

(Total: 25 marks)

(May 1994)

Benefits and drawbacks of the balanced scorecard

The main benefits are:

- It avoids management reliance on short-termist or incomplete financial measures.
- By identifying the non-financial measures, managers may be able to identify problems earlier. For example, managers may be measuring customer satisfaction directly as part of the balanced scorecard. If this changes, steps can be taken to improve it again before customers leave and it starts to impact on the company's finances.
- It can ensure that divisions develop success measures for their division that are related to the overall corporate goals of the organisation
- It can assist stakeholders in evaluating the firm if measures are communicated externally.

The drawbacks are:

- It does not provide a single overall view of performance. Measures like ROCE are popular because they conveniently summarise 'how things are going' into one convenient measure.
- There is no clear relation between the balanced scorecard and shareholder analysis.
- Measures may give conflicting signals and confuse management. For instance, if customer satisfaction is falling along with one of the financial indicators, which should management sacrifice?
- It often involves a substantial shift in corporate culture in order to implement it.

6 Benchmarking schemes

Benchmarking is 'the establishment, through data gathering, of targets and comparators, through whose use relative levels of performance (and particularly areas of underperformance) can be identified. By the adoption of identified best practices it is hoped that performance will improve.'

CIMA Official Terminology

Most organisations have systems in place to help management monitor key factors such as profits and sales. However, if the financial results or market share of the firm start to deteriorate, management needs to know the reasons why.

The purpose of benchmarking is to help management understand how well the firm is carrying out its key activities and how its performance compares with other, successful, organisations who carry out similar operations (often those considered **best in class**).

A famous example of this is the Rank Xerox company. In the 1970s, such was the dominance of the firm that the word 'Xerox' meant 'photocopier'. A decade later and they had serious competition, most notably from Canon. Something had gone wrong...but what?

Rank Xerox found that clients were switching to other providers because Rank Xerox machines were perceived to always be out of order. It used benchmarking to restore its fortunes.

Types of benchmarking

Seber identifies **three** basic types:

Internal

- This is where another branch or department of the organisation is used as the benchmark
- used where conformity of service is the critical issue – either threshold or core competence
- easily arranged, cheaper and culturally relevant
- but, culturally distorted and unlikely to provide innovative solutions.

Competitor

- Uses a direct competitor with the same or similar process
- essentially aims to render the competition core competence as threshold
- relevant for the industry and market
- but, will the competitor really be keen to hand over their basis for success?

Process or activity

- Focus upon a similar process in another company which is not a direct competitor, e.g. an airline and a health service
- looks for new, innovative ways to create advantage as well as solving threshold problems
- takes time and is expensive
- but, resistance likely to be less and can provide the new basis for advantage.

Implementing a scheme

This will involve:

(1) identifying what is wrong within the current organisation

(2) identifying best practice elsewhere

(3) contacting, preparing for an undertaking a site visit

(4) gathering, evaluating and communicating the results.

It will need:

- key executive commitment from the outset;
- establishment of teams for those ranges of opinions and expertise
- a team to manage the project
- a team for the site visit
- budget allocations and training to be given
- a formalised process.

Problems

- Best practice companies unwilling to share data
- what is 'best practice'?
- costly in terms of time and money – opportunity cost
- provides a retrospective view in a turbulent environment – what is best today may not be so tomorrow. As one writer put it: 'Benchmarking is the refuge of the manager who's afraid of the future.'
- successful benchmarking firms can find themselves inundated with requests for information from much less able firms from whom they can learn little
- managers may become demotivated if they are compared against a better-resourced rival.

Test your understanding 4

A company which manufactures and distributes industrial oils employs a team of salespeople who work directly from home and travel around different regions in the country. Each member of the sales team has his or her own geographical area to cover and they visit clients on a regular basis.

The sales team staff are each paid a basic monthly salary. Each member of the team is set an identical target for sales to be achieved in the month. A bonus payment, in addition to the basic salary, is made to any member of the team who exceeds his or her monthly sales target.

Generally, experience has been that the members of the sales team succeed in improving on their sales targets each month sufficiently to earn a small bonus. However, the managers are unclear whether all the team members are achieving their maximum potential level of sales. Consequently they are considering introducing a system of benchmarking to measure the performance of the sales team as a whole and its individual members.

Required:

Describe how a system of benchmarking could be introduced to measure the performance of the sales team:

(a) as a whole

(b) as individuals in comparison with each other.

The performance pyramid (Lynch and Cross)

The performance pyramid framework

The performance pyramid was developed by Lynch and Cross as a model to understand and define the links between objectives and performance measures at different levels in the organisation.

- The performance pyramid is designed to ensure that the activities of every department, system and business unit support the overall vision of the organisation.
- At the top of the pyramid is the vision through which the organisation describes how it will achieve long-term success and competitive advantage.

- The second level, the business unit, includes the critical success factors (CFSs) in terms of market-related measures and financial measures.
- The third level, the business operating systems, includes measures which relate to the internal systems and processes which are needed to meet the needs of customers. For example, measures of flexibility which relate to how responsive the system is to customer demands.
- The lowest level of the pyramid contains the day-to-day operational measures.
- The left-hand side of the pyramid contains measures which have an external focus and which are predominantly non-financial. Those on the right are focused on the internal efficiency of the organisation and are predominantly financial.
- Objectives cascade down through the organisation, while measures and information flow from the bottom up.
- The performance pyramid does tend to concentrate on two groups of stakeholders – shareholders and customers. It is necessary to ensure that measures are included which relate to other stakeholders as well.

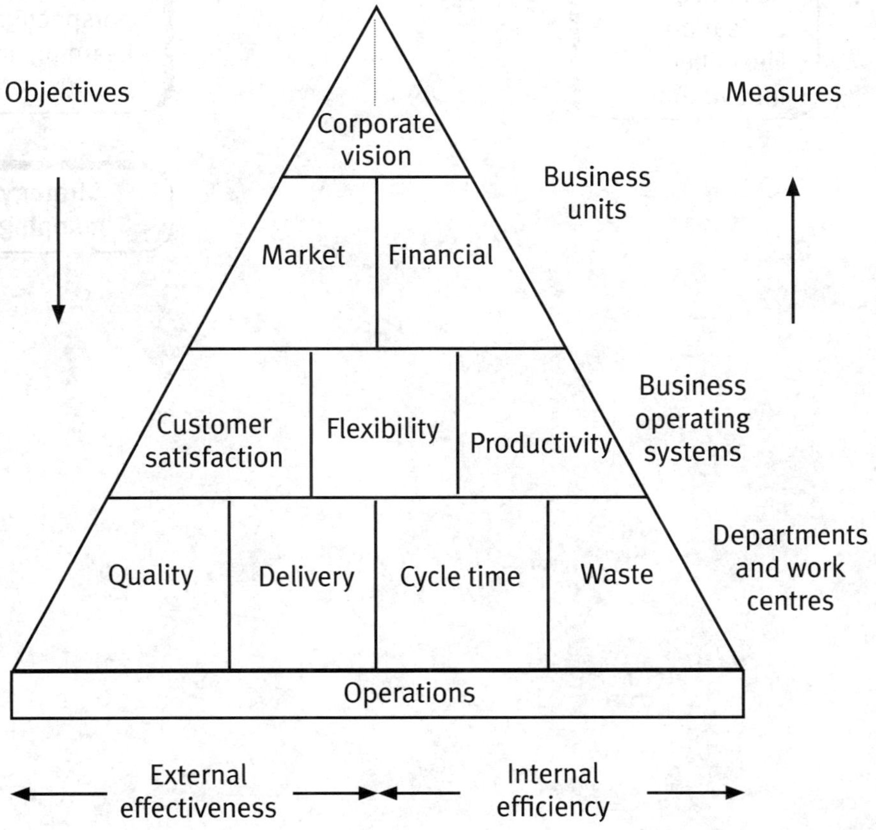

7 Summary

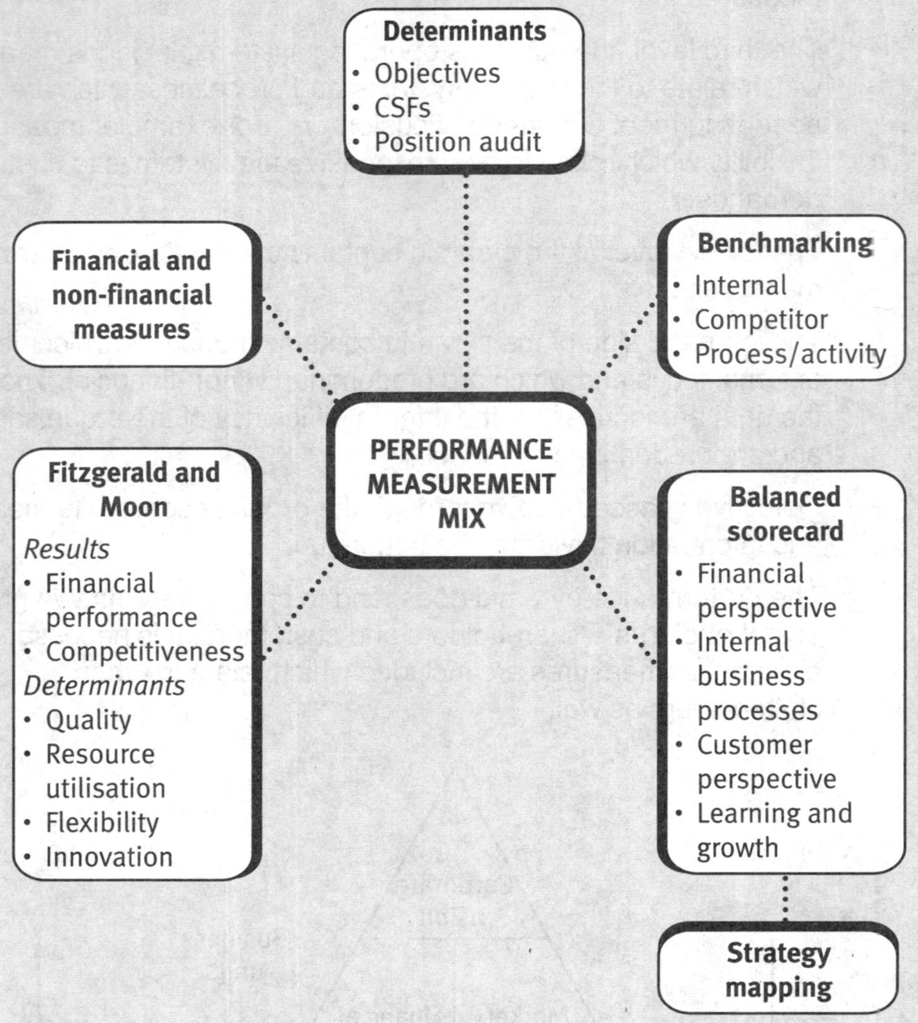
Determinants
• Objectives
• CSFs
• Position audit
Financial and non-financial measures
Benchmarking
• Internal
• Competitor
• Process/activity
PERFORMANCE MEASUREMENT MIX
Fitzgerald and Moon
Results
• Financial performance
• Competitiveness
Determinants
• Quality
• Resource utilisation
• Flexibility
• Innovation
Balanced scorecard
• Financial perspective
• Internal business processes
• Customer perspective
• Learning and growth
Strategy mapping

Test your understanding answers

Test your understanding 1

Dimension	Measures
Financial performance	• Profit per dealer • Average margins • Average discount agreed as a % of displayed list price
Competitive performance	• Local market share (e.g. look at new car registrations by postcode). • National market share (e.g. from published market research data).
Quality of service	• 'Mystery shopper data', i.e. outside consultants visit or ring dealerships posing as customers • Post-sale satisfaction surveys of customers
Flexibility	• Post-sale satisfaction surveys of customers to highlight whether they felt sales staff were flexible in getting different vehicle specifications, etc.
Resource utilisation	• Sales per employee • Sales per square metre of available floor space • Average length of time a second hand car (e.g. taken as part-exchange) remains unsold
Innovation	• Central inspection by senior staff could enable a subjective assessment of local innovation to be made

Test your understanding 2

Perspective	**Goals / CSFs**	**Measures / KPIs**
Customer	New products Responsive service Preferred supplier Partnership ventures	% of sales from new products % on-time delivery Customer ranking Number of cooperative operations
Internal	Manufacturing excellence Design productivity New product development	Production cycle time, unit cost engineering, etc. Material efficiency Introduction times, actual versus plan
Learning and growth	Time to market Product focus Manufacturing Learning technology	Introduction times v competition % of products giving 80% of sales Process time to maturity Time to develop next-generation products
Financial	Survival Success Prosperity	Cash flow Quarterly sales growth Increase in market share and return on equity (ROE)

Test your understanding 3

(a) **Arguments for using profit**

- Links with financial objectives
- system already exists and so is cheap
- regulatory system exists to guide preparation
- culturally expected and so minimal resistance
- follows the matching principle – the accruals concept
- many comparators exist.

(b) **Limitations and undue dependence**

- Suboptimal in that other areas are overlooked – non-financial objectives
- may lead to short-termist actions
- narrow focus onto financial objectives and so ignores the non-financial objectives
- communicates wrong emphasis – non-financial objectives
- subjective in preparation – provisioning and depreciation
- inflation distorts
- difficult to distinguish management performance from economic performance
- regulatory system varies over time and boundaries
- treats some assets as expenses.

(c) **Problems**

- Subjective in design and interpretation
- costly to develop and maintain – new information systems needed
- no regulatory guidelines
- lack of comparators

- indicator overload – you are measuring too much and are 'clouding the issue'
- slows the decision making process – 'paralysis by analysis'
- may meet resistance from some stakeholders as they lack understanding
- they may resist if they feel threatened
- results are likely to conflict and confuse the user
- still need an order of priority.

Test your understanding 4

The areas of the sales department as a whole which will be affected by the introduction of a system of benchmarking are:

Planning: It is important that the company's current practises are reviewed and assessed. If comparisons are made with similar organisations, it is essential that the present processes are understood to allow an objective view to be taken of the firm's current sales management function. An effort will need to be made to identify a firm which is prepared to share information that may be regarded as confidential by many firms.

Research: It will be necessary to identify the activities which can be compared. In a sales department this could include, for example, the number of calls per week, the distances covered by each salesperson, etc. These might be useful starting points for the benchmarking process.

Analysis: The method used and the specification of the variables should be established before comparisons are made with another organisation. It is likely that operating costs, past sales levels and new business generated could all be performance indicators that can be analysed to provide the basis on which benchmarking can be undertaken.

Implementation: The information obtained in the benchmarking exercise will be invaluable in the future in order to monitor the selling activities of the company. In addition it will assist in making better decisions regarding sales in the future.

The impact of benchmarking on individual salespeople would be in the following areas:

Planning: As the activities of each salesperson need to be monitored, it is essential to get their co–operation if the benchmarking process is to be successful. Staff may need to be reassured that it will not affect them adversely.

Research: It is necessary to establish performance measures in a flexible manner as it may be difficult to make direct comparisons. For example, travelling times and the size of purchases by customers are likely to be major performance measures. These targets are currently the same for each sales area, but this may need to be flexed in order to be fair to each salesperson.

Analysis: It will become possible to compare performance within the firm and with other firms operating in the same areas. This could make comparisons more realistic and more effective for determining bonuses.

Implementation: Benchmarking will provide a better appreciation of the factors involved in setting sales targets. By helping to improve the performance of individual salespeople, the performance of the company as a whole can be improved.

chapter

10

Business unit performance

Chapter learning objectives

Lead	Component
C1. Evaluate the process of strategy development	(c) Evaluate different organisational structures
D1. Evaluate the tools and processes of strategy implementation	(a) Recommend appropriate control measures (b) Evaluate alternative models of performance measurement (c) Recommend solutions to problems in performance measurement

Indicative syllabus content

- The relationship between strategy and organisational structure.
- Business unit performance and appraisal, including transfer pricing, reward systems and incentives.
- Project management: monitoring the implementation of plans.
- Theories of control within organisations and types of organisational structure (e.g. matrix, divisional, network).

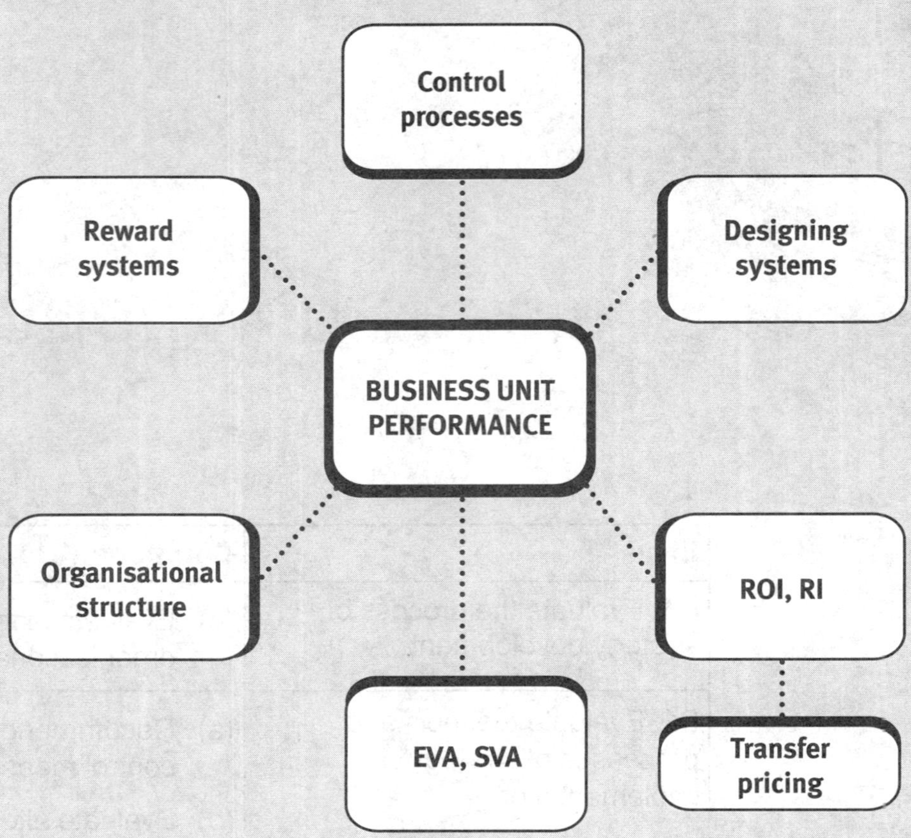

1 Strategy implementation

According to Johnson, Scholes and Whittington, a key aspect of strategy implementation is "organising for success":

- Does the firm need to change its organisational structure?
- How should key relationships be managed – e.g. degree of centralisation required?
- What control measures are required to ensure strategy is delivered?

2 Organising for success – organisational structure

Different types of organisational structure were studied in paper E2 (previously P5). In E3 you could be asked to evaluate existing structures and recommend new ones, so it is important that you understand the advantages and disadvantages of each type.

A structure is necessary in order to facilitate the implementation of strategy and the achievement of objectives. It has been described as the 'shape' of the business but can be defined as the established pattern of relationships between individuals, groups and departments within the organisation.

'Structure is a means for attaining the objectives and goals of an organisation' (Drucker).

Entrepreneurial structure

This is where everything revolves around one or a few central decision makers. There will be little in the way of formality as the owners tend to be the managers. Best exemplified by a small business. **Greiner** suggests that this will pose a problem as the organisation grows larger.

Functional structure

A functional structure divides the organisation up into activities or functions, e.g. production, sales, finance, personnel, etc. and places a manager in charge of each function which is then co-ordinated by a narrow band of senior management. This is a very common form of structure as it allows the deployment of specialisation principles.

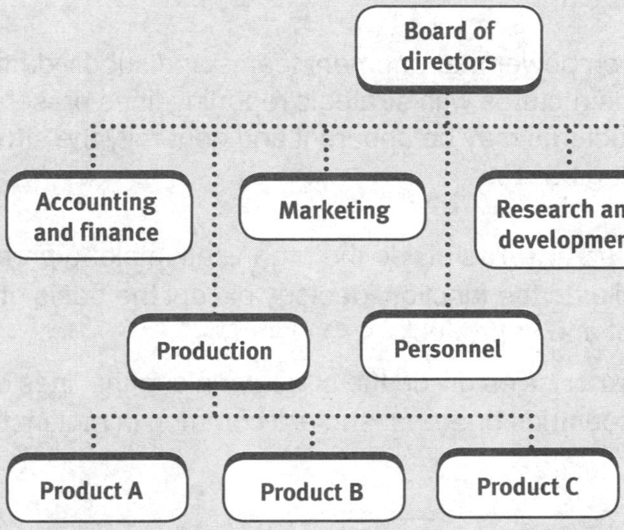

Pros and cons of functional structures

Advantages

- Pooling of expertise through the grouping of specialised tasks and staff.
- no duplication of functions and economies of scale
- senior managers are close to the operation of all functions
- the facilitation of management and control of functional specialists (suited to centralised organisations).

Disadvantages

- 'Vertical' barriers between functions that may affect work flow (creating co-ordination problems) and information flow (creating communication problems)
- focuses on internal processes/inputs rather than outputs such as quality and customer satisfaction through a horizontal value chain
- struggles to cope with change, growth and diversification
- senior management may not have time to address strategic planning issues.

Divisional structures

Divisional structures empower management teams and subdivide the structure into smaller structures with strategic reporting lines present. Holding company structures may be apparent and generally the structure divides on the following bases:

- **Product-based structures** divide the organisation along product lines. This is similar to the function ideology except the basis of division will be the market and or product.
- **Geographical structures** divide the structure along the lines of geography, i.e. countries or areas, and are common in multinational companies.

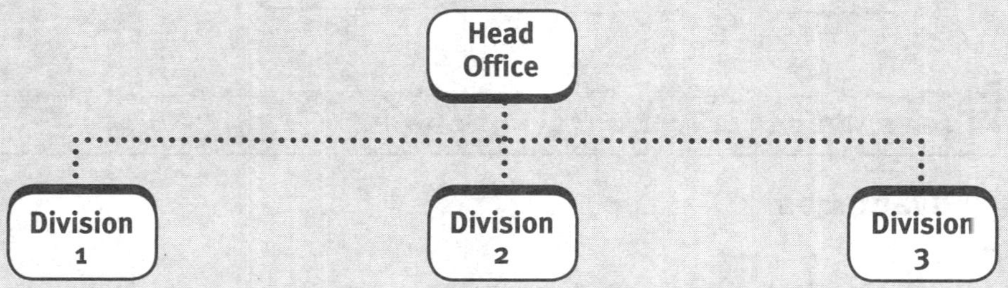

Pros and cons of divisional structures

Advantages

- A concentration of staff and management expertise
- faster response times to environment catalysts. Given the expertise and speed, better quality decisions must result
- improved managerial motivation via empowerment. The harnessing of the 'entrepreneurial' skills

- allows future divestment decisions – it becomes much easier to sell a complete business rather than to attempt to remove it from a centralised structure
- allows the development of subcultures for a better fit with local environments. This structure allows the development of disparate cultures.

Disadvantages

- Duplication of business functions – each division must have it own finance, personnel and sales manager. This results in more managers than if the company were centralised
- potential for sub optimisation as the divisions take decisions to benefit themselves, possibly to the detriment of the overall company
- increased cost arising from extra administration and the development and maintenance of the control system
- the design of the control system poses serious problems with regard to creating goal congruence between investment decisions made by managers and decisions which may be made to improve their own personal reward package – the risk of short-termist action or suboptimal behaviour
- loss of operational and tactical control requires increasing elements of formality which can stifle the operation of the divisionalised concept;
- designing a transfer pricing system where divisions are interdependent.

Matrix organisations

For the larger company the divisional structure is often the most appropriate but it may eventually have to move toward a structure which includes formal mechanisms to promote closer interdivisional collaboration – the result is the **matrix structure** in which dual reporting lines are recognised.

For example, a divisional financial controller has two reporting lines, one to group finance and the other to the divisional management team.

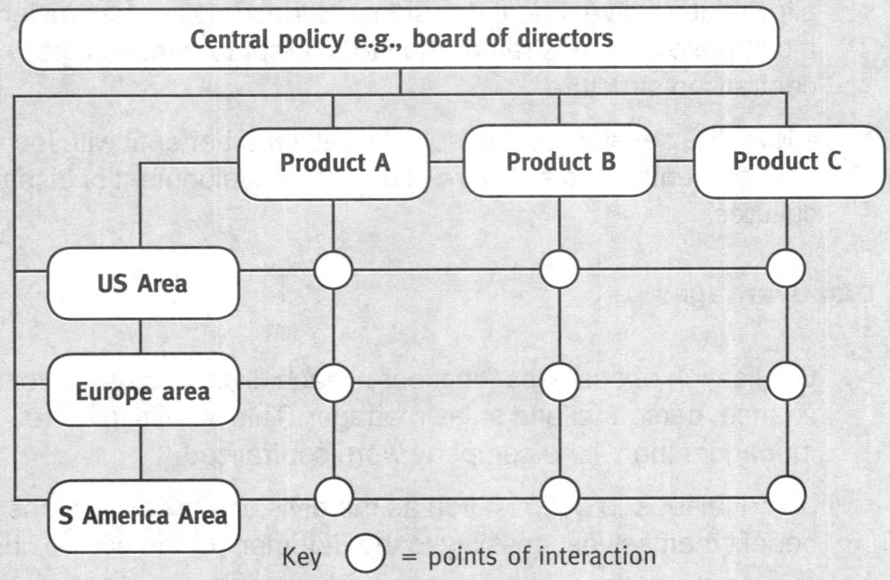

Matrix structures are also widely used for project management.

Pros and cons of matrix structures

Advantages

- Organise horizontal groupings of individuals or units into teams that operationally deal with the strategic matter at hand
- are organic with open communications and flexible goals
- may be established as a permanent structure or be temporary to address a particular strategic commitment, such as an export research group to study international markets in a multi-product trading company, or a unique product group for a limited-duration contract
- can creatively serve the needs of strategic change that otherwise might be constrained by more traditional structures
- retain functional economies and product, service or geographical co-ordination
- can improve motivation through:
  - people working participatively in teams
  - specialists broadening their outlook
  - encouraging competition within the organisation.

Disadvantages

- May lead to problems of dual authority with conflict between functional and product or geographical managers leading to individual stress arising from threats to occupational identity, reporting to more than one boss and unclear expectations
- may incur higher administrative costs.

3 Linking structure and strategy

The influences that have a bearing on organisational structure and design include:

- The organisation's strategic objectives – if co-ordination between specific parts of the organisation is of key importance then the structure should facilitate relationships between them.
- The nature of the environment in which the organisation is operating, now and in the future. Generally, product-based structures are more flexible and are more suitable in a dynamic or complex environment where organisations have to be adaptable.
- The diversity of the organisation – the needs of a multinational are different from those of a small company.
- The future strategy – for example, if a company may be making acquisitions in the future, then adopting a divisional structure now will make the acquired companies easier to assimilate.
- The technology available – IT has a significant impact on the structure, management and functioning of the organisation because of the effect it has on patterns of work, the formation and structure of groups, the nature of supervision and managerial roles. New technology has resulted in fewer management levels because it allows employees at clerical/operator level to take on a wider range of functions.
- The people within the organisation and their managerial skills.

4 Organising for success – decentralisation

Centralisation v decentralisation

One factor in determining the flexibility of a structure is the level at which decisions are made. In centralised organisations the upper levels of an organisation's hierarchy retain the authority to take most decisions. The choice of organisation will depend to a certain extent on the size of the organisation and the scale of its activities, such that the functional structure is likely to be centralised, and the divisional structure is likely to be decentralised.

Decentralisation:

- is more likely in large-scale organisations
- gives authority to make specific decisions to units and people at lower levels in the organisation's hierarchy
- allows front-line staff to respond flexibly to customer demands without reference upwards to senior management
- allows local management (of dispersed units) to respond flexibly to local market conditions without reference upwards to head office.

Pros and cons of decentralisation

Research shows that centralisation of strategic decisions and delegation of tactical and operating decisions can be very effective. Advantages of centralisation are:

- co-ordinated decisions and better management control, therefore less sub-optimising
- conformity with overall objectives – goal congruence is more likely to be achieved
- standardisation, e.g. variety reduction and rationalisation
- balance between functions, divisions, etc. – increased flexibility in use of resources
- economies of scale – general management, finance, purchasing, production, etc.
- top managers become better decision makers, because they have proven ability and they are more experienced
- speedier central decisions may be made in a crisis – delegation can be time-consuming.

There are a number of disadvantages.

- Those of lower rank experience reduced job satisfaction.
- Frequently, senior management do not possess sufficient knowledge of all organisational activities. Therefore, their ability to make decisions is narrowed and delegation becomes essential.

- Centralisation places stress and responsibility onto senior management.
- Subordinates experience restricted opportunity for career development toward senior management positions.
- Decisions often take considerable time. This restricts the flexibility of the organisation, as well as using valuable time. In addition, slower decision making impairs effective communication. Such communication problems may affect industrial relations.

Test your understanding 1

ALG TECHNOLOGY

John Hudson is the Managing Director of ALG Technology, a medium-sized high-tech company operating in several geographic markets. The company provides software and instrumentation, mainly for military projects but it does also have civilian interests. It currently has four key projects - (1) a command, communication and control system for the army's gunnery regiments, (2) avionics for the fighter aircraft within the airforce, (3) an air traffic control system for a regional airport and (4) radar installations for harbour authorities in the Middle East. All these projects were expected to have a life expectancy of at least five years before completion. However, Hudson was worried because each of these projects was increasingly falling behind schedule and the contracts which he had negotiated had late-delivery penalties.

Hudson is convinced that a significant cause of the problem is the way that the company is organised. It has been shown that a competitive advantage can be obtained by the way a firm organises and performs its activities. Hudson's organisation is currently structured on a functional basis, which does not seem to work well with complex technologies when operating in dynamic markets. The functional structure appears to result in a lack of integration of key activities, reduced loyalties and an absence of teamwork. Hudson has contemplated moving towards a divisionalised structure, either by product or by market so as to provide some element of focus, but his experience has suggested that such a structure might create internal rivalries and competition which could adversely affect the performance of the company. Furthermore, there is a risk that such a structure may lead to an over-emphasis on either the technology or the market conditions. He is seeking a structure which encourages both integration and efficiency. Any tendency towards decentralisation, whilst encouraging initiative and generating motivation may result in a failure to pursue a cohesive strategy, whereas a move towards centralisation could reduce flexibility and responsiveness.

The company is already relatively lean and so any move towards delayering, resulting in a flatter organisation, is likely to be resisted. Furthermore, the nature of the market – the need for high technical specifications and confidentiality – is likely to preclude outsourcing as a means of achieving both efficiency and rapidity of response.

Required:

(a) Provide an alternative organisational structure for ALG Technology, discussing both the benefits and problems which such a structure might bring.

(13 marks)

(b) Evaluate the main factors which can influence organisational design, relating these, where possible, to ALG Technology.

(12 marks)

(Total: 25 marks)

5 Organising for success – control processes

5.1 What are control processes and why are they important?

Controls are activities undertaken within an organisation that will increase the chance of the organisation achieving its objectives.

An organisation will not achieve its strategic goals, such as maximising profits or meeting growth targets, simply because it has stated its desire to do so. It will need to put in place control processes or systems to ensure all its activities are helping it to work towards these objectives.

Control systems help with the achievement of corporate objectives in several ways:

- They monitor whether the organisation is on track to achieve its goals. If not, corrective action can be taken.
- They help to identify unexpected problems or events that may have arisen through the year, which need managing.
- They help to remind staff of the organisation's objectives, focusing their attention on these key issues.

5.2 General control processes

Organisations and their strategies are managed and controlled by the informal and formal processes at work within them. There are a number of different processes that the organisation may use, any or all of which may operate alongside one another.

These processes may be:

- formal processes that are structured and documented
- informal, social: how people interact with other people
- focused on the control of resources and inputs, such as finance or staff
- results-oriented, based on targets or objectives
- direct processes, where the organisation's infrastructure such as hierarchies, relationships and culture are designed to produce certain behaviour within the organisation.

A number of typical, generic processes, or controls, are used within organisations to ensure the strategy is delivered, including:

- **direct supervision** of staff
- **planning processes**
- **targets**, based on key performance indicators
- **internal market processes** such as transfer pricing
- the **culture** of the organisation
- **self-control** by employees.

Generic control processes

A number of generic processes are used within organisations to ensure the strategy is delivered.

- **Direct supervision** – hands-on control of inputs by a small number of senior managers. This is typically found in small organisations, and is not possible in large or complex organisations.
- **Planning processes** that also control inputs by monitoring their utilisation. This could include the standardisation of work processes, for example.
- Performance management using **targets based on key performance indicators**. In large organisations these targets are usually set by the centre based on required outputs. Management of business units is hands-off, or indirect, with business units allowed to achieve the targets in their own way.

- **Internal market processes** such as transfer pricing and the use of service level agreements between individual business units. This method is particularly common with services such as information technology.
- The **culture** of the organisation, where a culture is deliberately developed by means such as training and personal development in order to indirectly encourage behaviour required by the strategy. This may have an impact both on the use of inputs and the results. While this can be very effective, once established the culture may be difficult to change if new behaviour is required at a later date.
- **Self-control** by individual employees – where leadership and support frameworks are used to encourage individuals to work independently and use their initiative to produce particular results.

Test your understanding 2

Jersey Ltd is a small business that manufactures high quality portable speakers. The business is small and has only twenty members of staff, with one supervisor. The work is highly skilled and complex, with staff divided into four teams – each with very different sets of required skills.

Currently there are no control procedures or any work guidance for employees, meaning that each member of staff often works in the way they individually feel is best. The twenty employees are moderately well paid, though there are few, if any, real promotion prospects and several employees have expressed their dissatisfaction with the working conditions within Jersey.

Jersey is owned and run by one person, H. She is concerned that the level of quality of production has fallen in recent months, as evidenced by an increase in wastage and a decrease in output. H is concerned about the effect this is having on the profitability of the company. As such, H is examining the possibility of introducing control processes to ensure that all units made are of adequate quality.

Required:

Discuss the appropriateness of each of the following possible controls for Jersey:

(a) Direct supervision of manufacturing staff

(b) Setting performance targets for employees based on quality of output

(c) Relying on individual employees to control their own work

5.3 Common organisational controls

The generic processes outlined above are often built into defined controls that can be used to monitor business activities and take corrective action where necessary.

There are three controls that are common to many organisations, each of which help the organisation to exert control over its activities within different time frames.

- **Corporate strategy** – this acts as a **long-term** control for the organisation. It gives direction to the organisation's activities at a **high level** (i.e. Board level). The activities of the organisation can be monitored in order to ensure that they are in line with this overall aim.
- **Budgetary control** – this acts as a **medium-term** control for the organisation. Management often set budgets for staff members, which will help to ensure that employees know what is expected of them as well as tying in staff goals with the organisation's overall strategy.
- **Variance analysis** – this can be used as a **short-term** control for the organisation. It involves regularly checking actual results against budget. Any departures from the budget can be identified and corrective action taken. This ensures that the organisation is not deviating from its stated strategic goals.

There can therefore be seen to be a strong link between these three controls. The strategy gives the overall direction for the organisation. The budgets are set based on this strategy and act as guidance for employees as to what is expected from them to ensure the organisation's strategy is met. Any variance from this budget can then be dealt with to ensure that the company remains on course.

e.g

Illustration 1 – Common organisational controls in action

Guernsey is a business that offers a range of accountancy services to its clients and is based in one city in country V. Guernsey's senior partners recently announced a new strategy, which involves expanding the business into two neighbouring cities over the coming year. This will involve hiring around fifty new members of staff.

The partners have therefore created a detailed budget for the coming year. This includes large amounts of expenditure for capital assets, such as buildings and fixtures, as well as additional wages costs for an additional fifty members of staff. This budget acts as authorisation for key managers to incur this expenditure, which is necessary for Guernsey's expansion.

At the end of each month, the partners can compare the actual expenditure with the budgets that were set at the start of the year. In the first month the expenditure on buildings was much higher than expected. Further investigation revealed that property prices were higher than expected. The partners were therefore able to secure additional bank funding to enable them to continue with Guernsey's overall expansion strategy.

6 Other contemporary approaches to organisational design

Many writers have commented on the need for change in how businesses are organised. Common themes include the following:

- a need for greater **flexibility**
- an increased emphasis on **teams**
- the growing importance of **knowledge workers**
- rising reliance on **network-**style solutions
- greater **delegation** and empowerment
- a need for new **MIS** to support the above.

Flexible firms

Introduction

Although the concept of flexible employment has been practised for some time in the form of casual work, shorter hours, shift work, overtime and other approaches to deal with fluctuating activity, there has been considerable interest in flexibility recently. Tight labour markets, weaker trade unions, increased labour supply and changing work patterns in families are major influences.

The need for flexibility

The need for flexibility generally arises from the need to remain competitive and adaptive in a dynamic globalised environment – the 'chaos' identified by **Peters** and discussed earlier. There are four main reasons for this:

- The need to be **adaptive** to ever more volatile external environments.
- The need to be more **competitive** in adapting to ever increasing numbers of competitors in the globalised world.

- The advent of new **organisational structures**, such as network organisations.
- The impact of new **technologies and working practices** changing production processes, employee/employer relations and customer service expectations.

There are various forms of flexibility including:

- **Functional flexibility** – requires employees to be multi-skilled and give the organisation the facility to redeploy employees.
- **Numerical flexibility** – where adjustments to the number of employees is made to deal with demand or the fluctuations in output.
- **Temporal flexibility** – variability of labour work time as flexible working hours, compressed hours or job sharing.

(1) **Numerical flexibility**

This refers to the ability of employers to match staffing levels to production demand without cost penalties. **Atkinson** has drawn attention to the division of employees into:

- *Core employees* who have critical and scarce skills – they deliver the **core competencies** of the firm (see Session 1). They receive good promotion, security and status prospects relative to others and are often managers, team leaders, professional staff, skilled technicians and skilled employees.
- *Interface (periphery) workers* are low skilled and form a buffer in relation to fluctuations in demand. These include temporary, part-time, seasonal and standby staff.
- *Suppliers (external workers)* such as contractors, temporary and self-employed staff with the general skills needed. Many are created by contracting out, a process where the firm trims headcounts and then re-employs them as consultants on more flexible hours.

Charles Handy in *The Age of Unreason* referred to this as the *shamrock organisation*.

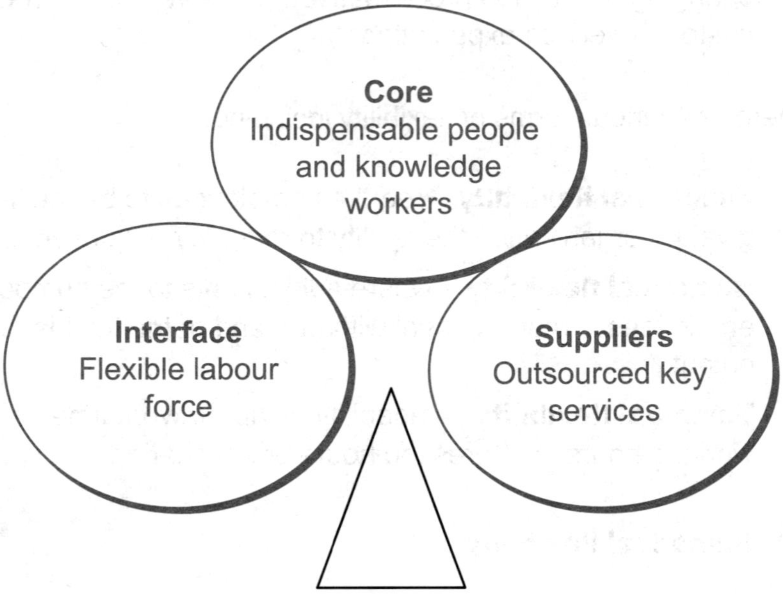

The ***knowledge worker*** will be a crucial strategic asset as part of the core indispensable people. These are intellectual, creative and innovative staff that need to be retained and, in terms of the resource-based view of strategy, are core competences that help to gain competitive advantage. Management, in terms of control, need to identify who these are, consider them as assets rather than expenses, and allow them enough freedom without losing control.

Dividing the employees in such a manner allows the employer to adjust manpower requirements without cost penalties in relation to changing demand, and core employees in whom the organisation has made substantial investment are protected as the periphery workers act as lines of defence.

Numerical flexibility requires a legal environment and framework that permits an employer to differentiate between employees, and non-unionism or single-unionism representing the core employees recognised by the employer. Multi-unions may restrict their members by demarcation to particular tasks.

(2) **Functional flexibility**

This refers to the ability of each employee to tackle a range of tasks which requires a quality workforce with high levels of commitment through:

- Participative and facilitative styles of management.
- High levels of team work.
- High levels of training to achieve multi-skilling.
- Decentralisation of operational decision making to the team and team leader.

(3) **Temporal flexibility**

Work time flexibility involves adjusting working periods in relation to changes in demand whilst avoiding costly overtime and short time. This may involve:

- Flexible working hours controlled by the employer.
- Flexitime arrangements where the employer provides a framework within which employees vary their hours.
- Shift working.
- Changing pattern of hours including compressing or extending the working week.
- Annualised hours where an average is achieved over a six-month or one-year period in situations where there are peaks and low levels of activity week by week.
- Homeworking, facilitated by information systems by recreating information resources available in the office at remote locations, e.g. provision of access to corporate database and communications through internet (or extranet) connections; e-mail; video calls and videoconferencing; mobile telephones.
- Hot-desks where staff do not have desks of their own but are assigned standard design desks on each visit to the office.

(4) **Financial flexibility**

This refers to organisations linking payment of employees to performance and includes profit sharing as well as other methods of performance-related pay. Government legislation has made financial flexibility easier to implement by weakening trade union and wage council power, introducing competitive tendering for public sector contracts, reluctance to sign up for the EU Social Charter and eliminating fair wage resolutions.

Certain aspects of financial flexibility need to be considered:

– The disappearance of notions of 'the rate for the job'.
– The need for pay to be viewed in the context of the 'total remuneration package' that includes employee benefits and job satisfaction.
– The need for total remuneration packages to be adjusted to the needs of individual employees including 'menu' or 'cafeteria' approaches where the employee is allowed to put together their own reward package up to a set limit.
– The decentralisation of pay and reward systems to take local conditions and requirements into account.

Flexibility in its different forms has its problems in sustaining the loyalty and commitment of periphery employees. Measuring individual job performance including the conflicts that performance-related pay have caused, the cost inefficiency of using skilled employees to do unskilled tasks, and the loss of specialisation implied by functional flexibility have also been problems.

Implications for the management accountant

The following aspects arising from flexible human resource strategies need to be considered by management accountants:

- Loss of management control.
- A participative culture in relation to strategic decision making particularly where performance-related pay is involved.
- Wider and additional performance measures.
- Impact on budgetary control systems in respect of lower fixed costs that are more difficult to estimate and problems of allocating flexible arrangements.
- Changes in the way management accountants are employed.

The concept of flexibility, although around for some time, has again come to the forefront in recent years. How can an organisation that faces fluctuating demand for its product ensure it has the right number of staff at the right time in order to minimise cost whilst providing a complete service to its customers?

Virtual organisations

Many organisations allow their staff to work from home to improve the flexibility of the workforce. Some writers believe this is moving many businesses towards becoming 'virtual' organisations where the organisation employs a small core of staff for essential tasks, while the remaining business activities are outsourced or performed by self–employed contract staff.

New wave management (Ezzamel)

In 1995 Ezzamel et al. summarised the likely changes managers would have to embrace in the management of their businesses. These were collectively termed "new wave management":

Historic emphasis	Future emphasis
Rules, regulation and clear supervision	Ambiguity, flexibility and contingency
Hierarchical control and chain of command	Emphasis on developing human resources
Discipline imposed by managers	Employee self-discipline
Directive approach to solving problems	Participative approach to problem solving
Specialists and individualism	Multi-functional teams
Well-defined job descriptions	Series of renegotiated assignments

The Boundaryless Organisation (Welch)

Jack Welch of General Electric (GE) coined the phrase "The Boundaryless Organisation". He believed, and has been proven correct, that GE would be much more effective if the cultural, geographical and organisational barriers that separated the employees become more permeable. He put emphasis on the boundaries' ability to enable business, rather than get in its way.

All organisations have external boundaries that separate them from suppliers and customers, and internal boundaries that provide demarcation to departments. This rigidity is removed in boundaryless organisations, where the goal is to develop greater flexibility and responsiveness to change and to facilitate the free exchange of information and ideas. The boundaryless organisation behaves more like an organism encouraging better integration between departments and closer partnerships with suppliers and customers.

Becoming boundaryless normally involves the creation of cross-functional teams, delayering, and empowerment of employees. Informality, fun and speed are encouraged, whereas managers should seek to eliminate bureaucracy.

This type of organisation is founded upon interdependency and trust. The individual working in a boundaryless environment must understand the importance of these characteristics. They must trust co-workers, recognise the importance of mutual accountability and share both credit and mistakes. The boundaryless person is one who sees the big picture and strives continually to build strong and lasting relationships with others.

Managers also have new roles, focusing on inspiring their people to connect with others, to make things happen, and to serve clients to the highest degree possible. The manager serves as a catalyst to their people with less reliance on managing things (i.e. doing things right) and more on leading people (doing the right thing).

Participating teams (Kanter)

Kanter surveyed over a hundred firms facing change and noted two distinct styles of thinking and problem solving:

- **Integrative thinking** – problems and change are viewed as a whole with multiple perspectives incorporated. Such thinking will facilitate innovation due to the fluidity of boundaries, the free flow of ideas and the empowerment of people.
- **Segmentalism** – problems are compartmentalised and given to specialists to solve. Innovation is difficult as change is seen as a threat to existing segmentation and divisions.

Kanter saw "participating teams" as key to integrative thinking and advised mangers to encourage the following:

- A **culture of pride** – a climate of success that highlights achievements. Experienced innovators serve as consultants to other parts of the organisation.
- Access to **power tools** (for example, management committees, research funds, etc) should be enlarged to improve support for innovative problem solving.
- **Lateral communication** should be improved through developing cross-functional links and encouraging staff mobility.
- Reduction of unnecessary levels of **hierarchy** with staff being empowered lower down the organisation.
- Increased, and earlier, **information** about company plans to enable people to contribute to changes before decisions are made.

Key management issues of the information age (Hope and Hope)

In their book 'Competing in the Third Wave', Jeremy and Tony Hope identified ten key management issues facing firms in the "information age":

(1) **Strategy**: pursue renewal not retrenchment and downsizing.

(2) **Customer value**: work on matching competencies to customer needs

(3) **Knowledge management**: leverage knowledge for competitive advantage.

(4) **Business organisation**: structure around networks and processes rather than traditional forms.

(5) **Market focus**: identify and retain customers who are strategic, profitable and loyal.

(6) **Management accounting**: focus on managing the business not the numbers. For example, look at customer account profitability; try to reduce costs through benchmarking and using the value chain.

(7) **Measurement and control**: try to strike a balance between control and empowerment by ensuring the firm does not become budget-constrained. Balanced scorecards can be useful here.

(8) **Shareholder value**: wealth is generated by intellectual capital and human resources rather than physical assets. Seek ways of measuring and developing these.

(9) **Productivity**: encourage and reward value-creating work.

(10) **Transformation**: adopt the "third wave model". Embracing the above is not simply a readjustment but will involve fundamental change in the organisation's culture and systems.

Extraordinary management (Stacey)

Chaos theory

Chaos theory is a branch of science that considers dynamic systems – systems capable of changing over time – and the predictability of their behaviour.

Stable and unstable behaviour are concepts that everyone is familiar with. What is novel is the concept of something in between – chaotic behaviour. Chaos here does not mean 'a state of utter confusion and disorder' (its common language usage). Instead it refers to systems that display behaviour which, though it has certain regularities, defies prediction.

Think of the weather as an example. Even the best weather forecasts are, in the short term, a little bit wrong and a little bit misleading. In the long run they can be deeply wrong. However, while weather sequences are irregular, they are not formless – there are patterns.

Another feature of chaotic systems is how a small change in the system can have wide-ranging effects. The often quoted example of this is the "butterfly effect" – how something as small as a butterfly's wings could alter the course ("trajectory") of a weather system and result in a monsoon on the other side of the planet.

Some have argued that chaos theory casts doubt over the veracity of any scientific theory or law as it challenges the predictability of systems. Much of science is thus a little bit wrong and a little bit misleading, according to such writers.

Application to management theory

Just as with science, theories relating to how organisations should be run are, at best, a little bit wrong and a little bit misleading. As the degree of complexity and change increase, the danger is that traditional approaches become deeply wrong and misleading.

Based on this understanding, Stacey makes a distinction between two types of management:

Ordinary management

- A legitimate system based on hierarchy, rules and procedures
- an emphasis on team-building, consensus and conformity
- incremental change based on a rational approach to strategic planning
- control based on negative feedback.

Extraordinary management

- A spontaneous system of self-organisation. This often involves a "shadow system" of contacts and political networks in contrast to (and even in opposition to) the official system
- an emphasis on organisational learning and innovation
- focus on the importance of tacit knowledge rather than detailed communication of plans
- best when deeply-held beliefs are challenged and the firm is on the edge of chaos.
- irrational decision making emphasising team commitment rather than organisational goals.

Stacey argued that ordinary management needed stability and certainty to work so was suitable for operational matters. In contrast extraordinary management was essential to strategic management and organisational development.

7 Designing control systems and performance measures

Problems in performance measurement and control in complex business structures

As stated above, a main feature in modern business management is the practice of splitting an enterprise into semi-autonomous units with devolved authority and responsibility.

Such units could be described as 'divisions', subsidiaries or SBUs, but the principles are the same.

This raises the following potential problems.

- How to co-ordinate different business units to achieve overall corporate objectives.
- Goal congruence – managers will be motivated to improve the performance of their local business unit, possibly at the expense of the larger organisation.
- The performance of one unit may depend to some extent on others, making it difficult to implement responsibility accounting effectively.
- Whether/how head office costs should be reapportioned.
- How transfer prices should be set as these effectively move profit from one division to another.

Controllability

Managers should be made accountable for those factors that they can control. This would see a focus onto divisional contribution. This issue of controllability and design poses a few problems:

- What exactly is controllable? Consider shared assets.
- Does controllability change when the long run is considered?
- Transfer pricing issues – should the sales and purchases be included?
- Managerial performance and divisional economic performance are not necessarily the same thing – uncontrollable factors would need to be included when considering economic performance.
- Where does the data originate from? The financial accounting system may not be suitable for performance evaluation of SBUs and may need to be adapted by the management accountant. Reporting or accuracy – which is most important? The faster you go the less reliable the information may become.
- The cultural situation and factors that are likely to motivate the divisional management team.

Cost centres, profit centres and investment centres

Key considerations

When assessing divisional performance it is vital that the measures used match the degree of decentralisation in the division:

Type of division	Description	Typical measures
Cost centre	• Division incurs costs but has no revenue stream	• Total cost • Cost variances • Cost per unit anc other cost ratios • NFPIs related to quality, productiv ty, efficiency, etc.
Profit centre	• Division has both costs and revenue • Manager does not have the authority to alter the level of investment in the division	All of the above PLUS • Sales • Profit • Sales variances • Margins • Market share • Working capital ratios (depending on the division concerned) • NFPIs related to customer satisfaction
Investment centre	• Division has both costs and revenue • Manager does have the authority to invest in new assets or dispose of existing ones	All of the above PLUS • ROI • RI • SVA / EVA These are discussed n more detail below

In most exam questions you will meet SBUs that are investment centres.

Sub-optimisation

Sub-optimisation refers to actions taken to improve the divisional situation at the expense of the company as a whole. This can arise for a number of reasons:

- **Short-termism**

  Short-termism refers to actions taken to improve the short-run performance at the expense of the long run. For example, cutting discretionary costs such as advertising and training budgets to hit a profit target.

- **Problems intrinsic to the targets used**

  ROI can lead to dysfunctional behaviour if a division has a high current return – see below.

  Most measures are linked to profit, which does not have a high correlation with shareholder value.

- **Wrong signals**

  Excessive pressure to hit targets may result in a culture where it is felt to be acceptable to use 'creative accounting' to achieve results.

Wrong signals and inappropriate action

There are many ways in which poorly designed performance management systems can send managers the wrong signals, resulting in dysfunctional behaviour. Berry, Broadbent and Otley identified the following problem areas:

- Misrepresentation – 'creative' reporting to suggest that a result is acceptable.
- Gaming – deliberate distortion of a measure to secure some strategic advantage.
- Misinterpretation – failure to recognise the complexity of the environment in which the organisation operates.
- Short-termism – leading to the neglect of longer-term objectives.

- Measure fixation – measures and behaviour in order to achieve specific performance indicators which may not be effective.
- Tunnel vision – undue focus on stated performance measures to the detriment of other areas.
- Sub-optimisation – focus on some objectives so that others are not achieved.
- Ossification – an unwillingness to change the performance measure scheme once it has been set up.

Test your understanding 3

HIH is a large, multinational chain of high-quality hotels. Recently they have expanded rapidly, with growth of over a hundred hotels in the last two years.

Each new hotel is fitted to a high standard by HIH. The head office of HIH is responsible for all advertising and special offers, the setting of prices and any branding changes.

The local hotel managers are responsible for operational decisions, such as which staff to hire and employee training.

HIH sets targets for local managers based on total sales and customer satisfaction feedback. The customer feedback is collected by hotel staff from customer questionnaires.

Required:

(a) Comment on the suitability of the targets set for managers.

(b) Identify the problems with HIH's current approach to collecting information on customer satisfaction and suggest two controls that HIH could implement to prevent problems occurring with customer satisfaction.

8 Dealing with control questions within E3

Although control is not a major written part of the E3 syllabus, it underlies many of the other key topics. This reflects the reality of a management accountant's role, which is intimately connected with control systems and issues.

You should have a very good understanding and an awareness of control systems and issues. It would be surprising if any management accountant did not spend some part of their time working with control issues, which is why it is an important part of E3.

However, the recent experience of candidates' performances is that they do not deal well with questions about control. For example, in question two of the E3 exam set in September 2011 candidates were required to:

'Evaluate the strengths and weaknesses of SAH's current control system.'

(9 marks)

Candidates performed badly on this section when:

- their answers focused only upon weaknesses, or
- they discussed organisational strengths and weaknesses, rather than control system weaknesses.

These two failings represent poor exam technique in that the candidates failed to address the very specific requirement. Some poor answers suggested a lack of familiarity with the concept of control and its applications. As control will continue to be a subject for examination, you would be well advised to ensure they you have a good grasp of this area.

One approach that might help you when answering future questions is to relate your own experiences to the circumstances described in the scenario. For instance, if the question asks for a discussion of strengths and weaknesses you could consider how the control system described in the scenario would work in your own organisation.

Alternatively, if a requirement asks for suggestions for improvements, you could think about the best features of the control systems you know well and apply these to the question.

Test your understanding 4

KWP is a large professional training organisation based primarily in country G, where competition in the market is fierce. Management has recently undertaken a review of the control systems in place within KWP and identified the following major procedures:

- An annual review is undertaken of the financial statements and variances from budget, allowing any unusual items or trends in income and expenditure to be identified.
- One senior customer services manager reviews all student complaints at the end of each year and flags any common issues that senior management need to take action on.
- Staff are interviewed as part of the annual appraisal process. Any comments they make are fed back by their managers to the Human Resource (HR) Director, who discusses any negative feedback with the employee and their line manager before deciding on whether to implement any changes.

These controls have been in place for a number of years and have not been subject to review, even though the company has grown and restructured many times since they were developed.

KWP has a strategic objective of increasing revenue and profits by five percent each year. However, in the last two years it has failed to achieve this. The management review has identified several key problems that may have contributed to this failure.

The amount of material printed by KWP (such as textbooks and question banks) has increased much faster than KWP's student numbers. Students are given this material on the first day of their training course, or can request the material from the college in advance or in person. No record is kept of these, meaning that students are often given material more than once.

In addition, KWP is often unsure of the number of students attending each course until the course actually commences. This has led to a number of classes being overbooked as well as regularly leading to KWP either under- or over-printing material for their courses. Any material printed but unused is wasted, as it is updated every six months for syllabus changes.

Finally, KWP has identified that there is a high level of staff turnover within the teaching staff. The management review was unsure for the reasons behind this, but several employees informally mentioned that they felt undervalued by the company. Teaching staff are a key resource for KWP, with some students following successful tutors if they move to a rival training provider.

Required:

(a) Explain how controls could aid KWP in achieving its strategic objectives.

(4 marks)

(b) Evaluate KWP's existing control systems and recommend improvements where possible.

(9 marks)

(c) Recommend and justify one control that KWP could put in place to help it deal with each of the three problems identified by the management review.

(12 marks)

9 Reward systems and incentives

There has been much debate over linking remuneration to performance targets.

Benefits of linking reward schemes and performance	Potential problems
• It gives individuals an incentive to achieve a good performance level • Schemes based on shares can motivate employees/managers to act in the long-term interests of the organisation by doing things to increase the organisation's market value	• Employees may be motivated more by intrinsic factors (such as achieving high quality) rather than financial gain • Employees may become demotivated if they feel that they were penalised financially for circumstances outside of their control

• Effective schemes also attract and keep the employees valuable to an organisation • By tying an organisation's key performance indicators to a scheme, it is clear to all employees that performance creates organisational success	• Employees may become highly stressed if a significant proportion of their income is performance related • Employees will have extra incentive towards the dysfunctional behaviour outlined above
• By rewarding performance, an effective scheme creates an organisation focused on continuous improvement	• Should targets be based on individual performance or team or division or group?

10 ROI and RI

Return on Investment (ROI)

$$\frac{\text{Controllable profit}}{\text{Controllable investment}} \times 100$$

- A readily accepted measure which relates the profit earned to the investment deployed.
- A powerful communication device which is a worthy inclusion in any scorecard but risky when used in isolation.

The measure can be improved from two possible directions:

- Increase profits:
  - increase sales, but may include socially-irresponsible sales
  - cuts costs, but may include discretionary expenses.
- Reduce investment:
  - improve working capital control but at a cost
  - divest stock and debtors but may lead to dissatisfied customers
  - defer fixed asset replacement but may lead to unsatisfied threshold competencies
  - divest fixed assets but may lead to that reduction in capacity.

The suboptimality issue in investment decisions and performance evaluation

	Division X	Division Y
Investment project available	$1m	$1m
Controllable profits	$200 k	$130 k
Return on the proposed project	20%	13%
Current ROI	25%	9%
The overall cost of capital is 15%		

The manager of X would be motivated not to invest whereas the manager of Y would be tempted to go ahead. Both are wrong from the company's perspective.

The ROI also suffers from the problem of 'age improvement'. This results from the impact of depreciation on the measurement system, e.g. assume that an investment costs £1m with a cost of capital of 10% and a positive NPV.

	Y1	Y2	Y3	Y4	Y5
Net cash flows	350	350	350	350	350
Depreciation	200	200	200	200	200
Profit	150	150	150	150	150
Opening WDV of asset	1,000	800	600	400	200
ROI	15%	19%	25%	38%	75%

The project has declining performance in real terms as the profits remain at 150 per annum. As the depreciation charge starts to reduce the value of the investment base, the measure naturally improves without any actual improvement in managerial or economic performance.

Possible solutions

(1) **Basic adjustment to accounting information**

Adjust the base measure to include original cost of the asset rather than the written-down value, i.e. ignore the issue of depreciation. This is one of many suggested adjustments to financial accounting data in an effort to improve the inputs. Depreciation is far too subjective and is ignored in many instances.

(2) **Use a residual income approach**

Controllable profit less a cost of capital charge on the controllable investment:

Profit – (Investment x K%)

This can be adapted to allow for the economic value-added (EVA) principle.

(3) **Use shareholder value analysis (SVA)**

A variation along the same theme as EVA. The main aim of the organisation is to add value to shareholder wealth. This can be defined in a variety of ways and usually results in a form of balanced scorecard being used.

Pros and cons of ROI and RI

ROI

Advantages	**Disadvantages**
Widely used and accepted As a relative measure it enables comparisons to be made with divisions or companies of different sizes It can be broken down into secondary ratios for more detailed analysis ROI forces managers to make good use of existing capital resources and focuses attention on them, particularly when funds for further investment are limited The nature of the measure is such that it can clearly be improved not just by increasing profit but by reducing capital employed. It therefore encourages reduction in the level of assets such as obsolete equipment and excessive working capital	May lead to dysfunctional decision making (see below). Different accounting policies can confuse comparisons Increases with age of asset if net book values (NBVs) are used Exclusion from capital employed of intangible assets, such as brands and reputation Disincentive to invest – a divisional manager will not wish to make an investment which provides an adequate return as far as the overall company is concerned if it reduces the division's current ROI

	ROI improves with age. This might encourage divisions to hang on to old assets and again deter them from investing in new ones. Alternatively, a division may try to improve its ROI still further by leasing its assets Corporate objectives of maximising total shareholders' wealth or the total profit of the company are not achieved by making decisions on the basis of ROI. In this way, as a relative measure, it can be compared with the internal rate of return (IRR), whose use is also dysfunctional

RI

Advantages	Disadvantages/problems
• It reduces the problem of under-investing seen in ROI • It is more consistent with the objective of maximising total profitability of the group • It is possible to use different rates of interest for different types of asset • The cost of financing a division is brought home to divisional managers	• It does not take into account the size of the investment or organisation • It is difficult to decide upon an appropriate measure of capital employed

Test your understanding 5 – RI/ROI

Sandy is a divisional manager. She gets paid a bonus based on how much her divisional ROI exceeds the company target of 15%. Her division currently generates profit of $37,500 and she has divisional capital of $187,500.

She has been offered a new project returning $15,000 of profit for a capital outlay of $90,000.

Required:

Will she accept the project? Would the company want her to?

If her bonus was linked to residual income (RI), would this change?

11 EVA and SVA

EVA

EVA is an estimate of true economic profit after making corrective adjustments to GAAP accounting.

Conventional divisional profit measure ± Adjustments for any divisional profit measures arising from using GAAP for external reporting − Cost of capital charge on divisional assets = EVA

- Adjustments are made to avoid the immediate write-off of value-building expenditure such as research and development R&D expenditure, advertising expenditure or the purchase of goodwill.
- Adjustments are intended to produce a figure for capital employed which is a more accurate reflection of the base upon which shareholders expect their returns to accrue and to provide a profit after tax figure which is a more realistic measure of the actual cash yield generated for shareholders from recurring business activities.

SVA

A variation along the same theme as EVA. The main aim of the organisation is to add value to shareholder wealth. This can be defined in a variety of ways and usually results in a form of balanced scorecard being used.

It is important to remember that value is not just a financial concept. Shareholders can attach non-financial value, e.g. social responsibility of the company – not testing on animals, positive human rights record or even football club membership.

Rappaport has a model that is frequently mentioned. He suggested that future cash flows should be discounted at a suitable cost of capital and that shareholder value would be increased if this measure were to increase.

In order to maximise future cash flows and reduce the cost of capital, he identified seven value drivers:

- **S**ales growth rate – assuming sales are profitable, this should increase cash flow.
- **L**ife of the project – if the firm can forecast growth over a longer period, there will be more cash flows to discount.
- **O**perating profit margin – if this is increased, the amount of cash generated from each sale should rise.
- **W**orking capital – this should be minimised to reduce the amount of cash tied up in inventory and receivables.
- **C**ost of capital – this should be minimised as this is the rate that will be used to discount the future cash flows. The lower the discount rate, the higher the present value.
- **A**sset investment – if growth demands high levels of capital investment, this will represent a large outflow of cash.
- **T**axation – clearly, any reduction in this rate will reduce cash outflow.

An easy way of remembering these drivers is using the acronym **SLOW CAT.**

Managers should set targets in each of these seven areas in order to ensure they are maximising shareholder wealth.

Later work has developed to include other stakeholders and also non-financial perspectives such as social responsibility. Remember, look after the environment in which you operate and you will get a longer life - the implications for increasing future cash flows as a result are substantial.

Advantages of EVA/SVA approaches

- Adjustments made to profit effectively mean we are looking at cash-flow based measures
- consistent with NPV so should ensure better goal congruence between divisional performance and maximising shareholder value. (Note: You can show that the present value of future EVA figures equates to the increase in shareholder value measured by discounted cashflows)
- cost of financing emphasised.

Drawbacks of the EVA/SVA Systems

- Uses accounting data which has been prepared for other purposes and involves subjective provisions and estimates
- it ignores items that don't appear on balance sheets such as brands, staff and inherent goodwill
- confuses management as they are seldom trained fully in its operation and it varies from one company to another
- costly to maintain and resistance is usually high when first deployed;
- assumes value can be measured in money terms
- judgement involved by users in evaluation and selection of cost of capital rate to be used.

12 Transfer pricing

(1) In larger multidivisional organisations, it is common to find SBUs trading with each other. This will involve the setting of transfer prices (TP). These prices are often set by the corporate unit and can prove to be problem areas when coming to asses SBU performance.

(2) TPs that are set at marginal cost do not offer the SBU manager an incentive to supply and they may chose to sell resources to outside parties who pay a higher margin. This can have quality implications for the group product who then take second place in terms of supply.

(3) Buying at marginal cost can also give a misrepresented position as performance appears to be better.

(4) In assessing managerial performance, it is usual to exclude the TPs from the performance measurement systems on the grounds that they are not controllable. This has the problem of suggesting that trading between group partners is not important ('what gets measured...')

(5) TPs can be used to assist entry into the international arena and can cause considerable controversy in the countries targeted as well as the divisional managers whose performance is being evaluated. TP can also be used as a basis to avoid taxation. By increasing or decreasing TP, profits can be relocated from high tax economies to low tax economies. As a result, tax authorities allocate substantial time and effort in attempting to identify these practices. One way that has been used in the past is to see whether the organisation concerned is excluding the TP items from the performance measurement mix. If they are doing so, this suggests that the TP is being centrally controlled and tax evasion is suspected.

(6) **The dilemma** – inclusion of the TP items in the measurement mix leads to problems in performance evaluation as uncontrollable items are included in the assessment. However, in so doing you could save millions in tax. To remove the TP items from the measurement system can lead to vastly increased taxation liabilities.

Test your understanding 6

Within a large group, divisional managers are paid a bonus which can represent a large proportion of their annual earnings. The bonus is paid when the budgeted divisional profit for the financial year is achieved or exceeded.

Meetings of divisional boards are held monthly and attended by the senior management of the division, and senior members of group management.

With the end of the financial year approaching, there had been discussions in all divisional board meetings of forecast profit for the year, and whether budgeted profit would be achieved. In three board meetings, for divisions that were having difficulty in achieving budgeted profits, the following divisional actions had been discussed. In each case, the amounts involved would have been material in determining whether the division would achieve its budget.

Division A had severely cut spending on training, and postponed routine repainting of premises.

Division B had renegotiated a contract for consultancy services. It was in the process of installing total quality management (TQM) systems, and had originally agreed to pay progress payments to the consultants, and had budgeted to make these payments. It had renegotiated that the consultancy would invoice the division with the total cost only when the work was completed in the next financial year.

Division C had persuaded some major customers to take early delivery, in the current financial year, of products originally ordered for delivery early in the next financial year. This would ensure virtually nil stock at year end.

Required:

Discuss the financial accounting, budgeting, ethical and motivational issues which arise from these divisional actions.

Comment on whether any group management action is necessary.

(25 marks)

13 Summary

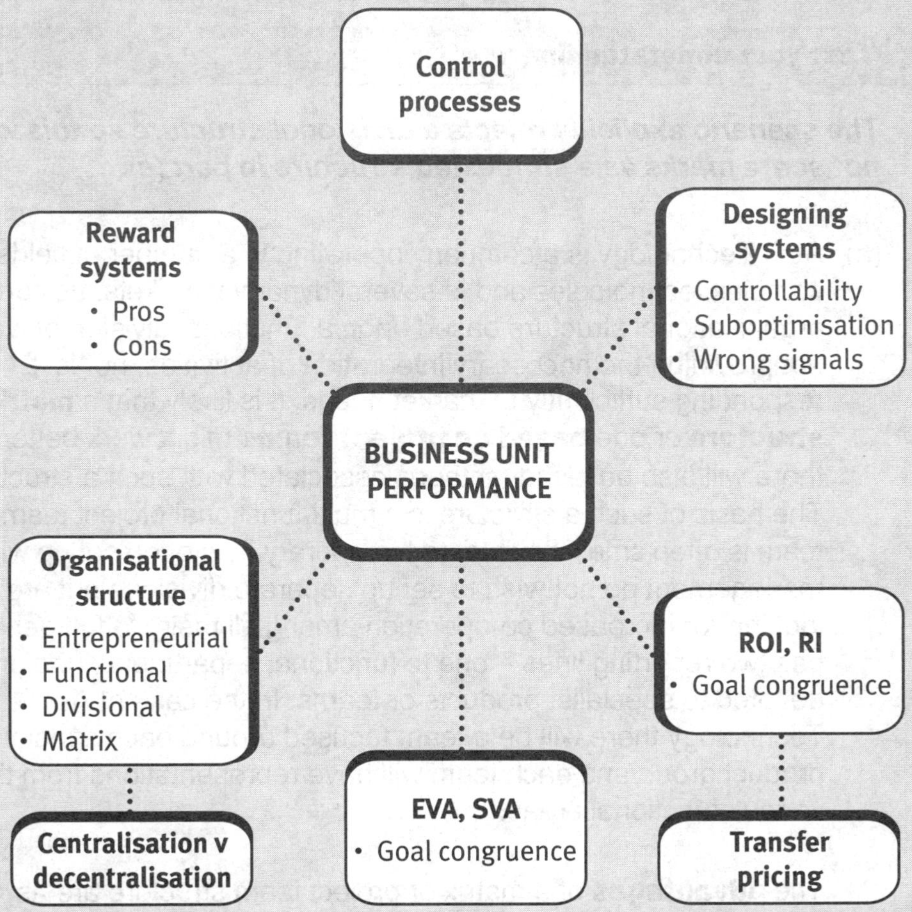
Control processes
Designing systems
• Controllability
• Suboptimisation
• Wrong signals
Reward systems
• Pros
• Cons
BUSINESS UNIT PERFORMANCE
Organisational structure
• Entrepreneurial
• Functional
• Divisional
• Matrix
ROI, RI
• Goal congruence
Centralisation v decentralisation
EVA, SVA
• Goal congruence
Transfer pricing

Test your understanding answers

Test your understanding 1

The scenario explicitly rejects a divisional structure so this would not score marks as a suggested structure in part (a).

(a) ALG Technology is a company operating in a number of fields of complex technologies and in several dynamic markets. Its current organisational structure based upon a functional division of work is not providing the necessary integration of activities, nor is it responding sufficiently to market needs. It is likely that a **matrix structure** or one **based on project teams** might work better but there will also be disadvantages associated with such a structure. The basis of such a structure is a multi-functional project team. The team is often small, flexible and temporary. It is often set up when management do not wish to set up separate divisions but are looking for increased co-operation among all their staff. It generally has two reporting lines – one to functional departments and one devoted to specialist products or teams. In the case of ALG Technology there will be a team focused around each specialist product group and each team will have representations from the various functional areas.

The **advantages** of a matrix or project team structure are as follows:

– The teams do not lose sight of their long-term objectives. They can remain more focused.

– There is more integration between the differing functional specialists – they become inter-disciplinary, resulting in greater co-operation and understand opposing or alternative opinions.

– Such a team is more responsive and flexible to environmental and technical change, so important for a company such as ALG. Because the team is now less bureaucratic and more focused, outcomes are much quicker as the bureaucracy is now replaced by a direct interplay between specialists – the interested parties.

– No one single functional area is likely to dominate. In a company such as ALG there is a danger that the views of scientists and engineers may triumph at the expense of prudent financial advice and market needs may also be ignored. There is a danger of the company becoming too product-orientated.

– Because staff are more directly involved in planning, control and decision making they become more motivated and commited – a key benefit for any company.

- Junior staff experience a wider range of inputs from a broad spectrum of areas. They lose their specialised isolation and become more valuable and 'rounded' employees. This provides a good training platform for future general managers.
- Experiences from one project team can easily and quickly be transmitted to other teams.

There are also **disadvantages**:

- Because of the dual representation within the teams there is a potential for conflict between project managers and functional heads.
- The two reporting lines can lead to confusion for members of the team. Where does their long-term future lie and where is it being determined?
- Because of the above there is increased complexity in reporting, making such a structure costly to administer.
- Decision making can be slower and not be more responsive if every participant insists on full participation. This is a problem with all democratic and participatory organisations, as has been experienced by a number of Japanese companies.
- Because of dual reporting, there is a problem of allocating responsibilities. Who is in charge?
- This proposed new structure may lead to a dilution of priorities, particularly in resource allocation.

As a guideline for organising innovative project teams it is essential that structures should be flexible so as to encourage experts to break through conventional boundaries into new areas. There should also be leadership within the team of staff with a good technical background (**expert power**) and the team should not be dominated by superiors armed only with authority (**position power**).

(b) Organisational design can be influenced by many factors which can generally be divided into two categories – internal and external influences.

The **internal influences** comprise:

- Poor performance in the past. If a company has had difficulties such as are currently being experienced by ALG Technology then it is not surprising that it is considering a change in its organisational structure.

- If a company is now heavily influenced by entrepreneurs and innovators, a more flexible structure would be welcome. A 'machine bureaucracy', which might be what ALG Technology has become, would not be sympathetic to this type of employee. An entrepreneurial structure might be more appropriate.
- A change in organisational ownership would inevitably have given the new shareholders a greater say on matters such as organisational design. Design will be more influenced by their management philosophy.
- There may have been a change in organisational goals. If quality of delivery is now given greater priority than product performance, as in the case of ALG, a structure more oriented to marketing might now be encouraged.
- A change in strategy will also help to influence the design of the organisation. If the company intends to compete with low prices then costs will now become critical. It is likely that there will be a more mechanistic approach to the structure with less focus on the individual. However, with a differentiation strategy there is a potential for more informality, with more decision making being devoted to junior managers. This will be reflected in a less bureaucratic organisational structure.

The **external factors** that might influence organisational design are as follows:

- A **change in knowledge available** to a company. An increase in the availability and application of information technology (IT) now enables organisations to have greater control and communication within an organisation while having a smaller infrastructure to accomplish these functions.
- **Economic opportunities** may change. The globalisation of markets will necessitate a change in organisational structure to reflect and respond to these changes. In certain parts of the world barter has been reintroduced because of shortages of liquidity within the banking system. Organisations must build into their structures recognition of this 'problem'. Certain companies have had to create whole departments to respond to this condition.
- **Socio-demographic changes** – as organisations now operate in different parts of the world, each with different demographics and social regimes, then differences such as attitudes to older people working, women in management, educational abilities matching requirements and labour force availability can all influence the design of organisational structures, resulting in more flexible and responsive organisations suiting local needs and cultures.

- **Ecological considerations** – 'green' issues are becoming more significant. Decisions on purchasing and distribution will be influenced by this and these, in turn, may affect the organisational structure. 'Just-in-time' supply techniques may be affected here (although just-in-time may be driven more by economic rather than ecological consideration).
- The **prevailing ideological beliefs** may also influence organisational design. In some countries planning may still be more dominant than a market culture. This could affect the organisational infrastructure with a greater reliance on planning departments than on a marketing and customer service. There has been much discussion on the differences between Japanese and Western-based companies. Concepts popular in Japan in the 1970s and 1980s such as jobs for life, promotion by seniority and job rotation have all affected the way in which organisations are configured. However, it is also true to say that with the recent increased tendency towards globalisation these ideological differences are being reduced.

As can be noted from the above discussion, a number of these factors can be used to justify ALG Technology's need to change its organisational structure. Probably the most pressing reason for the change is its current poor performance. Resulting from this, there will probably be changes in both objectives and strategies. Although the environmental factors may have limited relevance here, the fact that ALG is now operating in a dynamic and global marketplace means that it has to be more responsive to market needs. With improved IT, it can now control its enterprises from a distance without sacrificing responsiveness. It can do so with a relatively flat organisation without the need for an extensive supportive infrastructure.

Test your understanding 2

(a) **Direct supervision of staff**

Jersey could opt to directly monitor the activities of its staff in order to ensure their work is of appropriate quality. This could be effective at stopping the production of poor quality speakers and the associated waste that would be involved in this. The fact that Jersey only has a small number of staff would also tend to make this approach work well.

However, there would be several problems associated with this control. Firstly, each group of workers has highly specialised skills. This may make it difficult for Jersey's supervisor to understand what each group does and monitor their activities effectively. In addition, the fact that each worker may undertake the same job as their colleagues but using a different technique, will increase the complexity of the monitoring role.

While the workforce is small, there is only one supervisor. They may have insufficient time available to supervise all staff. Hiring of additional supervisors would have cost implications for Jersey.

Finally, additional supervision may have a negative impact on the motivation of employees, who are used to having autonomy over the way they perform their jobs. A sudden change to being closely monitored could cause further job dissatisfaction.

(b) **Performance targets**

Setting performance targets could be of great use to Jersey. This would likely involve offering incentives for staff (such as pay rises and bonuses) depending on how well they perform their jobs. For Jersey, the number of defective units produced by each employee could be measured and a bonus could be offered if this was below a pre-agreed level.

This could be a very practical approach for Jersey, as it links employee rewards with the objectives of the company itself. It should be easy to implement and would prevent the production of units that were defective, reducing waste. The offer of an additional bonus or extra pay may also help to improve general motivation as workers are currently only adequately paid and have few other benefits or prospects.

Note that this may not improve the output of each worker, which is another issue for Jersey. Workers may spend longer on each unit in order to ensure the quality and thus receive their bonus, leading to a further fall in productivity.

(c) **Reliance on self-control of workers**

Relying on individual staff to monitor their own activities may be problematic. It has the advantage of being cheap for Jersey, as it does not require any further staff to be hired. In addition, the staff are clearly skilled at their jobs, making it easier for them to understand the best way to approach individual tasks.

However, staff seem to be relatively de-motivated. This means that they are less likely to be concerned about the quality of their output. Unless they are offered an incentive by Jersey, there is no reason why they would focus on higher quality production.

In addition, there is no agreed 'best practice' for each of the four teams. Each worker is likely to see their method as superior to those of their colleagues, whether this is in fact correct or not. This means that they are unlikely to change their working practices to ones that would improve output and quality.

Test your understanding 3

Suitability of targets

Remember that targets set for managers need to be based around areas that they can directly control.

Managers do make the operational decisions in the hotel, meaning that they should have a large degree of control over the customer experience and therefore customer satisfaction.

However, as pricing and special offers are set by head office, they do not have total control over the sales made by the hotel. Should head office set an inappropriate price per room, sales will suffer. It would be unfair to blame the manager for this.

Controls

It is clearly important that customers are happy with their stay in HIH's hotels. If not, they will not book again for future accommodation and HIH's high-quality reputation will suffer.

While the business sets targets for managers based on customer feedback forms, this is easy to manipulate. Given that feedback is collected by the staff, they could easily destroy negative forms or falsify more favourable ones. In addition, a large number of satisfied customers may simply not bother to fill in a questionnaire, distorting the results.

Instead there are a number of controls that HIH could implement to prevent poor service from occurring. These could include:

Mystery shoppers

HIH could employ individuals to pretend to be customers in its hotels. They could then give impartial feedback on their stay. This may well be more reliable as a way of ascertaining the actual level of customer satisfaction in the hotels.

If staff are made aware that mystery shoppers will be in operation, it will encourage them to maintain high levels of customer service to avoid being identified as a poor worker.

Training

Staff performance is likely to be key to the customer experience. By having a formal training procedure for all staff members, rather than relying on local managers, HIH may be more able to ensure a consistent level of service across all its hotels.

Test your understanding 4

(a) **How controls can aid the achievement of corporate objectives**

Firstly, control systems can help to monitor the implementation of the strategic plan. KWP has a strategic goal of growing revenue and profits by five percent each year. Control systems can be created to monitor revenue and profitability throughout the year, enabling KWP to check that it is on course to meet these targets.

Controls can also help to identify any unexpected problems. Formal strategic plans often do not work perfectly in practice. Controls would allow KWP to identify any sudden drops in profitability or revenues and therefore investigate before taking corrective action.

Controls are also a way of ensuring that employees follow the corporate plans they are given. KWP's staff may not feel the need to work towards increased revenue and profits by themselves. Controls may help to remind or focus staff on key targets, as well as allowing management to look for ways to motivate employees by tying personal goals into strategic objectives. This currently appears to be a major issue for KWP, as staff motivation seems low.

(b) **Problems with existing controls**

Financial statement review

The aim of this control is presumably to help monitor whether the company is meeting its five percent growth targets and, if it is not, discover why not so that corrective action can be taken. As such this control should be useful for helping the company to meet its objectives.

However, the interval between reviews is clearly too long. Any number of unexpected events and problems could arise over the course of a year (such as special offers by competitors) and identifying these issues up to a year late is simply not good enough in a highly competitive market.

KWP should consider making the financial review more regular, perhaps monthly.

Customer service review

Again this can be seen to be linked to KWP's strategic objective of increasing revenue. Given the high levels of competition in the market, identifying and dealing with customer complaints may be crucial for retaining customers.

However, there are several major weaknesses. Again, as above, the review is undertaken annually. A major problem may arise mid-year and affect a large number of students. If action is not taken until the end of the year, many of these students may be lost and KWP's reputation damaged.

In addition, it should be noted that the person undertaking the review is a senior customer services manager. As such, they may be biased and may not wish to identify any major customer service failings that could reflect badly on them or their department.

KWP should consider monitoring complaints more frequently and ensuring they are reported to an independent third party, for example a member of the accounts department.

Staff appraisals

This control also ties in to KWP's strategic objectives. Teaching staff are highly regarded by students and loss of staff may mean loss of students, leading to reduced revenue and profitability.

However, the format is of concern. Any negative comments made by teaching staff are fed back to the HR Director, who then discusses them with the manager and the appropriate member of staff. Unfortunately this may lead to workers feeling victimised by management and may make staff reluctant to criticise the status quo.

KWP should consider creating an anonymous suggestion scheme for employees.

(c) **New controls**

Material for students

The lack of control over materials means that some students are able to collect several sets. This increases the print costs for KWP and lowers its profits.

KWP should consider having an online control system for material. Every time a member of staff sends or hands out material to a student, the student should be asked to sign for it. This could then be logged on the online system. Should the student ask for the same set of material again, the online register can identify that they have already received a copy.

Class numbers

KWP should create a central database of all classes being held across the company, along with the maximum number of students that can attend each one.

As enrolments are processed, this database would be updated. This will allow teaching staff and local administration to identify the number of students in each class and order material accordingly. This should significantly reduce wastage.

In addition, the system could be set to refuse to allow enrolments for courses that have reached their maximum size.

Staff turnover

Managers are currently unaware of the reason for employees leaving the business. They should therefore consider the use of exit interviews as a control system.

This would identify the reasons for staff leaving the company which can then be investigated and appropriate measures taken to deal with the problem.

Note that employees feeling 'undervalued' is unlikely to be insufficient information to allow KWP to take corrective action. The reason for this feeling needs to be found.

Test your understanding 5 – RI/ROI

Under ROI:

	Pre-project	Project itself	Post-project
Profit	$37,500	$15,000	$52,500
Capital employed	$187,500	$90,000	$277,500
ROI	($37,500/ $187,500) × 100 = **20%**	($15,000/ $90,000) × 100 = **16.7%**	($52,500/ $277,500) × 100 = **18.9%**

Looking at the project itself – it does offer a higher return than the 15% that the company requires. From the company's perspective it should therefore be accepted.

However, doing so will reduce the overall divisional ROI and therefore the manager's bonus. This means she will reject the project, regardless of the benefit to the company as a whole.

Under RI:

	Pre-project	Project itself	Post-project
Profit	$37,500	$15,000	$52,500
Capital employed	$187,500	$90,000	$277,500
Profit	$37,500	$15,000	$52,500
CE × 15% return	($28,125)	($13,500)	($41,625)
Residual income	$9,375	$1,500	$10,875

On a RI basis, the project has a positive RI and would therefore be beneficial to the company. It will also increase the division's RI, meaning that the manager will wish to accept it as it will increase her bonus.

Test your understanding 6

Key answer tips

This question deals with the possibility of management manipulating financial performance measures. To ensure a focused answer (and economic use of time) consider the three suggestions under the four headings in the question. Group management action is required to ensure such proposals being implemented prior to forthcoming bonus calculations.

Each of the divisions' actions can be discussed as follows:

Division A

In financial accounting terms, the reduction in discretionary expenditure will lead to higher reported divisional profits than would have been the case if the original planned expenditure had taken place. Discretionary expenditure should be charged against profits as it is incurred. No provisions or accruals need to be set up at the year end because the division is not compelled to make the expenditure.

There is some question as to whether the cut in training costs and repainting costs should be separately disclosed in the financial accounts in the overriding objective of giving a true and fair view. This depends on the materiality of the amounts involved, but is unlikely in the context of the group as a whole.

The ethical implications are more serious. The managers of Division A have deliberately manipulated the results in order to achieve the budget and be paid their bonuses. Their duty as managers is to serve the organisation, but they have served their own interests. Perhaps the two decisions can be distinguished from each other. The repainting of the premises is not important to the group; the timing of repainting is just the sort of matter than the group management should be happy to devolve to divisional management. The lack of training is more serious. It will probably lead to higher costs next year, which the group managers would not be happy about.

Division B

In financial accounting terms, the decision to defer payment to the consultants should make no difference to the division's reported profits. If work has been carried out but not yet paid for at the balance sheet date, the division must set up an accrual for the amounts due. This will be charged against profits. So this idea should have no effect on the divisional managers' bonus payable.

The only way that the idea would increase reported profits would be if the division abandoned the accruals concept and tried to defer the charging of the expense until the consultants were paid. This would be contrary to established accounting practices, and would attract criticism from the auditors if the amounts were sufficiently material.

If the divisional managers were familiar with accounting practices, but decided not to accrue for the payments in order to be paid their bonuses, an ethical question arises. These managers have shown themselves to act unethically, and the group managers should warn the divisional managers about their conduct.

If no accruals were made this year, then next year's profits would be lower when the total cost of the contract has to be charged against profits. To avoid this kind of shock, and in the interests of giving a true and fair view, an accrual for the work carried out at the balance sheet date should be set up.

Division C

In financial accounting terms the point of sale is the point when the purchaser starts to take responsibility for the risks and rewards of the goods. This is usually when the purchaser accepts delivery of the goods. So, by delivering goods which are accepted before the balance sheet date, the division has successfully moved the date of sale into the current financial year. The profit on such sales can therefore be included in this year's reported profits, which will help to trigger the bonus payments.

There would only be financial accounting implications to the scheme where it was decided that showing the higher profit this year, with next year's profit being lower than it would otherwise have been, destroys the true and fair view of the accounts. This is unlikely to be the case, particularly in the context of the group as a whole.

The nil stock at the year-end could cause problems at the start of the next financial year. Any large order received early next year could not be satisfied from stock; the purchaser might have to wait some time for the goods to be physically produced before they can be delivered. At best this is only an inconvenience to the purchaser. At the worst the sale may be lost altogether as the purchaser takes his custom elsewhere to a supplier who can deliver from stock. Thus a scheme that was designed to trigger bonus payments to the divisional managers in the current year could end up costing the group sales and consequent profits next year.

As in the other divisions, the divisional management have acted unethically. The possible loss of sales next year, and the pressuring of customers to accept early sales this year, simply so that managers can be paid bonuses this year, is not acceptable.

Group management action

The whole logic of establishing a divisionalised structure within a group is to allow local managements to manage their divisions as they think best, subject to meeting broad group criteria. Normally group management will adopt a hands-off attitude of observing procedures but not interfering. Interference would be resented by the divisional managers with adverse motivational consequences.

None of the proposals in the question is actually illegal, though division B's idea would be contrary to standard accounting practice, if an insufficient accrual were established. So, the group managers may feel unwilling to get involved and criticise the proposals.

However, there is a line to be drawn between legitimate 'income smoothing' (a good thing, since stock markets value highly companies with a smooth profit record) and manipulation of results to earn bonuses this year but which will depress profits next year. The idea of the bonus scheme is to reward good operational performance, not skills at profit manipulation.

So, however unwilling they may be to interfere unnecessarily, the group managers' responsibility to the stakeholders at large means that they must take up each of these issues with the divisional management, if only to prevent these proposals from being put in place every year as the bonus calculations are drawing near.

chapter

11

Information technology and e-business

Chapter learning objectives

Lead	Component
A2. Evaluate the impact of information systems on an organisation	(a) Evaluate the impact of the internet on an organisation & its strategy (b) Evaluate the strategic and competitive impact of information systems
D1. Evaluate the tools & processes of strategy implementation	(e) Recommend changes to information systems appropriate to the organisation's strategic requirements

Indicative syllabus content

- The impact of IT (including the internet) on an organisation (utilising frameworks such as Porter's Five Forces & the Value Chain).
- Contemporary developments in the commercial use of the internet (e.g. Web 2.0).
- Value chain analysis.
- The purpose and contents of information systems strategies and the need for strategy complementary to the corporate and individual business strategies.
- The critical success factors – links to performance indicators & corporate strategy, & their use as a basis for defining an organisation's information needs.

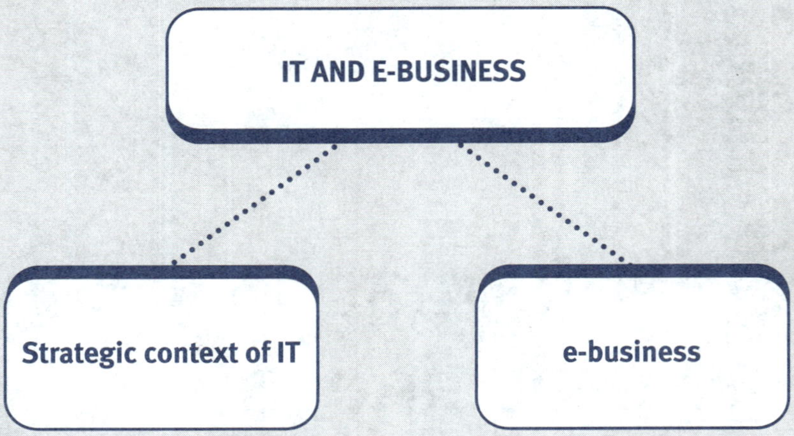

1 Introduction

This chapter covers two major themes:

(1) the strategic and competitive impact of information systems (IS)
(2) the impact of the Internet on organisations by looking at e-business.

On a related note, competing through exploiting information is covered in the chapter "Information for advantage and knowledge management".

2 IT, IS and IM strategies

Earl's three levels of strategy in IT

In 1989 **Earl** developed a framework to analyse the linkages between three interrelated types of strategy:

- information systems
- information technology
- information management.

Earl's three levels of information strategy

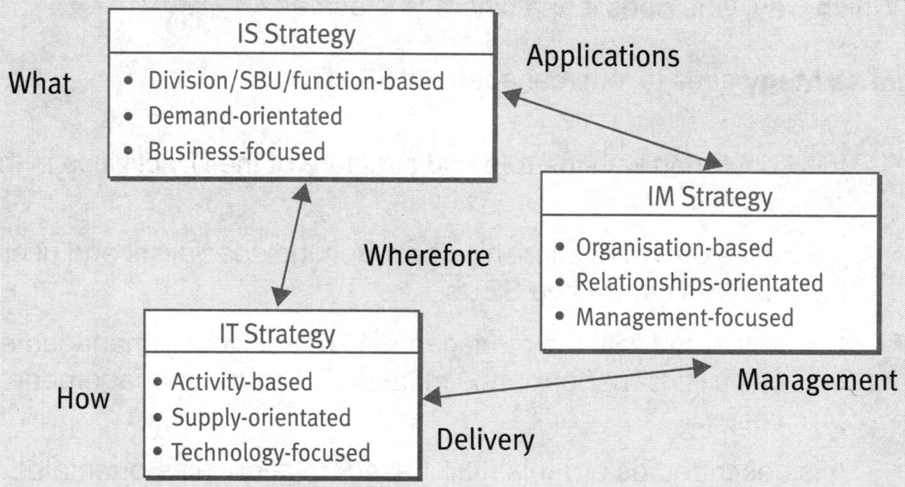

IS strategy

- **IS strategy** is concerned with aligning IS development with business needs and with seeking strategic advantage from IT. Formulated usually at the same level as product/market strategy for the SBU.
- Considered to be long-term in orientation. As the term 'systems' is often associated with tangible things (a central heating system, the Underground system, etc.) this part is often referred to as simply 'information strategy'.
- Refers to the interconnected organisational activities that gather and process data and provide information. Carried out by technology and/or human processes.
- The strategy is business-led and demand-orientated and is either supporting existing business strategies or developing new strategic choices.
- A strategy for information systems is concerned with identifying what information is needed by the organisation to enable it to achieve its business objectives. This includes considering the information needed at strategic, tactical and operational levels and the ways in which those levels of information should interconnect and interact.
- An effective IS strategy may be formed with the key objectives of using the information resource and generating new businesses.
- The strength of this type of strategy rests on it being demand-orientated where the managers of the divisions, business units or departments communicate their needs to the wider organisation.
- IS strategies must be business-driven and capable of delivering tangible benefits, e.g. increased productivity, enhanced profits and perhaps a reduction in the workforce.

IM strategy

'Which way, who does it and where is it located?'

IM strategy aims to 'put management into IT'.

- It is concerned with the role and structure of the IT activities in the organisation.
- It focuses on the relationships between the specialists and users and between the centre and SBUs.
- It is concerned with the management controls for IT, management responsibilities, performance measurement and management processes.
- It is described as organisation-based, relationships-orientated and management focused.
- Information management is a highly complex activity, concerned with:
  - identifying the sources of the information that are needed
  - collecting that information in appropriate formats
  - storing information
  - facilitating existing methods of using information
  - identifying new ways of using information
  - ensuring that information can be accessed by all who need it (but **only** by those people).

The burgeoning financial investment in IT provides the impetus for organisations to seek more effective control over the range of IT activities. In this context, IS and IT strategies can only be implemented if they are managed. Earl outlines the four tasks of information management:

(1) **Planning** – involves the integration of IS and IT strategies with other decision-making processes.

(2) **Organisation** – involves issues of decentralisation and centralisation of the IT function, the formation of steering committees, management education and training, reporting procedures and the responsibilities of IT managers.

(3) **Control** – issues relate to the relationship between IT and finance. Key management activities are performance measurement and investment appraisal of IT.

(4) **Technology** – is related to priorities of the IT strategy, e.g. the design and development of methodologies for IT, security practices and data management techniques.

Areas that underpin the formation of the IM strategy are:

- Information and technology need to be managed as efficiently and effectively as other resources.
- The organisational, business and management impact of IT requires these resources to be managed as an integral part of the organisation.
- The information function is too important to be managed without some formalisation when the business strategies are increasingly dependent on or created by IT.

IT strategy

IT strategy is described as activity-based, supply-orientated and technology-focused.

Information technology (IT) refers to the resources used to manage information:

- hardware and software used for everyday data processing
- communication
- office automation
- production automation.

IT describes any 'kit' concerned with the capture, storage, transmission, presentation or interpretation (e.g. by a robot) of information.

Earl writes that the architecture is a framework for making technological decisions and therefore must help firms to determine how the various elements or pieces of the IT jigsaw fit together.

The task of creating architectures can be justified by:

- Architecture provides a framework and a mechanism to consider and design interfaces and integration.
- Architecture provides a framework for resolving and reviewing technology choices over time.
- Architecture provides a structure for implementing the IS needs of the organisation.

The need for information systems strategies

Many organisations have historically viewed their IT and information systems as a necessary resource, but one that was not strategically significant. Nowadays, this attitude has changed as businesses have realised the value of having an IT strategy that fits into the overall corporate strategy.

The reasons for having an IT/IS strategy include:

- The cost of IT/IS is very high in many businesses. Without high-level management, there is a risk of costly mistakes.
- Strong IT/IS systems will help the business to create and maintain a competitive advantage.
- IT is fast-moving. By managing it strategically, a business can take advantage of new opportunities and technology as it becomes available.
- IT/IS systems are often expected by key stakeholders – for instance, many customers will expect a business to have a website. Failure to have reliable IT/IS systems may upset these stakeholders.

3 Information technology – the strategic context

Business strategy and information strategy

This section looks at IT/IS strategy in the context of the strategic planning tools met in earlier chapters.

Unlike many other resources, IS/IT evolves very quickly and will often play a large part in determining corporate strategy. On a SWOT analysis IS/IT can appear in any of the four quadrants and the appropriate responses have to be made. For example:

- **Strength:** A business has a very advanced IS/IT system that allows it to respond flexibly to orders while maintaining a low cost base.
- **Weakness:** An organisation's system is in disarray and customers are becoming irritated by its inability to deliver the proper goods on time.
- **Opportunity:** Set up new internet site that allows customers to buy over the Web.
- **Threat:** A competitor has spent heavily on IS/IT and can offer very high levels of service as a result.

e.g

Illustration 1 – Information technology - the strategic context

MP3 sound compression, the internet and fast broadband connections have forced companies like Sony and EMI to reassess their music-retailing strategies. Technology is a threat to these companies.

IS/IT and Porter's Five Forces

To analyse the SWOT factors relating to IS/IT, it can be useful to consider how IS/IT can be used to counter Porter's five forces so as to help an organisation have a more comfortable existence than some of its competitors.

- **Rivalry:** Use IT to reduce the effects of tough competition, for example by building strong relationships with customers and lowering costs.
- **Threat of new entrants:** Sophisticated IT applications are expensive, slow to develop and technically challenging. All of these are barriers to entry.
- **Supplier pressure:** Use IT to find new suppliers. Use IT to automatically rotate orders between suppliers. Compare prices on the internet.
- **Customer pressure:** Use IT to improve customer service, for example by allowing on-line ordering.
- **Threat of substitutes:** Use computer-aided design and manufacturing to develop new products first.

IT/IS and Porter's Five Forces

Porter's five forces model may be used to help clarify the overall business strategy. The model provides a framework to discuss areas where information technology and systems can yield competitive advantage. The advantages may be in defending the organisation against the forces or by attacking and influencing them in its favour.

Management should use the model to determine which of the forces poses a threat to the future success of the organisation. By ranking these threats in terms of intensity and immediacy, the most critical can then be considered in terms of how information technology or systems can be used to gain advantage or avoid disadvantage.

Threat of entry – new entrants into a market will bring extra capacity and intensify competition. The strength of the threat from new entrants will depend upon the strength of the barriers to entry and the likely response of existing competition to a new entrant. IT can have two possible roles to counteract the threat.

- *Defensively*, by creating barriers that new entrants to the market find difficult to overcome. IT can increase economies of scale by using computer-controlled production methods, requiring a similar investment in the technology of new entrants. Another defensive move is to colonise the distribution channels by tying customers and suppliers into the supply chain or the distribution chain. The harder the service is to emulate, the higher the barrier is for new entrants.

- *Offensively*, by breaking down the barriers to entry. An example is the use of telephone banking, which reduces the need to establish a branch network. Automated teller machines (ATMs) created new distribution channels enabling 'bank branches' to be set up in airports, out-of-town supermarkets and other areas where there are many potential customers. These machines provided not only expansion of the total market, but also a low-cost method of overcoming the barriers to entry in the areas where the cost of entry was high and space was at a premium.

Intensity of competitive rivalry – this is rivalry between firms making similar products, or offering the same services, and selling them in the same market. The most intense rivalry is where the business is more mature and the growth has slowed down.

IT can be used to compete. Cost leadership can be exploited by IT, for example, where IT is used to support just-in-time (JIT) systems. Alternatively IT can be used as a collaborative venture, changing the basis of competition by setting up new communications networks and forming alliances with complementary organisations for the purpose of information sharing. When Thomson Holidays introduced its on-line reservation system into travel agents' offices, it changed the basis of competition, allowing customers to ask about holiday availability and special deals and book a holiday in one visit to the travel agent.

Threat of substitute products – this threat applies both between industries (e.g. rail travel with bus travel and private car) and within an industry (e.g. long-life milk as substitute for delivered fresh milk). In many cases IS themselves are the substitute product. Word-processing packages are a substitute for typewriters.

IT-based products can be used to imitate existing goods as in electronic keyboards and organs. In the case of computer games, IT has formed the basis of a new leisure industry.

Computer-aided design and computer-aided manufacture (CAD/CAM) have helped competitors to bring innovative products to the market more quickly than in the past.

Interactive information systems add value by providing an extra service to an existing product. An example of this is provided by ICI's 'Counsellor', an expert system that advises farmers on disease control. It analyses data input by the farmer on areas such as crop varieties grown, soil type and previous history of disease and recommends fungicides or other suitable ICI products to solve the farmer's problems.

The threat from substitutes can be minimised by ensuring that an organisation develops a product before its rivals and then protects that product for a number of years by means of patents. This approach is widely used in the pharmaceutical and biotech industries where specialist software is now widely used in the drug discovery process, enabling drugs to be developed that target specific human and animal diseases.

Bargaining power of customers – the bargaining power of customers can be affected by using IT to create switching costs and 'lock' the buyer into products and services. The switching costs may be in both cash terms and operational inconvenience terms. For example, PCs run under Microsoft operating systems are not very efficient when using non-Microsoft application software.

Another form of locking customers in is to develop customer information systems that inform the organisation about the customer's behaviour, purchases and characteristics. This information enables the organisation to target customers in terms of direct marketing and other forms of incentive such as loyalty schemes, where methods of rewarding customer loyalty by giving them 'preferred customer' status are used. If a clothing retailer is launching a new collection it can offer its loyal customers a private viewing. Some airlines have deals such as frequent flyers and air miles as incentives.

The IT techniques at play here include 'data warehousing' – the collection and storage of large volumes of customer information on spending and purchasing patterns, social group, family make-up, etc. This then allows for 'data mining' – the extraction of relevant data from the warehouse as the source for target marketing drives. It was reported recently that Tesco, the UK's largest supermarket group, was mining its customer data to identify customers over the age of 60 who regularly purchased children's clothes, food and toys – possibly leading to a marketing push aimed at grandparents.

Bargaining power of suppliers – the bargaining power of suppliers, and hence their ability to charge higher prices, will be influenced by:

- the degree to which switching costs apply and substitutes are available
- the presence of one or two dominant suppliers controlling prices
- the products offered having a uniqueness of brand, technical performance or design not available elsewhere.

Reducing the suppliers' power to control the supply can erode this power. Where an organisation is dependent on components of a certain standard in a certain time, IT can provide a purchases database that enables easy scanning of prices from a number of suppliers. Suppliers' power can be shared so that the supplier and the organisation both benefit from performance improvements. The Ford Motor Company set up CAD links with its suppliers with the intention of reducing the costs of design specification and change. Both the time taken and the error rate were reduced because specifications did not have to be rekeyed into the suppliers' manufacturing tools.

How IT can play a role in generic strategies

IS/IT and Porter's generic strategies

Porter identified three generic strategies for dealing with the competitive forces. The two basic strategies are overall cost leadership and differentiation. The third strategy – a focus strategy – concentrates on a particular segment of a product line or geographical market – a niche. If it is known which strategy an organisation is currently using to promote their products and/or services, it should be possible to define a role for IS to enhance that strategy.

- **Overall cost leadership** is about competing by offering products or services at low cost and value for money. The emphasis is on cost reduction. For example, driving down inventory levels, with the assistance of IT for supply chain planning and scheduling, can reduce costs. Sales forecasting software that can be fed into manufacturing resources planning applications can be used in shop floor planning and scheduling applications to increase efficiency.
- **Differentiation** is about showing that your product or service is different from those of your competitors through, for example, brand image, customer service or design. A way of differentiating may be to make the ordering process as easy and flexible as possible. This can be done by providing on-line information services to identify the most appropriate product or service, followed up by a simple on-line ordering process. Where the differentiation is by customisation, CAD (computer-aided design) can reduce costs effectively.
- **Focus.** This strategy concentrates on a niche market, e.g. a particular buyer group, market, geographic area, segment or product line. The opportunities for IS/IT include providing access to customer information, trends and competitors so as to maximise competitive thrust and exclude competitors.

IT/IS and the value chain

IT/IS can impact the value chain in a number of different ways:

	Examples
Inbound logistics	• Stock control – MRP, ERP, JIT • Automated warehousing – Bar-coding systems • Virtual warehouses – several outlets, each connected to a system which indicates the total amount of stock available at different sites
Operations	• Robots – automate some of the process • CAM – computer aided manufacturing – production control, material and capacity planning • CIM – computer integrated manufacturing – machine tools, automated guided vehicles
Outbound logistics	• Automated warehousing – bar-coding systems • Order processing • Vehicle scheduling
Sales & marketing	• Customer databases – market segmentation, habits, trends • Electronic marketing • EPOS • CRM
Services	• Remote servicing • Computer scheduling of repairs • Expert systems • FAQ
Procurement	• EDI, e-procurement • Extranets
HR management	• Workforce planning • CBT
Technology development	• CAD – computer aided design • Design of extranets/intranets/Web-based products

Infrastructure	• Collaborative workflow • Intranets • Electronic scheduling • Office automation systems • ERP – enterprise resource planning – these systems are used for identifying and planning the enterprise-wide resources needed to record, produce, distribute and account for customer orders.

Test your understanding 1

Consider how an estate agent could use IS/IT to improve its competitive position.

The criticality of IT – McFarlan's grid

To assess the criticality of IT to the organisation, McFarlan's strategic grid can be used to identify the current and future dependence on information systems (IS).

Strategic impact of future systems

Strategic impact of current systems	Low	High
Low	**SUPPORT** Applications that improve management and performance but are not critical to the business	**TURNAROUND** (or high potential) Applications that may be of future strategic importance
High	**FACTORY** Applications that are critical to sustaining existing business	**STRATEGIC** Applications that are critical for future success

McFarlan's grid

(a) **Support**

- Information systems (IS) have a support role - a necessity to the working of the organisation. IS have little relevance to the organisation's existing or future success.
- May include accounting operations and payroll but there are no new developments which can contribute significantly to the competitiveness of the organisation.
- There is usually a low level of senior management involvement as the commitment to IS planning is low.
- Such organisations are not characterised by their high investment in IT and it is unlikely that IT plays a significant part in the strategic planning process.
- Earl cites a cement manufacturing company as an example in this sector. Information technology may be used to speed up administration and make occasional improvements to the processes but it is not vital or critical to the manufacture or distribution of cement.

(b) **Factory**

- The organisation depends heavily on IS for operations. However, there is little scope for future development and further IT developments are not likely to add to their competitive edge.
- McFarlan maintains that strategic goal setting and linkage of IS to the corporate plan are not too important if IT has a factory role. IT is critical to the current operation but not to the overall strategic direction.
- Some airlines and retailers would come into this category; Earl mentions a steelworks with an on-line real-time system for controlling production. Even one hour of disruption to these organisations' booking systems or order-processing systems could fundamentally damage their competitive performance.

(c) **Turnaround**

- Existing IT is not too important but future developments are likely to have a significant impact. Companies recognise the growing importance of IT as a means to improve competitive position.
- Possible applications have a high potential to contribute to the organisation's strategic objectives. For example, a professional accounting college.

- The current IT climate has forced firms to reassess their operations and the phrase 'automate or liquidate' can be used to sum up the approach companies need to take in order to stay in business. Significant change is expected.
- Earl identifies that IT budgets are being increased, leadership is coming from the boards and IT directors appear in the governance profile.
- E-commerce has opened up new possibilities for many industries. Consider the selling of books on-line and computer games. Insurance brokers, travel agents – the list goes on.

(d) **Strategic**

- Existing and future IT developments are at the heart of the organisation's success. These firms need significant amounts of planning as the firm would be at a disadvantage if the information processing did not perform well.
- They have applications which they rely on for the smooth running of their day-to-day activities and they have future developments which are vital to their competitive success and are integral to the organisation's strategic objectives. The future is shaped by potential IT activity. A substantial IT budget can be expected.
- Banks and insurance companies are typical of this sector. Earl cites a credit card company and a major bank as examples.

e.g

Illustration 2 – Information technology - the strategic context

Many insurance companies used IS/IT in a support role – accounting, sending out premium renewal notices, etc. The industry was very paper-based with customers submitting hand-written claims, accident diagrams and police reports. To save costs and give better customer service, many insurance companies now scan in documents so that they are available to call up on screen. Paper files no longer have to be moved around the office, with the potential of being mislaid. The role of IT in insurance companies went from support, to turnaround to strategic.

Forces that drive an organisation around the grid

Forces that drive an organisation round the strategic grid may be internal or external.

- Internal forces will be concerned with matching the potential of information technology to the organisation's operations and strategy, such as a decision to improve productivity. Porter's value chain is a good model to identify internal forces.
- External forces will be associated with changes in the competitive environment, such as actions of competitors, suppliers or customers. Porter's five forces model can be used to provide a framework to discuss areas where information technology and systems can yield competitive advantage. The advantages may be in defending the organisation against the competitive forces or by attacking and influencing them in its favour.

4 E-business

The meaning and use of e-business

E-commerce is described as 'all electronically mediated information exchanges between an organisation and its external stakeholders'. An e-commerce transaction can be considered from two perspectives.

E-business has been defined as the transformation of key business processes through the use of internet technologies.

So, e-commerce is a subset of e-business. The most generic description of e-commerce is trading on the internet, buying and selling products and services online.

Porter suggested three ways in which IS/IT in general can affect the competitive environment and an organisation's ability to compete. Though these points apply to IS/IT in general, they are particularly important when considering e-business.

- New businesses might become possible. For example, auction sites and photo-album sites.
- The industry structure can be changed. For example, in the music business it can be argued that the large CD publishers have less power because music can be self-published on the internet.
- IS/IT can provide an organisation with competitive advantage by providing new ways of operating. For example, airlines save money by encouraging internet bookings.

Terminology – buy and sell-side e-commerce

- 'Buy-side' e-commerce focuses on transactions between a purchasing organisation and its suppliers.
- 'Sell-side' e-commerce focuses on transactions between a purchasing organisation and its customers.

Stages of e-business

The stages of e-business can be described as:

Stage		Characteristics
1	Web presence	Static or dynamic web pages but no transactions are carried out. Would show information about the organisation, products, contact details, FAQs (Frequently Asked Questions). Faster updates are possible than with paper-based information and could be cheaper than paper-based catalogues.
2	E-commerce	Buying and selling transactions using e-commerce. Might cut out middlemen, but there is probably no fundamental change in the nature of the business.
3	Integrated e-commerce	Integrated e-commerce. For example, information can be gathered about each customer's buying habits. This can allow the organisation to target customers very precisely and to begin to predict demand.
4	E-business	E-business is now fundamental to the business strategy and may well determine the business strategy

This model helps businesses to understand where they are in the process of e-business, and this will help them to decide where to go next with further development.

The categories of e-business functions are shown below:

		Delivery by: Business	Delivery by: Consumer
Exchange initiated by:	Business	B2B Business models, e.g. VerticalNet	B2C Business models, e.g. Amazon.com
	Consumer	C2B Business models, e.g. Priceline.com	C2C Business models, e.g. eBay.com

- B2B (business to business). For example, a supermarket IS automatically placing orders into suppliers' IS.
- B2C (business to consumer). Selling over the internet – books, flights, music, etc.
- C2B (consumer to business). Some internet sites display a selection of suppliers' offerings from which the user can choose. A model that largely depends on the internet.
- C2C (consumer to consumer). Auction sites, such as eBay, putting consumers in touch with each other. Amazon does the same by offering second-hand books. This model largely depends on the internet.

Benefits of e-business

Most companies employ e-business to achieve the following:

- Cost reduction – e.g. lower overheads, cheaper procurement
- increased revenue – e.g. online sales, better CRM
- better information for control – e.g. monitoring website sales
- increased visibility
- enhanced customer service – e.g. via extranets
- improved marketing – e.g. emailing customers with special offers
- market penetration – e.g. even small suppliers can gain a global presence via the internet
- the combination of the above should be to enhance the company's competitive advantage.

e.g

Illustration 3 – E-business

Many supermarkets now offer a home-delivery service. Over the internet, inventory lists are displayed for customers who fill an electronic 'shopping trolley' and proceed to payment and checkout. A delivery period is chosen (say 4pm–6pm the following day). Supermarket staff pick the goods chosen and pack them for delivery.

Standard shopping lists can be set up by users to speed up the process. The standard lists can be amended each time (for example, extra milk, but no carrots).

Barriers to e-business

Barriers to e-business can be seen in both the organisation itself and in its suppliers and customers. They include:

- technophobia
- security concerns
- set-up costs
- running costs
- limited opportunities to exploit e-business
- limited IT resources in-house
- customers not likely to be interested in e-business.

Barriers to e-business

- Technophobia. Senior managers are distrustful and sceptical about the alleged benefits of e-business.
- Security concerns about hackers and electronic fraud.
- Set-up costs. Simple, static pages are cheap to set up, but dynamic pages, linking to e-commerce systems and databases, with impressive design values are expensive to set up.
- Running costs. Renting space on a web-server. Also, maintenance of websites is very important as most users are very unforgiving about out-of-date sites. Updating, say with special offers, is also needed to encourage return visits, perhaps linked to email campaigns.

- Limited opportunities to exploit e-business. Some businesses (such as selling books) are more suitable for e-business than others (such as selling carpets).
- Limited IT resources in-house (e.g. a lack of staff skills creating staff resistance) so recruitment is needed or all development and maintenance has to be subcontracted.
- Customers not likely to be interested in e-business (e.g. firms targeting retired pensioners).

Intranets and extranets

Intranets are internal internets. They exist inside the organisation only, using website and browser technology to display information.

Commonly they contain:

- information about customers
- information about products
- information about competitors
- news/updates
- procedure manuals.

However, there's no reason why accounting information cannot be delivered over intranets.

Extranets are intranets that are connected to external intranets.

For example, a supplier could give customers access to their order processing system so that orders can be placed and tracked. It is when these types of external connection are made that e-business can begin to produce spectacular results.

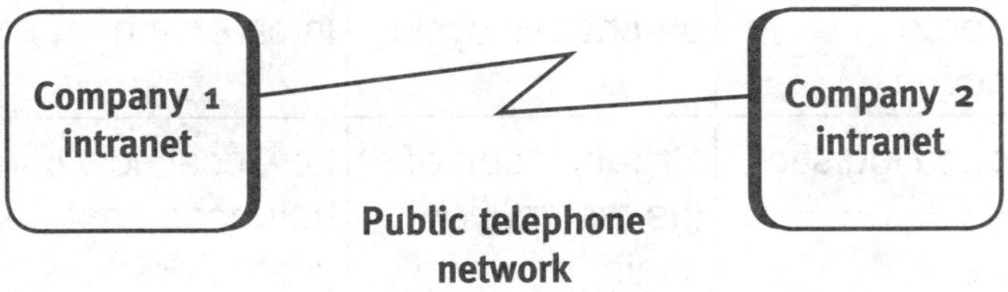

Other requirements needed to deliver an e-business strategy

Connection to the internet will not, of itself, deliver e-business. Suitable hardware, software and business processes have to be in place. Here are some examples of how e-business could affect various business areas.

Business area	Where e-business could impact	Strategic aim
Research and development	Internet used for research purposes. Access to research databases. Access to patent databases.	To be a leader in innovation. To develop unique, differentiated products
Design	Computer-aided design	Fast production of new designs and products. CAD will make designs cheaper (cost leading) and faster (differentiation)
Manufacturing/ service provision	Computer-aided manufacturing Just-in-time inventories	Flexible, low cost, but tailored to customers' requirements
Communication with customers	Website and email	
Inbound logistics	Organisation of the supply chain	Low cost, low inventory balances, flexible manufacturing
The buy-side e-commerce transactions	Automating the purchases cycle	Low cost as less human intervention
Outbound logistics	Organisation of the distribution chain	Low cost, low inventory balances, fast delivery to customers
The sell-side e-commerce transactions	Automating the sales cycle	Low cost as less human intervention. Greater accuracy

Making websites interactive

One of the most effective things you can do with your website is to give users power over it. Give them choices, tools and features that encourage them to interact with the site and provide them with a sense of control over it.

- Search: Provide users with the ability to search your website for words, phrases and/or provide them with key topics from which to choose. Consider in what format the results are to be presented.
- Online forms: How many, number of fields in each, what needs to be verified before the user submits the form – e.g. have they completed the field for email address?
- 'Members only' section: Is there a section that can only be accessed via a username and password? Where are the usernames and passwords to be stored? How will you handle people who forget their password?
- Interactive questionnaires/surveys/polls: How many, how long, how presented? What will you do with the information provided by the users?
- Animations: How can you (should you) use Flash or other programming devices to bring life into your site and illustrate products and services?
- Subscription email lists: What can users subscribe to by way of email lists, such as e-newsletters?
- Links to other sites: How many and what tools are to be employed during maintenance to check automatically on the veracity of the link?
- Downloadable files: PDFs, images, audio files – how many, in what format, with what restrictions?
- Contact us: What contact details should be on the site – e.g. email, telephone, street address?
- Site map: What is the site map of the website to look like? Just text as links or is a diagram preferred?
- Text-only version of the site: Will you need a text-only version of the website for customers who are visually impaired or with a slow/expensive connection?
- Multilingual requirements: How many languages? How much of the site is to be multilingual? At what point are users to nominate which language they want to view the site in – e.g. home page, a splash page?

- Provision for printing and bookmarking (i.e. allowing users to store the website address in their browser's memory or 'favourites' section). Are users to be able to bookmark specific pages or is the home page sufficient? Do you want any special print function other than the default function supplied by the browser?

5 Latest developments in e-business: Web 2.0

"Web 2.0" refers to a perceived second generation of web development and design that facilitates communication, secure information sharing, interoperability, and collaboration on the World Wide Web.

Although the term Web 2.0 suggests a new version of the World Wide Web, it does not refer to an update to any technical specifications, but rather to cumulative changes in the ways software developers and end-users utilize the Web.

Whereas Web 1.0 was primarily concerned with the web as a source of information, Web 2.0 is seen as the "participatory web" and includes the emergence of web-based communities, hosted services, and applications such as social-networking sites (e.g. Facebook), video-sharing sites (e.g. YouTube), wikis and blogs.

These can offer opportunities to firms in a number of different ways:

- **Advertising**

  For example, viral advertising via popular sites such as Facebook and YouTube.

- **Software as a service (SaaS):** With SaaS customers only pay for software when they need it. The service is provided on-demand via a web browser and is highly attractive to smaller users who cannot justify buying a full version of the software.

  For example, Fortiva offer an e-mail archiving service that complies with US legal requirements.

- **Mashups:** The term "mashup" originated in music where artists would combine parts from different songs to create a new track. The web equivalent is where developers can now mix, match, reuse, and morph web content, data, and services.

  For example, estate agent websites can now include interactive maps where users can see precisely where available properties are and also check local government information on school catchment areas and environmental issues such as flooding.

- **Competence syndication:** Web syndication is where firms make a portion of their website available to other firms, sites or individual subscribers. Competence syndication is where the different parties benefit from each other's competencies.

  For example, in 2001 Amazon opened zShops, providing virtual shelf space to online competitors. They could sell their goods through the same system Amazon used, paying a listing fee plus commissions on sales.

- **Using global network effects:** The network effect is the effect that one user of a good or service has on the value of that product to other people. A good example of this is the online auction site eBay – the more people use it the more attractive membership becomes.

  For example, IBM has capitalised on competencies across the world by dramatically changing their business model. Rather than trying to develop their own proprietary operating system to compete with Windows or Linux, IBM chose to get involved in the open-source movement by including open source software, contributing to the open-source community and adapting the open-source philosophy. IBM estimates that this alone has saved the company $1 billion per year.

Test your understanding 2 – Good Sports

Good Sports Limited is an independent sports goods retailer owned and operated by two partners, Alan and Bob. The sports retailing business in the UK has undergone a major change over the past ten years. First of all the supply side has been transformed by the emergence of a few global manufacturers of the core sports products, such as training shoes and football shirts. This consolidation has made them increasingly unwilling to provide good service to the independent sportswear retailers too small to buy in sufficiently large quantities. These independent retailers can stock popular global brands, but have to order using the Internet and have no opportunity to meet the manufacturer's sales representatives. Secondly, UK's sportswear retailing has undergone significant structural change with the rapid growth of a small number of national retail chains with the buying power to offset the power of the global manufacturers. These retail chains stock a limited range of high-volume branded products and charge low prices the independent retailer cannot hope to match.

Good Sports has survived by becoming a specialist niche retailer catering for less popular sports such as cricket and hockey. They are able to offer the specialist advice and stock the goods that their customers want. Increasingly since 2000 Good Sports has become aware of the growing impact of e-business in general, and e-retailing in particular. They employed a specialist website designer and created an online purchasing facility for their customers. The results were less than impressive, with the Internet search engines not picking up the company website. The seasonal nature of Good Sports' business, together with the variations in sizes and colours needed to meet an individual customer's needs, meant that the sales volumes were insufficient to justify the costs of running the site.

Bob, however, is convinced that developing an e-business strategy suited to the needs of the independent sports retailer such as Good Sports will be key to business survival. He has been encouraged by the growing interest of customers in other countries to the service and product range they offer. He is also aware of the need to integrate an e-business strategy with their current marketing, which to date has been limited to the sponsorship of local sports teams and advertisements taken in specialist sports magazines. Above all he wants to avoid head-on competition with the national retailers and their emphasis on popular branded sportswear sold at retail prices that are below the cost price at which Good Sports can buy the goods.

Required:

(a) Provide the partners with a short report on the advantages and disadvantages to Good Sports of developing an e-business strategy and the processes most likely to be affected by such a strategy.

(15 marks)

(b) Good Sports Limited has successfully followed a niche strategy to date. Assess the extent to which an appropriate e-business strategy could help support such a niche strategy.

(10 marks)

(Total: 25 marks)

Test your understanding 3 – H plc

H plc is a business that runs a national chain of high-street stores selling a wide range of furniture and household goods. While not a market leader, H has always traded profitably due to targeting the niche market for high-value, designer homewares.

H's revenues and profits have been static for several years and the directors are under pressure from investors to find ways of increasing shareholder returns.

The market for household goods is a saturated one, but the Sales Director (SD) has identified that H could start selling goods online. None of H's competitors have a significant online presence and H itself only has a basic website that lists locations of its stores.

The Managing Director is uncertain about this approach. He is aware that H has had problems implementing information systems in the past. Most recently, the company attempted to implement an online stock system, which would have allowed stores to check stock levels in other, nearby, H stores. This was in response to a number of customer requests.

The system was abandoned due to spiralling costs and problems with the software, which was written in-house by H plc's small IT department.

The SD feels that the problems with the earlier projects were caused by a lack of control. H plc has never employed an IT director and the SD has therefore recommended that if H decides to expand into online retailing, this role will need to be filled.

Required:

(a) Using H plc as an example, distinguish between the different levels of information systems strategy

(6 marks)

(b) Identify the problems that H plc may encounter when launching its online retail website

(10 marks)

(c) Explain the need for IT to be a strategic decision within H plc

(9 marks)

(Total: 25 marks)

6 Summary

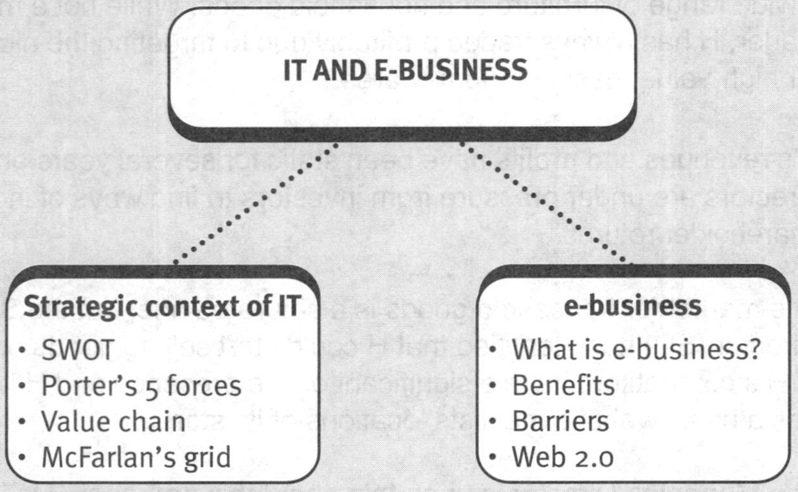
IT AND E-BUSINESS
Strategic context of IT
• SWOT
• Porter's 5 forces
• Value chain
• McFarlan's grid
e-business
• What is e-business?
• Benefits
• Barriers
• Web 2.0

Test your understanding answers

Test your understanding 1

All of the following technologies could help either to save costs or provide enhanced (and differentiated) service.

- Use of digital cameras to photograph property. The images would then be made available over the web.
- Video of properties that can be downloaded or viewed over the web.
- Graphics programs designed to make floor diagrams easy to produce.
- Standard descriptive phrases ('deceptively large' – or do they mean 'deceptively small'?) that can be used for property write-ups.
- A database of properties, searchable by price, bedrooms, type, area, age, etc.
- Properties linked to an interactive map.
- A database of recent property prices in the area.
- Buyer requirements database.
- Automatic mailing lists to circulate information to buyers.
- Electronic appointments system.
- Computerised accounting system used for property management.

Test your understanding 2 – Good Sports

GOOD SPORTS

(a) **To:** Good Sports Limited

From: xxxxx

E–business strategy

Clearly, the markets that Good Sports operates in are being affected by the development of e-business and its experiences to date are mixed to say the least. In many ways the advantages and disadvantages of e-business are best related to the benefit the customer gets from the activity.

- First, through integrating and accelerating business processes, e-business technologies enable response and delivery times to be speeded up.
- Second, there are new business opportunities for information-based products and services.
- Third, websites can be linked with customer databases and provide much greater insights into customer buying behaviour and needs.
- Fourth, there is far greater ability for interaction with the customer, which enables customisation and a dialogue to be developed.
- Finally, customers may themselves form communities able to contact one another.

There is considerable evidence to show how small operators like Good Sports are able to base their whole strategy on e-business and achieve high rates of growth. The key to Good Sports' survival is customer service – in strategic terms they are very much niche marketers supplying specialist service and advice to a small section of the local market. The nature of the business means that face-to-face contact is crucial in moving customers from awareness to action (AIDA – awareness, interest, desire and action). There are therefore limits to the ability of e-business to replace such contact.

Yours, etc.

(b) Good Sports has pursued a conscious niche or focus differentiation strategy, seeking to serve a local market in a way that isolates it from the competition of the large national sports good retailers competing on the basis of supplying famous brands at highly competitive prices. Does it make strategic sense for Good Sports to make the heavy investment necessary to supply goods online? Will this enhance its ability to supply its chosen market?

In terms of price, e-business is bringing much greater price transparency – the problem for companies like Good Sports is that customers may use their expertise to research into a particular type and brand of sports equipment and then simply search the Internet for the cheapest supply. Porter, in an article examining the impact of the Internet, argues that rather than making strategy obsolete it has in fact made it more important. The Internet has tended to weaken industry profitability and made it more difficult to hold onto operational advantages. Choosing which customers you serve and how are even more critical decisions.

However, the personal advice and performance side of the business could be linked to new ways of promoting the product and communicating with the customer. The development of customer communities referred to above could be a real way of increasing customer loyalty. The partners are anxious to avoid head-on competition with the national retailers. One way of increasing the size and strength of the niche they occupy is to use the Internet as a means of targeting their particular customers and providing insights into the use and performance of certain types of equipment by local clubs and users. There is considerable scope for innovation that enhances the service offered to their customers. As always there is a need to balance the costs and benefits of time spent. The Internet can provide a relatively cost-effective way of providing greater service to their customers. There is little in the scenario to suggest they have reached saturation point in their chosen niche market. Overall there is a need for Good Sports to decide what and where its market is and how this can be improved by the use of e-business.

Test your understanding 3 – H plc

(a) **Distinguish between the levels of IS strategy within H plc**

According to Earl, there are three levels of information systems strategy.

Information systems (IS) strategy

In the scenario, H plc is under pressure to grow its returns to investors. This is an over-riding business objective.

IS strategy involves deciding on which systems, broadly, will enable H plc to achieve this objective. The SD's suggestion to expand into online retailing is an example of this.

Information management (IM) strategy

This looks at the roles of management and other members of staff within the overall IS strategy – in other words, who controls and uses the information systems.

For H plc, it will involve deciding on how existing staff will be used in the new IT system, such as who will be responsible for inventory data entry. It will also include the recruitment of an IT director to oversee the process.

Information technology (IT) strategy

This level looks at the practical application of the IS strategy. Given that H plc has decided to expand into online retail, IT strategy will specify the technological requirements of these new systems.

For H plc, this may include new hardware, such as computers and servers. Inventory control and website design software will also be required. This will need to be written internally or purchased externally.

(b) **Identification of problems H plc may encounter when launching online**

As with any major project, there will be problems that H will face with its proposed move into online retailing. These may include:

Setup and running costs

Investors in H are keen to see an increase in their returns. However, the cost of setting up and running an online retailing system may be significant.

H plc will need to determine whether the additional profit it can make by reaching new customers online will exceed these costs. Certainly in the short term the setup costs may well mean that shareholder returns fall.

Any further investment in staff will also increase the IT costs to the company.

Lack of in–house IT resources

The business currently lacks an IT director to take control of the project. While the company may be able to hire someone quickly to fill this role, they will lack experience of H's business by the time the new project is started.

The current IT department is small. They may well lack the time or skills for a project of this magnitude. This indicates further investment will be required to hire additional staff or to buy the new systems from external software houses.

It should also be noted that an online retail system would require H plc to have precise information about its stock levels. It currently does not have an automated inventory control system as this was abandoned.

Lack of customer interest

It is always possible that H's customers will not be interested in purchasing goods online. They may, for example, wish to try out furniture or physically see it for themselves rather than buying it online.

It is unclear from the scenario whether the SD has undertaken any market research. This would be vital before making the decision about beginning online retailing, to avoid launching an expensive website that fails to attract customers.

Technophobia

Given the lack of IT currently in place at H, employees may not see the need for new IT systems and may resist being retrained.

In addition, the MD has expressed concerns about the launch of a new IT system, given the problems H has faced in the past. A project of this scale will require management support in order to be successful.

Security concerns

As H will be processing transactions through its website, it will need to ensure that customers are protected from viruses and that their details are protected from hackers.

(c) **Explanation of the need for IT to be a strategic decision in H plc.**

It is crucial that H has information systems represented at the strategic or board level for several reasons:

Cost of IT/IS

Setting up an online retail store will involve high levels of expenditure for H. There is the risk of costly mistakes if it is not carefully managed. This is evidenced by the failure of its inventory control system.

Failure of such a major project could have a significant impact on the company's financial position.

Competitive advantage

The market H operates in is described as saturated. It will be difficult for H to increase its market share unless it finds a way to differentiate itself.

If the website is a success, it will give H a competitive advantage over its rivals and as such it should be part of H's strategic decision–making process.

Stakeholders

Expansion of H is of great interest to H's shareholders. As such it is crucial that the directors monitor its progress.

In addition, customers are currently unable to check the stock of goods within H plc. They may be very interested in a system that would enable them to save unnecessary journeys into H's stores for goods that are not in stock.

Fast–moving

Technology is a fast-moving area and even if becomes a successful first mover in the market by selling online, competitors are likely to follow H into the online market.

As such, H's IT systems will need to be continually monitored and kept up-to-date to ensure it remains competitive.

chapter

12

Information for advantage and knowledge management

Chapter learning objectives

Lead	Component
D1. Evaluate the tools and processes of strategy implementation	(d) Advise managers on the development of strategies for knowledge management and information systems that support the organisation's strategic requirements

Indicative syllabus content

- The purpose and contents of information systems strategies, and the need for strategy complementary to the corporate and individual business strategies.
- Competing through exploiting information (rather than technology), e.g. use of databases to identify potential customers or market segments, and the management of data (warehousing and mining).

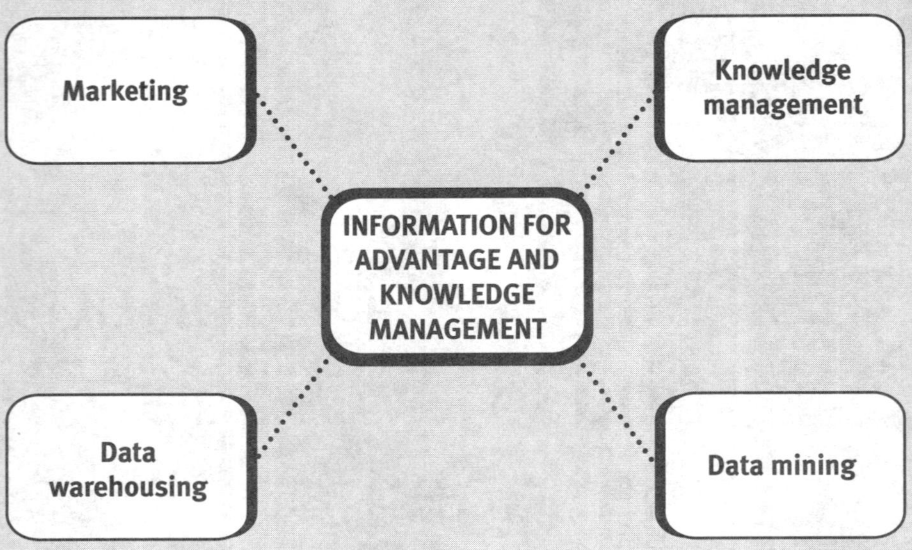

1 Marketing

In order to meet the critical success factors in target segments and develop sustainable competitive advantage over competitors, information is needed.

In chapter 3, the systematic gathering, recording and analysing of information about problems relating to the marketing of goods and services is described. Such marketing research is a crucial early stage in strategic planning.

The gathering of information is therefore an essential activity for a business in order to get to know their market and to remain ahead of the competition. Information is also required to monitor the success of any strategy.

Information issues

The two prime characteristics of information are relevance and reliability. The management accountant is involved in each.

Relevant information assists the decision-making process – the management accountant decides what is relevant.

Reliable information is as accurate as needed – the management accountant decides again and establishes control systems to ensure that accuracy is achieved.

Sources of information

Internal sources – considered to be more reliable as it is known:

- who provided the information
- when
- why
- what assumptions were used in its preparation.

Questions exist over relevance as there is likely to be:

- narrow focus
- cultural distortion of issues.

External sources – considered to be more relevant as a wider range of issues with less cultural distortion. However the 'who, why, when and what' is questionable this time as these are unknown factors.

2 Data warehousing

A data warehouse is a subject-oriented, integrated, time-variant, non-volatile collection of data in support of management's decision-making process.

Put more simply, it is a large relational database that collates a vast amount of data from a variety of sources and makes it available to end-users in an understandable fashion.

A data warehouse supports information processing by providing a solid platform of integrated, historical data from which analysis can be done.

It is:

- a database
- a data extraction tool
- a decision support system
- other analysis tools which extract data from the organisation's production database, reformat and load it into a database designed for querying with an on-line analytical processing systems (OLAP). OLAP allows users to dynamically extract pertinent summary information.

The conventional data warehousing model is a system in which a large centralised store of consolidated business data is maintained by constant updates from the operational systems (branches/stores).

Since operational data are likely to reside in a range of very different systems, e.g. cash register tapes, invoice printing systems and order entry systems, the process of collecting the data needs to be customised and automated. Each store or branch must be responsible for ensuring the timely and accurate delivery of this information. In enterprises where the information is managed centrally, the problem is simpler.

For very large enterprises, the act of centralising all data in a single data warehouse may not be feasible or may even be impossible.

The purpose of data warehousing

Data warehouses traditionally have three primary purposes:

(1) Presentation of standard reports and graphs, consolidating data from a variety of sources into a standard format.

(2) Enabling of comparisons between different factors – for example, how have customer buying habits changed over the last several years?

(3) To allow data mining (see below).

3 Data mining

Data mining is the analysis of data to unearth unsuspected or unknown relationships, patterns and associations.

There are many different definitions of data mining. Almost all of them involve using advanced analytical techniques to discover useful relationships in large databases. Some people's definition of data mining is linked with their definition of data warehousing. **Data warehouses are for storing data, not turning it into information, whereas data mining turns data into information.**

For example, the sales records for a particular brand of tennis racquet might, if sufficiently analysed and related to other market data, reveal a seasonal correlation with the purchase of golf equipment by the same people.

The process uses statistical techniques and technologies to discover relationships and then builds models based on them. Data mining results include:

- **Associations** – when one event can be correlated to another event, e.g. beer purchasers buy peanuts a certain percentage of the time.
- **Sequences** – one event leading to another later event, e.g. a rug purchase followed by a purchase of curtains.

- **Classification** – the recognition of patterns and a resulting new organisation of data, e.g. profiles of customers who make purchases.
- **Clustering** – finding and visualising groups of facts not previously known.
- **Forecasting** – simply discovering patterns in the data that can lead to predictions about the future.

There are two main kinds of models in data mining:

(1) **Predictive models** can be used to forecast explicit values, based on patterns determined from known results. For example, from a database of customers who have already responded to a particular offer, a model can be built that predicts which prospects are likely to respond to the same offer.

(2) **Descriptive models** describe patterns in existing data and are generally used to create meaningful subgroups such as demographic clusters. These could then be used for marketing purposes.

Benefits of data warehousing and data mining

- Faster transaction and query execution can provide competitive advantage. A data warehouse is a large database, regularly updated and organised to permit a high level of query activity. Not all organisations will have a need for this; it will depend on the organisation and what it does.
- With relatively small amounts of data, the specialist data warehouse software and hardware will not be required, as downloading subsets of data from production systems to PCs is a workable solution. However, many organisations need to manage large amounts of data which, when properly analysed, can provide information that leads to competitive advantage.

Disadvantages

- The systems used in different departments will often be incompatible, and that is likely to mean that data is in a wide variety of different formats.
- There are likely to be inconsistencies between different databases where duplicated items of data should, in theory, be identical, but in practice are not.
- The data will need to be analysed and 'cleansed' before it can be integrated into a warehouse. This will not be easy, quick or cheap to achieve.

- Incompatible systems may mean that most of the departments will need to be furnished with new hardware and software before they can use the data warehouse. This is likely to be expensive and disruptive to the day-to-day work of each department.
- Almost all staff who want to use the new system will need training.
- Individual departments may use data in widely different ways and require all manner of different reports. It could be very difficult to create a common interface that is capable of delivering information in every format that may be required. Report formats that are only needed in a single department may not be catered for, and this may cause resentment.
- As the new system proves its worth, more and more demands will be made of it, so ongoing maintenance, adequate network bandwidth, sufficient storage space, and highly flexible upgrade capability are all essential.
- With all data in a single main source, it is vital to ensure that effective back-up arrangements are made and strictly adhered to.

e.g

Illustration 1 – Tesco

Tesco is the UK's largest supermarket with a 30% market share. In addition it has global interests and is now the world's second most profitable retailer. One of the reasons for the company's success is its loyalty card, the Clubcard.

The Clubcard is used to gather information about the spending patterns of Tesco's customers. Around five billion pieces of information each week are captured, and this number is constantly growing.

This information is stored in an enormous search engine (a data warehouse) that can be accessed by Tesco and other select partners, such as Coca-Cola and Unilever. The information can be used to assess the success of new product launches as well as which demographics of customer are making the purchases.

The system also allows Tesco to tailor its special offers to particular segments of the market. For example, many families shop at several different supermarkets. Clearly, Tesco would prefer customers to only buy their groceries from its stores. To help it achieve this, it can identify common products that are 'missing' from a customer's shopping. They will then send the customer special offers to encourage the customer to buy these goods at Tesco.

At one Tesco store where this approach was adopted, turnover rose by 12%.

4 Knowledge management

Mayo defines knowledge management as the management of the information, knowledge and experience available to an organisation – its creation, capture, storage, availability and utilisation – in order that organisational activities build on what is already known and extend it further.

Knowledge management is a relatively new approach to business in which an organisation consciously and comprehensively gathers, organises, shares and analyses its knowledge to further its aims.

Where the knowledge resides

The intellectual capital can be divided between:

(1) **Human capital,** which comprises: human resources – the knowledge, skills and experience possessed by employees can be easily overlooked in times of crisis, just when it is most needed; this knowledge is vital to all service companies.

(2) **Structural capital**, which is in turn divided into:

- innovation capital – intellectual property
- customer capital – address lists and client records
- organisational capital – e.g. systems for processing policies and claims.

Implementing a knowledge management strategy

There are five main steps in the development and implementation of a knowledge management strategy.

(1) **Gaining top management support.** Like any major strategy, knowledge management will fail unless it has the clear support of the 'top team'.

(2) **Creating the technological infrastructure.** Hardware and software must be acquired and installed in order for the knowledge to be communicated and stored.

(3) **Creating the database structures.** Advanced database management systems may be required. These will need to be specifically designed for the type of knowledge the company is looking to capture.

(4) **Creating a sharing culture.** This involves convincing staff of the benefits, both to the organisation and to themselves, of sharing knowledge for the common good. This is often the most difficult stage.

(5) **Populating the databases and using the knowledge.** The knowledge must be captured and recorded and individuals trained and encouraged to use it.

The benefits of a knowledge management system

These will include:

- higher workforce motivation and reduction in inefficiencies
- increased ability to compete and add value
- a culture where employees are encouraged to innovate and use knowledge to improve efficiency.

Steve Jobs, one of the founders of Apple technology company, is quoted as saying:

'It doesn't make sense to hire smart people and then tell them what to do. We hired smart people so they could tell us what to do.'

Problems in implementing a knowledge-sharing system

- It is not always necessary to invest in expensive technology to address problems in information sharing: often the problem will arise because of organisational matters such as an **inappropriate organisation structure**.
- There may be some **technological barriers** to overcome, such as the need to roll out a suitable modern network across an organisation, if one is not in place already.
- There will be situations in which problems arise because of **incompatible systems** and working methods in different parts of the organisation.
- It is inevitable that some data will have to be **transferred into a new common format** and this can lead to errors, omissions and inconsistencies if not done with great care.
- In certain systems it is possible that **older information will not be held in digital form at all**, or not in a format that can easily be converted into a suitable modern equivalent. Examples include architect's drawings, medical notes written by hand and so on.
- A decision is needed about **how to archive this material**. Will individual older systems be maintained and thoroughly indexed, or will it be accepted that such material has to be recreated from paper records on an ad hoc basis, if it is ever needed? Will archives be held locally or centrally?
- There are **social barriers to information sharing**. For some staff the notion of making their information available to other staff in other offices may be difficult. They will have their own established and familiar methods of organising their information and may even refuse to change their current practices to fall in line with a centrally imposed system.

- There is likely to be some **demotivation amongst staff**. Some may resent having to give up a system that they know and like and learn a new one, especially if they are not given adequate training and adequate time to adapt.
- There may be **political issues and inter office rivalries.** Information is power and some staff may fear that their own status within the organisation will be impaired if they have to share the source of their power with others.

Appropriate systems

(1) Networks

Most organisations connect their PCs and other computers together in local area networks (LANs), enabling them to share data and peripherals such as printers.

LANs may be grouped together into 'work groups' which, in addition to sharing information and software facilities such as email, can run software such as groupware and/or an intranet.

LANs themselves are also being interconnected using sophisticated new hardware to create wide area networks (WANs), sometimes called enterprise networks.

(2) Groupware

Groupware is a generic term for software that helps work groups to collaborate on projects. For example a groupware system might have the following features for individual time management.

- a **scheduler** or **calendar** allowing users to timetable their activities for the day and plan meetings with others. It will also be able to generate reminders, for example when a deadline is approaching, or the date of a meeting
- an **address book**
- **to do** lists
- a **journal**. This can automatically record interactions with people involved in a project, such as e-mail messages, and record and time actions such as creating and working on files. The journal will keep track of all of this and is useful both as a record of work done and as a quick way of finding relevant files and messages without having to remember where each one is saved
- a **jotter** for jotting down notes as quick reminders of questions, ideas, and so on.

The advantage is that all this information is available at the touch of a button, rather than relying on Post-it notes, memo pads, hard-copy out-of-date address books, and company telephone directories.

(3) **Intranet**

An intranet is a private network that is contained within an organisation. It may consist of many interlinked local area networks and also use leased lines in the wide area network. Typically, an intranet includes connections through one or more gateway computers to the outside Internet.

The main objective of an intranet is to make information flow more freely by sharing company information and computing resources among employees.

(4) **Extranet**

An extranet is a private, secure extension of the enterprise via the corporate intranet. It allows the organisation to share part of its business information or operations with suppliers, customers, and other business partners using the Internet. For example, an organisation could connect its browser-based purchase order system to the product catalogue database on a supplier's intranet.

e.g

Illustration 2

Modern IT systems have made sharing and distributing knowledge easier.

The UK government has a massive project in progress to computerise the health records of every UK resident. The aim is that a patient's medical history will be available instantly to any health professional in any hospital or clinic.

Test your understanding 1

A barrier to knowledge management is that many people believe that keeping knowledge secret gives them unique power. Knowledge management, however, requires that knowledge is uncovered and shared.

What arguments could be used to encourage individuals to freely give up and share information?

Test your understanding 2 – PR University

The PR University provides tuition to degree level to 12,000 students, both on campus and by distance-learning courses. The university has 34 different departments, each of which specialises in one specific area, such as economics, geography or astronomy.

Over the past ten years, information systems have been developed in each department to meet the specific needs of that department. However, the systems are incompatible with each other and use a wide range of software applications.

The information systems are becoming expensive to operate, as well as requiring duplication of input where students study in more than one department. Additional duplication occurs when student details have to be entered into the central university database, which is used for monitoring total student numbers.

The Board of Management of the university has decided that the university should develop and implement an integrated database for future information requirements and place all existing data into a single data warehouse.

Moreover, any new system must meet the information requirements of the central database as well as those of the individual departments.

Required:

(a) (i) Evaluate the use of data within the university.

(7 marks)

(ii) Explain how the Board of Management should use Critical Success Factors (CSFs) in revising the current information system.

(8 marks)

(b) Discuss the disadvantages of data warehousing with specific reference to the situation at PR University.

(10 marks)

(Total: 25 marks)

Test your understanding 3 – M-HK

M-HK provides a passenger ferry service between two large cities separated by the mouth of a major river. The ferries are frequent, well-supported by passengers and cover the distance between the cities in one hour. M-HK also transports passengers and goods by ferry to other cities located on the river mouth. There are other ferry operators besides M-HK providing services between each of these locations.

Required:

(a) Explain what strategic information is required by M-HK's management in respect of customer demand, competition, competitiveness and finance in order to plan its future ferry services.

(10 marks)

(b) Using the information in your answer to part (a), discuss how M-HK's chartered management accountant should provide reports to M-HK's senior management for operational and strategic planning purposes.

(15 marks)

(Total: 25 marks)

(May 2001)

5 Summary

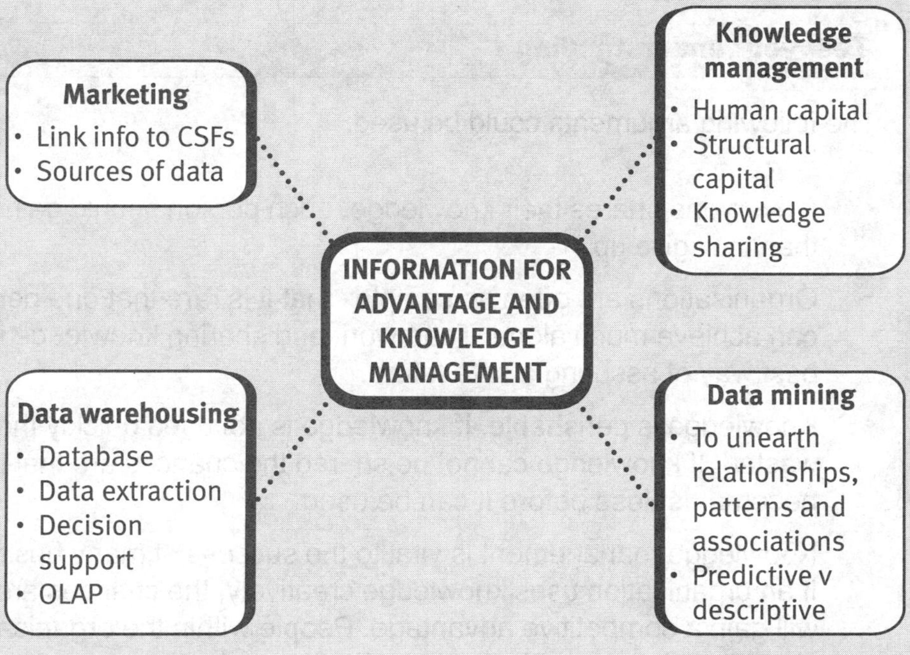
Marketing
• Link info to CSFs
• Sources of data
Knowledge management
• Human capital
• Structural capital
• Knowledge sharing
INFORMATION FOR ADVANTAGE AND KNOWLEDGE MANAGEMENT
Data warehousing
• Database
• Data extraction
• Decision support
• OLAP
Data mining
• To unearth relationships, patterns and associations
• Predictive v descriptive

Test your understanding answers

Test your understanding 1

The following arguments could be used:

- If everyone shares their knowledge, each person should gain more than they give up.
- Organisations are often so complex that it is rare that one person can achieve much alone. Teamwork and sharing knowledge is the best way of assuring a safe future.
- Knowledge is perishable. If knowledge is not used quickly then it is wasted. If knowledge cannot be shared the chances are that it will become useless before it can be used.
- Knowledge management is vital to the success of many businesses. If an organisation uses knowledge creatively, the chances are that it will gain a competitive advantage. People within the organisation should not be competing with each other at the expense of the company.

Test your understanding 2 – PR University

Key answer tips

There are some positive points that can be made about current data use within the university, for instance staff appear to be happy with what they have, so beware of suggesting change just for the sake of change. Be sure to link your CSFs to the overall mission of the university or to the performance indicators needed to enable appropriate information systems to be developed. In part (b) some candidates discussed centralised systems in general: however, the question is about data warehousing.

(a) (i) **Data use within the university**

Although the data needs of individual departments are being met there are a number of problems that make information systems in the university as a whole cumbersome and expensive.

Above all the problem is duplication, both of effort and of data. The same data has to be input separately to the system of each department in which a student studies. This is a waste of time and there is a possibility of inconsistency between the records held by different departments.

The various systems are incompatible so information cannot be transferred between them and it will be difficult to develop the proposed integrated database.

Incompatible systems and diversity of applications also mean that it will be difficult for administrative staff to transfer between departments: they will need retraining each time. This may limit career opportunities within the university.

On the other hand staff will be used to their own systems and may resent or resist any centrally imposed change that requires them to abandon a working system and learn new skills.

(ii) **Critical Success Factors for revising the system**

Critical Success Factors (CSFs) are the limited number of areas in which results, if they are satisfactory, will ensure successful performance. They are the vital areas where 'things must go right' for the organisation to flourish.

There is no indication in the scenario of any respect in which the university as a whole is not flourishing or individual departments are performing unsuccessfully. This is not to say that there are no improvements to be made, however, especially as the systems are becoming expensive to operate.

The aims of individual departments are likely to be broadly similar – for instance, to attract sufficient numbers of students, provide X number of teaching hours per week, achieve certain standards in terms of exam results and future employability of graduates. Some departments may also have research interests and goals.

An overriding aim of the university's Board of Management will be to ensure that the entire organisation is on a sound financial footing and its activities are properly funded, and therefore any means of reducing costs (or getting better value from new investment in information systems) will be important.

The Board of Management can establish CSFs in each of these areas and then identify suitable performance indicators that will show whether CSFs are being met. This in turn will help to define what information will be needed in the future to monitor whether CSFs are being achieved.

It is likely that this analysis will reveal a gap between current information provision and required information provision, and appropriate revisions to the current information system, to close the gap, can then be specified.

(b) **Disadvantages of data warehousing**

A data warehouse supports information processing by providing a solid platform of integrated, historical data from which to do analysis. It is a database, data extraction tool, decision support system, or other analysis tool or procedure that extracts data from one or more of the organisation's existing databases, reformats it and loads it into a database designed for querying with an on-line analytical processing system (OLAP). OLAP allows users to dynamically extract pertinent summary information.

Although the concept of data warehousing appears to offer considerable advantages, especially to organisations such as PR University with a large number of disparate legacy systems, there may be considerable problems when trying to implement such a system.

The systems used in different departments of the PR University are incompatible, and that is likely to mean that data is in a wide variety of different formats. As noted earlier there are also likely to be inconsistencies between different databases where duplicated items of data should in theory be identical, but in practice are not.

The data will either need to be analysed and 'cleansed' before it can be integrated into a warehouse, or else some kind of middleware will be required, probably converting all data to a common format such as XML. Whichever option is chosen, with 34 different departments this will not be easy, quick or cheap to achieve.

Incompatible systems will also mean that most of the departments will need to be furnished with new hardware and software before they can use the data warehouse. This is likely to be expensive and disruptive to the day-to-day work of each department.

Moreover, almost all staff who want to use the new system will need training, both in the use of the data warehouse itself, and probably also in the use of new hardware, operating systems and applications software.

Individual departments may use data in widely different ways and require all manner of different reports. It could be very difficult to create a common interface that is capable of delivering information in every format that may be required. Report formats that are only needed in a single department may not be catered for, and this will cause resentment.

Even if the above problems are overcome, scalability is a key issue. As the new system proves its worth, more and more demands will be made of it, so ongoing maintenance, adequate network bandwidth, sufficient storage space, and highly flexible upgrade capability are all essential.

Finally it is worth pointing out that with all the university's data in a single main source it is vital to ensure that effective backup arrangements are made and strictly adhered to. Depending on how the data warehouse is implemented, loss or serious corruption of data could be disastrous.

Test your understanding 3 – M-HK

M-HK

Approach

Brief introduction with regard to data sources – internal v. external. Then group answer around the four areas.

Demand

- Segment volumes and prices
- price elasticity
- timing of demand (rush hour?)
- research – forecast growth/decline in numbers by segment.

Competition

- PROSAC
- who are they?
- how do they compete?
- where do they compete?
- customer perceptions of them.

Competitiveness

- Consider their marketing mix and ours
- what are their core competencies and ours?
- any thresholds exposed?
- any chance of exposing?
- customer perceptions of M-HK
- barriers to exit and entry.

Finance

- Funding needs
- sources of finance
- cost of capital
- costings of product
- contribution analysis – actual, forecast and budget.

How to provide reports (Note 'discuss')

Basically, 'how can the management accountant assist' would be a useful planning tool.

- Periodic reporting which would include:
  - narrative
  - numericals with both financial and non-financial (BSC?)
  - comparators provided – past data
  - forecast, budgets, KPIs and variances
  - competitor data
- Face-to-face meeting/discussions with budget centre managers to allow presentation of report and "Q&A" session from centre manager. Can offer advice as necessary and also allows for any corrections or amendments before final publication.
- Benchmarking data can be provided or data from a competitor analysis. Pricing and elasticity of demand.

For operational purposes

- Using predominately internal sources
- on a daily or weekly basis – keep it simple
- focus onto actual v. plan with easy KPIs (easy to understand and prepare) e.g.:
  - revenue by service
  - passenger numbers
  - number of complaints.

For strategic purposes

- Uses more external sources
- on a monthly or quarterly basis
- more elaborate using database of information
- forecasts and budgets with scenario planning
- competitive reviews and competitor analysis.

chapter

13

Customers, suppliers and supply chain management

Chapter learning objectives

Lead	Component
A1. Evaluate the key external factors affecting an organisation's strategy	(e) Recommend how to interact with suppliers and customers

Indicative syllabus content

- Strategic supply chain management
- Implications of these interactions for Chartered Management Accountants and the management accounting system
- The customer portfolio: Customer analysis and behaviour, including the marketing audit and customer profitability analysis as well as customer retention and loyalty.

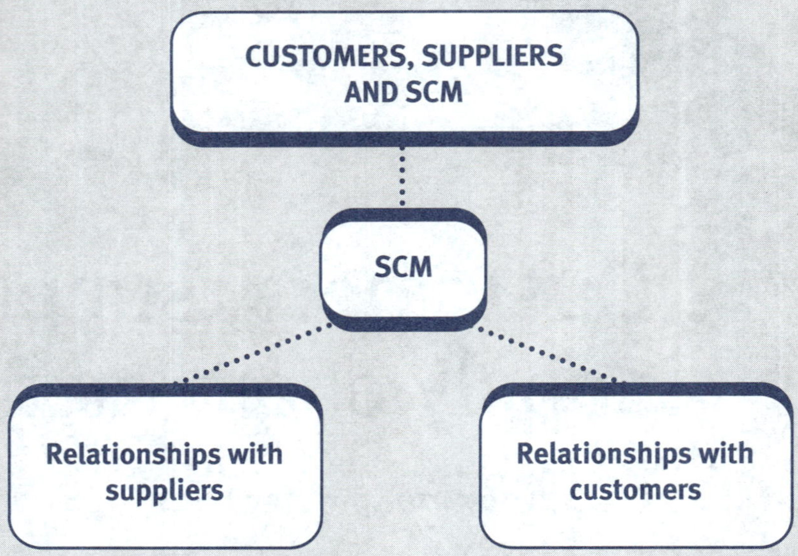

1 Introduction

Customers and suppliers are often key stakeholder groups for an organisation. Two frameworks that we have already met – Mendelow's power / interest matrix and Porter's five forces model – are useful for assessing the power of customers and suppliers and suggesting suitable strategies for dealing with them.

In this chapter the practicalities of managing the relationships with suppliers and customers is considered. In particular the role of e-business in supply chain management is analysed in detail.

2 Supply chain management (SCM)

A supply chain encompasses all activities and information flows necessary for the transformation of goods from the origin of the raw material to when the product is finally consumed or discarded.

This typically involves distribution of the product from the supplier to the manufacturer to the wholesaler to the retailer and to the final consumer, otherwise known as nodes in the supply chain.

It is helpful to make a distinction between upstream and downstream supply chain management. For an Internet retailer, for example, upstream SCM would involve transactions between the firm and its suppliers (equivalent to buy-side e-commerce) and downstream, customers (equivalent to sell-side e-commerce).

The transformation of product from node to node includes activities such as:

- production planning
- purchasing
- materials management
- distribution
- customer service
- forecasting.

While each firm can be competitive through improvements to its internal practices, ultimately the ability to do business effectively depends on the efficient functioning of the entire supply chain.

e.g

Illustration 1 – Supply chain management (SCM)

For example, a wholesaler's inability to adequately maintain inventory control or respond to sudden changes in demand for stock may mean that a retailer cannot meet final consumer demand. Conversely, poor sales data from retailers may result in inadequate forecasting of manufacturing requirements.

Push and pull supply chain models

In the traditional supply chain model, the raw material suppliers are at one end of the supply chain.

- They are connected to manufacturers and distributors, who are in turn connected to a retailer and the end-customer.
- Although customers are the source of the profits, they are at the end of the chain in the 'push' model.

Driven by e-commerce's capabilities to empower clients, many companies are moving from the traditional 'push' business model, where manufacturers, suppliers, distributors and marketers have most of the power, to a customer-driven 'pull' model.

This new business model is less product-centric and more directly focused on the individual consumer – a more marketing-oriented approach.

- In the pull model, customers use electronic connections to pull whatever they need out of the system.

- Electronic supply chain connectivity gives end customers the opportunity to give direction to suppliers, for example about the precise specifications of the products they want.
- Ultimately, customers have a direct voice in the functioning of the supply chain.

E-commerce creates a much more efficient supply chain that benefits both customers and manufacturers. Companies can better serve customer needs, carry fewer inventories, and send products to market more quickly.

e.g

Illustration 2 – Supply chain management (SCM)

Several personal computer manufacturers allow users to order over the internet and to customise their machines (for example Lenovo and Dell). PCs are then made to customers' orders.

3 Relationships with suppliers

Supplier strategy

A supply strategy is likely to take account of matters such as the following.

- **Sources**

  What sources are available and where are they located? Are suppliers' businesses larger or smaller than the buying organisation (this affects bargaining power). Will different suppliers need to be used in different parts of the world?

- **Number of suppliers**

  If there is only a single source of supply this may bring the advantage of bulk purchase discounts, but the organisation may prefer to have several or multiple suppliers to avoid the risk of failed deliveries and to prevent a single supplier from getting either too powerful or/and complacent.

- **Cost, quality and speed of delivery**

  These factors are closely interrelated and the strategy will probably need to make compromises to achieve the right balance.

- **Make or buy and outsourcing**

  The outsourcing decision is effectively the same as the strategy of vertical integration discussed in the chapter "Strategic analysis and choice". The decision will depend on the above factors and whether or not the firm has the required competences and resources to bring the supply in-house.

Factors to consider when choosing suppliers

- What does the company charge?
- Does it offer discounts or other incentives?
- Can it deliver the required quality of product or service (for example is it ISO 9001 certified)?
- Is the supplier willing to customise orders or handle other special needs?
- How will it ship its products, and how much will that cost?
- How quickly will orders be delivered?
- Will delivery quantities be accurate?
- How will the supplier handle returns or other problems?
- Is technical support available, if required?
- How will the supplier manage the account?
- Do they have adequate technology?
- Are they financially secure? Credit reports can help here.
- Are they reliable? Can references be obtained?
- What credit period is offered?

Antagonism or partnership?

Antagonism

In the past the supply chain was typically defined by antagonistic relationships.

- The purchasing function sought out the lowest-price suppliers, often through a process of tendering, the use of 'power' and the constant switching of supply sources to prevent getting too close to any individual source.
- Supplier contracts featured heavy penalty clauses and were drawn up in a spirit of general mistrust of all external providers.

- The knowledge and skills of the supplier could not be exploited effectively: information was deliberately withheld in case the supplier used it to gain power during price negotiations.

Hence no single supplier ever knew enough about the ultimate customer to suggest ways of improving the cost-effectiveness of the trading relationship, for instance buying additional manufacturing capacity or investing in quality improvement activities.

Partnership

It is now recognised that successful management of suppliers is based upon collaboration and offers benefits to an organisation's suppliers as well as to the organisation itself. By working together organisations can make a much better job of satisfying the requirements of their end market, and thus both can increase their market share.

- Organisations seek to enter into partnerships with key customers and suppliers so as to better understand how to provide value and customer service.
- Organisations' product design processes include discussions that involve both customers and suppliers. By opening up design departments and supply problems to selected suppliers a synergy results, generating new ideas, solutions, and new innovative products.
- To enhance the nature of collaboration the organisation may reward suppliers with long-term sole sourcing agreements in return for a greater level of support to the business and a commitment to ongoing improvements of materials, deliveries and relationships.

Service level agreements

Service level agreements should include the following factors:

- A detailed explanation of exactly what service the supplier is offering to provide.
- The targets / benchmarks to be used and the consequences of failing to meet them.
- Expected response time to technical queries.
- The expected time to recover the operations in the event of a disaster such as a systems crash, terrorist attack, etc.
- The procedure for dealing with complaints.
- The information and reporting procedures to be adopted.
- The procedures for cancelling the contract.

4 Upstream SCM

The key activities of upstream SCM are procurement and upstream logistics. A good example of how the upstream supply chain can be improved using IT is Tesco:

e.g

Illustration 3 – Upstream SCM

Tesco

- Largest grocery retailer in the UK
- a typical store stocks 50,000 products
- over 2,000 suppliers, each of which will supply, at most, 200 products.

Date	**Objective**	**Solution**	**Comments**
1980s	Streamline store replenishment	Goods ordered via Electronic Data Interchange (EDI)	
1989	Help suppliers forecast demand	Suppliers sent EDI messages	Suppliers receive messages detailing Actual store sales Depot stockholdings Tesco's forecasts
1997	Better two-way collaboration Shift responsibility for managing products to suppliers	Tesco Information Exchange (TIE) allowing suppliers to view EPOS data	Suppliers can monitor actual sales in real time (almost!), allowing them to identify changes in demand (by product, store and region) and react accordingly
1999	More effective promotions	Promotions management module added	Suppliers are involved in planning and executing promotions

What is e-procurement?

The term 'procurement' covers all the activities needed to obtain items from a supplier: the whole purchases cycle.

The benefits of e-procurement

The more of the procurement process that can be automated, the better, as there will be considerable financial benefits.

- Labour costs will be greatly reduced.
- Inventory holding costs will be reduced. Not only should overstocking be less likely, but if orders are cheap to place and process, they can be placed much more frequently, so average inventories can be lower.
- Production and sales should be higher as there will be fewer stock-outs because of more accurate monitoring of demand and greater ordering accuracy.

Other benefits include the following:

- The firm may benefit from a much wider choice of suppliers rather than relying on local ones.
- Greater financial transparency and accountability
- Greater control over inventories
- Quicker ordering, making it easier to operate lean or JiT manufacturing systems
- There are also considerable benefits to the suppliers concerned, such as reduced ordering costs, reduced paperwork and improved cash flow, that should strengthen the relationship between the firm and its suppliers.

Potential risks of e-procurement

There are some risks associated with e-procurement. These are:

- technology risks. There is a risk that the system (whether software or hardware) will not function correctly. There are risks that it might not interface properly with the organisation's system. There are very high risks that it will not communicate properly with a wide range of supplier systems
- organisational risks. Staff might be reluctant to accept the new procurement methods

- no cost savings realised. As with all IS/IT projects, it is very difficult to predict all the benefits that can arise. Tangible benefits (such as might arise if fewer staff have to be employed) are relatively easy to forecast. However, intangible benefits (such as better customer service giving rise to an improved reputation) are very difficult to estimate with any accuracy.

E-sourcing, e-purchasing and e-payment

E-procurement is the term used to describe the electronic methods used in every stage of the procurement process, from identification of requirement through to payment. It can be broken down into the stages of e-sourcing, e-purchasing and e-payment.

E-sourcing covers electronic methods for finding new suppliers and establishing contracts.

Not only can e-sourcing save administrative time and money, it can enable companies to discover new suppliers and to source more easily from other countries.

Issuing electronic invitations to tender and requests for quotations reduces:

- administration overheads
- potentially costly errors, as the re-keying of information is minimised
- the time to respond.

E-purchasing covers product selection and ordering.

Buying and selling online streamlines procurement and reduces overheads through spending less on administration time and cutting down on bureaucracy. E-purchasing transfers effort from a central ordering department to those who need the products. Features of an e-purchasing system include:

- electronic catalogues for core/standard items
- recurring requisitions/shopping lists for regularly purchased items. The standard shopping lists form the basis of regular orders and the lists can have items added or deleted for each specific order
- electronic purchase orders despatched automatically through an extranet to suppliers
- detailed management information reporting capabilities.

Improvements in customer service can result from being able to place and track orders at any time of day. An e-catalogue is an electronic version of a supplier's paper catalogue including product name, description, an illustration, balance in hand and so on. User expectations have increased dramatically in recent years as a result of their personal experiences of shopping on the internet. Well-designed websites and web interfaces are essential to offer good functionality so as to maintain user satisfaction.

E-payment includes tools such as electronic invoicing and electronic funds transfers. Again, e-payment can make the payment processes more efficient for both the purchaser and supplier, reducing costs and errors that can occur as a result of information being transferred manually from and into their respective accounting systems. These efficiency savings can result in cost reductions to be shared by both parties.

Test your understanding 1 – XL Travel

XL Travel are a tour operator based in the capital city of country S. They run weekly trips to the seaside resort of Black Rock (around 140km away) for four–day visits (typically from Friday to Monday).

The tours are very popular, especially with people aged over 65 (who make up over 90% of XL's customers). The company has traded profitably for many years on the back of premium pricing. However, recently profits have started to fall, coinciding with a minority of complaints from regular users. Some users feel that the quality of the trips have fallen and are not up to previous high standards. Other users feel that, whilst XL itself has invested (with attractive new offices, better marketing, more staff and easier booking systems) this investment has gone on the wrong areas.

XL has built up a large cash surplus for further investment. One of the ways it is considering using this cash is to invest in and improve its supply chain.

Required:

What are likely to be the element's of XL's upstream supply chain? Give some examples of what areas XL could aim to change?

5 Relationships with customers

Relationship marketing

Customer retention is a critical issue for many businesses.

Customers can be lost by a number of factors:

- unhelpful staff
- poor quality of service
- inappropriate prices
- lack of customer care.

The concept of relationship marketing has been defined as the technique of maintaining and exploiting the firm's customer base as a means of developing new business opportunities.

Transaction marketing	Relationship marketing
• concentrates on products	• concentrates on retention and loyalty
• little knowledge of customer	• considerable customer commitment
• product quality a key issue	• considerable customer contact
• little effort on customer retention	• emphasis on quality service

Customer relationship management

Customer relationship management (CRM) consists of the processes a company uses to track and organize its contacts with its current and prospective customers, with particular emphasis on software-based approaches.

The six markets model (Payne)

The six markets model advocates that an organisation has six key markets, not just the traditional customer market. Marketing activity should be extended to build and manage relationships in all these areas.

- **Customer markets**

  The final destination for the product. This ability to reach the customer in a highly competitive environment depends on other parties or relationships.

- **Referral markets**

  This is the institution or person who refers the customer to the supplier. A bank refers customers to providers of insurance services. The Automobile Association (AA) refers members to a bank or hire purchase company.

- **Supplier markets**

  Partnerships with suppliers have replaced old adversarial relationships. A supermarket sets up a JIT arrangement with a supplier for short-life articles, such as ready-made salads, in order to retain customer interest in an instant healthy food product.

- **Recruitment markets**

  A service provider such as PriceWaterhouseCoopers depends on quality staff to deliver quality service. Such an organisation will build up a relationship with careers advisers, professional bodies and others to supply the necessary human resources.

- **Influence markets**

  Influence marketing used to be called public relations – a new low fat spread depends upon the sponsorship of a body that promotes healthy eating (Weightwatchers).

- **Internal markets**

  This concept is not dissimilar to the concept of internal quality management. Every department has a customer provider relationship with others. The UK corporate lending market recognises that the supplier of banking services (transaction processing) supports the manager of the client account (the relationship manager).

Customer account profitability (CAP)

CAP is 'analysis of the revenue streams and service costs associated with specific customers or customer groups.'

CIMA Official Terminology

CAP could also be defined as 'the total sales revenue generated from a customer or customer group, less all the costs that are incurred in servicing that customer or customer group'.

The essence of CAP is that it focuses on profits generated by customers and does not automatically equate increases in sales revenues with increases in profitability.

If an analysis of customer profitability is provided then marketing decisions are more easily made on such matters as:

- discounts
- special credit terms
- special after-sales servicing
- whether any efforts are required on a sector given its lack of profitability.

Stages of CAP

The normal approach to CAP is as follows:

(1) **Analyse the customer base and divide it into segments**. This will normally not be into the same segments as used for marketing, but rather based on factors such as order size or annual purchase volume.

(2) **Calculate the annual revenues earned from the customer segments**. Any discounts granted should be taken into account here.

(3) **Calculate the annual costs of serving the segment**. This will require a detailed analysis of the firm's overheads as well as its direct costs.

(4) **Identify and retain the quality customers**. The quality customers are those that provide earnings in excess of costs. They may either be willing to pay a premium price or they may require only a basic level of service.

(5) **Eliminate or re–engineer the unprofitable customer groups.** This may mean ceasing to supply certain customer groups, or alternatively looking at ways of reducing the level of service provided or increasing sales prices.

e.g

Illustration 4 – CAP

An insurance company was concerned about the poor profit performance of one of its types of policy. By using CAP analysis, it discovered that the policy was unprofitable when sold to recently retired people. Otherwise, it was profitable.

The reason was discovered to be that recently retired policyholders had more free time with which to ask for information and alter their finances. Dealing with this consumed a higher proportion of the insurance company's time and resources than other customer groups.

The company therefore reduced agents commission on the policies according to the age of the policyholder to deter them from selling to the unprofitable segment.

Advantages and disadvantages of CAP

Advantages

- CAP takes account of non-production costs when determining profitability. Differences between the profitability of different groups of customers are often attributable to the costs of supporting their accounts rather than the production costs of what they buy.

  For example, banks often find that pensioners are more likely to be unprofitable customers as they take up a higher proportion of staff time and are less likely to use internet-based services.

- CAP provides a method of identifying customer groups who are of value to the firm, allowing the organisation to decide which customers may be worth additional expenditure to retain – such as through advertising and discounts.
- It provides a technique for assessing the financial value of marketing and product development expenditures. For example, Ferrari invests millions of pounds in supporting its Formula One racing team. CAP analysis would question whether this gives Ferrari additional revenues to justify the costs.

Disadvantages

- CAP can encourage ill-judged product changes. Deciding to remove a product feature based on CAP can have unintended consequences if the customer's behaviour is not fully understood.

  One luxury car company removed the cover of the car's ashtray on the understanding that most customers no longer smoked and those that did preferred to keep the ashtray permanently open. However, customers felt that the cheaper ashtray mechanism indicated that the company was cutting corners on quality. This caused significant damage to the company's reputation.

- Obtaining reliable customer revenue and customer cost figures can be extremely difficult.

  CAP requires a system to accumulate information across all business functions and geographic areas. Most systems used today are unable to perform this necessary function.

- CAP may overlook combinations of products bought.

  For example, although bank accounts lose money when provided to 80 per cent of customers, they are essential if the bank is to sell its credit products, insurance and foreign exchange services.

- CAP can also overlook the life cycle value of the customer. The value of a customer is not restricted to their present revenue and costs.

  For instance, Kotler (1997) cites the example of Taco Bell, an American fast-food restaurant chain. The chain sells tacos for less than $1 each, but estimates that a loyal customer generates up to $11,000 over their lifetime.

  In addition, a customer's value may increase over time. Student accounts may costs banks large amounts of money, but they may become profitable once they enter employment and need credit cards, mortgages and other products from the bank.

Test your understanding 2 – CAP

C1 is a major customer of ABC Manufacturing plc. Forecasts for next year are as follows:

Sales revenue (before discounts) ($000s)	12,000
Target contribution margin (before discounts)	30%
Number of sales visits (2 per month)	24
Number of purchase orders (30 per month)	360
Number of normal deliveries (80% of orders)	288
Number of last-minute "rush" deliveries (20% of orders)	72
Typical discount given	10%

Using Activity Based Costing the following cost driver rates have been estimated:

	$
Making a sales visit	500
Processing a purchase order	100
Making normal delivery	800
Making a last-minute "rush" delivery	2,000

Required:

Calculate the net customer account profitability for C1.

6 Customer lifetime value (CLV)

Customer lifetime value (CLV) is the present value of the future cash flows attributed to the customer relationship. Use of customer lifetime value as a marketing metric tends to place greater emphasis on customer service and long-term customer satisfaction, rather than on maximizing short-term sales.

In theory CLV represents exactly how much each customer is worth in monetary terms, and therefore exactly how much a marketing department should be willing to spend to acquire each customer.

In reality, it is difficult to make accurate calculations of CLV due to the complexity of and uncertainty surrounding customer relationships.

Inputs to CLV

Most models to calculate CLV apply to the contractual or customer retention situation. These models make several simplifying assumptions and often involve the following inputs:

- **Churn rate**

  The percentage of customers who end their relationship with a company in a given period. The assumption is that the churn rate is constant across the life of the customer relationship.

- **Discount rate**

  The cost of capital used to discount future revenue from a customer.

- **Retention cost**

  The amount of money a company has to spend in a given period to retain an existing customer. Retention costs include customer support, billing, promotional incentives, etc.

- **Period**

  The unit of time into which a customer relationship is divided for analysis. A year is the most commonly used period. Customer lifetime value is a multi-period calculation, usually stretching 3–7 years into the future. In practice, analysis beyond this point is viewed as too speculative to be reliable. The number of periods used in the calculation is sometimes referred to as the model horizon.

- **Periodic revenue**

  The amount of revenue collected from a customer in the period.

- **Profit Margin Profit as a percentage of revenue.**

  Depending on circumstances this may be reflected as a percentage of gross or net profit. For incremental marketing that does not incur any incremental overhead that would be allocated against profit, gross profit margins are acceptable.

Marketing audits

The marketing audit is a particular form of position audit which focuses on the products of the firm and the relationship it has with customers.

It helps to not only give the company a deeper understanding of the market it operates in, but also the strategies it will need to implement in order to gain competitive advantage.

The normal stages in a marketing audit include:

(1) **Define the market.** This involves the firm describing the products or services it wishes to offer in the market, as well as the key characteristics of the market itself. These could include size, growth rate and the strategies most likely to succeed in it.

(2) **Determine performance differentials.** The purpose here is to look for segments of the market that are currently not being fulfilled and which may provide an entry-point for the business (or a rival). For example, Subway exploited a niche in the fast-food market by attracting health conscious consumers who were not having their needs met by existing suppliers.

(3) **Profile the strategies of competitors.** This involves 'getting to know your enemy'. Major competitors should be identified, along with a profile of their products, services and style of competitive strategy. The firm's own strategy can then be compared against those of its competitors.

(4) **Determine the strategic planning structure.** This involves deciding how the strategic marketing effort is to be organised, including the assignment of staff and the goals and objectives of the marketing department.

7 Downstream SCM

Examples of how e-business affects relationships with customers

The following are the main ways in which e-business can affect an organisation's relationship with its customers.

- Tie-in/switching costs. A good e-business arrangement can make customers reluctant to switch supplier. For example, time and effort might have gone into automating most of a customer's purchase transactions. If this works well, not only would customers not want to switch away from an efficient process, but there would be expense and disruption if they did.
- E-commerce can lead to **disintermediation**. In this process intermediate organisations (middlemen) can be taken out of the supply chain.

- The process of **reintermediation** is also found, i.e. new intermediaries are introduced to the value chain, or at least to some aspects of it.
- **Countermediation** is where established firms create their own new intermediaries to compete with established intermediaries.
- Continual updates – products, prices, news.
- Easy, fast, cheap, two-way communication.
- User communities. The users of some complex products, such as software, set up user communities where members help each other and where pressure on the product supplier can be organised. Strong user communities are valued by their members and the organisation would be wise to look at the comments and queries on the bulletin boards.
- Tracking customer internet activity and buyer habits. Every click on a website can be recorded and analysed.
- Customer preferences can be acted on.
- Customers can specify precisely the features they might want in their product.

e.g

Illustration 5 – Downstream SCM

An example of disintermediation is seen in the travel industry where travel agents have been cut out of many transactions as the public can book directly with hotels, airlines and rail companies.

The travel industry also gives an example of reintermediation. Companies like lastminute.com and expedia.com are like new travel agents, presenting a wide choice of products and services.

An example of countermediation is Opodo.com, set up by a collaboration of European airlines to encourage customers to book flights directly with them rather than using cost-comparison intermediaries such as lastminute.com.

The use of intranets and extranets

An intranet is a private network within a single company using Internet standards to enable employees to share information using e-mail and web publishing.

An extranet is formed by extending an intranet beyond a company to customers, suppliers and other collaborators.

The benefits of using an extranet are as follows:

- **Information sharing in a secure environment**

  For example, the advertising agency Saatchi allows customers to view draft advertising material during a project.

- **Cost reduction**

  Savings can arise from need fewer people in the ordering process and the elimination of the need to rekey information from paper documents.

- **Order processing and distribution**

  For example, a customer's point of sales terminals can be linked to a supplier's delivery system, ensuring prompt replenishment of goods sold. this results in fewer lost sales due to stock-outs and lower inventory holding.

- **Improved customer service**

  Customer service can be improved through easier / quicker access to information, increased accuracy and consistency of information and quicker response times. Together these build customer confidence and may result in increased revenue.

8 Customer acquisition, retention and extension

Customer acquisition

Methods of acquiring customers can be split between traditional off-line techniques (e.g. advertising, direct mail, sponsorship, etc) and rapidly-evolving on-line techniques:

Search engine marketing

- Search engine optimisation – improving the position of a company in search engine listings for key terms or phrases. For example, increasing the number of inbound links to a page through 'link building' can improve the ranking with Google.

- Pay per click (PPC) – an advert is displayed by search engines as a 'sponsored link' when particular phrases are entered. The advertiser typically pays a fee to the search engine each time the advert is clicked.
- Trusted feed – database-driven sites such as travel, shopping and auctions are very difficult to optimise for search engines and consequently haven't enjoyed much visibility in the free listings. Trusted Feed works by allowing a 'trusted' third party, usually a search engine marketing company, to 'feed' a website's entire online inventory directly into the search engine's own database, bypassing the usual submission process.

Online PR

- Media alerting services – using online media and journalists for press releases.
- Portal representation – portals are websites that act as gateways to information and services. They typically contain search engines and directories.
- Businesses blogs (effectively online journals) can be used to showcase the expertise of its employees.
- Community C2C portals (effectively the e-equivalent of a village notice board) – e.g. an oil company could set up a discussion forum on its website to facilitate discussion on issues including pollution.

Online partnerships

- Link-building – reciprocal links can be created by having quality content and linking to other sites with quality content. The objective is that they will then link to your site.
- Affiliate marketing – a commission-based arrangement where an e-retailer pays sites that link to it for sales. For example, hundreds of thousands of sites direct customers to Amazon to buy the books or CDs that they have mentioned on their pages.
- Sponsorship – web surfers are more likely to trust the integrity of a firm sponsoring a website than those who use straight ads.
- Co-branding – a lower cost form of sponsorship where products are labelled with two brand names. For example, as well as including details about their cars, the website Subaru.com also includes immediate co-branded insurance quotes with Liberty Mutual Insurance and pages devoted to outdoor lifestyles developed with LL Bean.

- Aggregators – these are comparison sites allowing customers to compare different product features and prices. For example, moneysupermarket.com allows analysis of financial services products. Clearly a mortgage lender would want their products included in such comparisons.

Interactive adverts

- Banners – banners are simply advertisements on websites with a click through facility so customers can surf to the advertiser's website.
- Rich-media – many web users have become immune to conventional banner ads so firms have tried increasingly to make their ads more noticeable through the use of animation, larger formats, overlays, etc. For example, an animated ad for Barclays banking services will appear on some business start-up sites.
- Some ads are more interactive and will change depending on user mouse movements, for example generating a slide show.

Opt-in e-mail

It is estimated that 80% of all e-mails are spam or viruses. Despite this, e-mail marketing can still deliver good response rates. One survey found only 10% of e-mails were not delivered (e.g. due to spam filters), 30% were opened and 8% resulted in 'clickthroughs'. Options for e-mail include the following.

- Cold, rented lists – here the retailer buys an e-mail list from a provider such as Experian.
- Co-branded e-mail – for example, your bank sends you an e-mail advertising a mobile phone.
- 3rd party newsletters – the retailers advertises itself in a 3rd party's newsletter.
- House list e-mails – lists built up in-house from previous customers, for example.

Viral marketing

- Viral marketing is where e-mail is used to transmit a promotional message from one person to another.
- Ideally the viral ad should be a clever idea, a game or a shocking idea that is compulsive viewing so people send it to their friends.

Customer satisfaction and retention

Key to retention is understanding and delivering the drivers of customer satisfaction as satisfaction drives loyalty and loyalty drives profitability.

The 'SERVQUAL' approach to service quality developed by **Parasuraman et al** focuses on the following factors.

Tangibles

- The 'tangibles' heading considers the appearance of physical facilities, equipment, personnel and communications.
- For online quality the key issue is the appearance and appeal of websites – customers will revisit websites that they find appealing.
- This can include factors such as structural and graphic design, quality of content, ease of use, speed to upload and frequency of update.

Reliability

- Reliability is the ability to provide a promised service dependably and accurately and is usually the most important of the different aspects being discussed here.
- For online service quality, reliability is mainly concerned with how easy it is to connect to the website.
- If websites are inaccessible some of the time and/or e-mails are bounced back, then customers will lose confidence in the retailer.

Responsiveness

- Responsiveness looks at the willingness of a firm to help customers and provide prompt service.
- In the context of e-business, excessive delays can cause customers to 'bail-out' of websites and/or transactions and go elsewhere.
- This could relate to how long it takes for e-mails to be answered or even how long it takes for information to be downloaded to a user's browser.

Assurance

- Assurance is the knowledge and courtesy of employees and their ability to inspire trust and confidence.
- For an online retailer, assurance looks at two issues – the quality of responses and the privacy/security of customer information.
- Quality of response includes competence, credibility and courtesy and could involve looking at whether replies to e-mails are automatic or personalised and whether questions have been answered satisfactorily.

Empathy

- Empathy considers the caring, individualised attention a firm gives its customers.
- Most people would assume that empathy can only occur through personal human contact but it can be achieved to some degree through personalising websites and e-mail.
- Key here is whether customers feel understood. For example, being recommended products that they would never dream of buying can erode empathy.

Techniques for retaining customers

Given the above consideration of service quality, firms use the following e-techniques to try to retain customers.

- Personalisation – delivering individualised content through web-pages or e-mail. For example, portals such as Yahoo! enable users to configure their home pages to give them the information they are most interested in.
- Mass customisation – delivering customised content to groups of users through web-pages or e-mail. For example, Amazon may recommend a particular book based on what other customers in a particular segment have been buying.
- Extranets – for example, Dell Computers uses an extranet to provide additional services to its 'Dell Premier' customers.
- Opt-in e-mail – asking customers whether they wish to receive further offers.

- Online communities – firms can set up communities where customers create the content. These could be focussed on purpose (e.g. Autotrader is for people buying/selling cars), positions (e.g. the teenage chat site Doobedo), interest (e.g. Football365) or profession. Despite the potential for criticism of a company's products on a community, firms will understand where service quality can be improved, gain a better understanding of customer needs and be in a position to answer criticism.

Customer extension

Customer extension has the objective of increasing the lifetime value of a customer and typically involves the following.

- 'Re-sell' similar products to previous sales.
- 'Cross sell' closely related products.
- 'Up sell' more expensive products.
- For example, having bought a book from Amazon you could be contacted with offers of other books, DVDs or DVD players.
- Reactivate customers who have not bought anything for some time.

Key to these is propensity modelling.

Propensity modelling

Propensity modelling involves evaluating customer behaviour and then making recommendations to them for future products. For example, if you have bought products from Amazon, then each time you log on there will be a recommendation of other products you may be interested in.

This can involve the following.

- Create automatic product relationships – e.g. through monitoring which products are typically bought together.
- Using trigger words or phrases – e.g. 'customers who bought …also bought…'.
- Offering related products at checkout – e.g. batteries for electronic goods

Test your understanding 3 – DRB

DRB ELECTRONIC SERVICES

DRB Electronic Services operates in a high labour cost environment in Western Europe and imports electronic products from the Republic of Korea. It re-brands and re-packages them as DRB products and then sells them to business and domestic customers in the local geographical region. Its only current source of supply is ISAS electronics based in a factory on the outskirts of Seoul, the capital of the Republic of Korea.DRB regularly places orders for ISAS products through the ISAS web-site and pays for them by credit card. As soon as the payment is confirmed ISAS automatically e-mails DRB a confirmation of order, an order reference number and likely shipping date. When the order is actually despatched, ISAS send DRB a notice of despatch e-mail and a container reference number. ISAS currently organises all the shipping of the products. The products are sent in containers and then trans-shipped to EIF, the logistics company used by ISAS to distribute its products. EIF then delivers the products to the DRB factory. Once they arrive, they are quality inspected and products that pass the inspection are re-branded as DRB products (by adding appropriate logos) and packaged in specially fabricated DRB boxes. These products are then stored ready for sale. All customer sales are from stock. Products that fail the inspection are returned to ISAS.

Currently 60% of sales are made to domestic customers and 40% to business customers. Most domestic customers pick up their products from DRB and set them up themselves. In contrast, most business customers ask DRB to set up the electronic equipment at their offices, for which DRB makes a small charge. DRB currently advertises its products in local and regional newspapers. DRB also has a web site which provides product details. Potential customers can enquire about the specification and availability of products through an e-mail facility in the web site. DRB then e-mails an appropriate response directly to the person making the enquiry. Payment for products cannot currently be made through the web site.

Feedback from existing customers suggests that they particularly value the installation and support offered by the company. The company employs specialist technicians who (for a fee) will install equipment in both homes and offices. They will also come out and troubleshoot problems with equipment that is still under warranty. DRB also offer a helpline and a back to base facility for customers whose products are out of warranty. Feedback from current customers suggests that this support is highly valued. One commented that 'it contrasts favourably with your large customers who offer support through impersonal off-shore call centres and a time-consuming returns policy'. Customers can also pay for technicians to come on-site to sort out problems with out-of-warranty equipment.

DRB now plans to increase their product range and market share. It plans to grow from its current turnover of £5m per annum to £12m per annum in two years time. Dilip Masood, the owner of DRB, believes that DRB must change its business model if it is to achieve this growth. He believes that these changes will also have to tackle problems associated with:

- Missing, or potentially missing shipments. Shipments can only be tracked through contacting the shipment account holder, ISAS, and on occasions they have been reluctant or unable to help. The trans-shipment to EIF has also caused problems and this has usually been identified as the point where goods have been lost. ISAS does not appear to be able to reliably track the relationship between the container shipment and the Waybills used in the EIF system.
- The likely delivery dates of orders, the progress of orders and the progress of shipments is poorly specified and monitored. Hence deliveries are relatively unpredictable and this can cause congestion problems in the delivery bay.

Dilip also recognises that growth will mean that the company has to sell more products outside its region and the technical installation and support so valued by local customers will be difficult to maintain. He is also adamant that DRB will continue to import only fully configured products. It is not interested in importing components and assembling them. DRB also does not wish to build or invest in assembly plants overseas or to commit to a long-term contract with one supplier.

Required:

(a) Draw the primary activities of DRB on a value chain. Comment on the significance of each of these activities and the value that they offer to customers.

(9 marks)

(b) Explain how DRB might re-structure its upstream supply chain to achieve the growth required by DRB and to tackle the problems that Dilip Masood has identified.

(10 marks)

(c) Explain how DRB might re-structure its downstream supply chain to achieve the growth required.

(6 marks)

(Total: 25 marks)

9 Brand strategy

What is a brand?

A brand usually has three elements:

- a name and/or logo – e.g. McDonald's
- a colour scheme – e.g. McDonald's has a gold letter M on a red background and the M is shaped like arches.
- associations – attributes, benefits and values associated with the brand – e.g. Volvo cars are associated with safety.

Brand strategies (Kotler)

Kotler identified 5 brand strategies:

(1) Line extensions
   - an existing brand is applied to new variants/products within the same product category
   - e.g. Ford Fusion and Ford Focus are both small cars

(2) Brand extensions
   - an existing brand is applied to products in a new product category
   - e.g. Honda cars and motorcycles

(3) Multibrands
   - having many different brands in the same product category
   - e.g. Kellogs breakfast cereals include Cornflakes, Frosties, Special K, etc

(4) New brands
   - new brands are created for new products and/or markets, usually because existing brands are not deemed suitable.
   - e.g. when the banking arm of the Prudential expanded into internet banking they created a new brand, Egg Banking

(5) Cobrands
   - two brands are combined in an offer so the brands reinforce each other.
   - e.g. Dell Computers with Intel Processors

10 Summary

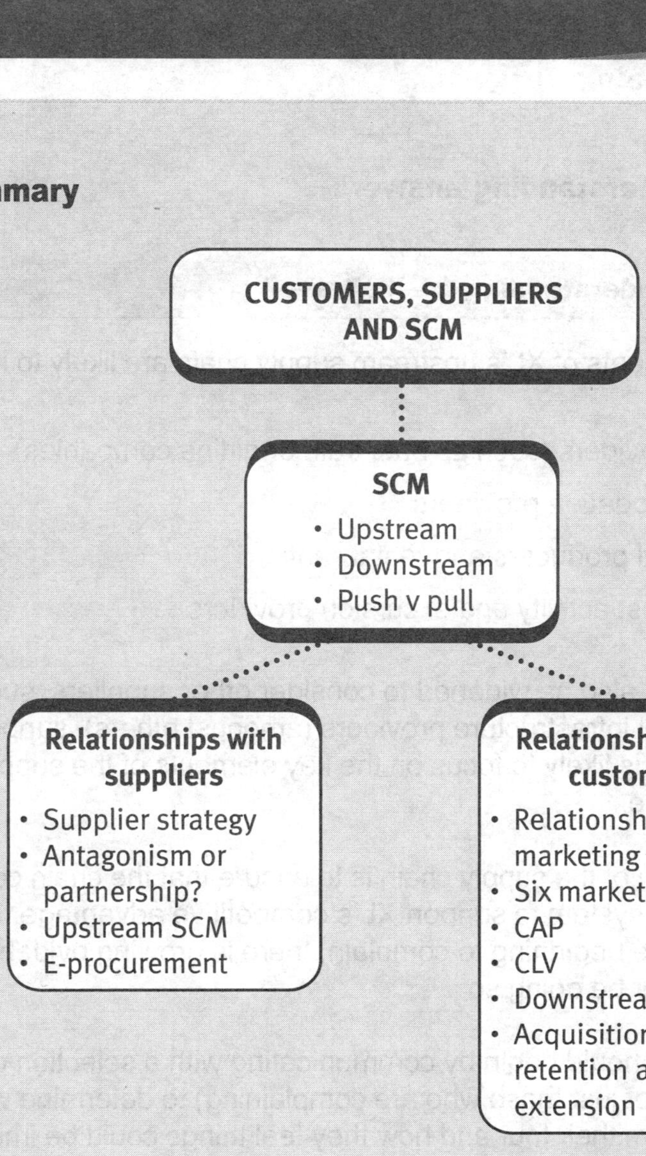
CUSTOMERS, SUPPLIERS AND SCM
SCM
• Upstream
• Downstream
• Push v pull
Relationships with suppliers
• Supplier strategy
• Antagonism or partnership?
• Upstream SCM
• E-procurement
Relationships with customers
• Relationship marketing
• Six markets model
• CAP
• CLV
• Downstream SCM
• Acquisition, retention and extension

Test your understanding answers

Test your understanding 1 – XL Travel

The key elements of XL's upstream supply chain are likely to include:

- travel providers (such as bus, train or airline companies)
- accommodation providers
- local food producers and restaurants
- attractions, activity and excursion providers

While it could also be widened to consider other suppliers, such as local bars and local infrastructure providers (amongst others), supply chain management is likely to focus on the key elements of the supply chain outlined above.

A key function of the supply chain is to ensure that the chain contains the correct value system to support XL's competitive advantage. As some customers are beginning to complain, there is growing evidence that it may no longer be doing so.

As such, XL should begin by communicating with a selection of customers (not just those who are complaining) to determine what they would like from their tour and how they feel things could be improved.

XL can then use this information to provide suppliers with areas that they will need to focus on to improve the customer experience.

For example, XL could examine the accommodation it offers. It could consider issues such as location, ease of access, appearance, staffing and facilities.

For travel providers, XL may wish to examine the safety measures, the ease of check-in, luggage facilities and in-journey refreshments and facilities.

Should there be any problem areas for customers that a supplier is either unwilling or unable to change, XL could consider attempting to switch to an alternative supplier.

Test your understanding 2 – CAP

	$000
Sales revenue (before discounts)	**12,000**
Target contribution margin (before discounts) – 30% × 12,000	(3,600)
Contribution (before discounts)	8,400
Discounts (10% × revenue)	(1,200)
Contribution (after discounts)	**7,200**
Cost of sales visits (24 × 500)	(12)
Cost of purchase orders (360 × 100)	(36)
Cost of normal deliveries (288 × 800)	(230.4)
Cost of last-minute "rush" deliveries (72 × 2,000)	(144)
Net customer profitability	**6,777.6**

Test your understanding 3 – DRB

DRB ELECTRONIC SERVICES

(a) A simple value chain of the primary activities of DRB is shown below.

Handling and storing inbound fully configured equipment Quality inspection	Re-branding of products Re-packaging of products	Customer collection Technician delivery and installation	Local advertising Web-based enquiries	On-site technical support Back to base support
Inbound logistics	**Operations**	**Outbound logistics**	**Marketing and sales**	**Service**

Comments about value might include:

Inbound logistics: Excellent quality assurance is required in inbound logistics. This is essential for pre-configured equipment where customers have high expectations of reliability. As well as contributing to customer satisfaction, high quality also reduces service costs.

Operations: This is a relatively small component in the DRB value chain and actually adds little value to the customer. It is also being undertaken in a relatively high cost country. DRB might wish to re-visit the current arrangement.

Outbound logistics: Customer feedback shows that this is greatly valued. Products can be picked up from stock and delivery and installation is provided if required. Most of the company's larger competitors cannot offer this service. However, it is unlikely that this value can be retained when DRB begins to increasingly supply outside the geographical region it is in.

Marketing and sales: This is very low-key at DRB and will have to be developed if the company is to deliver the proposed growth. The limited functionality of the website offers little value to customers.

Service: Customer feedback shows that this is greatly valued. Most of the company's competitors cannot offer this level of service. They offer support from off-shore call centres and a returns policy that is both time consuming to undertake and slow in rectification. However, it is unlikely that this value can be retained when DRB begins to increasingly supply outside the geographical region it is in.

(b) DRB has already gained efficiencies by procuring products through the supplier's website. However, the website has restricted functionality. When DRB places the order it is not informed of the expected delivery date until it receives the confirmation e-mail from ISAS. It is also unable to track the status of their order and so it is only when it receives a despatch email from ISAS that it knows that it is on its way. Because DRB is not the owner of the shipment, it is unable to track the delivery and so the physical arrival of the goods cannot be easily predicted. On occasions where shipments have appeared to have been lost, DRB has had to ask ISAS to track the shipment and report on its status. This has not been very satisfactory and the problem has been exacerbated by having two shippers involved. ISAS has not been able to reliably track the transhipment of goods from their shipper to EIF, the logistics company used to distribute their products in the country. Some shipments have been lost and it is time-consuming to track and follow-up shipments which are causing concern. Finally, because DRB has no long term contract with ISAS, it has to pay when it places the order through a credit card transaction on the ISAS website.

DRB has stated that it wishes to continue importing fully configured products. It is not interested in importing components and assembling them. It also does not wish to build or invest in assembly plants in other countries. However, it may wish to consider the following changes to its upstream supply chain:

– Seek to identify a wider range of suppliers and so trade through other sell-side websites. Clearly there are costs associated with this. Suppliers have to be identified and evaluated and financial and trading arrangements have to be established. However, it removes the risk of single-sourcing and other suppliers may have better systems in place to support order and delivery tracking.
– Seek to identify suppliers who are willing and able to re-brand and package their products with DRB material at the production plant. This should reduce DRB costs as this is currently undertaken in a country where wage rates are high.
– Re-consider the decision not to negotiate long-term contracts with suppliers (including ISAS) and so explore the possibility of more favourable payment terms. DRB has avoided long-term contracts up to now. It may also not be possible to enter into such contracts if DRB begins to trade with a number of suppliers.
– Seek to identify suppliers (including ISAS) who are able to provide information about delivery dates prior to purchase and who are able to provide internet-based order tracking systems to their customers. This should allow much better planning.
– Consider replacing the two supplier shippers with a contracted logistics company which will collect the goods from the supplier and transport the goods directly to DRB. This should reduce physical transhipment problems and allow seamless monitoring of the progress of the order from despatch to arrival. It will also allow DRB to plan for the arrival of goods and to schedule its re-packaging.

DRB might also wish to consider two other procurement models; buy-side and the independent marketplace.

In the buy-side model DRB would use its website to invite potential suppliers to bid for contract requirements posted on the site. This places the onus on suppliers to spend time completing details and making commitments. It should also attract a much wider range of suppliers than would have been possible through DRB searching sell-side sites for potential suppliers. Unfortunately, it is unlikely that DRB is large enough to host such a model. However, it may wish to prototype it to see if it is viable and whether it uncovers potential suppliers who have not been found in sell-side websites searches.

In the independent marketplace model, DRB places its requirements on an intermediary website. These are essentially B2B electronic marketplaces which allow, on the one hand, potential customers to search products being offered by suppliers and, on the other hand, customers to place their requirements and be contacted by potential suppliers. Such marketplaces promise greater supplier choice with reduced costs. They also provide an opportunity for aggregation where smaller organisations (such as DRB) can get together with companies that have the same requirement to place larger orders to gain cheaper prices and better purchasing terms. It is also likely that such marketplaces will increasingly offer algorithms that automatically match customers and suppliers, so reducing the search costs associated with the sell-side model. The independent marketplace model may be a useful approach for DRB. Many of the suppliers participating in these marketplaces are electronics companies.

(c) DRB's downstream supply chain is also very simple at the moment It has a website that shows information about DRB products. Customers can make enquiries about the specification and availability of these products through an e-mail facility. Conventional marketing is undertaken through local advertising and buyers either collect their products or they are delivered and installed by a specialist group of technicians. DRB could tune its downstream supply chain by using many of the approaches mentioned in the previous section.

For example:

- Developing the website so that it not only shows products but also product availability. Customers would be able to place orders and pay for them securely over the website. The site could be integrated with a logistics system so that orders and deliveries can be tracked by the customer. DRB must recognise that most of its competitors already have such systems. However, DRB will have to put a similar system in place to be able to support its growth plans.
- Participating in independent marketplace websites as a supplier. DRB may also be able to exploit aggregation by combining with other suppliers in consortia to bid for large contracts.
- DRB may also consider participating in B2C marketplaces such as ebay. Many organisations use this as their route to market for commodity products.

DRB may also wish to consider replacing its sales from stock approach with sales from order. In the current approach, DRB purchases products in advance and re-packages and stores these products before selling them to customers. This leads to very quick order fulfilment but high storage and financing costs. These costs will become greater if the planned growth occurs. DRB may wish to consider offering products on its website at a discount but with specified delivery terms. This would allow the company to supply to order rather than supply from stock.

chapter

14

Lean systems and innovation

Chapter learning objectives

Lead	Component
D1. Evaluate the tools and processes of strategy implementation.	(a) Advise managers on the development of strategies.

Specific areas of indicative syllabus content of relevance here are the following:

- D1: The implementation of lean systems across an organisation

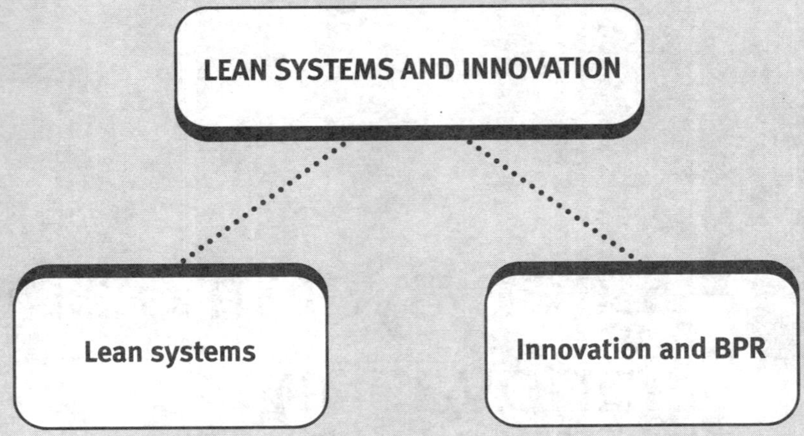

1 Introduction

Many organisations are facing business environments that are changing in some or all of the following ways:

- increasing competition
- greater globalisation
- more rapid change (dynamism)
- increasingly complex
- greater perceived risk.

Dealing with these challenges has involved a mixture of the following:

- a switch to more emergent styles of strategic planning
- a greater awareness of the need for a clear, sustainable competitive strategy
- a greater emphasis on innovation as a critical success factor
- a greater emphasis on quality (e.g. the adoption of six-sigma methodologies)
- a drive for cost reductions (e.g. through outsourcing to countries with lower wage costs)
- the use of greater automation in manufacturing systems
- a need for greater flexibility
- an increase in the strategic significance of IT and IS
- a switch to more flexible organisational forms.

Many of these have resulted in a drive towards "lean systems". You have studied these before in paper E1 (previously P4), so much of this chapter is revision. As with other areas in E3 the emphasis now is on **evaluating** an enterprise's position and making recommendations.

2 Lean systems

What is lean production?

The concept of lean production (sometimes called lean manufacturing) developed out of the Toyota Production System, the Japanese approach to operations management that emerged during the 1950s.

It can be described as an operational strategy oriented towards achieving the shortest possible cycle time by eliminating waste in every area of production, including customer relations, product design, supplier networks and factory management.

Its goal is to incorporate less human effort, less inventory, less time to develop products and less space to become highly responsive to customer demand while producing top-quality products in the most efficient and economical manner possible'.

Four principles

- Minimise waste
- Perfect first time quality
- Flexible production lines
- Continuous improvement

The characteristics of lean manufacturing

- zero waiting time
- zero inventory
- scheduling production – production is initiated by external or internal customer demand rather than the ability and capacity to produce. In other words, production is initiated by 'demand-pull' rather than 'supply-push'
- moving from batch production to continuous flow production, or cutting batch sizes to one
- continually finding ways of reducing process times.

The seven wastes to be eliminated

(1) Overproduction and early production – producing over customer requirements, producing unnecessary materials / products

(2) Waiting – time delays, idle time (time during which value is not added to the product)

(3) Transportation – multiple handling, delay in materials handling, unnecessary handling

(4) Inventory – holding or purchasing unnecessary raw materials, work in process, and finished goods

(5) Motion – actions of people or equipment that do not add value to the product

(6) Over-processing – unnecessary steps or work elements / procedures (non added value work)

(7) Defective units – production of a part that is scrapped or requires rework.

3 Implementing lean systems

While there are a number of specific tools that organisations use to implement lean production systems, the six core methods listed below are most typically used. Most of these lean methods are interrelated and some can occur concurrently. Implementation is often sequenced in the order presented below. Most organisations begin by implementing lean techniques in a particular production area or at a pilot facility and then expand use of the methods over time.

(1) Just in time

(2) Kaizen – continuous improvement

(3) 5S

(4) Total Productive Maintenance (TPM)

(5) Cellular manufacturing/One-piece flow production systems

(6) Six Sigma

Step 1: Just in time (JIT)

The JIT concept

JIT is a system whose objective is to produce or to procure products or components as they are required by a customer or for use, rather than for stock.

The basic elements of JIT were developed by Toyota in the 1950s, as part of the Toyota Production System (TPS). JIT is based on the Kaizen philosophy of continuous improvement.

- Pull system – respond to demand
- Driven by demand – each component is produced only when needed
- Applies to production and to purchasing from suppliers.

The elements of a JIT system

A JIT system has a number of key characteristics.

- Attention to product design
- Good relationships with suppliers
- Quality and delivery being reliable
- Productive maintenance
- Elimination of all non-value-added costs and waste
- Monitoring of progress
- All parts of the productive process should be operated at a speed.

The benefits of JIT

Organisations which have introduced JIT systems have seen a number of benefits:

- reduced inventory levels, leading to lower costs
- improved quality
- faster throughput

- better utilisation of the workforce as they are trained to be more flexible
- the development of better relationships with suppliers, which is necessary for the JIT system to work effectively
- shorter delivery times and improved customer satisfaction.

Implementation issues

Although it might be difficult to argue against the philosophy of JIT, there can be problems with applying the theory in practice.

- It is not always easy to predict patterns of demand.
- The concept of zero inventories and make-to-order is inapplicable in some industries. For example, retailing businesses such as supermarkets must obtain inventory in anticipation of future customer demand.
- JIT makes the organisation far more vulnerable to disruptions in the supply chain.
- JIT was designed at a time when all of Toyota's manufacturing was done within a 50 km radius of its headquarters. Wide geographical spread, however, makes this more difficult.
- The success of JIT depends on employees and suppliers embracing the concept and the culture. Without their full support and commitment, a system that operates with zero inventories (or close-to-zero inventories) will be vulnerable to disruptions.

Step 2: Kaizen

Kaizen – continuous improvement

'Kaizen' is a Japanese term meaning to improve processes via small, incremental amounts rather than through large innovations.

- Kaizen processes focus on eliminating waste in the targeted systems and processes of an organisation, improving productivity, and achieving sustained continual improvement.
- This philosophy implies that small, incremental changes routinely applied and sustained over a long period result in significant improvements.
- The Kaizen strategy aims to involve workers from multiple functions and levels in the organisation in working together to address a problem or improve a particular process.

- The team uses analytical techniques, such as value stream mapping, to quickly identify opportunities to eliminate waste in a targeted process.
- The team works to rapidly implement chosen improvements (often within 72 hours of initiating the Kaizen event), typically focusing on ways that do not involve large capital outlays. Periodic follow-up events aim to ensure that the improvements from the Kaizen blitz are sustained over time.
- Kaizen, or rapid improvement processes, are often considered to be the building blocks of all lean production methods. Kaizen can be used as an implementation tool for most of the other lean methods.
- Although incremental changes can often be too small to be seen, Kaizen can be very effective in the long run and lead to sustainable improvements.

Step 3: 5S

The '5S' practice is an approach to achieving and maintaining a high-quality work environment. The 5S model provides the foundation on which other lean methods, such as total productive maintenance, cellular manufacturing, just-in-time production, and Six Sigma, can be introduced.

The 5Ss (Japanese words) are used to outline improvement actions that workers/teams can apply in their work area. Translated these are:

- **Seiri** – straighten up/sort – eliminate unnecessary things in the workplace. Decide what you need to do the work and what is not needed. Keep what is needed and remove what is not needed. Mark unwanted items with a red tag, so that they can be taken away to a central storage location.
- **Seiton** – put things in order – arrange things properly. Place things where they will be easily found and reached whenever they are needed. 'A place for everything and everything in its place.'
- **Seiso** – clean up – when you have got rid of all the unwanted items and stored everything else in a tidy way, the next step is to clean the work place thoroughly every day. When the workplace is clean, it becomes easier to spot problems such as oil leaks or water leaks.
- **Seiketsu** – standardise – concentrate on standardising work practices to achieve 'best practice'.

- **Shitsuke** – sustain or self-discipline – having established a clean and efficient working environment, and established best practice, make sure that this is sustained. Do not slip back into old habits. Maintain the new work culture.

In the daily work of a company, routines that maintain organisation and orderliness are essential to a smooth and efficient flow of activities. This lean method encourages workers to improve their working conditions and facilitates their efforts to reduce waste, unplanned downtime and in-process inventory.

Step 4: Total productive maintenance (TPM)

Total productive maintenance (TPM) seeks to engage all levels and functions in an organisation in maximising the overall effectiveness of production equipment.

- Whereas traditional preventive maintenance programs are centered in the maintenance departments, TPM seeks to involve workers in all departments and levels, from the plant-floor to senior executives, in ensuring the effective operation of equipment.
- Autonomous maintenance, a key aspect of TPM, trains and focuses workers to take care of the equipment and machines with which they work.
- TPM addresses the entire production system life-cycle and builds a solid, plant-floor based system to prevent accidents, defects, and breakdowns.
- TPM focuses on preventing breakdowns (preventive maintenance), 'mistake-proofing' equipment (or poka-yoke) to prevent breakdowns or to make maintenance easier (corrective maintenance), designing and installing equipment that needs little or no maintenance (maintenance prevention), and quickly repairing equipment after breakdowns occur (breakdown maintenance).
- TPM's goal is the total elimination of all losses, including breakdowns, equipment setup and adjustment losses, idling and minor stoppages, reduced speed, defects and rework, spills and process upset conditions, and start-up and yield losses.

Step 5: Cellular manufacturing

Cellular manufacturing/one-piece flow systems are work units arranged in a sequence that supports a smooth flow of materials and components through the production process with minimal transport or delay.

- Rather than processing multiple parts before sending them on to the next machine or process step (as is the case in batch-and-queue, or large-lot production), cellular manufacturing aims to move products through the manufacturing process one piece at a time, at a rate determined by customers' needs.
- Cellular manufacturing can also provide companies with the flexibility to vary product type or features on the production line in response to specific customer demands.
- To make the cellular design work, an organisation must often replace large, high volume production machines with small, flexible, 'right-sized' machines to fit well in the process 'cell'. Equipment often must be modified to stop and signal when a cycle is complete or when problems occur, using a technique called autonomation (or jidoka). This transformation often shifts worker responsibilities from watching a single machine, to managing multiple machines in production cell.
- While plant-floor workers may need to feed or unload pieces at the beginning or end of the process sequence, they are generally freed to focus on implementing TPM and process improvements.

Step 6: Six Sigma

The Six Sigma approach

Six Sigma is a quality management programme to achieve 'six sigma' levels of quality, derived from TQM.

- It is a performance measurement framework first pioneered by Motorola in the 1980s which has developed into an system for process improvement.
- It has been used by both manufacturing and service businesses.
- It can be implemented across the whole business, but in practice it is generally used for individual processes.
- It is designed to decrease wastage and improve products and services, leading to greater customer satisfaction and lower costs. Companies implementing Six Sigma report high levels of savings from projects.

- It is a data-driven approach, based on statistical measurements of variation from a standard or a norm and the use of quantitative data for processes.
- Its aim is to achieve a reduction in variations and the number of 'faults' that go beyond an accepted tolerance limit. The ultimate aim of a Six Sigma project is to reduce the variation in process output so that there are no more than 3.4 defects per million opportunities – the Six Sigma (6σ) level of performance.
- Performance measures are based on customer requirements. While targets may appear very high at first, it should be remembered that just one defect can result in a lost customer.

Key requirements for successful Six Sigma implementation

There are a number of key requirements for the implementation of Six Sigma.

- Six Sigma should be focused on the customer and based on the level of performance acceptable to the customer.
- Six Sigma targets for a process should be related to the main drivers of performance.
- To maximise savings Six Sigma needs to be part of a wider performance management programme which is linked to the strategy of the organisation. It should not be just about doing things better but about doing things differently.
- Senior managers within the organisation have a key role in driving the process.
- Training and education about the process throughout the organisation are essential for success.
- Six Sigma sets a tight target, but accepts some failure – the target is not zero defects.

Some criticisms and limitations of Six Sigma

Literature on Six Sigma contains some criticisms of the process and identifies a number of limitations as follows.

- Six Sigma has been criticised for its focus on current processes and reliance on data. It is suggested that this could become too rigid and limit process innovation.
- Six Sigma is based on the use of models which are by their nature simplifications of real life. Judgement needs to be used in applying the models in the context of business objectives.

- The approach can be very time consuming and expensive. Organisations need to be prepared to put time and effort into its implementation.
- The culture of the organisation must be supportive – not all organisations are ready for such a scientific process.
- The process is heavily data-driven. This can be a strength, but can become over-bureaucratic.
- Six Sigma can give all parts of the organisation a common language for process improvement, however it is important to ensure that this does not become jargon but is expressed in terms specific to the organisation and its business.
- There is an underlying assumption in Six Sigma that the existing business processes meet customers' expectations. It does not ask whether it is the right process.

Criticisms and limitations of lean production

The concept of lean production has many supporters, but it also has critics. The alleged limitations of lean production include the following.

- It might involve a large initial expenditure to switch from 'traditional' production systems to a system based on work cells. All the tools and equipment needed to manufacture a product need to be re-located to the same area of the factory floor. Employees need to be trained in multiple skills.
- Lean manufacturing, like TQM, is a philosophy or culture of working, and it might be difficult for management and employees to acquire this culture. Employees might not be prepared to give the necessary commitment.
- It might be tempting for companies to select some elements of lean manufacturing (such as production based on work cells), but not to adopt others (such as empowering employees to make on-the-spot decisions).
- In practice, the expected benefits of lean manufacturing (lower costs and shorter cycle times) have not always materialised, or might not have been as large as expected.

4 Enabling success – innovation and BPR

Process Innovation and Business Process Re-engineering

Process Innovation (PI) and Business Process Re-engineering (BPR) are similar concepts that emerged in the early 1990s from the writings of various management gurus. BPR in particular has been interpreted in a wide variety of ways and was much criticised because in some interpretations it took no account of human issues.

- BPR is the fundamental rethinking and rational redesign of the business processes to achieve dramatic improvements in critical contemporary measures of performance such as cost, quality, service and speed.
- PI emphasises the invention of entirely new processes, rather than tweaking existing ones. There is more emphasis on human resource management and the approach may involve rethinking the entire business and its mission rather than focusing on individual processes.

From this point of view PI is a more radical approach. It should be noted that there is no general agreement about the precise meanings of the terms or the difference between them.

Process innovation

Innovation can apply to product and/or process design and is aimed at the development of new core competences or as a response to competitor action.

The development of IT capabilities over the recent decade has seen the pace of innovation increase. Increasing sophistication of demand and levels of competition has seen the ability to innovate becoming a threshold competence in itself. The idea that 'what is good today, will not be so tomorrow' has never been so relevant.

Innovation can be used to:

- Reduce costs;
- Provide a basis for differentiation.

An organisation will need to exploit its creative ideas. This can be done via certain organisational dimensions:

- **Structure** – a flexible structure to avoid the stifling of initiative;
- **Culture** – sees failure as a learning experience and to be expected;

- **Leadership** – to lead the organisation via communication and the creation of vision;
- **People** – the team-based approach creating ownership and participation;
- **Communication** – creating awareness within the organisation of the ideas created.

Thomas Davenport, a leading writer on Process Innovation, suggests the following framework for assessing the priority for investment:

- Identify processes that are suitable for innovation.
- Identify 'change levers' (e.g. enabling or transformation technologies).
- Develop 'process visions' – where do we want to be?
- Understand and improve existing processes.
- Design and prototype new processes.

Business process re-engineering

As stated above, BPR is the fundamental rethinking and radical redesign of business processes:

- to achieve dramatic improvements in performance
- to increase the ability of the organisation to meet the needs of its customers
- to challenge existing ways of doing business and eradicate inefficient processes
- to use technology innovatively to carry out business in totally new ways.

BPR draws on the insights of Porter's value chain by viewing the organisation as a set of value-adding processes rather than as a segmented structure of departments and divisions. As such, the 'Value Chain' is commonly used in BPR as a tool to identify and analyse processes that are of strategic significance to the organisation.

Business process re-engineering (BPR)

The main stages of BPR

(1) **Process identification**

Each task performed within the organisation or department being re-engineered is broken down into a series of processes. Each process is recorded and analysed to find out whether it is:

– Necessary
– Adding value
– Supporting another value adding process.

It is important that a complete and detailed model of the processes is created (often this is software-based as the complexity of even simple business processes makes a paper based model unworkable) as it is to this that post-BPR performance improvements can be compared.

(2) **Process rationalisation**

Those processes which are not adding value, or which are not essential to supporting a value-adding process are discarded.

(3) **Process redesign**

The remaining processes are redesigned (IT based – WP, Spreadsheet, Accounting packages, CAD/CAM, EDI) so that they work in the most efficient way possible. At this stage detailed operating procedures need to be produced for all processes that are to be performed manually.

(4) **Process reassembly**

The re-engineered processes are implemented, resulting in tasks, departments and an organisation that work in the most efficient manner.

BPR Example – Mortgage processing

- Prior to BPR: In one organisation it was found that the processing of a mortgage application involved eight different application form with 217 questions, 750 steps, four IT systems, five functional areas of business, and four interviews with the customer. The whole process culminated in a mortgage offer being offered, on average, some 30 days from form completion.
- Post BPR: The process involved one interview, completion of one application form, and resulted in an offer being made within 24 hours.

Advantages of BPR

- It is useful in providing an organisation with cost advantages over competitors, and with improved customer service. Because significant, rather than incremental, changes in working practices are sought, an approach is encouraged which is more strategic than operational.
- It helps to reduce organisational complexity by focusing on core processes and driving out unnecessary or uneconomic activities.
- It offers an alternative perspective on formulating strategy based upon operating processes, rather than on products and markets (e.g. are we in the train business or the transport business?).
- It helps to link together the functional areas of an organisation by focusing on processes that cut across the value chain from inputs of materials and services to creating customer satisfaction.

Disadvantages OF BPR

- It is often used as the pretext for staff reductions;
- It is viewed as a 'quick fix' to organisational problems – one-off cost savings;
- It delegates decision making to lower levels of management – may affect employee attitudes and behaviour;
- Senior management may lose commitment, once the programme has been implemented;
- It may destroy existing controls within the organisation – reduced internal controls, quality of staff and accounting procedures, combining procedures, reduced segregation of duties;

- It overlooks the impact on human resources – BPR is a very time-consuming exercise. Introduction of new processes will involve new patterns of work, break-up of traditional workgroups, redundancies, loss of staff goodwill;
- It increases stress on staff – reduction in staff numbers at middle and line management levels – overload the remaining staff, resulting in reduced effectiveness;
- BPR focuses too much on improving existing business rather than developing new and better lines of business.

Test your understanding 1 – WOWR

The WOWR organisation produces books and magazines. It employs 560 staff in 7 different locations. The organisation has been using IT in various departments as follows:

Production – stock control, including real-time stock and finished goods levels

Sales – historical record of books and magazines sold for the last 15 years

Finance and administration – maintenance of all ledgers, cash book and wages details

Human resources – factual information on employees, such as rate of pay, department, home address and date of birth.

In other words, most of the basic transaction systems within the organisation have been computerised. Additional investment in IT has been limited, partly as a result of the success of the organisation's core businesses, and partly from a lack of desire for change on the part of existing managers.

Recent changes in the senior management of the organisation now mean that additional appropriate IT investment is seen as being a key success criterion.

Required:

(a) Using a suitable framework, advise the managers how to assess the priority for investment in competing IT systems within the WOWR organisation.

(10 marks)

(b) Compare and contrast Process Innovation (PI) and Business Process Reengineering (BPR).

(5 marks)

(c) Explain the reasons why PI and BPR are important in an organisation, making reference to the situation in the WOWR organisation where appropriate.

(10 marks)

(Total: 25 marks)

5 Summary

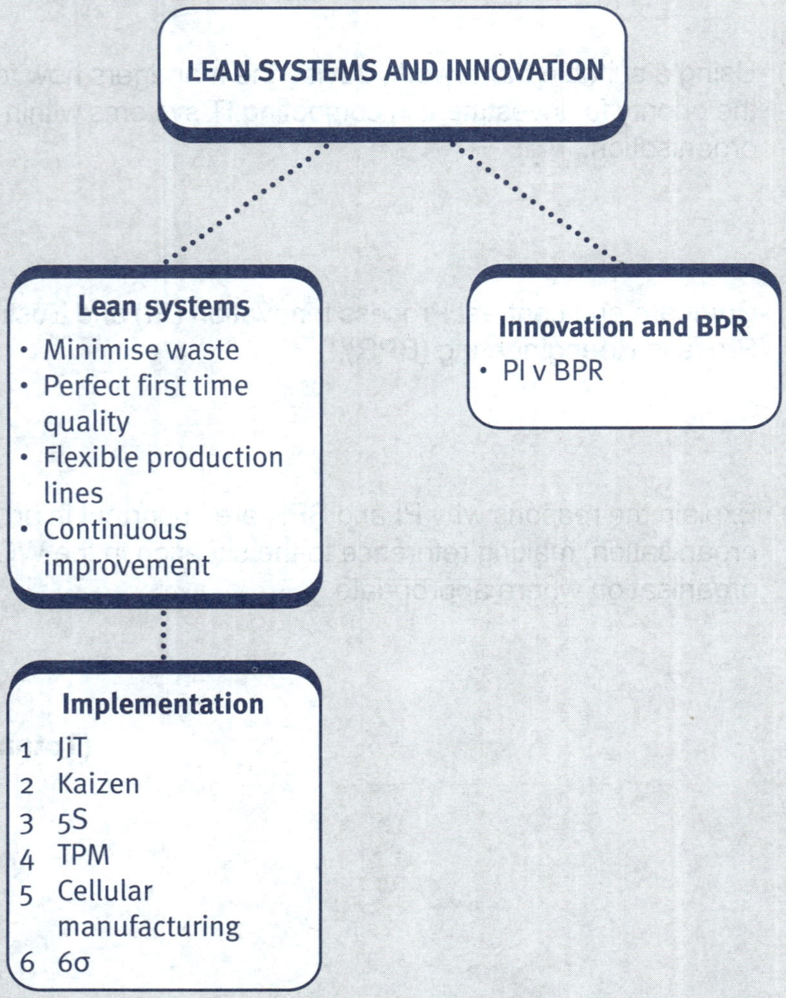
LEAN SYSTEMS AND INNOVATION
Lean systems
• Minimise waste
• Perfect first time quality
• Flexible production lines
• Continuous improvement
Innovation and BPR
• PI v BPR
Implementation
1 JiT
2 Kaizen
3 5S
4 TPM
5 Cellular manufacturing
6 6σ

Test your understanding answers

Test your understanding 1 – WOWR

WOWR ORGANISATION

Key answer tips

For Part (a) a wide range of different systems and theories can be used (CSF and PI analysis; the value chain; SWOT; McFarlan; CBA) as long as they assess the priority for IT investment. Our answer below uses the framework proposed by Thomas Davenport in *Process Innovation: Reengineering Work Through Information Technology*, 1993, as in the official CIMA answer, since this seems most appropriate in the overall context of the question.

(a) Thomas Davenport, a leading writer on Process Innovation, suggests the following framework for assessing the priority for investment in competing IT systems:

- Identify processes that are suitable for innovation.
- Identify 'change levers' (enabling or transformation technologies).
- Develop 'process visions'.
- Understand and improve existing processes.
- Design and prototype new processes.

Processes that are suitable for innovation

Most of the basic transaction systems in the organisation have already been computerised, although it seems likely that the systems are nothing more than computerised versions of the previous manual system. It may be possible to establish closer links between the separate systems such as production, sales and finance. Production systems relate to books and magazines – in other words text and graphics – and these may well benefit from investment in newer technologies such as project management software and groupware for collaborative working.

Change levers

WOWR have made little investment in IT in recent years, during a time of great technological change, particularly in communications technology. It is likely that Internet-enabled systems, Enterprise Resource Planning systems and Customer Relationship Management systems could offer considerable benefits to a company such as WOWR. The company's products themselves (text and graphics) are perfect candidates for items that could be distributed online.

Process visions

This stage involves looking at processes as the means of achieving the company's mission. For instance WOWR may decide that, above all, it wishes to 'stick to the knitting' and not get involved in online publication. Nevertheless it is possible that its current products could be improved and better targeted and the company has a wealth of historical sales records that could be mined to identify hidden trends and other useful information.

Understand existing processes

This stage would look at the benefits and drawbacks of existing information flows and technologies. Any new process should not prevent the company from carrying out tasks that it can currently do, so long as those tasks add value. There may be some small steps that need to be taken before more radical process redesign is feasible, such as upgrading operating systems or cleansing of existing data stores.

Design and prototype new processes

This stage takes the change levers and uses them to alter the existing processes, for instance using ERP software to integrate production, sales and finance or creating subscription-based on-line versions of magazines.

(b) Process Innovation and Business Process Re-engineering

Process Innovation (PI) and Business Process Re-engineering (BPR) are similar concepts that emerged in the early 1990s from the writings of various management gurus. BPR in particular has been interpreted in a wide variety of ways and was much criticised because in some interpretations it took no account of human issues.

BPR is the fundamental rethinking and rational redesign of the business processes to achieve dramatic improvements in critical contemporary measures of performance such as cost, quality, service and speed.

PI emphasises the invention of entirely new processes, rather than tweaking existing ones. There is more emphasis on human resource management and the approach may involve rethinking the entire business and its mission rather than focusing on individual processes.

From this point of view PI is a more radical approach. It should be noted that there is no general agreement about the precise meanings of the terms or the difference between them.

(c) **Why PI and BPR are important an organisation**

Changes in information and communications technology have come at an astonishing pace since the late 1990s and there is no sign of a slowdown. Each new development offers new opportunities to businesses and it is the businesses that embrace such change that are most likely to survive and thrive.

WOWR appears to be well-established in a mature industry, but its previous managers lacked the desire for change. From the limited information in the scenario it appears that the new management understand the importance of IT to the future of the business.

At the very least WOWR needs to invest to maintain its competitive position. If other publishers have amended their processes so that they can offer services such as on-line ordering, then WOWR will need to do the same.

Preferably WOWR should attempt to gain competitive advantage. For example, innovation in products is a source of differentiation, which enables maintenance of this strategy: for example WOWR may be able to offer on-line supplements to its books and publications, adding value for purchasers and subscribers.

However, innovation must be continuous because it is only a matter of time before competitors catch up with or improve upon another company's innovative ideas.

Innovation in production processes might reduce production costs and hence support a cost-leadership strategy. Innovation in sales and marketing processes may lead to better decisions about which publications to target at which markets.

Innovative organisations tend to attract and retain higher-quality staff, who want to gain experience with the market leader and want the opportunity to contribute to the development of a forward-looking organisation. Or, from the opposite point of view, lack of change tends to demotivate staff, especially if they are aware that other companies have better systems and are able to produce higher quality products and give better service.

chapter

15

Change management – understanding the context of change

Chapter learning objectives

Lead	Component
B1. Advise on important elements in the change process.	(a) Discuss the concept of organisational change.
B2. Evaluate tools and methods for successfully implementing a change programme.	(a) Evaluate approaches to managing change. (b) Compare and contrast continuous and discontinuous change.
B3. Recommend change management processes in support of strategy implementation.	(a) Evaluate the role of change management in the context of strategy implementation.

Indicative syllabus content

- External and internal change triggers (e.g. environmental factors, mergers and acquisitions, reorganisation and rationalisation)
- Problem identification as a precursor to change
- Cultural processes of change
- The importance of managing critical periods of discontinuous change
- Change management and its role in the successful implementation of change.

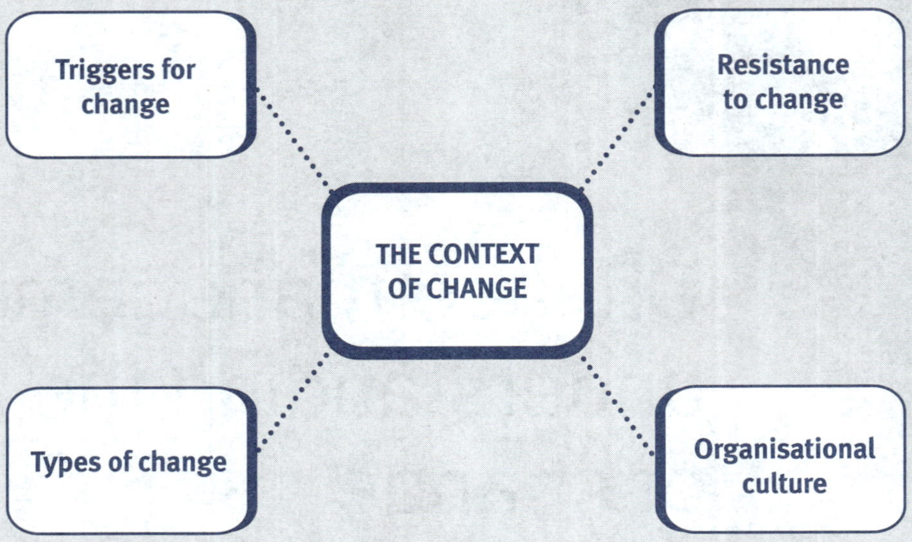

1 Introduction

Internal and external pressures make change inevitable. 'Adapt or die' is the motto of almost every organisation. Some strive to meet the challenge by leading those in the marketplace whilst others hide in niches, snapping at the heels of the major players.

The key questions for all companies are not whether to change or not but rather:

- **What to change?**
- **What to change to?**
- **How to change successfully?**

2 Triggers for change

External triggers

Environmental pressure for change can be divided into two groups.

- General (indirect action) environmental factors – these can be identified using the familiar PEST framework and
- Task (direct action) factors – these can be assessed using Porter's five forces model

Examples of external triggers

Indirect triggers (PEST)

Political/legal	Changes in government New environmental protection policies New labour laws European directives Private/public partnerships
Economic	Growth or recession Changes in currency and interest rates Local labour costs Regional prosperity/opportunities Disposable income
Social	Attitudes to work and leisure Environmentalism Attitudes to health/education Fashion trends Changing national/regional culture
Technological	Growth in Internet Public use of IT Global sourcing/call centres Innovations

Direct triggers (Porter's five forces)

Competitive rivalry	Powerful rivals may force the firm to have to adapt to survive, either through innovation, if a differentiator, or cost cutting if a cost-leader.
Power of customers	Powerful customers could trigger a firm to consider forwards vertical integration
Power of suppliers	Supplier power could encourage a firm to redesign products in order to reduce the reliance on specialist components and thus facilitate multi-sourcing
Threat of new entrants	New entrants may force incumbent firms to improve quality to maintain market share
Threat of substitutes	New technologies may result in substitutes that render existing products obsolete. this could lead to factory closure and reorganisation.

Internal triggers

The reasons for change within the organisation could span any functional area of operation or level of control from strategic to operational.

Philosophy	New ownership
	New CEO
	New initiative/management style
Reorganisation	Takeover/merger
	Divisional restructuring
	Rationalisation/cost reduction
Personnel	Promotions/transfers
	Rules/procedures
	Training/development
Conditions	Location change
	Outsourcing
	Rosters/flexible working
Technology	New procedures/systems
	Changing information demands
	Integration of roles

Problem identification as a precursor to change

The above triggers can be reasons **why** change is considered or even necessary. However, further strategic analysis is needed to determine **what** needs changing.

e.g

Illustration 1 – Problem identification as a precursor to change

For example, TGH Textiles is a UK-based clothing manufacturer that has seen falling profits, declining margins and a loss of market share over the last two years. The main reason for this decline is increasing competition from manufacturers in China and India.

The external trigger for change is increased competitive rivalry, but what needs changing?

The first step would involve analysing the firm's cost base and determining customer perceptions regarding relative quality. This should help TGH to see how it's competitive advantage is being eroded. Suppose poor quality is identified as the underlying problem.

Even then, it is not obvious what needs changing. "Poor quality" could be an underlying problem of customer perception related to brand or design flaws, the quality of raw materials, production problems or an underlying culture where quality is not valued highly enough. Determining the main cause(s) could involve discussions with customers, competitor analysis, Porter's value chain analysis, SWOT and /or benchmarking.

Only then will the directors have a clear idea of what needs changing.

3 Classifying change

Types of organisational change

Change can be classified by the extent of the change required, and the speed with which the change is to be achieved:

Types of change

Speed of change	Extent of change: Transformation	Extent of change: Realignment
Incremental	**Evolution:** Transformational change implemented gradually through inter-related initiatives; likely to be proactive change undertaken in participation of the need for future change	**Adaptation:** Change undertaken to realign the way in which the organisation operates; implemented in a series of steps
Big Bang	**Revolution:** Transformational change that occurs via simultaneous initiatives on many fronts: • more likely to be forced and reactive because of the changing competitive conditions that the organisation is facing	**Reconstruction:** Change undertaken to realign the way in which the organisation operates with many initiatives implemented simultaneously: • often forced and reactive because of a changing competitive context

Note that incremental change is also known as "continuous" change while "discontinuous change" refers to the big bang above.

- Transformation entails changing an organisation's culture. It is a fundamental change that cannot be handled within the existing organisational paradigm.

- Realignment does not involve a fundamental reappraisal of the central assumptions and beliefs.
- Evolution can take a long period of time, but results in a fundamentally different organisation once completed.
- Revolution is likely to be a forced, reactive transformation using simultaneous initiatives on many fronts, and often in a relatively short space of time. It is critical that this type of change is managed effectively.

e.g

Illustration 2 – Strategic change

Strategic change is by definition far-reaching. We speak of strategic change when fundamental alterations are made to the business system or the organisational system. Adding a lemon-flavoured Coke to the product portfolio is interesting, maybe important, but not a strategic change, while branching out into bottled water was a major departure from Coca-Cola's traditional business system.

Evolution or revolution?

Another way that evolution can be explained is by conceiving of the organisation as a learning system. However, within incremental change there may be a danger of strategic drift, because change is based on the existing paradigm and routines of the organisation, even when environmental or competitive pressure might suggest the need for more fundamental change.

In selecting an approach to strategic change, most managers struggle with the question of how bold they should be. On the one hand, they usually realise that to fundamentally transform the organisation, a break with the past is needed. To achieve strategic renewal it is essential to turn away from the firm's heritage and to start with a clean slate. On the other hand, they also recognise the value of continuity, building on past experiences, investments and loyalties. To achieve lasting strategic renewal, people in the organisation will need time to learn, adapt and grow into a new organisational reality.

The 'window of opportunity' for achieving a revolutionary strategic change can be small for a number of reasons. Some of the most common triggers are:

- competitive pressure – when a firm is under intense competitive pressure and its market position starts to erode quickly, a rapid and dramatic response might be the only approach possible. Especially when the organisation threatens to slip into a downward spiral towards insolvency, a bold turnaround can be the only option left to the firm.

- regulatory pressure – firms can also be put under pressure by the government or regulatory agencies to push through major changes within a short period of time. Such externally imposed revolutions can be witnessed among public sector organisations (e.g. hospitals and schools) and highly regulated industries (e.g. utilities and telecommunications), but in other sectors of the economy as well (e.g. public health regulations). Some larger organisations will, however, seek to influence and control regulation.
- first mover advantage – a more proactive reason for instigating revolutionary change, is to be the first firm to introduce a new product, service or technology and to build up barriers to entry for late movers.

Test your understanding 1 – Zed Bank

Historically the directors of Zed Bank have resisted change, seeking to offer a traditional approach to its customers. However, recent problems within the banking industry and an increasingly competitive market has forced the Board to consider a number of important initiatives, including:

- enhancing its current services to customers by providing them with on-line internet and telephone banking services; and
- reducing costs by closing many of its rural and smaller branches (outlets).

In an attempt to pacify the employee representatives (the Banking Trade Union) and to reduce expected protests by the communities affected by branch closure, a senior bank spokesperson has announced that the changes will be 'incremental' in nature. In particular, she has stressed that:

- the change will be implemented over a lengthy time period
- there will be no compulsory redundancies
- banking staff ready to take on new roles and opportunities in the online operations will be retrained and offered generous relocation expenses.

For customers, the bank has promised that automatic cash dispensing machines will be available in all the localities where branches (outlets) close. Customers will also be provided with the software needed for Internet banking and other assistance necessary to give them quick and easy access to banking services.

The leader of the Banking Trade Union is 'appalled' at the initiatives announced. He has argued that the so-called 'incremental' change is in fact the start of a 'transformational' change that will have serious repercussions, not only for the Union's members but also for many of the bank's customers.

Required:

Distinguish incremental change from transformational change. Explain why the bank spokesperson and the trade union leader disagree over their description of the change.

Greiner's growth model

Greiner suggests that organisations grow through an evolutionary process punctuated by periods of crisis. The model assumes that as an organisation ages it grows in size. This growth is characterised by:

Evolution: There is a distinctive factor that drives organisational growth.

Revolution: There is a distinctive factor that creates crisis marring the ability to change.

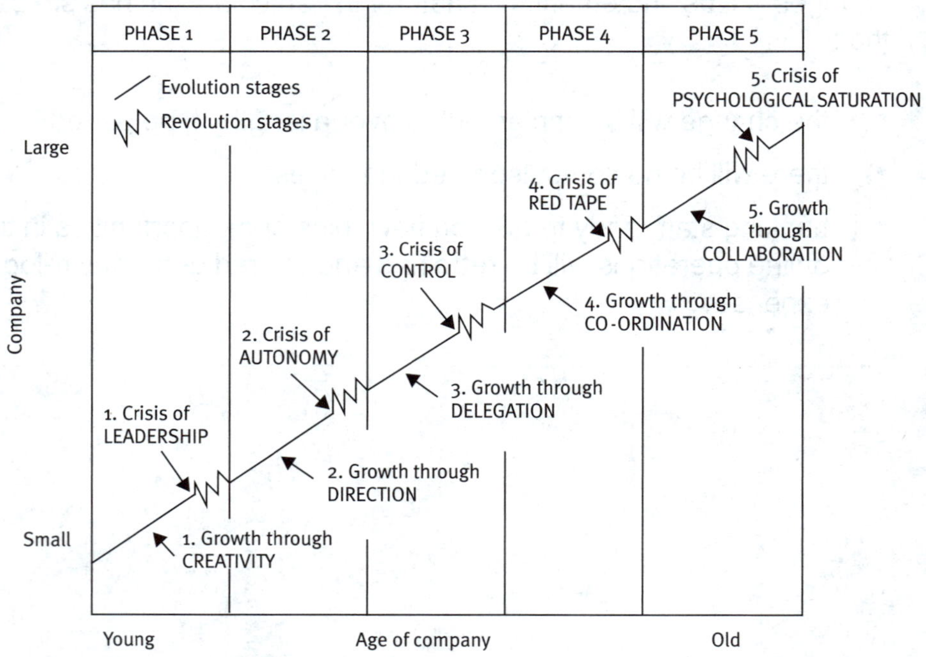

Phase 1

(a) Growth through creativity

The goal is survival for the small dynamically-led organisation.

(b) Crisis of leadership

A need for distinct management skills emerges beyond the abilities of one person.

Phase 2

(a) Growth through direction

Professionalisation leads to structure and direction of activity.

(b) Crisis of autonomy

Employees resent the loss of autonomy, senior management find delegation difficult.

Phase 3

(a) Growth through delegation

Decentralisation of management and decision making is the basis for growth.

(b) Crisis of control

Sub-optimal activity and problems of co-ordination and control.

Phase 4

(a) Growth through co-ordination

Internal systems for co-ordination and control to optimise use of resources.

(b) Crisis of red tape

Over-zealous control aggravates grievances and restricts activity.

Phase 5

(a) Growth through collaboration

Increased informal collaboration, a cultural shift.

(b) Crisis of psychological saturation

Exhaustion of teamwork and longing for new horizons.

4 Organisational culture

Definition

Culture is the set of values, guiding beliefs, understandings and ways of thinking that are shared by the members of an organisation and is taught to new members as correct. It represents the unwritten, feeling part of the organisation.

Culture is 'the way we do things around here' (Charles Handy).

Culture is a set of 'taken-for-granted' assumptions, views of the environment, behaviours and routines (Schein).

Cultural processes of change

The inherent culture of the organisation is important for two reasons:

Firstly the existing culture can become "embedded" and hence resistant to change. Overcoming this resistance can be a major challenge.

Secondly the existing culture can limit the types of strategy development and change that are considered.

- Faced with forces for change, managers will seek to minimise the extent to which they are faced with ambiguity and uncertainty by defining the situation in terms of that which is familiar.
- This can explain why some firms adopt incremental strategies and, worse, why some fail to address the impact of environmental triggers, resulting in strategic drift.

e.g

Illustration 3 – Cultural process of change

Faced with a change trigger such as declining performance, management are likely to react as follows:

(1) First managers will try to improve the effectiveness and efficiency of the existing strategy

e.g. through tighter controls

(2) If this is not effective, then a change in strategy may occur but in line with existing strategies

e.g. through market development, selling existing products into markets that are similar to existing ones and managing the process in the same way as they are used to.

(3) Even when managers know intellectually that more radical change is needed, they find themselves constrained by existing routines, assumptions and political processes.

The cultural web

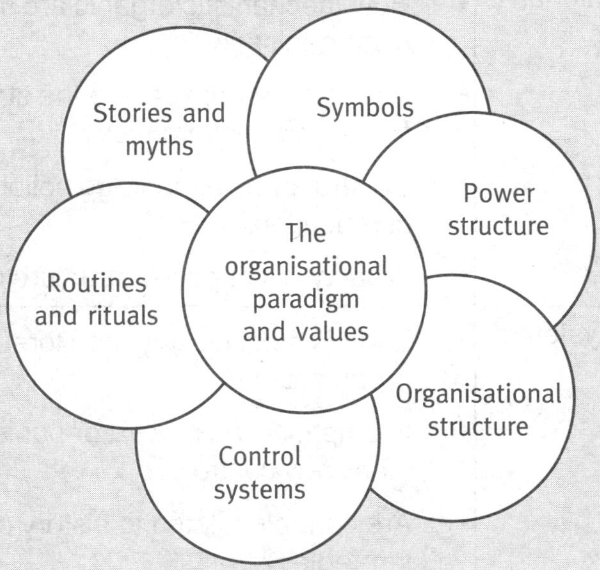

The cultural web was devised by Gerry Johnson as part of his work to attempt to explain why firms often failed to adjust to environmental change as quickly as they needed to. He concluded that firms developed a way of understanding their organisation – called a paradigm – and found it difficult to think and act outside this paradigm if it was particularly strong.

Using the cultural web to map change

The concept of the cultural web is a useful device for mapping out change but its real worth is in the fact that we can identify which elements of culture need to change.

Key questions to ask include:

Stories	• What core belief do the stories in my place reflect? • How pervasive are these beliefs (through the levels of the organisation)? • Do stories relate to: strengths or weaknesses, successes or failures, conformity or mavericks? Who are the heroes and villains? • What norms do the mavericks deviate from?
Routines and rituals	• What behaviour do routines encourage? Which would look odd if changed? • What are the key rituals? What core beliefs do they reflect? • What do training programmes emphasise? • How easy are the rituals/routines to change?
Organisational structures	• How mechanistic/organic are the structures in my organisation? • How flat/hierarchical are the structures? How formal/informal are they? • Do structures encourage collaboration or competition? • What types of power structure do they support?
Control systems	• What is most closely monitored/controlled in my organisation? • Is emphasis on reward or punishment? Are there many/few controls? • Are controls related to history or current strategies?
Power structures	• What are the core beliefs of the leadership in my organisation? • How strongly held are these beliefs (idealists or pragmatists)? • How is power distributed in the organisation? • What are the main blockages to change?

Symbols	• What language and jargon are used in my place of work? • How internal or accessible are they? • What aspects of strategy are highlighted in publicity? • What status symbols are there? • Are there particular symbols that denote the organisation?
Overall	• What are the (four) key underlying assumptions that are the paradigm? • What is the dominant culture? • How easy is this to change?

e.g

Illustration 4 – The cultural web

Suppose you are acting as a consultant to the technical services department of a local government authority. You have found that departments are not very responsive to the needs of users and that service is inconsistent from one branch to another.

A strategic change workshop with managers resulted in the following cultural web:

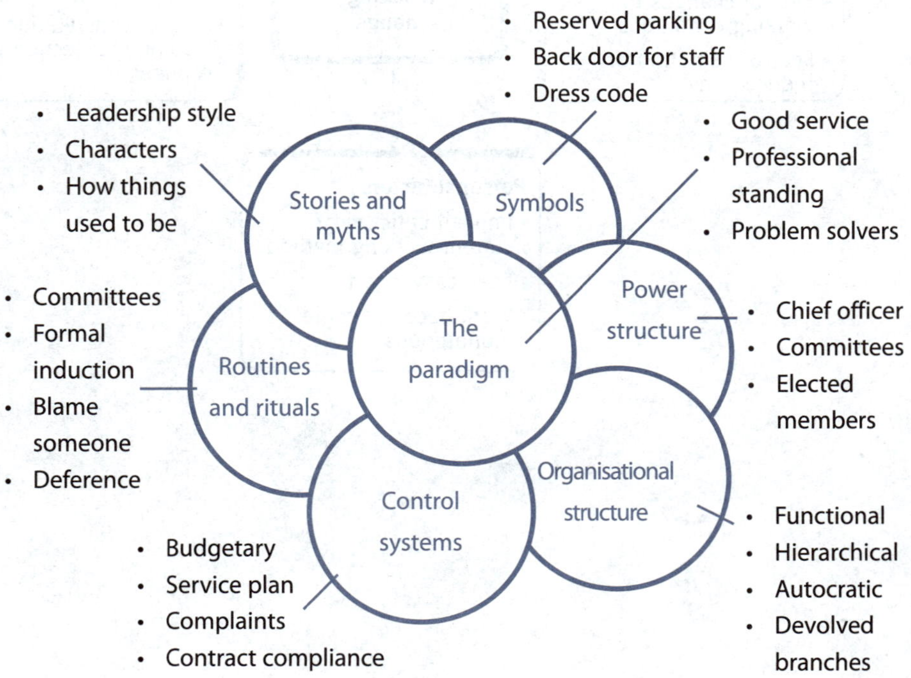

What is notable about the paradigm is that staff believe they are providing a "good service", that they have a high professional standing and see themselves as problem solvers. Unfortunately their problem solving and professional standards do not appear to be customer focused. The fact that stories and myths focus on how things "used to be" indicate staff are out of touch with user needs.

Furthermore, given the degree of local autonomy, an emphasis on status symbols such as parking spaces and a blame culture, it is hardly surprising that co-operation and standardisation across branches is poor.

These are the cultural challenges that must be met if effective change is to be implemented.

5 Resistance to change

Resistance to change is the action taken by individuals and groups when they perceive that a change that is occurring is a threat to them.

Resistance is 'any attitude or behaviour that reflects a person's unwillingness to make or support a desired change'.

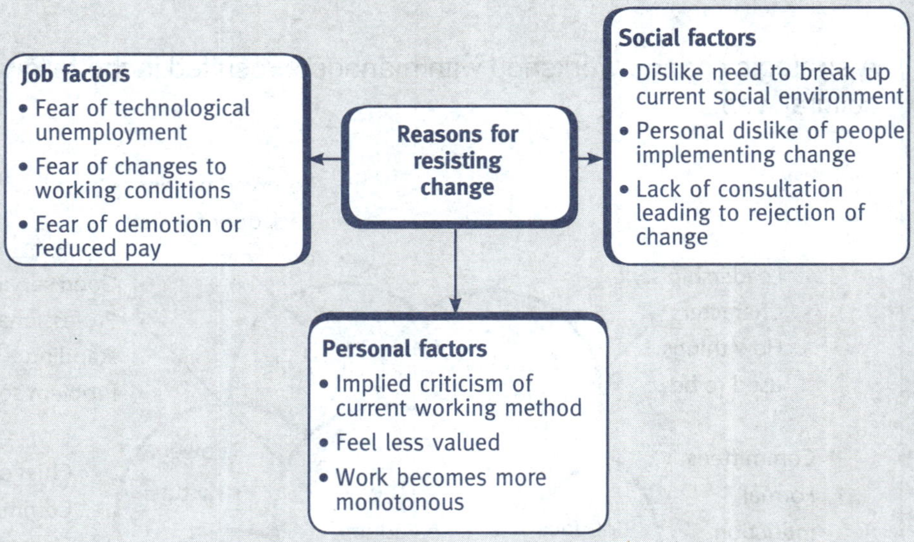

Resistance may take many forms, including active or passive, overt or covert, individual or organised, aggressive or timid. For each source of resistance, management need to provide an appropriate response, e.g.:

Source of resistance	Possible response
• The need for security and the familiar	• Provide information and encouragement, invite involvement
• Having the opinion that no change is needed	• Clarify the purpose of the change and how it will be made
• Trying to protect vested interests	• Demonstrate the problem or the opportunity that makes changes desirable

Reasons for resisting change (Kotter and Schlesinger)

According to Kotter and Schlesinger (1979) there are four reasons that explain why certain people resist change.

- Parochial self-interest (some people are concerned with the implication of the change for themselves and how it may affect their own interests, rather than considering the effects for the success of the business).
- Misunderstanding (communication problems; inadequate information).
- Low tolerance to change (certain people are very keen on security and stability in their work).
- Different assessments of the situation (some employees may disagree on the reasons for the change and on the advantages and disadvantages of the change process).

Test your understanding 2 – M Magazines

M Magazines (M) publishes several major magazines in country A. M's best-selling title is a fashion magazine – Mean – although it also produces magazines on other topics, such as sport and technology.

The majority of M's shares are held by members of the founding family, who have traditionally occupied all of the senior positions within management, although most key decisions are made in consultation with the staff.

M currently employs around 2,500 staff in one large office building in country A's capital city.

The family has always been concerned with maintaining the family name and have focused on the quality of the magazines. Unfortunately, in recent years this has not prevented a significant reduction in M's profitability leading to M's first ever loss being made in the last financial year.

This has led M to hire a Finance Director (FD) who is not a member of the owning family for the first time in its history. After a careful review of M's expenditure he has discovered a large amount of unnecessary expenditure.

He has therefore proposed centralising a number of key functions, such as accounting, printing and proof-reading which are currently duplicated in each magazine. This will lead to around 300 job losses.

In addition he has suggested that the magazines should be produced using cheaper paper and inks, that the large expense accounts offered to senior managers should be cut and that M should start making use of intranets and groupware to allow staff to share ideas quickly and easily.

The FD's proposals have been met with significant resistance from M employees, as well as a number of members of the owning family.

Required:

Discuss the reasons that the FD's proposals are likely to have met with resistance.

6 Summary

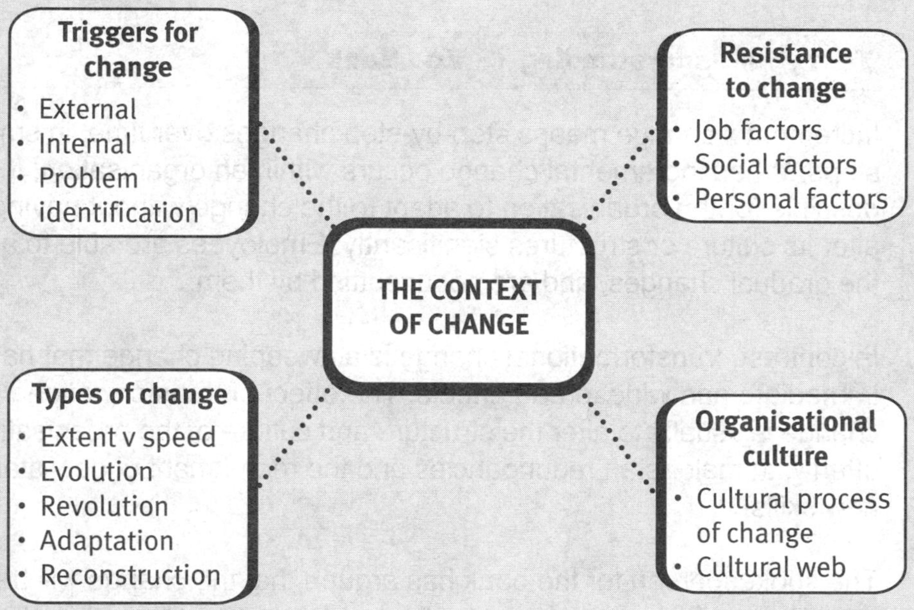
Triggers for change
• External
• Internal
• Problem identification
Resistance to change
• Job factors
• Social factors
• Personal factors
THE CONTEXT OF CHANGE
Types of change
• Extent v speed
• Evolution
• Revolution
• Adaptation
• Reconstruction
Organisational culture
• Cultural process of change
• Cultural web

Test your understanding answers

Test your understanding 1 – Zed Bank

Incremental change means step-by-step changes over time, in small steps. When incremental change occurs within an organisation, it is possible for the organisation to adapt to the change without having to alter its culture or structures significantly. Employees are able to adapt to the gradual changes, and are not unsettled by them.

In contrast, transformational change is a sweeping change that has immediate and widespread effects. The effect of transformational change is usually to alter the structure and culture of the organisation, often with major staff redundancies and the recruitment of new staff with new skills.

The spokesperson for the bank has argued that the change will be incremental. Since the change will take place over a long period of time, staff will have time to adapt to the new structure. There will be no compulsory redundancies and staff will be re-trained in new skills. Although some branches will close, others will remain open, and customers will be offered additional facilities through on-line banking.

The trade union leader believes that the change will be much more dramatic. He might believe that many employees will leave the bank because they are unable to adapt to the new service, or because they are unwilling to re-locate from the branches that are closed down. The bank might push through the branch closure programme more quickly than it has currently proposed, and staff redundancies could be made compulsory if there are not enough individuals willing to take voluntary redundancy.

Essentially, the two individuals take differing viewpoints because they are looking at change differently. The spokesperson for the bank wants to persuade employees to accept the change, and even welcome it. The trade union representative wants to warn employees about the potential consequences, and has therefore stressed the risks.

Test your understanding 2 – M Magazines

Reasons for resistance

There may be many reasons why the new FD is meeting resistance from M Magazines when trying to push through a change management process.

Job factors

Many employees may be resisting due to concerns about their jobs. For 300 employees, the FD's proposals will mean unemployment, which means they are likely to be strongly resistant to them.

Many other employees will be affected by the plans to centralise key functions. Those members of staff who remain may be forced to take on a heavier workload to cover the roles of employees made redundant. This may also cause resistance.

Senior managers will be unhappy due to the reduction in their expense accounts as this will be perceived as a loss of their status within the business.

In addition, the FD is proposing increased use of intranets and groupware. Staff may well be unfamiliar with these systems and dislike the idea of having to learn how to use them. They may also have concerns over the impact they will have on their jobs.

Personal factors

The changes suggested by the FD may well be seen as an implied criticism of the long-standing methods of the business. This may well cause resistance from not only the staff, but the owners who have been heavily involved in running the business.

Senior managers may feel less valued under the proposals due to the cuts to their expense accounts, leading to further resistance.

The owners of the company have traditionally focused on the quality of the magazines as they feel this reflects on their family name. The proposals to reduce the quality of the paper and ink is therefore likely to be poorly received by them.

Social factors

The family has normally made key decisions within the company in full consultation with the employees. This does not seem to have been the case with the FD's proposals, reducing the likelihood that employees will accept the changes.

The FD is also new in his role and, for the first time, not a member of the owning family. This may reduce his perceived authority, making it more likely that employees, managers and owners will feel that they do not have to follow his suggestions.

chapter

16

Change management – managing the change process

Chapter learning objectives

Lead	Component
B1. Advise on important elements in the change process.	(b) Recommend techniques to manage resistance to change.
B2. Evaluate tools and methods for successfully implementing a change programme.	(c) Evaluate tools, techniques and strategies for managing the change process. (d) Evaluate the role of leadership in managing the change process.
B3. Recommend change management processes in support of strategy implementation.	(b) Evaluate ethical issues and their resolution in the context of organisational change.

Indicative syllabus content

- Stage models of change
- Tools, techniques and models associated with organisational change
- Approaches, styles and strategies of change management
- Importance of adaptation and continuous change
- Leading change
- The advantages and disadvantages of different styles of management on the successful implementation of strategy

- Group formation within an organisation and its impact on change processes within organisations
- Business ethics in general and the CIMA Code of Ethics for Professional Accountants (Parts A and B) in the context of implementation of strategic plans.

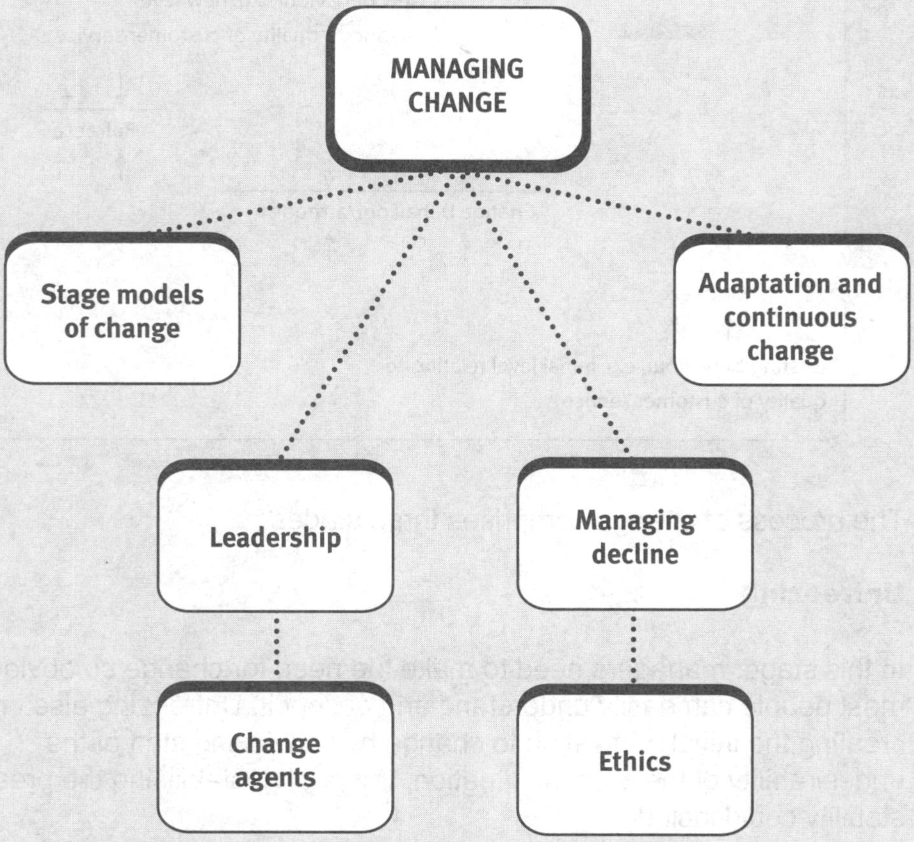

1 Introduction

As can be seen from the previous chapter, understanding the factors that impact on change management can be complex. However, even when a manager has a good understanding of the context of change within their organisation, they still need to be able to successfully implement the change itself.

Given the conflicting views of different stakeholders – such as shareholders, employees and customers – achieving change within an organisation is often difficult and prone to failure. Due to this, a number of different theorists have examined the issue and identified possible approaches to managing the change process within the organisation.

2 Stage models of the change process

Lewin's three-stage model

The three-stage model of change was proposed by Kurt Lewin in the 1950's. He argued that, in order for change to occur successfully, organisations need to progress through three stages.

This process, shown in the following diagram, includes unfreezing habits or standard operating procedures, changing to new patterns and refreezing to ensure lasting effects.

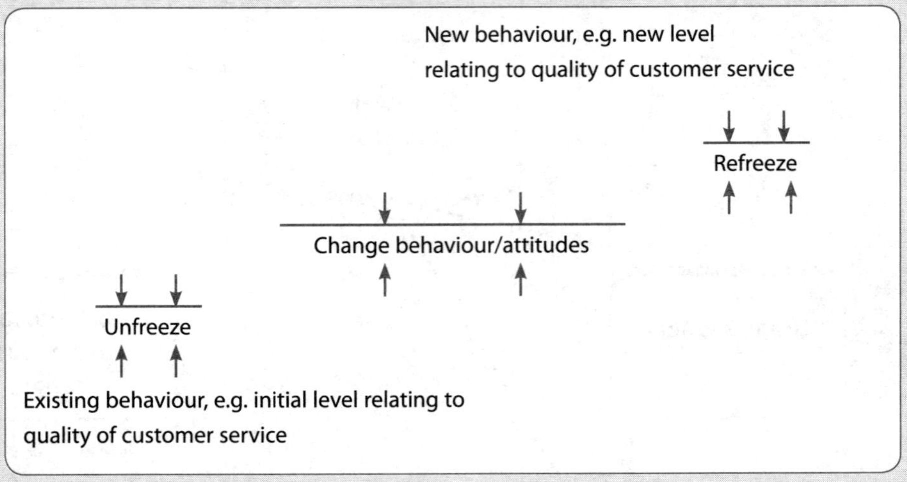

The process of change comprises three stages.

Unfreezing

In this stage, managers need to make the need for change so obvious that most people can easily understand and accept it. Unfreezing also involves creating the initial motivation to change by convincing staff of the undesirability of the present situation. Ways of destabilising the present stability could include:

- Identifying and exploiting existing areas of stress or dissatisfaction.
- Creating or introducing additional forces for change, such as tighter budgets and targets or new personnel in favour of the change.
- Increasing employee knowledge about markets, competitors and the need for change.

Change

The change process itself is mainly concerned with identifying what the new behaviour or norm should be. This stage will often involve

- Establishing new patterns of behaviour
- Setting up new reporting relationships
- Creating new reward / incentive schemes
- introducing a new style of management

It is vital that new information is communicated concerning the new attitudes, culture and concepts that the organisation wants to be adopted, so that these are internalised by employees.

Refreezing

Refreezing or stabilising the change involves ensuring that people do not slip back into old ways. As such it involves reinforcement of the new pattern of work or behaviour by:

- Larger rewards (salary, bonuses, promotion) for those employees who have fully embraced the new culture
- Publicity of success stories and new "heroes" – e.g. through employee of the month

Bank automation

During the recent economic problems across the world, many companies have been faced with the need to restructure their organisations in order to cut costs and improve efficiency – with many banks being particularly hard-hit.

A number of banks have been increasing the amount of automation in their branches. This involves the purchase of cash machines that are able to process deposits of cash and cheques as well as performing other basic account management functions. Many other traditional branch functions now require customers to telephone central call centres rather than going into a branch. These changes allow the bank to reduce the number of staff in their branches, saving money.

However, such an approach is likely to create significant resistance from staff – especially employees who work within the branches themselves. The bank may wish to use Lewin's three-stage model as a way of managing the change process.

Unfreezing

This involves convincing employees of the initial need for the increased automation in the branches. While this may be difficult to do, especially if employees are heavily unionised, it is a crucial step in the change management process.

The bank may choose to explain to employees about its current position in the market and the effect that the economic downturn has had on profits. If reducing costs will help to secure the long-term survival of the entire bank, many employees may be convinced of the need to proceed with the change.

The directors of the bank may also stress any potential benefits of the proposals for the remaining branch employees. For example, a reduction in the number of basic account queries from customers may free up time for more interesting work, such as helping customers review their finances.

Change

This is the stage where the proposed change actually occurs. It will involve the reduction in the number of branch employees and the installation of new machinery into the branches.

This will require training for employees. They will need to be able to deal with customer queries and complaints about the new branch procedures as well as how to maintain the new cash machines.

Communication is vital at this stage. Employees must know what is expected of them during and after the change management process.

Refreezing

This stage tries to ensure that bank staff do not return to the old systems. In this case managers need to prevent staff from processing basic customer transactions themselves rather than convincing customers to use the new automated systems.

This may involve the creation of new reward schemes to encourage staff to adopt the new procedures. For instance, branch staff could receive an increased bonus if a high proportion of their customers start maintaining their accounts using the automated system. They may be penalised if they continue using the old systems.

Managers can also reinforce the new approach by publicising success stories of branches that have embraced the change and by promoting key members of staff who supported the automation process.

Criticisms of Lewin's ice cube model

Kanter et al suggest that Lewin's ice cube model is too simplistic.

They argue that the model is based on the assumptions that organisations are stable and static so change results only from concentrated effort and only in one direction.

Kanter et al argue that change is 'multi-directional and ubiquitous', that it happens in all directions simultaneously and is often a continuous process.

Test your understanding 1 – WW

WW is a company specialising in industrial paint manufacturing. It has recently experienced significant growth in turnover and has opened two new factories to help it cope with the additional demand.

The managers of WW have become concerned that their current accounting software is no longer adequate for their needs. The current system is a basic one, which is mainly designed to record transactions and produce financial statements at the end of each period. Given the growth in the business, the managers of WW now need additional information, such as the production of monthly management reports and the ability to accurately cost each unit of their products.

The current accounting system does not support these functions, meaning the accounting department is required to produce the information manually, which is both complex and time-consuming. WW's managers are concerned that this delay in obtaining management information may be putting the firm at a disadvantage in the marketplace.

The managers are therefore currently considering the purchase of a new, more complex, accounting package that will easily allow the production of the management accounting information that they need.

WW has a small accounting department with six members of staff. All of these staff members have been employees of the company for many years. The current accounting package has been in use within WW for the last seven years.

Required:

Using Lewin's three-stage model, explain how WW could manage the changeover to the new accounting package.

Force field analysis

Lewin also emphasised the importance of force field analysis. He argued that managers should consider any change situation in terms of:

- the factors encouraging and facilitating the change (the driving forces)
- the factors that hinder change (the restraining forces).

Change will only be successful if the driving forces are larger than the restraining forces.

If we want to bring about change we must change the equilibrium by:

- strengthening the driving forces
- weakening the restraining forces
- or both.

The model encourages us to identify the various forces impinging on the target of change, to consider the relative strengths of these forces and to explore alternative strategies for modifying the force field.

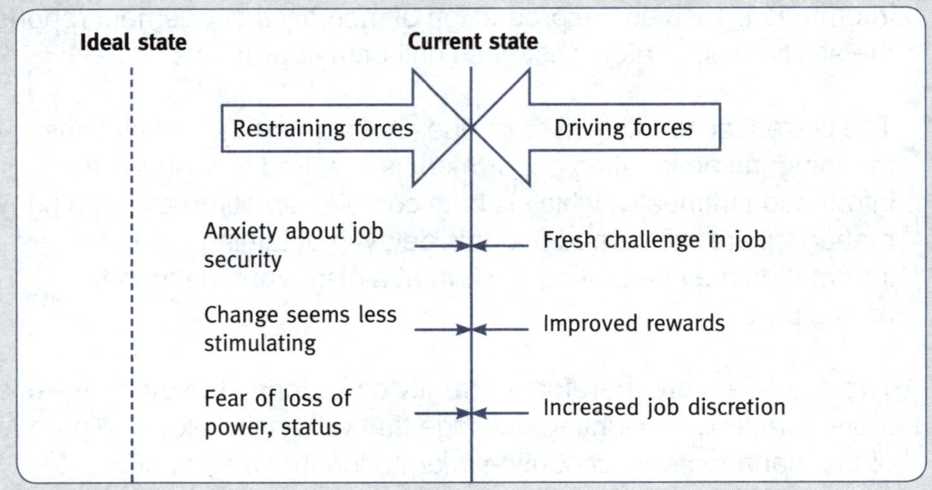

Test your understanding 2 – GVF

Great Value Foods (GVF) is one of Bigland's leading supermarket chains, having traded for over fifty years. Though fierce competitive activity had reduced the major players in the industry to six large chains in the last twenty years, the competitive pressures and large-scale capital investment required had not prevented all new entrants to the market. A high proportion of all workers in the supermarket industry are unionised.

A few foreign competitors seeking new markets had managed to secure a market share by offering unbranded goods at extremely low prices. This development increased the pressure on GVF as these new entrants were attracting consumers that had been part of GVF's traditional customer base.

In the midst of these difficulties, GVF was presented with a major opportunity. One of its competitors was experiencing difficulties and offered GVF the chance to purchase 60 of their stores in the south of the country. GVF borrowed $800m and made the purchase, doubling its number of outlets.

As GVF took over management of the new stores, however, it realised that considerable time and funds would be required to convert them to its own distinctive format and to the modern standards now expected by customers. This not only delayed the expected revenue stream, but also required additional borrowing, raising GVF's gearing to uncomfortably high levels. The government of Bigland subsequently raised interest rates, increasing the financial pressure on GVF.

During all this, GVF had been seeking to catch up with its competitors in a number of ways. This had included increasing the number of own-brand products it offered, along with the development of a new central distribution system that experts agreed was one of the best in the country. However, there were delays in distribution of supplies to some stores during the run up to the country's most important festive period. This resulted in a considerable loss for the company and three of the directors considered responsible for the problems were sacked.

These problems, together with an accompanying decline in profits, resulted in a fall in GVF's share price. Investors were concerned that GVF had paid too much for its 60 southern stores and that a rights issue would be needed to reduce the company's debt burden.

GVF has recently appointed a new CEO and she has spent her first few weeks reviewing the company and its problems, She has found that the company has too many layers of management, narrow functional attitudes and a controlling, bureaucratic head office culture. She feels that the business is no longer effective or responding to customer needs.

Required:

(a) Summarise the measures required to turn the company around

(5 marks)

(b) Describe:

(i) the most likely sources of resistance to change;

(ii) Lewin's force field analysis model and explain how it might be used to implement change in GVF.

(15 marks)

(Total: 20 marks)

Beer and Nohria – Theory E & Theory O

Beer and Nohria (2000) identified that a large proportion of all business change initiatives fail. They believed that this was caused by managers becoming overwhelmed by the detail of the change management process and failing to focus on the overall goals of the change itself.

Beer and Nohria identified that every organisational change conforms to a variant of either:

- **Theory E strategies** – these are based on measures where shareholder value is the main concern. Change usually involves incentives, layoffs, downsizing and restructuring.
- **Theory O strategies** – these are 'softer' approaches to change, often involving cultural adjustment or enhancing employee capabilities through individual and organisational learning. This involves changing, obtaining feedback, reflecting and then making further changes. This requires involving employees in the change process.

Both approaches have drawbacks. A Theory E approach will tend to ignore the feelings and attitudes of their employees, which will often lead to a loss of motivation and commitment from staff members. This can damage the competitive advantage of the organisation.

Theory O organisations, on the other hand, will often fail to take the 'tough' decisions that may be needed.

To solve these problems, Beer and Nohria recommended that organisations should implement both Theory E and Theory O approaches simultaneously and try to balance the associated tensions.

e.g

Illustration 1 – Beer and Nohria

Due to the recent economic slowdown, many high-street retailers have seen a significant reduction in their profits, forcing them to consider a number of strategies to improve their results.

A **Theory E** approach means that the retailer is only concerned with the effect that falling profits has on shareholders – such as reduced dividends and share prices. The managers of the company will usually try to improve this quickly by laying off staff, reducing employee pay or closing stores that are seen as underperforming.

While this can have a positive impact on profits in the short-term, it fails to consider the needs of other stakeholders, such as employees. This can cause problems with employee motivation and commitment as staff members will not feel that the company is acting in their best interests. As such, the company may suffer from poor performance in the long-term.

A **Theory O** approach would see the retailer attempt to improve their profits by developing the organisation's capabilities and culture. For instance, a high-street retailer may train its staff to provide better customer service for shoppers. This will improve the customer experience and therefore, in the longer-term, should improve the profitability of the business. The retailer may well choose to involve staff in the decision-making process, asking for suggestions as to how customer service could be improved.

All of this is likely to make the employees feel more valued and should improve the commitment and motivation of the workforce. However, it may be insufficient in the short–term to deal with the fall in profitability and shareholders may expect more drastic, Theory E action in order to quickly improve their returns.

Beer and Nohria suggested that companies needed to be prepared to take both approaches simultaneously. This could, for example, involve some restructuring as well as a development of remaining employees. This would still need careful management as it would be easy to get the 'worst of all worlds' where staff are demotivated by the job losses while investors feel the cost cuts have not gone far enough.

Balance is needed!

Test your understanding 3

In what circumstances would Theory E be a successful approach?

3 Leadership

Kotter and Schlesinger

Kotter and Schlesinger set out the following change approaches to deal with resistance:

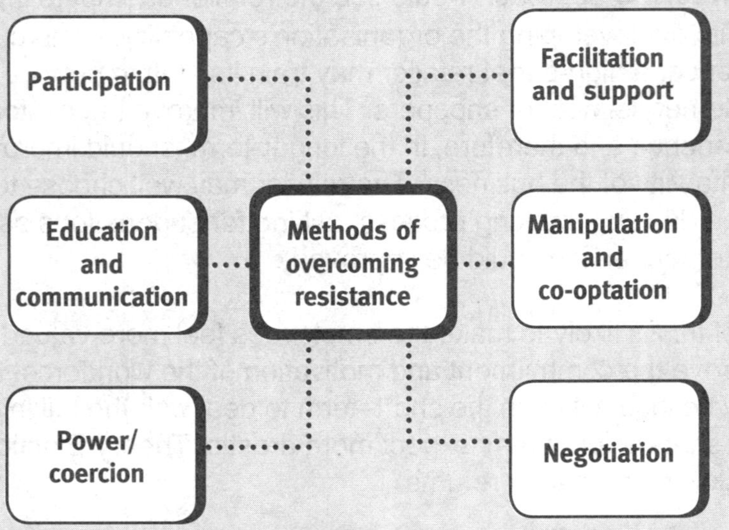

Key considerations when deciding upon a leadership style

- The speed at which change must be introduced
- The strength of the pressure for change
- The level of resistance expected
- The amount of power you hold
- How much information you need before you can implement the change and how long it will take to get that information

Approach/ style	Situations used	Advantages	Disadvantages
Education + Communication	Where there is a lack of or inaccurate information and analysis	If persuaded, people will help with the implementation of change	Can be time consuming if many people are involved
Participation + Involvement	Where initiators do not have all information to design change, and where others have power to resist	Participants are committed to implementing change including their relevant contribution	Can be very time consuming with possibly inappropriate changes made

Facilitation + Support	Where resistance comes from adjustment problems	Best approach for adjustment issues	Can be time consuming, expensive and still fail
Negotiation + Agreement	Where one group will lose out and has power to resist	Can be an easy way to avoid major resistance	Can be too expensive if it leads to general compliance
Manipulation + Co-optation	Where other tactics won't work or are too costly	Can be a relatively quick and inexpensive solution to resistance	Can lead to future problems if people feel they have been manipulated
Explicit + Implicit Coercion	Where speed is essential, and the change initiators possess considerable power	It is speedy and can overcome any kind of resistance	Can be risky if it leaves people angry at the initiators

Explanation of the Kotter and Schlesinger styles

- Participation – aims to involve employees, usually by allowing some input into decision making. This could easily result in employees enjoying raised levels of autonomy, by allowing them to design their own jobs, pay structures, etc.
- Education and communication – used as a background factor to reinforce another approach. This strategy relies upon the hopeful belief that communication about the benefits of change to employees will result in their acceptance of the need to exercise the changes necessary.
- Power/coercion – involves the compulsory approach by management to implement change. This method finds its roots from the formal authority that management possesses, together with legislative support.

- Facilitation and support – employees may need to be counselled to help them overcome their fears and anxieties about change. Management may find it necessary to develop individual awareness of the need for change.
- Manipulation and co-optation – involves covert attempts to sidestep potential resistance. The information that is disseminated is selective and distorted to only emphasise the benefits of the change. Co-optation involves giving key people access to the decision-making process.
- Negotiation – is often practised in unionised companies. Simply, the process of negotiation is exercised, enabling several parties with opposing interests to bargain. This bargaining leads to a situation of compromise and agreement.

Test your understanding 4 – Grey Limited

Grey Limited is a conglomerate organisation with two major divisions: A and B. The two divisions are run as autonomous business units as they operate in completely different markets. Both are entering a period of organisational change and the directors of Grey are considering what style of management would be the most effective for each division.

Division A is currently highly profitable. However, it is looking at ways of increasing its efficiency. The managers of A have decided to centralise the accounting function within the business, which will reduce overheads and allow for a reduction in the number of employees. Division A has always had an excellent relationship with its relatively small number of highly skilled staff and is concerned about how these plans may affect that.

Division B is currently loss-making. It is also planning on reducing the number of staff it employs, but wishes to do so across all departments. B has a large number of workers and initial estimates are that 18% of all staff members will be made redundant. B has undertaken similar exercises in previous years, leading to significant conflict between the relatively unskilled staff and managers. The directors of Grey have informed the managers of B that if the division does not move back into profit in the near future, the division will be closed.

Required:

For each division of Grey Limited, suggest which of Kotter and Schlesinger's leadership style(s) would be most appropriate. Justify your answer.

Test your understanding 5

A manager is in charge of a team that has been given the task of introducing a new management reporting system into regional offices. There is considerable resistance to the changes from the office managers, and comments that you have heard include the following.

- I have more important work priorities to take up my time.
- I'm used to the old system.
- The new system is too complicated.
- The new system will create more paperwork.
- The new system will make me more accountable.
- My job in the new system is not clear.

How would you try to deal with this resistance to change?

4 Change agents

Many organisations seek to identify and reward change agents to encourage and facilitate change. They can play a major role in helping deal with resistance to change. Usually change agents are figures who are familiar and non-threatening to other people.

The quality of the relationship between the change agent and key decision makers is very important, so the choice of change agent is critical.

Whether internal or external, the change agent is central to the process, and is useful in helping the organisation to:

- **Define the problem and its cause** – the change agent should be able to identify restraining forces or potential resistance and help management to understand the root causes behind them.
- **Diagnose solutions and select appropriate courses of action** – the change agent will be responsible for proposing ways in which these problems can be overcome and then helping management to select the most appropriate course of action.
- **Implement change** – once management have made their decision about which course of action to take, it will need to be implemented. Given that the change agent will be well informed about the proposed change and the reasons behind it, they are likely to be the best person to take the lead in implementing the change.

- **Transmit the learning process to others and the organisation overall** – the change agent should document the learning process and discussions which the company has undergone during the change process. They can then take the lead in spreading this information throughout the company.

Skills and attributes of change agents

The skills and attributes of the change agent would include:

Goals	• Clarity in defining the achievable • Sensitive to the impact of change on all stakeholders • Flexibility to adapt to internal and external triggers
Roles	• Team-building skills to establish work groups • Networking skills inside and outside the company • Tolerance of ambiguity and uncertainty
Communication	• Skills with colleagues and subordinates • Personal enthusiasm, stimulating commitment • Meeting management
Negotiation	• Creating vision and selling plans • Resolving conflict • Contract negotiation
Managing up	• Political awareness and influencing skills • Balancing goals and perceptions • Helicopter perspective

"Power skills" of change agents (Kanter)

Kanter identified seven 'power skills' that change agents require to enable them to overcome apathy or resistance to change, and enable them to introduce new ideas:

- ability to work independently, without the power and sanction of the senior management hierarchy behind them, providing visible support
- ability to collaborate effectively
- ability to develop relationships based on trust, with high ethical standards
- self-confidence, tempered with humility
- being respectful of the process of change, as well as the substance of the change
- ability to work across different business functions and units
- a willingness to stake personal rewards on results, and gain satisfaction from success.

Using external consultants as change agents

Advantages of using external consultants as change agents are as follows:

- They can bring a fresh perspective to the problem
- May have state-of-the-art knowledge of the required change – e.g. introducing TQM
- Being a dedicated resource they may be able to give it more time and energy
- They may have more experience and hence be better able to avoid traps and pitfalls.
- Greater objectivity as they have no personal stake in the outcomes of the change.

Test your understanding 6 – MMM

MMM is a small company based in country A. It is currently considering the acquisition of a rival company, POR, which is based in country D. Unfortunately, the employees in country D speak a different language to staff members in country A. The directors of MMM are concerned about the effect that this could have on the viability of the acquisition.

They have decided to appoint a change agent to help control the process.

Required:

Explain how a change agent could aid in the acquisition of POR.

5 Managing decline

In reality, businesses are not always successful at expanding their business. Many managers may therefore find themselves having to manage decline rather than growth. The changes required during a period of decline pose particular dilemmas for managers as decisions often affect the organisation's workforce – its pay, conditions and job security.

When attempting to help a business recover from a period of decline, a manager's strategic priorities are likely to be:

- reducing costs to improve efficiency, and
- improving competitiveness in order to increase revenue.

Initially, when facing a downturn, the typical management response is to cut costs. While these can be cut from anywhere in the supply chain, the most obvious starting point is to reduce labour costs. At first, this may simply involve altering working patterns, such as the elimination of paid overtime or the replacement of full-time with part-time jobs. If this does not produce a sufficient cost reduction, management may move on to a program of voluntary or compulsory redundancies.

There is, however, a danger that if staff cuts are too severe then there will be reductions in the quality of the product and services provided to customers. There is also likely to be a serious impact on staff morale, potentially leading to a loss of commitment, a loss of skilled staff and an increase in conflict within the organisation.

Test your understanding 7

A business has found itself entering a period of decline. What measures could it consider as alternatives to reducing its labour costs?

Illustration 2 – UK public sector

It is not just businesses that have been affected by the global economic slow-down in recent years. Many governments have had to reduce their level of spending – leading to many public departments having to lay off staff.

In the UK, local and central government departments have shed hundreds of thousands of posts in an effort to cope with the tight budget restrictions that have been imposed upon them, while attempting to continue to maintain their level of service provision.

This has led to angry reactions from the heavily unionised public sector employees, with a number of strikes and protests across the country. The long-term effects of this are unknown, but the government may find it harder to attract good quality staff members in the future as public sector jobs may no longer be seen as secure.

It should be noted that many of the changes that a business may wish to make during a period of decline, such as compulsory redundancies or improving factory layout, may require some initial expenditure. The business may be unable to afford this if it is experiencing falling revenues.

In this case, managers may have to consider a fundamental change to the business strategy. This may involve:

- **Retrenchment** – this involves doing the same as before, but drastically cutting costs.
- **Turnaround** – the organisation repositions itself within the market for competitive advantage.
- **Divestment** – this involves the external sale of part of the organisation, or the internal closure of units as part of a rationalisation programme.
- **Liquidation** – the organisation is sold to one or more buyers. This is an admission of failure by the senior managers and is normally a last resort.

All four of these strategies require managers to make difficult decisions, which may have adverse effects on the organisation's stakeholders – especially employees. Whichever approach is taken, it is important that the business acts ethically towards its stakeholders when making tough decisions.

Test your understanding 8 – AV Ltd

AV Ltd is a high-quality board game manufacturer. It is part of a larger group of companies that manufacture toys and computer games. While these other businesses have prospered over the last few years, this has been at the expense of the traditional board games that AV manufactures and AV's sales have declined each year for the last several years. In addition, AV has seen increased competition from cheaper board game manufacturers, further reducing demand.

The directors of AV's parent company have met to discuss their approach to AV's problems. They have all agreed that a fundamental change is needed to their strategy with regards to the company, but they are not sure what that change should be.

Required:

Discuss four possible strategies that the directors may consider, given AV's continuing decline.

6 Ethics and change management

Most ethical issues focus on how one stakeholder group is benefited at the expense of another, so within any change process there will be a number of potential ethical dilemmas that need managing:

- Whether the change is justified – for example, boosting shareholder profits at the expense of widespread job cuts. If the change involves re-engineering and/or downsizing, then there will usually be redundancies. Ethical issues include:
  - Deciding on who to make redundant (e.g. preference to keep younger employees).
  - Fair treatment of all employees (e.g. discrimination by race, sex or age).
  - What severance package and assistance to offer.
  - Skills obsolescence.
  - Do remember that making employees redundant is not always unjustified. If it is necessary to safeguard the business in the long-term, it cannot be classed as being unethical.

- Management approach used – e.g. manipulation v participation.
- Some managers may seek to exploit change to ensure they benefit personally from new power structures and reward schemes.
- Similarly some may resist change to protect their own interests.
- The extent to which plans are made available or if a "need to know" culture is adopted.
- Whether "misinformation" is used to drive certain phases of the change process – e.g. to unfreeze the existing culture
- Accountants may be asked to manipulate figures to exaggerate the case for change

This list is not exhaustive. The CIMA E3 syllabus requires you to apply the Code of Ethics in the context of business change. This means that whenever you read through a scenario, you need to consider whether there are any issues that may impact on the fundamental principles, which were dealt with earlier in this text.

e.g

Illustration 3 – Chrysler

Even when tough decisions need to be made, the actions of a business do not have to be uncaring or disrespectful to the individual employees affected. As part of a US government plan to save the struggling Chrysler motor company, Chrysler's CEO was faced with having to close a number of plants.

The CEO decided to soften the blow through a series of associated plans designed to get the employees into self-employment or into other forms of work. Some employees reskilled and moved to jobs in other parts of the Chrysler group, but the majority found employment elsewhere locally.

Test your understanding 9

How far should a CIMA member use manipulation and coercion?

7 The importance of adaptation and continuous change

Many authors have argued that firms need to look beyond change as an event and develop a culture where change is embraced as an ongoing process. These include:

- change-adept organisations (Kanter)
- excellent firms that thrive on chaos (Peters)
- learning organisations (Senge)

Change-adept organisations – Kanter

Attributes of companies that manage change successfully.

- The imagination to innovate.
- The professionalism to perform.
- The openness to collaborate.

Skills for leaders in change-adept organisations – skills identified by Kanter.

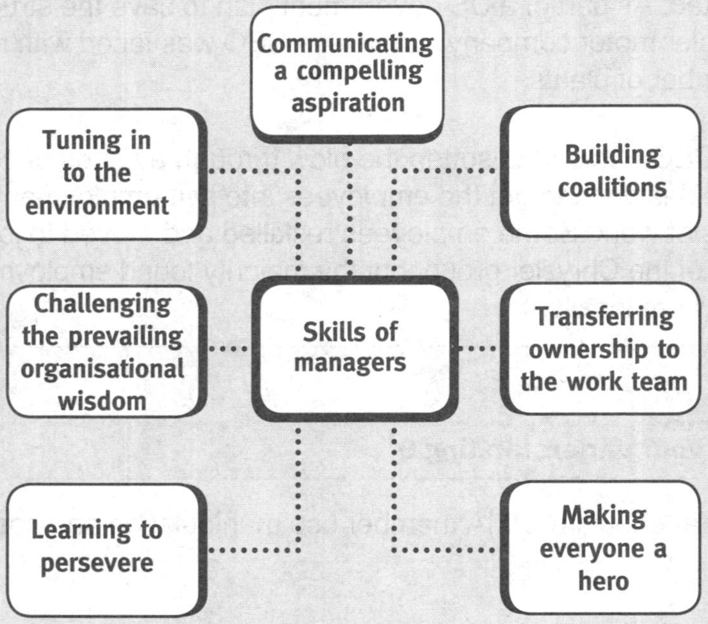

Change adept organisations

Rosabeth Moss Kanter looked at the characteristics of organisations that managed change successfully ('change-adept organisations'), and the qualities of their leaders and managers. She suggested that change-adept organisations share three key attributes:

- The imagination to innovate.

  Effective leaders help to develop new concepts, which are a requirement for successful change.

- The professionalism to perform.

  Leaders provide both personal competence and competence in the organisation as a whole, which is supported by workforce training and development. This enables the organisation to perform strongly and deliver value to ever-more-demanding customers.

- The openness to collaborate.

  Leaders in change-adept organisations make connections with 'partners' outside the organisation, who can extend the organisation's reach, enhance its products and services, and 'energise its practices'. 'Partners' will include suppliers working in close collaboration, joint venture partners, and so on.

Kanter argued that change should be accepted naturally by organisations, as a natural part of their existence. Change that is compelled by a crisis is usually seen as a threat, rather than as an opportunity for successful development. Mastering change means being the first with the best service or products, anticipating and then meeting customer requirements (which continually change) and applying new technology. This requires organisations to be 'fast, agile, intuitive and innovative'.

Skills for leaders in change-adept organisations

- Tuning in to the environment.

  A leader can actively gather information that might suggest new approaches, by tuning in to what is happening in the environment. Leaders can create a network of 'listening posts', such as satellite offices and joint ventures.

- Challenging the prevailing organisational wisdom.

  Leaders should be able to look at matters from a different perspective, and should not necessarily accept the current view of what is right or appropriate.

- Communicating a compelling aspiration.

  Leaders should have a clear vision of what they want to achieve, and should communicate it with conviction to the people they deal with. A manager cannot 'sell' change to other people without genuine conviction, because there is usually too much resistance to overcome. Without the conviction, a manager will not have the strength of leadership to persuade others.

- Building coalitions.

  Change leaders need the support and involvement of other individuals who have the resources, knowledge or 'political clout' to make things happen. There are usually individuals within the organisation who have the ability to influence others – 'opinion shapers', 'values leaders' and experts in the field. Getting the support of these individuals calls for an understanding of the politics of change in organisations.

- Transferring ownership to the work team.

  Leaders cannot introduce change on their own. At some stage, the responsibility for introducing change will be handed to others. Kanter suggested that a successful leader, having created a coalition in favour of the change, should enlist a team of other people to introduce the change.

- Learning to persevere.

  Something will probably go wrong, and there will be setbacks. Change leaders should not give up too quickly, but should persevere with the change.

- Making everyone a hero.

  A successful leader recognises, rewards and celebrates the accomplishments of others who have helped to introduce a change successfully. Making others feel appreciated for their contribution helps to sustain their motivation, and their willingness to attempt further changes in the future.

Thriving on Chaos (Tom Peters)

Tom Peters has written extensively on management theory. One of his ideas relates to 'excellent' companies that have succeeded by seeking to create a climate of continual and radical change. Peters called this 'thriving on chaos'. He suggested that:

- Incremental change is the enemy of true innovation, because it makes an organisation less willing to be truly innovative.
- Excellent firms don't believe in excellence, only in constant improvement and constant change.
- A constantly changing environment does not necessarily mean chaos: instead, it may mean that companies can handle the introduction of change successfully.

Peters suggested that the advantages of having a climate of change are as follows:

- Innovation and the introduction of new products and new methods are actively sought and welcomed.
- People who are used to change tend to accept it without resistance.
- Employees develop an external viewpoint, and are less insular and defensive in their outlook.

However, there are possible disadvantages:

- With a climate of change morale might be damaged
- Staff might become involved in office politics because of their concerns about the possible changes that might occur in the organisation.

Learning organisations

A learning organisation is an organisation skilled at creating, acquiring and transferring knowledge and at modifying its behaviour to reflect new knowledge and insights. It is an organisation that facilitates the learning of all its members and continuously transforms itself.

Learning organisations encourage questions and explicitly recognise mistakes as part of the learning process. They encourage testing and experimentation. Because they want to find new answers they recognise that failed answers are as important as successful ones.

Peter Senge outlines five disciplines that individuals and groups should be encouraged to learn to create a learning organisation.

(a) Systems thinking – is the ability to see particular problems as part of a wider whole and to devise appropriate solutions to them.

(b) Personal learning and growth – individuals should be encouraged to acquire skills and knowledge.

(c) Mental models – are deeply ingrained assumptions that determine what people think, e.g. a marketing group may think that price is more important than quality. Learning organisations can use a number of group techniques to make these models explicit and to challenge them.

(d) A shared vision that does not filter knowledge which undermines learning.

(e) Team learning – teams must be trained to learn because there are factors in group dynamics that impede learning.

8 Conclusion

The management of change is never an easy process and it is rare that the final outcome exactly matches the original plans. Remember that there is no recipe for success – it simply does not exist.

However, change is more likely to succeed if there is/are:

- clearly understandable goals,
- realistic time frames, rather than merely looking for a 'quick fix'
- clear guidance as to how each individual's behaviour needs to change
- clear, unified leadership with no conflict between managers
- management support for training and other necessary investment.

Test your understanding 10 – T Company

T Company was, until recently, a national telephone company that enjoyed monopoly status, but a decision to deregulate by the government means that it is now exposed to aggressive competition from new entrants. T Company's competitive position has also been undermined by developments in wireless technology. As customers increasingly choose to use mobile phones, T Company's vast investment in fixed line technology is becoming increasingly uneconomic. This change in technology and the associated shift in consumer tastes have left T Company with no option but to invest in mobile technology itself.

T Company also suffers from its history as a monopoly provider; its bureaucratic culture and structure means that it tends to be slower to respond to market changes than the new entrants. The high proportion of telephone engineers who belong to the telecoms trade union does not help this situation. When earlier this year, T Company announced job cuts, the trade union members voted for industrial action that lasted for several weeks and cost the company millions in lost revenue.

The development of broadband digital technology, however, allows high speed access to the Internet. This has meant a new lease of life for fixed line operators like T Company because existing fixed line systems can be adapted for broadband use. This opportunity has been seized by T Company's senior management. The company has been successful in attracting 50,000 subscribers to the new broadband service in its first year of operation. The company has also introduced a service that allows people on the move to access the Internet at selected public venues using a wireless enabled laptop.

This installation of broadband does, however, require training in new skills and the engineers required to undertake this training have threatened strike action in support of a large pay increase to compensate them for using the new skills required for the job.

Required:

(a) Identify the internal and external triggers for change in the strategy and operations of T Company. Discuss the difficulties that the company is likely to experience in introducing the change programme.

(5 marks)

(b) Evaluate the success of T Company in managing the change process to date. By application of any model of change management, explain how T Company might go about managing change in the future.

(12 marks)

(c) Assuming that the need to transform T Company was identified and championed by senior management, describe some of the political mechanisms that they might have used to deal with any reluctance of middle managers to resist change.

(8 marks)

(Total: 30 marks)

Test your understanding 11 – C Company

C is a large multinational confectionary manufacturer which was purchased in a hostile takeover bid one year ago. The new owners, R Co, have been surprised at the number of key staff who have left over the last year. A total of 120 out of 170 managers and executives have resigned since R Co took control of the two-hundred-year-old company. The acquisition of C completed R Co's ten year geographical expansion strategy.

In particular, there have been departures among creative, design and marketing specialists. While some resignations are normal after such a bitterly fought takeover battle, industry specialists are shocked at the extent of the staff losses.

A group of remaining managers have been questioned by the board of R Co on why they think so many employees have left. The managers explained that the rate of change in C was historically slow, with a great deal of pride taken in making confectionary the old-fashioned way. C's products are considered part of the national identity of its home country and the company even has a royal license to make chocolate for the queen.

Since R Co took over, the company has changed suppliers for many of the key ingredients used in C's products, and despite pre-takeover promises to the contrary, begun devising strategies to move production overseas. Many of the managers who have left made it clear they were resisting these changes before their resignation.

R Co is a cost leader in the global confectionary market and wishes to bring C in line with the rest of the group. The board of R Co have also announced plans to remove the C name altogether and bring the newly acquired company into its own functional structure, rather than allowing it to operate as a stand-alone division.

The managers stated that in their view, the rate of change has been a problem for many employees together with what they perceive to be a 'selling out' of the C name and values.

Required:

(a) Explain what is meant by the phrase 'resistance to change' and discuss the resistance to change at C which led to so many managers leaving

(9 marks)

(b) Evaluate the change management process which has been undertaken at C over the last year

(10 marks)

(c) Advise the board of R Co on an alternative strategy for C, which may avoid further loss of staff

(6 marks)

(Total: 25 marks)

9 Summary

By the end of this chapter you should be able to discuss the following:

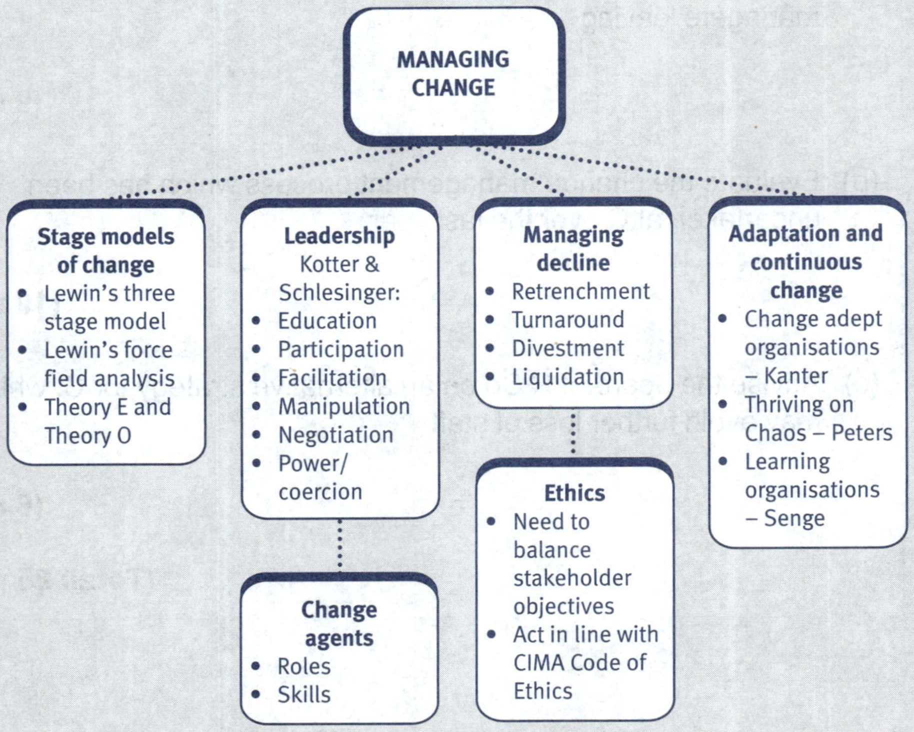

Test your understanding answers

Test your understanding 1 – WW

Lewin's model suggests that, in order to be successful, WW will need to follow three stages in the change-over to a new accounting package.

Unfreeze

Staff need to be convinced of the need for the new accounting package. This could be difficult within WW for several reasons.

WW's six employees have used the current accounting system for many years. This may mean that they are 'stuck in their ways' and unwilling to learn the new skills required for the new system.

In addition, currently management accounting information can only be produced after a time-consuming and complex process. If a new system improves the efficiency of this process, employees may fear that they will become redundant.

To help with this, WW need to convince them of the superiority of the new system. For instance, it appears that it will make the production of management reports much faster, easing the workload for the employees.

WW also needs to communicate well with its employees. Resistance is often caused by a fear of the unknown. Managers could discuss with staff about the level of training that they will be given on the new system and attempt to allay any fears they may have about potential redundancies.

Finally, WW's managers could also stress to staff members that it will benefit the business as a whole. The current system may cause WW to be less competitive in the marketplace, which could threaten the business as a whole.

Change

This involves actually moving staff onto the new accounting system.

This stage will involve training all members of the accounting department on how to use the new system. Enough time must be allowed for employees to be reasonably comfortable with the new system before the change-over is made.

Communication is also vital here – employees must know when the new system will be installed and what will be expected from them. For example, what new reports will the managers expect from the system and when they will need to be prepared.

Refreeze

Finally, WW's managers must ensure that employees do not slip back into old habits and start using the old systems again.

Clearly, if the old accounting system is entirely replaced by the new one, it should be easy to ensure that staff members do not continue to use the original accounting system. However, employees may still continue preparing the management reports manually.

To avoid this, managers could refuse to accept reports in the old, manual format – instead requiring that they be produced from the new system. Staff could be rewarded for using the new system and penalised if the old methods are still used.

Test your understanding 2 – GVF

(a) **Summary of measures needed to turn around GVF**

The inefficiency of GVF management seems to be related to the structure of the company. According to the CEO, there is a need to reduce the number of layers of management, to reduce head office controls and to change attitudes from a narrow concern with departmental objectives to a broader concern for the needs of GVF as a whole.

The reduction in the layers of management will help to reduce costs and to improve communications within the business. Store managers and others may well welcome reduced interference from head office and the increased autonomy may help to motivate them.

The CEO's comment that the company was 'no longer effective or responding to customer needs' is clear from the scenario. Given its loss of customers to new entrants to the market, GVF needs to determine precisely what the needs of its customers are. This may need further investigation – although by increasing the number of own–brand products, it appears to be at least part way through this process already.

(b) (i) **Likely sources of resistance**

Resistance to change in organisations can be considered according to whether the resistance comes from individuals, groups or the organisations themselves.

Individual level

At the individual level, resistance is often caused by fear of the unknown, long-held existing habits and possible threats to position or livelihood.

In GVF, all of the above are likely to be factors. Given the present circumstances of GVF, employees are likely to fear for their job security and whether or not they will be able to continue in their current role or will have to learn a new one.

Managers will be particularly fearful, given the CEO's statement regarding the need to reduce the number of layers of management within GVF. Given that many of these managers may have much to lose and little to gain from such a restructuring, GVF could expect to see significant resistance from them.

Group level

At a group level, there will be collections of individuals who see their positions as threatened and who will join forces to resist and make mutual threats. This will particularly be the case in GVF as many of its employees are unionised, increasing the amount of co-ordinated resistance they are capable of.

Even where trade unions do not exist, it is possible for groups of employees, including managers, to collude informally to resist changes. This may be achieved by withholding information or refusing to co-operate with those seeking to implement change.

For GVF, managers and employees are unlikely to co-operate unless they can see some long-term benefits for themselves.

Organisational level

At the level of the organisation, a number of factors will combine to make the change process difficult. These include the existing culture and structure of the organisation, as well as any past agreements with stakeholders.

Given that the company has traded for over fifty years, the company may be 'set in its ways', with staff unwilling to see significant changes made to longstanding arrangements or ways of working.

The proposed de-layering in GVF will threaten the jobs and status of some layers of management. This will again increase resistance.

(ii) **Models of organisational change**

The new CEO of GVF might use the force-field theory of change proposed by Lewin. Lewin's theory suggests that there are two forces present in a change management scenario. One set he refers to as driving forces because they are forces attempting to bring about change; the other set are referred to as restraining forces as they act in the opposite direction and seek to maintain the status quo.

For GVF, the driving forces are likely to include the need for the business to be competitive. Unless GVF can improve its efficiency, its competitors will continue to take its market share. Unless GVF becomes flatter, leaner and more responsive to the market, it may ultimately collapse – especially given its high level of financial gearing.

The restraining forces will include the reasons for employee resistance mentioned above, such as loss of job security and management levels within GVF.

To be successful, the CEO will need to increase the driving forces – perhaps by improved communication with all employees, laying out the benefits of her proposed changes and the potentially dire consequences to the whole of GVF if they are not implemented.

Alternatively, the CEO may look at reducing the restraining forces. This could involve looking at ways of avoiding voluntary redundancies among managers or by supporting employees who are to be made redundant as they try to find alternative employment.

Test your understanding 3

Theory E is often the approach taken in a crisis. If a business needed to make drastic or rapid cuts to its business, or undertake a major restructuring, management may have to make tough decisions in order to secure the long–term survival of the business.

In these circumstances, there may be insufficient time to involve staff in the decision–making process and doing so would likely make it harder to make the difficult choices, such as the number of job losses in the organisation.

Test your understanding 4 – Grey Limited

Division A

Division A appears to be making a relatively small change to its business. It is currently highly profitable – indicating that it is not currently experiencing a crisis.

As such, education and communication may be the best approach. This involves explaining the reasons behind the proposed centralisation of the accounting function and attempts to persuade the employees that this is a beneficial idea. While this is often time-consuming, A has a relatively small number of staff, which makes this approach more realistic. In addition, as the company currently has a good relationship with its workers (and likely needs to maintain this given that its staff are highly skilled and therefore very important to the company), this approach is most likely to keep the majority of staff happy.

It is possible that staff may not be convinced by the need to cut costs given that the division is highly profitable. In this case, A could choose facilitation and support – perhaps helping the staff who will be made redundant to find new jobs, such as by giving them time off for job interviews.

Finally, A could consider participation and involvement. This would see A getting its employees involved in the change process. Perhaps job losses can be avoided if employees are able to think of alternative ways of improving efficiency. This may be very time consuming, although there is no evidence of time-pressure in the scenario.

Division B

Division B is clearly in a crisis, with poor industrial relations and the potential threat of closure.

Given the serious nature of its situation, B could also adopt an education and communication style. If the alternative to job losses is a total closure of the division, this may be enough to convince employees of the need for the change. However, given the poor relations between staff and managers, as well as the tight time-constraints that B is under, this may not be realistic.

As an alternative, B could choose a manipulation and co-optation style. This involves undermining resistance in a more covert manner, perhaps by stressing the potential for the division to be closed, or down-playing the number of job losses that would be involved. It is a faster way of dealing with resistance than education and communication, but if employees feel that they are being manipulated, it may damage industrial relations further.

Finally, B could opt for coercion. This involves the managers of B forcing the staff to accept the changes. Any individuals who resist can be threatened with redundancy. Given the urgent nature of the needed change, this may be the easiest and most effective way of dealing with resistance. However, it will be likely to leave employees angry and may lead to demotivation and high employee turnover.

B may decide that its industrial relations are less important than its long-term survival, especially as employees are low skilled and will therefore be easy to replace.

Test your understanding 5

Change introduced through the use of power or manipulation is likely to add to anxiety. Education and communication will rarely succeed on their own when introducing major change. However, they are useful as a support for a negotiation or participation approach. The negotiation approach requires the existence of organised representatives and a formal procedure that is suitable for some items such as change in employment terms but would be inadvisable for other items of changing procedures, organisational changes, decentralisation, etc. In these cases, participation offers the best opportunity of allaying staff anxieties by involving them early in the change process and continuing that involvement through to completion.

Test your understanding 6 – MMM

A change agent is a person, or group of people, who help an organisation to achieve its strategic change. If MMM appoints a change agent, he or she would carry out a number of useful functions, including:

Identify any problems and their causes

This is likely to be relatively straightforward for MMM. The biggest problem with their proposed purchase of POR is the language barrier between their staff. MMM and POR will find it almost impossible to work together as they do not understand each other's language.

This could cause the acquisition to fail.

Diagnose solutions and select appropriate courses of action

The change agent is responsible for proposing ways in which the problems that they have identified could be overcome.

For MMM, it could consider:

- sending key members of staff in both companies on external language courses, or
- hiring some additional staff members in both companies who are bilingual.

In many cases there will be a number of possible solutions. The change agent will be responsible for presenting these to management and helping them to decide which option is most appropriate for MMM.

Implement change

Once the management have selected an appropriate strategy, they will need someone to implement it. As the change agent has been part of the decision-making process, they will be the most logical choice to actually carry out the plan. In MMM, the change agent may, for example, investigate and book language courses for appropriate members of staff.

Transmit the learning process to others and the organisation overall

There may be some resistance to the proposed changes. A change agent can champion the proposals, explaining to employees why it is necessary and what the advantages will be.

The change agent will also document the decision-making process and communicate to all members of staff in both MMM and POR. This is a vital step, as employees in both businesses will need to be kept informed about the developments in the company.

Test your understanding 7

The business could attempt to:

- generate additional revenue through more effective marketing
- improve purchasing policies and procedures
- redesign the product or service offered in order to reduce production costs
- contract out services that are not considered essential to the core business (although this may result in job losses)
- consider changes to reduce duplication and improve financial control systems.

Test your understanding 8 – AV Ltd

There are four major approaches that the directors could consider with regards to AV:

Retrenchment

This would involve AV continuing to make board games, but looking at ways to significantly cut costs. This would help increase profits and offset the decline in results that the business is experiencing.

Given that the company currently produces high-quality board games, there may be scope for the business to save money by reducing the quality of materials. This may also allow it to cut its prices and compete with the new, lower-cost market entrants.

Turnaround

For AV this would probably involve much the same approach as retrenchment. AV could attempt to reposition itself within the board games market as a low-cost manufacturer.

Liquidation

The directors could choose to sell AV to one or more investors. Given the current level of decline, they may not realise a high price for the business. This would normally be a last resort for the directors.

Divestment

As an alternative to selling the business, the directors could decide to close the business unit down. The assets could then be sold or transferred to other parts of the organisation.

Test your understanding 9

While manipulation and coercion are legitimate approaches to dealing with resistance, a CIMA member must ensure that they do not breach any of their ethical requirements.

Manipulation, for example, may involve presenting information in such a way as to support a company's position. For example, if a business is planning to make a number of redundancies, they may wish to make the company's financial position look as weak as possible in order to convince staff of the need for cost savings and the associated job losses.

Remember, however, that the CIMA Code of Ethics demands that accountants act with *integrity*. That implies fair dealing and truthfulness. Deliberately manipulating figures to present a misleading view would breach this requirement.

The other potential threat here is that an accountant could be pressured by management into presenting misleading figures. This could be a threat to the accountant's *objectivity*, as self-interest could then cloud their judgement.

Coercion, or an exercise of power, may also be a tool that a management accountant must use in a crisis. If a business is about to become insolvent, for example, job losses may be necessary.

However, the accountant should always treat others with dignity and respect, as they are required to act with *professional behaviour*. This involves avoiding any actions that could bring the profession into disrepute. An unnecessarily harsh approach to dealing with resistance from employees may well do this.

In either case, should CIMA members be uncertain as to what action they should take, they can consult with senior managers within their organisation or with CIMA itself to determine the best course of action.

Test your understanding 10 – T Company

(a) **Triggers for change**

Organisational change can be driven by both external developments and/or internal organisational factors. The key triggers for change in T Company are as follows:

External triggers	*Internal triggers*
• Government decisions to deregulate the telecommunications industry • Technological developments in wireless technology (mobile phones!) • Development of broadband Internet technology • Shift in consumer tastes away from fixed line telephones to mobile phones	• Senior management decisions to enter the mobile telephone market and, later, broadband internet services • Managers' decision to sack workers • Workers' decision to take industrial action to preserve jobs • Trade union's decision to support the actions of T Company employees

The key difficulties that T Company is likely to face in making all the necessary changes are as follows.

Existing culture

The inherited bureaucratic culture of the organisation with its rules and procedures is likely to act as a barrier to change.

Employees' resistance to change

Employees will resist change due to:

- fear of being unable to cope with the new technology
- unwillingness to throw away existing skills and learn new ones
- fear of job losses
- fear that new jobs will be more specialised and more boring.

Action of trade unions

The threat of action by the trade union will make change even more difficult.

(b) **The change process**

Success to date

T Company has had a mixed record of success in the management of change to date. The main success is that it has managed to change from being a provider of only fixed line telephone services to one that now also provides mobile and broadband Internet services. This is despite the old bureaucratic culture and structure.

The main failures have been as follows:

- Attempts to downsize the workforce resulted in industrial action that cost T Company many millions.
- The current implementation of broadband services is also meeting with resistance. Engineers have threatened industrial action in support of a large pay rise.

Managing future change

There is no universal plan for the successful management of change as each situation is different. At best, there are useful models and principles to help in the design of the change process. One such model was developed by Lewin.

Lewin argued that some (usually external) forces are outside management's control and so management should concentrate on the internal forces driving change and those resisting change. Lewin suggested a three-step process to then manage the change as follows:

(1) 'Unfreezing' – which involves reducing forces that resist change. This involves providing people with an understanding of why change needs to occur so that they can more easily accept it.

(2) 'Changing behaviour' – in such a way that new attitudes, values and behaviour become part of employees' new ways of thinking.

(3) 'Refreezing' – introducing mechanisms, such as reward systems and structures, to ensure that the new behaviour pattern is maintained.

In the case of T Company, many of the forces for change are outside the control of the senior management. Management needs to accept the changes in the market place and adopt strategies to deal with the threats and opportunities the changes present.

Unfreezing

Management can use the threat of competition to persuade employees and the trade union that, unless changes are made, the very survival of the company and, therefore, the jobs of employees, are at risk. This should create dissatisfaction with existing methods.

Changing behaviour

Changing behaviour is difficult and will require a range of methods:

- effective communication of what needs to be changed and why
- regular meetings involving all employees
- negotiation with unions to ensure their participation in the change process.

The directors may be tempted to force changes through regardless of the reasons for resistance. The danger of this approach is that employees often return to the old ways of working once the pressure is removed.

Refreezing

- To consolidate changes made, appropriate incentives and penalties must be put in place.
- Rather than sitting still there should be an emphasis on constant improvement to raise levels of productivity even further.

(c) The most obvious mechanism is the control and manipulation of organisational resources. Senior management can allocate resources in such a way that managers and departments are encouraged to embrace the new culture. This might be combined with the development of revised internal reporting systems so that resistance to change is highlighted and penalised in terms of performance measures.

Management might publicise its desire to change the culture within the company. Amongst other things, this could be raised as an issue by board members who are participating in interviews for promoted posts. Middle management might, therefore, be encouraged to align itself with the interests of this elite.

The company's systems need to be consistent with the whole process of change. If reporting and decision-making systems are based on the outmoded culture then it will persist and will, indeed, be viewed as the board's preferred approach.

The board might even resort to symbolic devices. Creating positive messages in support of those who embrace the changes and adapt to it will speed implementation more quickly.

Test your understanding 11 – C Company

(a) **Resistance to change**

Resistance to change is the action taken by individuals and groups when they perceive that a change that is occurring is a threat to them.

Resistance is any attitude or behaviour that reflects an individual's unwillingness to make or support a desired change.

Reasons for resisting change can stem from three factors. These are discussed below with reference to the situation at C:

Job factors

Employees may resist change because they fear changes to their working conditions, demotion or reduced pay. The managers in question at C took pride in the traditional ways of making confectionary and obviously saw these methods were under threat from R Co. In particular, the creative managers may have foreseen cuts to design and marketing budgets, since these costs are often viewed as discretionary by cost leader organisations like R.

Reduced pay, demotion and certainly inferior working conditions would all be suggested by R's aggressive strategy over the first few months of ownership.

Personal factors

Managers may have resisted changes as they saw them as a perceived criticism of their performance in C. Changing suppliers of raw materials as well as beginning to move production overseas suggests that R Co sees C as inefficient and its cost base as too high. Altering the supply chain and sourcing overseas partners are typical strategies to reduce variable costs. It is likely that the managers felt less valued under the new management than the old.

The development of C into a cost leader would also signal more monotonous roles for many of its staff, with the emphasis on reducing costs rather than being creative with products.

Social factors

C was a well established part of the national culture in its home nation. The staff's social environment at work would have reflected this, with a great deal of pride being taken in working methods pre-takeover. For new owners to come in and disregard this heritage would lead to personal dislike of R's staff on the part of the C employees. The lack of consultation carried out by R's executives is also likely to have led to rejection of change.

(b) **Evaluation of change management process carried out at C**

There are some positives to the way change management has been carried out at C. Employees are in no doubt as to the intentions of R Co, and although acceptance of that may be difficult in some cases, it could be argued that, the sooner processes of change are begun, the sooner staff can get used to new methods of working.

R Co clearly has a track record of cost leadership, and to maintain a subsidiary which has a different strategy would detract from their corporate image and possibly confuse investors and customers. The sooner this mismatch is dealt with the better.

There is also a clear reason for R Co's rapid changes, in that it is possible for them to save money through moving production abroad and changing suppliers. Such rapid change will in fact increase profit margins and, arguably, benefit stakeholders in C.

C has given a clear message that it is in charge of C and again, this strategic clarity is equivalent to a 'short, sharp shock'. Once the message is communicated, there can be no doubt or confusion as to the company's intentions.

However, the results of such rapid change show that there are significant disadvantages to altering strategy upon acquisition in such a fashion. Firstly, C is a highly valued national institution, with a royal endorsement. R's actions may be seen as disrespectful and result in a consumer backlash.

Rapid transformational change only works if employees believe it is necessary to benefit the company and safeguard their jobs. In the case of C, the opposite is true, with managers feeling so strongly that the change is a mistake and that they would rather resign than see it through. The loss of so many staff, particularly in creative areas, means that new strategies will be harder to implement.

R Co is taking significant risks by adopting a cost leadership strategy for C. If in fact, it is impossible to complete the transfer of C from a differentiator to a cost leader, there will be no return to the previous strategy. C's brand names are, at best, likely to be devalued once it becomes part of the functional structure of R and at worst, completely lost.

In conclusion, the unpopularity of R's actions means they will find it harder to push continued change through and high staff turnover together with resistance to change will both remain as key obstacles to their aims.

(c) **Alternative strategy for C**

Since R Co has purchased C as part of a geographical expansion programme, the simplest alternative is to allow C to continue to operate as a division of R but to use its distribution channels to introduce some of R's products into its markets.

This parallel strategy could work well for some time and R could slowly introduce cost-cutting measures, trying to keep any promises, such as not moving production overseas for the foreseeable future.

It is likely with a slower approach that many managers could be brought on-side. The board of R Co are clearly not averse to consulting with C's staff, since they have asked for their views on the staff turnover issue. If these consultations could be extended to strategic aims and intent, the 'old' C workforce would be much happier to work under R's board, particularly if they saw the attributes of C protected rather than dismantled.

Of course, if R Co is determined to make C part of their empire and remove its identity completely, any kind of change management is likely to meet fierce resistance.

chapter

17

How to prepare for the exam

Chapter learning objectives

HOW TO PREPARE FOR THE EXAM

Section A of the Enterprise Strategy exam accounts for 50% of the paper, and it relates to a pre-seen case study which is common to all three Strategic Level papers. It is vital that you study the pre-seen material carefully before the exam. This chapter explains how you should prepare for the exam and what you should do with the pre-seen material.

1 Introduction

About two months before the May or November exam sittings for the strategic level, a pre-seen case study will be released by CIMA.

It will be background information regarding a particular company in an industry which should be reasonably familiar to everyone. The case study is typically about seven pages long and includes information that would be useful when answering a range of unknown questions on any of the three strategic level papers – E3, P3 and F3.

The case study question is for 50 marks (50% of the exam). Since the exam is 3 hours long with 20 minutes reading time, you should spend one and a half hours only on answering the case study question.

No questions will be asked at this stage. They will be disclosed on the day of the exam.

Preparing for the exam

This chapter explains how to use the pre-seen information, starting from the moment you receive it and going through to the exam day. Towards the end of the chapter, you will find the real CIMA pre-seen material for the May 2010 and September 2010 exams, some detailed analysis of it, and then a question and answer based on it.

The idea is that if you follow the process through right to the end of the chapter, this should give you an invaluable practice run which you can repeat when the real pre-seen material is released.

2 Two months before the exam

Initial reading

You should start by reading the pre-seen case study several times to assimilate the large amount of information.

While reading, keep asking yourself the question

> "If I were the management accountant in this organisation, what would I be interested in?"

Further research

Students are expected to research the industry and gain a wider knowledge which they can demonstrate in an exam question. This can be achieved in several ways:

- Research on the internet – try to think of a similar real world company and look on its website. In particular the financial statements will be useful.
- Swap ideas and information with friends who are also sitting the exam. You may be lucky enough to have someone in your peer group who works in that industry. (Don't worry that they might fare better than you in the exam. The examiners have commented that those who do work in the industry specified in the case study appear to fare no better than others.) Industries so far have included electronics and an airport.
- Speak to your colleagues and managers at work.
- Discuss with your training provider if you are enrolled on a course covering these exams.
- Watch the television and read quality newspapers which may cover the industry or a similar company in the months preceding the exam.

Objectives of your reading and research

While it important to understand the organisation in the pre-seen, and the industry in which it operates, you shouldn't spend too long researching the industry. In previous exams, all the information needed to answer the question has been contained within the pre-seen and the unseen information received on the exam day.

Your key objectives at this stage of the process should be to:

- analyse the context of the case organisation – what industry is it in? (With DEF airport in November 2010, several students seemed to think that DEF was an airline, rather than an airport – lack of awareness)
- analyse the current position of the case organisation (perhaps using SWOT)
- identify and analyse key issues facing the case organisation
- identify key issues from the pre-seen and consider how they might be developed in the unseen and the requirement – consider each chapter of this text and try to think how the examiner might fit that particular topic into the case study, and how it could be examined.

3 One month before the exam

Question practice

Students are expected to be able to answer a range of questions based on this scenario in all of the three strategic level papers. The only way to achieve this is to practise as many potential questions as possible.

Past questions and answers are available on the CIMA website for:

- The specimen exam paper released when the case study question was launched;
- The May 2010/September 2010 real exam
- The November 2010/ March 2011 real exam
- The May 2011 real exam.

When you have attempted any real past exam questions, make sure you read the relevant post-exam guidance produced by CIMA. This is written by the marking team after each sitting and analyses each question, looking in particular at areas that candidate were weak. This can give you some valuable tips for how to improve your answers and pick up additional marks. Post exam guidance for past exams is available on the CIMA website.

Your training provider will also have produced several practice papers covering other areas of the syllabus which may be tested.

While attempting these practice questions, you should start to think about how best to tackle the exam paper in its entirety.

There is no clear evidence that tackling the A or B sections first significantly increases the pass rates. By practising a few mock papers you will find which order best suits you for each paper. The critical point in all papers is that you must allocate time carefully and strictly. Make sure you decide on your approach **before** you get into the exam hall.

For any question you attempt, you should always write down (on the exam paper possibly) the time you should start and stop that question. You should further break this down into what time to finish each individual requirement so that you have covered the whole paper at the end of the three hours.

4 The night before the exam

Last minute preparation

On the night before the exam, you should reread the case study scenario fully and try to separate in your mind the real CIMA material from the practice scenarios you may have attempted in the previous weeks – you must make sure that you don't get confused in the exam and bring in fictional scenarios which you have seen during your revision.

Then get a good night's sleep to ensure you are alert and ready for the exam.

5 The day of the exam

Unseen material

On the day of the exam, further unseen material will be supplied by CIMA along with the question paper. The unseen material tends to be about two further pages of information. (You will also receive a clean copy of the case study pre-seen material in the exam.)

There are commonly three or four requirements on each exam paper, which may be further broken down into parts (i), (ii), etc.

The requirements are likely to cover a range of topics across the syllabus.

Time management

For each mark available you have 1.8 minutes available. So for a 10-mark requirement you should spend no longer than 18 minutes answering it.

Remember to write down your start and stop times for each question / requirement.

There is a law of diminishing returns when answering exam questions – you will probably score the first half of the available marks in the early minutes of your answer. The last few minutes will probably score far fewer as you may have gone off on a tangent or be waffling. Stop! Move on to the next requirement where you will start to score rapidly once again.

Planning

For E3 and P3 your answer will probably be predominantly written although some calculations may be required that you will then need to discuss. In F3 the split between calculations and discussion is more even.

Planning your answers is absolutely critical if the requirement is for a large number of marks.

Most students can write a coherent answer for a requirement of, say, 5 marks. But when the requirement is larger than this many students will ramble, or move away from the actual question asked.

It is recommended that in your answer booklet, possibly on the middle two pages (which you could pull out, but need to put back at the end of the exam) you should plan your answer to each requirement.

Try considering:

- Information from the pre-seen material
- Information from the unseen material
- Technical topics from your study text
- Past exam questions you may have done which might just cover the same topic if you are lucky (but be careful if they are slightly different not to answer the question you had earlier rather than the one asked in the exam)
- Common sense.

Writing up your answer

Write up your answer once your plan is complete. Remember that your plan should be very brief, so that you don't waste time rewriting it out in full without adding very much.

As you use points on your plan tick them off. Do not obliterate them since if you fail to use all of them in the time allowed, markers are allowed to consider whether any further marks are available within them for a marginal candidate.

The layout of your answer needs to be professional. Use full English sentences and avoid notes. Never use the word 'etc'. This indicates that you know more but that you can't be bothered to tell the examiner!

Other exam tips

- Leave plenty of space between each answer (possibly start a fresh page for each) so that you can go back to add to your answer later if need be.
- You can answer the requirements in any order, however, you should clearly mark which is (a), (b), (c) or (d), or part (i), (ii), etc.
- Keep looking at your watch to ensure that you do not run over your allocated time. Stop when you are supposed to. Many students think 'just two more minutes' and the next time they look at their watch ten minutes have passed. This can mean that whole requirements are not attempted later, which is a recipe for failure.

- It is unlikely, but you may have time at the end of the exam to review what you have written. You should really make time to do this, but few students do since they think it is better to keep writing. At the end of the day, there is no negative marking, and therefore the more you write the more possible marks you might get.
- As a rough guide, a student with average sized writing might score about 6 marks per page, so aim to write about 2 sides for a ten mark requirement. (This includes the use of headings, and spacing between each point made.)
- Underline your headings and any key words which you are sure will gain marks (but don't go wild underlining everything).
- Use a black or blue biro. Never use red or green biro or highlighter pens anywhere in your answer booklet. Pencil can be used for diagrams.
- Leave plenty of space between different requirements in the answer booklet, so that you can add to your answer later if necessary. This also makes your answer much tidier and more professional.

6 Practice exam – pre-seen material

The pre-seen information below is the real CIMA pre-seen case study for the May 2010 and September 2010 exams. It describes an electronic components manufacturer called Aybe.

Follow the steps above in order to prepare yourself for a requirement based on this pre-seen material and the following unseen material.

Read the pre-seen material first, prepare some analysis of it and compare this with our analysis in the next section. Then, when you feel that you are ready to spend 90 minutes attempting the question, start to look at the unseen material.

Pre-seen material – Aybe

Background

Aybe, located in Country C, was formed by the merger of two companies in 2001. It is a listed company which manufactures, markets and distributes a large range of components throughout Europe and the United States of America. Aybe employs approximately 700 people at its three factories in Eastern Europe and supplies products to over 0.5 million customers in 20 countries. Aybe holds stocks of about 100,000 different electronic components.

Aybe is regarded within its industry as being a well-established business. Company Ay had operated successfully for nearly 17 years before its merger with Company Be. Company Ay can therefore trace its history back for 25 years, which is a long time in the fast moving electronic component business. The company is organised into three divisions, the Domestic Electronic Components division (DEC), the Industrial Electronic Components division (IEC) and the Specialist Components division (SC).

The Domestic and Industrial Electronic Components divisions supply standard electronic components for domestic and industrial use whereas the Specialist Components division supplies components which are often unique and made to specific customer requirements. Each of the three divisions has its own factory in Country C.

Composition of the Board of Directors

The Board of Directors has three executive directors, the Company Secretary and five non-executive directors. The Chairman is one of the five independent non-executive directors. The executive directors are the Chief Executive, Finance Director and Director of Operations. There is also an Audit Committee, a Remuneration Committee and a Nominations Committee. All three committees are made up entirely of the non-executive directors.

Organisational structure

Aybe is organised along traditional functional/unitary lines. The Board considers continuity to be a very important value. The present structure was established by Company Ay in 1990 and continued after the merger with Company Be. Many of Aybe's competitors have carried out structural reorganisations since then. In 2008, Aybe commissioned a review of its organisational structure from a human resource consultancy. The consultants suggested alternative structures which they thought Aybe could employ to its advantage. However, Aybe's Board felt that continuity was more important and no change to the organisational structure took place.

Product and service delivery

Customers are increasingly seeking assistance from their component suppliers with the design of their products and the associated manufacturing and assembly processes. Aybe's Board views this as a growth area. The Board has recognised that Aybe needs to develop web-based services and tools which can be accessed by customers. The traditional method of listing the company's range of components in a catalogue is becoming less effective because customers are increasingly seeking specially designed custom made components as the electronics industry becomes more sophisticated.

Financial data

Aybe's historical financial record, denominated in C's currency of C$, over the last five years is shown below.

Year ended 31/12	**2009**	**2008**	**2007**	**2006**	**2005**
	C$m	C$m	C$m	C$m	C$m
Revenue	620	600	475	433	360
Operating profit	41	39	35	20	13
Profit for the year	23	21	16	9	5
Earnings per share (C$)	0.128	0.117	0.089	0.050	0.028
Dividend per share (C$)	0.064	0.058	0	0	0

Extracts from the 2009 financial statements are given at Appendix A. There are currently 180 million ordinary shares in issue with a nominal value of C$0.10 each. The share price at 31 December 2009 was C$0.64. No dividend was paid in the three years 2005 to 2007 due to losses sustained in the first few years after the merger in 2001. Aybe's bank has imposed an overdraft limit of C$10 million and two covenants: (i) that its interest cover must not fall below 5 and (ii) its ratio of non-current liabilities to equity must not increase beyond 0.75:1. Aybe's Finance Director is comfortable with this overdraft limit and the two covenants.

The ordinary shareholding of Aybe is broken down as follows:

	% holding at 31/12/09
Institutional investors	55
Executive directors and company secretary	10
Employees	5
Individual investors	30

The Executive Directors, Company Secretary and other senior managers are entitled to take part in an Executive Share Option Scheme offered by Aybe.

Performance Review

Aybe's three divisions have been profitable throughout the last five years. The revenue and operating profit of the three divisions of Aybe for 2009 were as follows:

	DEC division	**IEC division**	**SC division**
	C$m	C$m	C$m
Revenue	212	284	124
Operating profit	14	15	11

Financial objectives of Aybe

The Board has generally taken a cautious approach to providing strategic direction for the company. Most board members feel that this has been appropriate because the company was unprofitable for the three year period after the merger and needed to be turned around. Also, most board members think a cautious approach has been justified given the constrained economic circumstances which have affected Aybe's markets since 2008. While shareholders have been disappointed with Aybe's performance over the last five years, they have remained loyal and supported the Board in its attempts to move the company into profit. The institutional shareholders however are now looking for increased growth and profitability.

The Board has set the following financial objectives which it considers reflect the caution for which Aybe is well known:

(i) Dividend payout to remain at 50% of profit for the year;

(ii) No further equity shares to be issued over the next five years in order to avoid diluting earnings per share.

Capital budget overspends

Aybe has an internal audit department. The Chief Internal Auditor, who leads this department, reports directly to the Finance Director. Investigation by the Internal Audit department has revealed that managers with responsibility for capital expenditure have often paid little attention to expenditure authorisation levels approved by the Board. They have justified overspending on the grounds that the original budgets were inadequate and in order not to jeopardise the capital projects, the overspends were necessary.

An example of this was the building of an extension to the main factory at the DEC division that was completed in 2009 at a final cost of nearly C$3 million which was almost 50% over budget. The capital budget for the extension was set at the outset and the capital investment appraisal showed a positive net present value. It subsequently became apparent that the site clearance costs and on-going construction expenditure were under-estimated. These estimates were provided by a qualified quantity surveyor who was a contractor to Aybe. The estimates supplied by the quantity surveyor were accurately included in Aybe's capital investment appraisal system which was performed on a spreadsheet. However, no regular checks were carried out to compare the phased budgeted expenditure with actual costs incurred. It came as a surprise to the Board when the Finance Director finally produced the capital expenditure project report which showed the cost of the extension was nearly 50% overspent.

Strategic development

Aybe applies a traditional rational model in carrying out its strategic planning process. This encompasses an annual exercise to review the previous plan, creation of a revenue and capital budget for the next five years and instruction to managers within Aybe to maintain their expenditure within the budget limits approved by the Board.

Debates have taken place within the Board regarding the strategic direction in which Aybe should move. Most board members are generally satisfied that Aybe has been turned around over the last five years and were pleased that the company increased its profit in 2009 even though the global economy slowed down. Aybe benefited from a number of long-term contractual arrangements with customers throughout 2009 which were agreed in previous years. However, many of these are not being renewed due to the current economic climate.

The Board stated in its annual report, published in March 2010, that the overall strategic aim of the company is to:

"Achieve growth and increase shareholder returns by continuing to produce and distribute high quality electronic components and develop our international presence through expansion into new overseas markets."

Aybe's Chief Executive said in the annual report that the strategic aim is clear and straightforward. He said "Aybe will strive to maintain its share of the electronic development, operational, maintenance and repair markets in which it is engaged. This is despite the global economic difficulties which Aybe, along with its competitors, has faced since 2008. Aybe will continue to apply the highest ethical standards in its business activities."

In order to facilitate the achievement of the strategic aim, Aybe's Board has established the following strategic goals:

(1) Enhance the provision of products and services which are demanded by customers;

(2) Invest in engineering and web-based support for customers;

(3) Maintain the search for environmentally friendly products;

(4) Pursue options for expansion into new overseas markets.

The Board has also stated that Aybe is a responsible corporate organisation and recognises the social and environmental effects of its operational activities.

Concern over the rate of growth

Aybe's recently appointed Director of Operations and one of its Non-Executive Directors have privately expressed their concern to the Chief Executive at what they perceive to be the very slow growth of the company. While they accept that shareholder expectations should not be raised too high, they feel that the Board is not providing sufficient impetus to move the company forward. They fear that the results for 2010 will be worse than for 2009. They think that Aybe should be much more ambitious and fear that the institutional shareholders in particular, will not remain patient if Aybe does not create stronger earnings growth than has previously been achieved.

Development approaches

The Board has discussed different ways of expanding overseas in order to meet the overall strategic aim. It has, in the past, been reluctant to move from the current approach of exporting components. However the Director of Operations has now begun preparing a plan for the IEC division to open up a trading company in Asia. The DEC division is also establishing a subsidiary in Africa.

APPENDIX A

Extracts of Aybe's Income Statement and Statement of Financial Position

Income statement for the year ended 31/12/09

	C$m
Revenue	620
Operating costs	(579)
Finance costs	(4)
Profit before tax	37
Income tax expense	(14)
Profit for the year	23

Statement of financial position at 31/12/09

	C$m
ASSETS	
Non current assets	111
Current assets:	
Inventories	40
Trade and other receivables	81
Cash and cash equivalents	3
	124
Total assets	235

EQUITY AND LIABILITIES

Equity:	
Share capital	18
Share premium	9
Other reserves	8
Retained earnings	75
Total equity	110
Non current liabilities	
Bank loan (8% interest, repayable 2015)	40
Current liabilities	
Trade and other payables	73
Current tax payable	8
Bank overdraft	4
Total current liabilities	85
Total liabilities	125
Total equity and liabilities	235

End of pre-seen material

7 Sample unseen material

Note: You should only read this unseen information and the associated question when you have already read and analysed the Aybe pre-seen material in detail. For maximum benefit (to simulate the time you will have in the real exam), you should aim to spend 10 minutes reading the unseen material and the requirement, and then 90 minutes preparing and writing up your answer.

Unseen material for the Aybe Case Study

Introduction

Aybe is organised into three divisions. Institutional shareholders are looking for increased growth and better profitability. At a recent meeting involving the Board of Directors and senior managers a number of key areas for improvement were discussed.

Divisional performance

The first issue on the agenda was Aybe's divisional strategy. The latest forecast figures for 2010 by division were presented as follows:

	DEC	**IEC**	**SC**	**Total**
	C$m	C$m	C$m	C$m
Revenue	221	270	140	631
Operating profit	15	13	15	43
Operating margin	**6.8%**	**4.8%**	**10.7%**	**6.8%**

The Director of Operations confirmed that overall profit is expected to be roughly the same as 2009, a creditable result given difficult economic circumstances. However, this has already led to the following problems:

- The Finance Director argued that this was unlikely to satisfy shareholders and emphasized the need to improve the profitability of the company further.
- The HR Director commented that if the performance was static as suggested, then none of the employees in any division will be paid a bonus. This led to heated discussion with the Manager of the SC division arguing that his staff were being penalized for the poor performance of the other two divisions.

Organisational Structure

The Industrial Division of Aybe (IED) is considered to be the market leading provider of industrial components in its chosen market niches. In contrast the DEC and SC divisions are not market leaders yet.

The Chief Executive of Aybe is convinced that a significant cause of the problems within the company is due to the way that the company is organised.

Aybe is currently structured on a functional basis, with all functional departments being centralised except for production where there are 3 separate factories.

The functional structure appears to result in a lack of integration of key activities, reduced loyalties and an absence of team work. The Chief Executive has contemplated moving towards a divisionalised structure, so as to provide some element of focus, but his experience has suggested that such a structure might create internal rivalries and competition which could adversely affect the performance of the company.

He is interested in revisiting alternative structures suggested by consultants in 2008 that are designed to encourage both integration and efficiency.

Project overspends

During 2010 to date, further project overspends have occurred and the board of directors feel that this issue needs addressing urgently.

The Chief Executive commented that, in his opinion, divisions look to make as much profit as they can but don't seem to care how much money they use to do it. He argued that divisional managers needed to be more aware of the funds they are using, that there is a cost to using these funds, and that implementing a system of measures including ROI and RI could help. He also added "Money doesn't grow on trees and our shareholders demand that we add value to their investment!"

The factory manager of the Domestic division (DEC) responded, "People seem to be getting annoyed with my division because of our recent refit and factory extension, but I didn't approve the project and I'm not responsible for making capital decisions. We only incur costs here in the factory and the way I see it our job is to keep these down to give the centralised sales team the best chance of making a profit on our goods."

Other issues

The Director of Operations is also under pressure from his fellow Board members to take action following a series of minor accidents during March and April at three factories. Maintenance has been reduced and machine breakdown is common. In most cases the repairs are simple and straightforward and the machine is up and running again very quickly. However, there are a growing number of minor accidents that are happening on an almost daily basis and the employees are frustrated that management is ignoring these incidents. The general feeling in the factories is that a major accident will occur before the management team either replaces the faulty and aged machinery, or improves the level of maintenance.

Furthermore, Aybe employs a high proportion of skilled female employees in the IEC factory and many are unhappy and have complained that they are paid a lower pay rate than their male colleagues who are doing the same work. However, the factory manager explained to the HR Director that this was due to the extra responsibilities that many of the male employees undertake.

8 Analysis of the pre-seen

Introduction

Now that you have had chance to read the pre-seen material, you should do some further research into the industry and try to pick out key themes which might form the basis of the exam questions.

You will find below:

- a SWOT analysis on Aybe
- stakeholder analysis
- quantitative analysis
- a consideration of potential examinable E3 topics.

Before reading this information, try to do your own analysis first and then compare your analysis to the information below.

The examiners have commented that students really need to do their own analysis. Simply copying analysis from your tutors or colleagues will not necessarily help you to understand the pre-seen properly.

Aybe pre-seen analysis – SWOT

Strengths

- Steady financials – growth in revenue and margins
- Seems to comply with Governance "best practice" (e.g. many NEDs although should have executive input to nominations committee)
- Share option plan should motivate directors

Weaknesses

- Board lacks ambition
- Aybe may have outgrown its functional structure
- Restrictive bank covenant limits financing opportunities
- Poor MIS (e.g. Board surprised about capex overspend)
- Poor budgetary control processes

Opportunities

- Expansion into Asian and /or African markets
- Enhance CRM – especially for specialist components division
- Develop website and e-business – especially for managing customer relationship
- Switch manufacturing to be closer to markets or to cheaper countries
- Improve information systems
- Sell a division

Threats

- Increasing competitive pressure
- Further loss of major customers
- High risk of takeover as shareholders may become dissatisfied
- Risk of breaching covenant
- Political risks – e.g. Eastern European country, African target
- Currency and interest rate risks.

Aybe pre-seen analysis – Stakeholders

Key stakeholders

- Institutional Shareholders (since privatisation) are becoming dissatisfied with current levels of growth and returns
- Major customers may threaten to move their business elsewhere

Aybe pre-seen analysis – Quantitative analysis

Divisions

- IEC contributes the most to both revenue and profit and SC the least
- Operating margins are DEC 6.6%, IEC 5.6% and SC 8.9%

Overall company

Profitability

- Fairly steady and unexciting
- Average revenue growth of 14.6% pa since 2005
- Operating margin has grown from 3.6% in 2005 to 6.6% (41/620) in 2009
- ROCE = 41/150 = 27.3% (no comparisons)

Liquidity

- Current ratio = 124 / 85 = 1.46
- Quick ratio = (81+3) / 85 = 0.99
- Receivables days = 81/620 × 365 = 48 days – seems high

- Payables days using operating costs = 73/579 × 365 = 46 days
- Inventory days using operating costs = 40/579 × 365 = 25 days
- Length of operating cycle = 25 + 48 – 46 = 27
- All fairly unexciting except Aybe has low cash reserves

Investor ratios

- Market capitalisation = 180m × 0.64 = C$115.2m
- Eps growth of 9.4% in 2009
- Dividend payout ratio set at 50% in 2008 and 2009
- Gearing based on book value of debt/equity = 40 / 110 = 36% which seems low enough. Slightly lower if use market values.

Aybe Case Study – Key examinable issues for paper E3

Note: It is important that in the real exam you fully incorporate the new unseen information into your answers and do not rely too much on your analysis of the pre-seen. However, based on the pre-seen the following potential issues can be identified.

Porter's Five Forces and Customer Relationship Management (CRM)

A Porter's 5 forces analysis would be useful to assess the relationship between Aybe and its main customers as well as indicating the key threats to Aybe's profitability arising from rivalry. This could be part of a discussion of customer relationship management, especially in the context of closer working relationships with customers (e.g. SC division) and investment in e–business.

Stakeholder concerns

Institutional investors may want higher growth. This could be quantified, allowing gap analysis and a review of whether new plans close the gap. If 2010 results are worse than 2009, as expected, then immediate action may be necessary.

Strategy evaluation

The scenario makes it clear that Aybe is considering expansion. The unseen could give you some options to evaluate. The suitability/feasibility/acceptability framework would be useful, but also be aware of Porter's diamond if specific country information is given.

How Aybe is run

The pre–seen suggests an unambitious Board who are very traditional in their thinking (functional structures, traditional rational planning model, etc). While this has been successful to date, events in the unseen may force a more flexible approach with the associated change management issues.

Divisional performance

The fact that there appears to be very little overlap between the three divisions could be a clue that you have to discuss **divisional** performance and strategy as distinct from a company–wide perspective.

Make sure you revise divisional performance issues (e.g. ROI/RI) and strategic portfolio models such as BCG matrix.

Ethics

Ethics is likely to crop up in your exam somewhere. This will either be personal ethics linking to the CIMA Code or corporate ethics and CSR. Given the references in the pre–seen that Aybe is looking to have the highest ethical standards, the pre–seen could include evidence of ethical problems such as poor working relationships in factories, possible redundancies, pollution from factories and so on.

Test your understanding 1

Required:

(a) Evaluate the existing product portfolio of Aybe using the BCG matrix and advise on a potential strategic direction for each division.

(18 marks)

(b) Evaluate Aybe's existing organisational structure and recommend appropriate alternative structures that Aybe could implement.

(12 marks)

(c) (i) Advise the Board of Aybe of the potential advantages and disadvantages of using Return on Investment (ROI) or Residual Income (RI) to measure performance.

(10 marks)

(ii) Discuss how the directors of Aybe can use shareholder value analysis to assist with the future strategic direction of the business.

(4 marks)

(d) Explain any ethical issues facing Aybe and make recommendations for how the company should deal with them.

(6 marks)

Total: 50 marks

9 Calculations in section A questions

The E3 examination typically has one or more sections in the compulsory question one which require candidates to perform calculations. The published syllabus for E3 does not explicitly define any numerical models or approaches that may be examined. However, the syllabus does state that 'material included in the syllabus for any of the past papers at the management or operational levels may also be relevant for the purposes of assessment.' Thus, recent papers have required candidates to use ratio analysis, discounted cash flows (DCF) and payback, amongst others.

As well as requiring the use of existing models, the E3 paper is set in the wider context of management accounting, which often requires the provision of prompt decision support and guidance to managerial colleagues. Often the situation where the management accountant is asked to provide such guidance does not fit into a model, instead requiring the accountant to use their skills of numeracy, analysis and creativity. An example of this was Question One from the November 2011 exam:

(a) **Advise the Web Division's Managing Director whether he should change the Daily News website to a subscription-only basis.**

(20 marks)

You should base your answer on a 364 day year.

10 marks in this section are for calculations.

In the unseen scenario some alternative strategies are described as a way of improving business performance. The requirement above reflects what strategic decision-makers might ask a management accountant to do in practise – given a set of incomplete information, they will need to estimate the likely consequences of a proposal and give some guidance as to future action. As the specifics of any real-life proposal will be unique no model can be prescribed to deal with it. However, management accountants should be pragmatic, numerate, flexible, creative and possessing a good grounding in business skills. Question One, part (a) above attempts to replicate what candidates might have to deal with in their jobs.

Below are five examples of typical section A numerical requirements for you to practise.

Test your understanding 2

ARG is a medium-sized company that writes business software. It is currently considering the purchase of a small rival company, CHG. After an initial review of CHG's financial statements, however, ARG's Finance Director has stated that 'there are clear signs that CHG is in financial distress.' He has recommended that CHG is therefore not a suitable acquisition target.

The most recent financial statements published by CHG are shown below.

Statement of financial position	**2012**	**2011**
	$000	$000
Assets		
Non-current assets		
Property, plant and equipment	30	25
Goodwill	215	133
	245	158
Current assets		
Inventories	3	2
Trade receivables	205	185
	208	187
Total assets	453	345

Equity and liabilities		
Equity		
Share capital	105	105
Liabilities		
Current liabilities		
Trade payables	257	178
Tax liability	1	2
Bank overdraft	10	25
	268	205
Non-current liabilities		
Bank loans	80	35
Total equity and liabilities	453	345

Statement of comprehensive income		
Revenue	2,650	2,350
Cost of sales	(2,600)	(2,300)
Gross profit	50	50
Other costs	(30)	(20)
Finance costs	(10)	(4)
Profit before tax	10	26
Income tax expense	(1)	(2)
Profit for the year	9	24
Number of staff	90	70

Required:

Assess, using the financial information available, the validity of the Finance Director's statement.

Test your understanding 3

E plc provides a satellite television service to residents across the UK. The UK economy is currently enjoying a period of growth, although some analysts are concerned that it will shortly fall into recession.

E's market is highly competitive, with E facing four major rivals who all offer similar services. The average price charged by E's rivals is around £56 per month. New customers contact E, which installs satellite receiving equipment in the customer's home, enabling them to watch around four hundred standard television channels. E currently offers this service for around £38 per month to each of its two million customers.

E also offers an additional ten 'premium' channels, including sports, that viewers must pay an additional £10 per month to watch. Currently around 50% of all of E's customers subscribe to these premium channels.

E pays a licence fee to the broadcasters who produce the television channels that are viewed by its customers. Currently, this licence fee averages around £0.05 per person per channel per month for each standard channel, and an additional £0.25 per person per channel per month for each premium channel.

E has been considering changing its pricing structure and has discovered that its sales volume is fairly price sensitive. The price charged by E also appears to have an effect on the proportion of customers subscribing to the premium channels. Market research undertaken on the existing industry has identified the following information:

Average price charged per customer per month for standard channels	Number of subscribers (m)	Proportion of customers subscribing to premium channels
£25	3.1	68%
£45	1.8	45%
£55	1.3	30%

If E's customer numbers fall below 1.5 million, E will only have to pay £0.04 per channel per person per month in licence fees to broadcasters. If customer numbers rise above 3 million, the fee will rise to £0.06 per channel per person per month. The licence fee and selling price for premium channels will be unchanged.

Required:

Calculate which of the three new pricing structures, if any, should be adopted and discuss your findings.
Work to the nearest £m.

Test your understanding 4

SNB plc is a large chain of supermarkets that operates throughout the UK, selling groceries. It is currently undergoing a major expansion as part of its strategy to expand into every town and city across the entire country, as well as increase its overall long-term profitability. SNB is currently considering opening a new store in Hexsham, a town where SNB currently has no presence.

SNB is investigating three potential sites for the new supermarket. Market research has indicated the following information about expected customer numbers and average spend:

Site:	One-off setup costs	Average number of customer visits per week	Average spend per customer visit	Marketing spend required per month
Out of town	£3.5m	18,000	£60	£12,000
Residential area	£4.0m	17,000	£75	£6,000
Town centre	£5.0m	32,000	£45	£5,000

Running costs will vary for each of the three locations. Excluding marketing, SNB expects that the profit margin on sales will be around 4.5% on the town centre location. The residential area would expect to earn a 5.5% margin, while an out of town store would have a margin of around 6.5%. These figures would be expected to stay constant for the foreseeable future.

SNB uses payback to assess its projects and insists that any new site achieves payback within one year. It also expects stores that open in a new area to achieve at least a thirty percent market share. The grocery market in Hexsham is estimated to be worth, in revenue terms, around £220m each year.

Required:

Evaluate the three proposed sites and recommend which SNB should select.

Test your understanding 5

FBV is a large company that makes and sells televisions and computer monitors around the world. This is a fiercely competitive industry, with dozens of rival manufacturers selling similar products to FBV and each spending large sums on research and development of new products.

FBV's research and development department has recently created a new type of display – the DCL. This will allow FBV's products to be lighter and thinner than those made by its rivals, potentially providing the company with a significant competitive advantage.

If FBV decides to proceed with the manufacture of the new display, it will cost around $200m to redesign the company's existing factories. FBV will depreciate this on a straight line basis over five years.

FBV estimates that the DCL will boost the company's revenue by $80m a year (in current values) starting in one year's time. This revenue is expected to rise by around five percent per annum each year until the end of year five, after which time FBV feels that its rivals will have designed similar systems and FBV will no longer gain any competitive advantage or benefits from the DCL.

Production costs will rise by $15m (in current terms) each year. These costs are expected to rise by around eight percent per annum due to rising raw material prices.

The CEO of FBV is excited about the new product and has claimed to the Board that shareholders in FBV can expect to see a rise of up to $0.33 in FBV's earnings per share (EPS) if the new displays are produced. Several members of the Board have expressed concern that they have not been provided with detailed evidence to back up the cost and revenue predictions that they have been given.

FBV currently has 120m shares in issue.

Required:

Evaluate whether the CEO's claims are correct.

Test your understanding 6

OPO Ltd is a manufacturing company that makes domestic boilers in three factories at different locations in the UK. In recent years the company has struggled financially and OPO recorded a significant loss in its last financial year.

OPO's management is deeply concerned about the company's situation and is looking for ways to reduce the organisation's costs. Two of OPO's factories (B and C) currently have some spare capacity. OPO's managers are currently analysing whether the closure of the third factory (factory A) and the transfer of its workload to the other two factories would be of financial benefit to the company.

OPO's managers wish to assess the financial viability of this proposal, using a net present value (NPV) calculation. They believe that the project should be assessed over a six year period and they typically use a 12% discount rate to appraise projects.

The factory site to be closed is owned by OPO. The company estimates that it could be sold for £400,000. The one-off costs of reorganising the remaining factories to enable them to take on A's workload has been estimated at £1,085,000.

Closure of factory A is expected to save around £45,000 per annum in local taxes, as well as around £55,000 per annum of administration costs. However, the proposal will lead to additional administrative costs of £20,000 per annum in each of the other two factories.

Factory A currently employs around 300 members of staff, at an average salary of £10,000 each. Around 95% of these will be made redundant if the factory closes, with an immediate redundancy payment having to be made to them of around £1,100 each. The remaining 5% of workers will be relocated to factories B and C on their current pay, but will be given a £5,000 relocation allowance each.

Factories B and C will need some additional members of staff to enable them to fully take on A's workload. An estimated 260 workers (in addition to those relocated from factory A) will be needed to be hired by OPO at an estimated annual cost of £10,000 each.

Required:

Calculate whether the proposed closure is financially viable, using the criteria provided.

Test your understanding answers

Test your understanding 1

(a) **Product portfolio evaluation**

The product portfolio can be assessed using the BCG framework as follows:

Specialist components division

The specialist components division has seen sales growth on the prior year of 13% and has a lot of potential for further growth as the board has indicated. Aybe is currently, however, a relatively small player in this market. This classifies it as a problem child within the BCG.

The idea with products of this type is to "get big or get out". This division will need further investment if it is to become a big force in this specialised area as high growth markets are also attractive to the competition. Alternatively if we cannot invest further we may need to consider divesting as the competition may surpass our capabilities and secure competitive advantage that we cannot compete with.

The key to growth would seem to be working more closely with customers and being better able to service their needs.

The company currently operates in a B2C manner, by manufacturing components and listing them in a catalogue. This is easy for Aybe as it can gain production economies through making a known range of items and schedule production more easily.

However as customers are seeking specially designed custom-made components the SC division in particular needs to work on a more flexible "pull" basis rather than with this old "push" system.

Technology can play a key part in allowing this, with web based services allowing customers to upload designs and input dimensions so as to get the exact part required.

The problem with this for Aybe will come in pricing components, which will require a specialist team to review uploads and quote as accurately as possible. This will need to be communicated back to the customer swiftly to ensure that response times do not cause the customer to go elsewhere.

The pricing policy will need to be carefully overseen and for a differentiated product of this nature it would make sense to adopt a premium pricing approach. However, customers will only pay a premium if the product delivered meets their needs.

Working more closely in partnership with the customers more closely would help ensure that they are getting what they want. The division could also make use of an extranet to allow the customer to view designs for components following initial enquiry being logged and ensure that the customer is satisfied with the product and has the opportunity to make any changes prior to wasting any actual production resources.

This would both save on cost and build customer goodwill, both of which will benefit the profitability of this business area.

Domestic components division

The domestic division has extensive competition and has only seen small growth in sales on prior year of 4%. It would therefore appear that the market is quite saturated and that growth and opportunities here have slowed down. It is therefore classified as a dog product within the BCG matrix.

It would be assumed by the BCG that this division would therefore lack the economies of scale required to compete with its larger rivals and this division should be divested.

However it can be seen that the division does generate a higher profit margin and more profit in absolute terms than the Industrial division. This is mainly due to the fact that industrial markets are more difficult and involve dealing with expert buyers, ordering large quantities. As such the margins in domestic markets are usually higher.

Given the recent refit undertaken to extend the factory in the domestic division, it is unlikely that we would now want to simply cease production for this market.

It would be hoped that following this refit Aybe can now generate greater economies of scale and this should lower the company's unit costs and make it better positioned to compete with its rivals. It can be seen that a slight increase in profit margin has occurred year on year, but perhaps not enough given the size of the capital investments.

The alternative to divesting is therefore to continue to try to generate greater profitability from domestic markets in order to keep shareholders happy.

This could be done by improving efficiency in the factory through the use of lean systems. Working more closely with suppliers could enable greater flexibility in upstream supply chain and the company could look to move towards a JIT system or even move towards a process of total quality management.

Given that only a small increase in profitability has been seen though it could be that a more dramatic solution, such as BPR or process innovation, may be appropriate to bring a significant change in margins.

Industrial components division (IEC)

The industrial division is the market leader, but in what would appear to be a declining area. Its sales have decreased 5% on prior year and the economic conditions will likely prevent further growth. According to the BCG matrix this would be classified as a cash cow.

The normal assumption here would be that this type of division would therefore be generating a lot of surplus cash which can be used to fund some alternative ventures and that therefore this division could be harvested.

However, the profit margin within the industrial area is the lowest of the three divisions and has deteriorated year on year. As stated above this is likely due to the demanding nature of large industrial businesses and the pressure they can put on Aybe to secure competitive prices.

Given the change in market conditions due to the recession, there is now likely to be even greater pressure on margins, and potentially fewer contracts around to compete for.

The key issue facing the division is that of customer retention. Promotional marketing direct to existing customers to reassure them of the quality of Aybe's products and the competitive pricing offered could help to prevent customers looking elsewhere for cheaper, but potentially inferior, substitutes.

Given Aybe's position as the market leader in this area it may well be that rivals are hit harder and could even be forced to withdraw from the market. Detailed competition analysis would be required to see the likely responses of rivals to the new market conditions.

Competitor analysis would also help Aybe to understand the core competences of its rivals. Given the increased pressure to impress remaining customers it will be more important than ever to focus on CSFs and ensure its own competitive advantage.

If Aybe cannot retain a sufficient portfolio of profitable industrial customers, then consideration should be given to divesting the division. Given a return of only 4.8% the division requires significant effort for only a limited return. This is not likely to be enough for the shareholders and may only get worse.

If the business unit is divested then it may be possible to sell off the division as a whole to a rival given the fixed asset base and remaining customer contracts that the division has in place.

The funds generated from this sale could then be invested in the high-growth specialist components area which generates greater profits and could yield more impressive returns for shareholders. The board would however need to consider the loss of $270m out of $631m of revenue if other sales can't be boosted.

(b) **Organisational structure**

Functional

The current functional structure has been in place for a long time, but is potentially restricting the business from achieving further growth.

A functional structure works very well in a single product and single market environment. The departments can all specialise in their roles and the business can grow to develop economies of scale.

However, given the three different markets that Aybe serves, it is likely that a functional structure will struggle to work in a diversified environment. The specific markets will need more specialised sales teams, marketing teams and design teams. This could help the divisions to tailor their services better to customer needs (e.g. specialist division).

Divisional

A divisional structure would appear more suitable for Aybe as it would give the divisional managers autonomy to make more decisions.

Having a central marketing and sales function as is currently the case may see the factories cut off from the needs of customers. Aybe currently manufactures over 100,000 different components in the factories, however, if divisional managers had their own sales team then they could capture and interpret sales data to maybe streamline this number.

Domestic customers may have certain products that are very regularly consumed which could be produced in high volumes and others which are only demanded occasionally. Such products could be made to order instead.

By capturing individual divisional data for sales and marketing purposes the company could gain further advantage in each of the individual markets through its use of information.

The risk with a divisional structure is that there could be potential for empire building by one of the divisional managers, and also the company could lose out on central economies of scale. For example, when purchasing raw materials for the factories to manufacture components it would make sense to place one bulk order rather than three separate ones to maximise discounts.

To minimise this risk, some of the departments within Aybe could be kept as central shared service functions, for example finance, IT and HR. This would allow the company to continue to benefit from economies of scale and avoid any duplication of effort.

Matrix

Aybe could consider using a matrix structure to try to gain the benefits of both functional and divisional ideas. Given that the company has wanted to maintain continuity as far as possible this could be an interesting compromise.

Existing functional managers in the areas of sales and marketing and purchasing could remain in place, but separate divisional managers for industrial, domestic and specialist divisions could be put alongside this.

The role of the divisional managers in this would be to oversee the strategy for each division and ensure that the various functions are doing their task in a way which suits that divisional customers' needs.

The functional managers could then oversee their respective teams and ensure that they are working as efficiently as possible, and allocate resources and staff from the function to each division in a more flexible way.

The key disadvantage of implementing this structure is that dual control and many time-consuming meetings are likely to occur.

Each divisional manager will have the specialist knowledge of their division, but for example all three will need to talk to the sales director so he can consider the total requirements of the whole company before he allocates staff to each.

(c) (i) **Performance appraisal**

The employees within Aybe are currently focused on achieving cost targets, sales targets and increasing operating profit. However, this focus on financial factors only has led to the managers thinking about short-term goals and failing to consider the use of long-term funds.

Aybe have had trouble in recent years with capital overspend as was evidenced by the DEC factory extension in 2009.

A move to a divisional structure as suggested above would mean the divisions could be appraised as investment centres rather than merely cost centres then this would force divisional managers to consider also the amount of money they spend when generating returns.

The use of ROI as a performance appraisal measure would make the divisional managers more aware of capital budgets and the need to achieve required levels of return when investing funds.

The target ROI set by the company indicates to the managers a minimum acceptable return from the company's point of view. Managers can therefore aim to beat this and further rewards can be attached based on the relative performance of the divisions.

The bonus structure rewards managers for achieving performance above the target and so divisional managers should strive to maximise ROI. This measure is also good for comparing divisional performance and will show which division is doing best with the funds it has available.

The fact that the managers' bonuses are based on this could lead to dysfunctional decisions, however. A manager may make suboptimal decisions in order to maximise his own personal benefits and could potentially reject suitable projects from the company point of view if it would diminish the divisional position.

The use of RI would help to eliminate the issue of sub-optimality, as it takes profit and deducts the cost of the finance used within the division to see if the division is generating enough profit to cover financing costs.

Using RI leads to goal-congruent decisions as now managers will accept any project returning more than the company target as this will generate positive residual income.

Residual income cannot be used for comparisons however as divisions of vastly different sizes may end up delivering the same residual income, however the smaller division will have performed significantly better than the larger one in achieving this.

Overall, linking bonus and reward structures to these two measures would mean that any overspend in the project would cause managers not to get a bonus.

Another advantage of switching to a divisional structure from a performance appraisal point of view is that it becomes easier to reward one division even if the others have not performed so well, thus avoiding the current feeling that SC employees are being "penalised".

(ii) **Shareholder value analysis**

The term 'shareholder value' reflects the view that when a person invests his or her money in a company, they do so in the expectation that their wealth will increase. It is generally assumed for profit-making entities that the principle strategic aim of the company is to generate long-term economic value.

Changes in shareholder value can be measured crudely by looking at earnings per share. Future shareholder value is concerned with the economic value of an investment and by discounting forecast cash flows at an appropriate cost of capital, one can work on the assumption that cash flows provide dividends and therefore lead to expected changes in share price.

However, whilst shareholder value analysis (SVA) purports to be only concerned with increasing shareholder wealth, the directors must look beyond the purely financial to decide what will impact ultimately on the company's value and share price.

Investing in wider stakeholder concerns would no doubt add to costs in the short term (and therefore decrease shareholder wealth) but in the long term the directors may see increases in employee motivation, customer satisfaction and a strengthening of supplier relations that benefit the company and its cash flows long into the future.

The performance of employees, for example, impacts directly on customer satisfaction and hence income. So the directors need to know how wealth is generated and what impacts on each factor.

The concept of shareholder value analysis links closely with the idea of NPV. If managers understand the factors that drive NPV then they can attempt to improve on these drivers and bonuses could even be linked to these factors instead of the standard profit-based performance measures.

(d) **Ethical issues**

The key ethical issues facing Aybe are as follows:

Claims of sexual discrimination

Many skilled female workers have complained that they are paid a lower wage rate than their male colleagues who are doing the same work. The factory manager has suggested that this reflects differing responsibility levels but that argument could result in female employees, particularly skilled ones, claiming that they have not been promoted on the grounds of gender.

Either way there appears to be a case for Aybe to answer. It is unethical for Aybe to discriminate on the grounds of gender.

It is recommended that:

– Aybe introduces a system of job evaluation to ensure that employees get the same pay if they do jobs of equal value

– Aybe reviews responsibilities to ensure that there is no discrimination.

Accidents

In every factory older machinery is not being maintained sufficiently to prevent minor accidents from occurring. It is unethical for Aybe to boost shareholder profit by cutting costs at the expense of employee safety. It is also probably illegal under relevant health and safety legislation.

It is recommended that the maintenance budget be increased immediately. In addition suspect machinery should be replaced when financing constraints permit.

Test your understanding 2

When analysing the financial statements of an organisation, it is useful to identify key ratios from the industry the business operates within. Unfortunately, this information has not been provided, meaning that the only meaningful comparison that can be made for CHG is between the 2011 and 2012 financial statements.

General issues

Firstly, goodwill is the most significant non-current asset. The company may have difficulty raising further finance in the future, as they seem to have few tangible assets that can be offered as security. It can be seen that goodwill has increased significantly in the year, which could suggest that CHG has made an acquisition. Further investigation would be required to confirm this.

Secondly, it should be noted that the financial statements show no retained profit, suggesting that all profits are being distributed to shareholders as dividends. This should be investigated further.

Profitability

The net profit margin (before tax) has fallen by more than half, from 1.1% in 2011 to 0.4% in 2012. This seems to have been caused by a number of factors, including:

- While sales increased by 12.8% in the year, the gross profit margin has fallen by 0.2% to just 1.9% in 2012. This may have been caused by the large increase in employees in the year. Staff numbers rose by almost 30% in the year, which is likely to have put a strain on CHG's margins.
- Other costs have risen by 50% between the two years. This has had a significant effect on the bottom-line profit of the organisation and the reason for this rise in other costs should be investigated.

Note that the absolute net profit margin before tax seems low. It should be compared with industry averages to see if it is a cause for concern.

The return on capital employed (ROCE) has fallen from 21.4% in 2011 to just 10.8% in 2012. This is caused partly by the fall in profits (as outlined above), but also because of the sharp rise in borrowing seen in the year. ROCE is a key investor ratio and such a large fall may make it difficult for CHG to attract further investment.

Efficiency

Trade receivables have increased at a roughly similar rate as sales. However, the trade payables payment period has seen a sharp rise from 28 days in 2011 to 36 days in 2012. This may indicate that CHG is slowing payments down to its suppliers in order to improve its cash flows (which is supported by the deteriorating cash position of the business).

Sales revenue per employee has dropped from approximately $33,500 in 2011 to under $29,500 in 2012, indicating a significant drop in the efficiency of the employees. It may be due to the large rise in employee numbers, but the reason for the large increase in staff numbers needs to be investigated.

Liquidity

Liquidity, as measured by the current ratio, has fallen from 0.91 in 2011 to just 0.78 in 2011. This seems low, indicating that CHG may not have sufficient short-term funds to meet its short-term obligations. Again, this is a cause for concern and would need investigating further and comparing with industry averages.

(Tutorial note: There would be little point in calculating the quick ratio here, due to the relatively insignificant amount of inventory. Doing so would simply waste time.)

Note that the cash position has improved marginally, with the overdraft falling by $15,000. However, the long-term debt in the company has risen by $45,000. This suggests that the core activities of the company are actually losing cash and CHG is borrowing money in order to deal with this. This would not be supportable in the long term.

Financial gearing

Both of CHG's gearing ratios give cause for concern. Gearing (as measured by debt/equity) has risen from 57.1% in 2011 to 85.7% in 2012 (note that this includes the overdraft figure). Interest cover has dropped from 7.5 to just 2 in 2012. Again, while this needs comparing to industry averages, such large increases cannot continue indefinitely and may cast doubts on CHG's long-term going concern.

This is compounded by the likely problems (low non-current assets and falling ROCE) that CHG will face if it needs to raise future finance.

Overall

There are very clear signals that CHG may be in financial distress. Rising debt, cash flow issues and poor profitability mean that the company may indeed not be a suitable target for takeover, as identified by the Finance Director.

However, more work should be carried out to ensure that CHG is not simply typical of its industry.

Test your understanding 3

We first need to identify how much profit is being made each month at the current pricing structure.

		Total (£m)
Standard subscription revenue	2m × £38	76
Premium revenue	2m × 50% × £10	10
Standard channel licence fees	400 × £0.05 × 2m	(40)
Premium channel licence fees	2m × 50% × £0.25 × 10	(3)
Monthly profit		43

Monthly profits under the proposed new pricing structures would be:

		At £25 per month (£m)		At £45 per month (£m)		At £55 per month (£m)
Standard subs rev.	£25 × 3.1m	78	£45 × 1.8m	81	£55 × 1.3m	72
Premium subs rev.	£10 × 3.1m × 68%	21	£10 × 1.8m × 45%	8	£10 × 1.3m × 30%	4
Standard licence fees	400 × £0.06 × 3.1m	(74)	400 × £0.05 × 1.8m	(36)	400 × £0.04 × 1.3m	(21)
Premium licence fees	(£0.25 × 10) × 3.1m × 68%	(5)	1.8m × 45% × (£0.25 × 10)	(2)	(£0.25 × 10) × 1.3m × 30%	(1)
Monthly profit		20		51		54
% movement vs. current profit		**–53.5%**		**+18.6%**		**+25.6%**

The option that maximises E's profits can be seen to be the £55 per month selling price.

Arguments for increasing prices to £55

At this price, while the number of subscribers is significantly lower than at present, E is earning far higher profits per subscriber. In addition, the costs of licensing the channels have fallen by almost a half from their current levels. Taken together, this leads to a significant rise in profit for E.

A rise to £55 (an approximately 45% rise on the current selling price) may seem significant, but it can be argued that this is simply bringing E in line with its existing rivals.

While the premium channel uptake will be disappointing at this higher price, it is still an area with high margins for E. If the standard package price rises to £55 per month, E could consider lowering its prices for the premium package to encourage a higher uptake – hopefully boosting profitability.

Arguments against raising prices to £55

There is no indication that E will offer any improvements to its services in exchange for the price rise. Customers are likely to be upset by such a move, even if it merely brings E in line with competitors. This could seriously damage E's reputation.

There appears to be no analysis of what competitor reaction will be. Given the elastic nature of the market, if E's competitors cut their prices to below £55, they may gain customers at E's expense.

It should also be noted that the UK economy is predicted to enter a recession in the near future. This may mean that subscribers will see a reduction in their disposable incomes. If E charges a much higher price for its services, it may be seen as an unnecessary luxury by many customers and could see a steep fall in custom.

Overall

E needs to proceed with care. While the £55 selling price appears to be fair for the market, it will increase E's risks in an uncertain market. E may be losing its unique selling point of being cheaply priced, which could lead to loss of custom in the future.

Test your understanding 4

SNB has two main selection criteria – payback must be achieved within one year and the store must achieve a market share of at least 30%.

		Out of town		Residential		Town centre
Revenue (£)	18,000 × 60 × 52	56,160,000	17,000 × 75 × 52	66,300,000	32,000 × 45 × 52	74,880,000
Contribution margin		6.5%		5.5%		4.5%
Profit before marketing (£)		3,650,400		3,646,500		3,369,600
Marketing (£)	12,000 × 12	(144,000)	6,000 × 12	(72,000)	5,000 × 12	(60,000)
Profit after marketing (£)		3,506,400		3,574,500		3,309,600
Setup costs		(3,500,000)		(4,000,000)		(5,000,000)
Year one profit/(loss)		**6,400**		**(425,500)**		**(1,690,400)**
Market share	56.2/220	**25.5%**	66.3/220	**30.1%**	74.9/220	**34.0%**

The picture provided by SNB's market research is not straightforward, with none of the three sites managing to achieve both of SNB's investment criteria.

Out of town

The out of town development is the cheapest to set up and enjoys the highest profit margins. However, due to its high required marketing, as well as its moderate spend per customer, it only just manages to break even within a one year period. Note that any slight variation in income or expenditure from budget could wipe this out, meaning that it could easily fail this requirement.

The out of town site only provides a market share of 24.4%, which is well below SNB's requirement of 30%.

Residential

While this provides the lowest number of shoppers, the spend per shopper is significantly above that of the other two stores. However, this is insufficient to enable the residential site to achieve payback within one year, though it manages to just produce a market share of above 30%.

Town centre

It appears that the running costs are higher in the town centre, leading to a reduction in the margin achieved. The spend per customer is also lower than the other sites, perhaps due to accessibility issues. This means that, even with the low marketing and high customer numbers, it fails to achieve the annual profitability of the other sites.

Due to the high setup costs, the town centre site also fails to achieve payback within the specified one year. However, it does provide the highest market share, exceeding SNB's investment criteria of 30%.

Overall

While there is no clear candidate, one of the three must be selected in order to meet SNB's overall strategy of expanding into every town and city in the country.

It should be noted that SNB may wish to consider the appropriateness of its one year payback criterion. Only the out of town development achieves this, but selecting this option will not maximise the long-term profitability of the company (which is one of SNB's strategic goals). The residential development, in spite of failing the payback test, has the highest annual profit of the three sites. As such, it will be more suitable to help the company achieve its goal of maximising long term profitability.

The town centre development, while offering a slightly higher market share than the residential development, offers the lowest annual profit and fails the one year payback test by a wide margin.

SNB should therefore consider choosing the residential development site, as it achieves the required market share as well as offering a higher annual profit than the other two sites for the foreseeable future.

Test your understanding 5

	Yr 1	Yr 2	Yr 3	Yr 4	Yr 5
	$000	$000	$000	$000	$000
Revenue (+5% inflation)	84,000	88,200	92,610	97,241	102,103
Production costs (+8% inflation)	(16,200)	(17,496)	(18,896)	(20,407)	(22,040)
Depreciation	(40,000)	(40,000)	(40,000)	(40,000)	(40,000)
Profit	27,800	30,704	33,714	36,834	40,063
EPS ($)	0.23	0.26	0.28	0.31	0.33

The figures provided would indicate a rise of up to $0.33 in EPS over the next five years, as suggested by the CEO.

However, this assumes that the projections themselves are correct. The other members of the Board appear to be concerned that there is a lack of evidence supporting these figures. Certainly there are several key areas that need further investigation.

Competitors

Each of FBV's rivals are spending large sums of money on research and development. FBV's figures assume that its rivals will be unable to develop a similar product to the DCL for the next five years. In reality, this may be over-optimistic. Should alternative products be produced even one year earlier than predicted, FBV may not achieve the $0.33 rise in EPS.

FBV could also face a similar problem if its rivals are currently working on a new or better system that the DCL. Any new innovations in the market over the next five years could seriously compromise the profitability of the DCL.

Inflation

It can be extremely difficult to predict inflation rates, even in the short term. Over a five year period there is significant scope for error. If inflation rates change, this could have a significant effect on whether a $0.33 rise in EPS is achievable for the DCL project.

Overall

While the existing figures do support the CEO's statement, more careful research is needed before informing the shareholders of the possible rise in EPS. Failing to achieve the results that have been promised to investors will likely cause a drop in confidence and a fall in FBV's share price.

Test your understanding 6

	Year 0	Years 1 to 6
	£000	£000
Site disposal	400	
Reorganisation costs	(1,085)	
Redundancy costs (W1)	(314)	
Relocation costs (W2)	(75)	
Annual impact on costs (W3)		310
Total	(1,074)	310
Discount factor at 12%	1	4.111
Present value	(1,074)	1,274

The proposed closure of factory A has a NPV of £200k and should therefore be accepted.

(W1) **Redundancy costs**

300 × 95% × £1,100 = £314k

(W2) **Relocation costs**

300 × 5% × £5,000 = £75k

(W3) **Annual impact on costs**

Local tax saving		£45,000
Administration cost savings (A)		£55,000
Additional administration costs (B and C)	£20,000 × 2 factories	(£40,000)
Labour savings	((95% x 300) – 260) × £10,000	£250,000
Total annual cost saving		£310,000

chapter

18

Section A-style practice questions

1 T plc (Multinational)

PRESEEN INFORMATION

Introduction

T plc is a well-established company providing telecommunications services both nationally and internationally. Its business has been concerned with telephone calls, the provision of telephone lines and equipment, and private telecommunication networks. T plc has supplemented these services recently by offering mobile phones, which is an expanding market worldwide

The company maintains a diverse customer base, including residential users, multi-national companies, government agencies and public sector organisations. The company handles approximately 100 million calls each working day, and employs nearly 140,000 personnel.

Strategic development

The Chairman of T plc stated within the latest Annual Report that there are three main areas in which the company aims to develop in order to remain a world leader in the telecommunications market. He believes that the three main growth areas reflect the evolving nature of the telecommunications market and will provide scope for development.

The areas in which development is planned are:

- expansion of the telecommunications business in the national and overseas markets, both by the company acting on its own and through partnership arrangements with other suppliers
- diversification into television and multi-media services, providing the hardware to permit telephone shopping from home and broadcasting services
- extension of the joint ventures and strategic alliances which have already been established with companies in North America, Europe, India and the Far East.

The Chairman explained that the company is intent on becoming a world leader in communications. This will be achieved through maintaining its focus on long-term development by improving its services to customers, developing high quality up-to-date products and being innovative, flexible and market-driven. His aim is to deliver a world-class service at competitive cost.

Financial information

Comparative statistics showing extracts from the company's financial performance in its national telecommunications market over the last two years are as follows:

	Last year	*Previous year*
	$ million	$ million
Turnover	16,613	15,977
Profit before interest and tax	3,323	2,876
Capital employed	22,150	21,300

The company estimates its cost of capital to be approximately 11%.

The Chairman expressed satisfaction with the increase in turnover and stated that cost efficiencies were now being generated following completion of a staff reduction programme. This would assist the company in achieving a target return on capital employed (ROCE) in this market of 20% over the next three years.

Business opportunities

The Chief Executive of T plc has stated that the major opportunities for the company lie in the following areas:

- encouraging greater use of the telephone
- provision of advanced services, and research and development into new technology, including the internet and systems integration
- the increasing freedom from government control of worldwide telecommunication services.

An extensive television and poster advertising campaign has been used by the company. This was in order to penetrate further the residential market by encouraging greater use of the telephone with various charging incentives being offered to residential customers.

Markets and competition

The company is currently experiencing an erosion of its market share and faces increasingly strong competition in the mobile phone market. While T plc is the leader in its national market, with an 85% share of the telecommunications business, it has experienced a reduced demand for the supply of residential lines in the last five years as competition has increased.

UNSEEN INFORMATION

At a recent Board meeting the following issues were highlighted.

Business opportunities

To further the objective of increasing long-term shareholder value, the company is actively considering investment of $200 million in each of the next three years in new technology and quality improvements in its national market. Because of its specialist technical nature, the investment is not expected to have any residual value at the end of the three-year period.

Following the investment, the directors of T plc believe that its rate of profit before interest and tax to turnover in its national telecommunications market will remain constant. This rate will be at the same level as last year for each of the three years of the investment.

Markets and competition

The market for the supply of equipment in the national telecommunications market is perceived to be static. The investment of $200 million in each of the next three years is estimated to increase T plc's share of this market to a level of 95%. The full improvement of 10% is expected to be received by T plc next year, and its market share will then remain at this level for the full three-year period. It is anticipated that unless further investment is made after the three-year period, T plc's market share will revert to its current level as a consequence of the expected competitive response.

Industry regulation

The government has established an industry regulatory organisation to promote competition and deter anti-competitive behaviour

As a result of the activities of the regulator and aggressive pricing strategies, it is anticipated that charges to customers will remain constant for the full three-year period of the new investment.

All cash flows can be assumed to occur at the end of the year to which they relate. The cash flows and discount rate are in real terms.

Question – T plc – PEST

Explain the nature of the political, economic, social, and technical forces which influence T plc in developing its business and increasing its market share.

(10 marks)

Question – T plc – ANSOFF

(a) Apply Ansoff's Product/Market Growth Vector matrix to assess the extent of the potential market development opportunities available to T plc.

(15 marks)

(b) Explain how this matrix may be incorporated into the strategic planning process to determine the extent of the planning gap.

(5 marks)

Question – T plc – Closing a planning gap

(a) Evaluate and comment on T plc's proposed investment in new technology and quality improvements in its national telecommunications market.

Assume that variable costs are 80% of the incremental revenue, and that fixed costs will not increase. Ignore working capital.

(15 marks)

(b) Assess to what extent the investment in new technology and quality improvements in T plc's national telecommunications market contributes towards the closure of the company's planning gap in respect of its target ROCE.

(5 marks)

Note: You may assume that the entire capital investment is written off at the end of the three-year period.

2 The National Museum (not for profit)

PRESEEN INFORMATION

Introduction

The National Museum (NM) was established in 1857 to house collections of art, textiles and metalware for the nation. It remains in its original building which is itself of architectural importance. Unfortunately, the passage of time has meant that the condition of the building has deteriorated and so it requires continual repair and maintenance. Alterations have also been made to ensure that the building complies with the disability access and health and safety laws of the country. However, these alterations have been criticised as being unsympathetic and out of character with the rest of the building. The building is in a previously affluent area of the capital city. However, what were once large middle-class family houses have now become multi-occupied apartments and the socio-economic structure of the area has radically changed. The area also suffers from an increasing crime rate. A visitor to the museum was recently assaulted whilst waiting for a bus to take her home. The assault was reported in both local and national newspapers.

Thirty years ago, the government identified museums that held significant Heritage Collections. These are collections that are deemed to be very significant to the country. Three Heritage Collections were identified at the NM, a figure that has risen to seven in the intervening years as the museum has acquired new items.

Funding and structure

The NM is currently 90% funded by direct grants from government. The rest of its income comes from a nominal admission charge and from private sponsorship of exhibitions. The direct funding from the government is based on a number of factors, but the number of Heritage Collections held by the museum is a significant funding influence. The Board of Trustees of the NM divide the museum's income between departments roughly on the basis of the previous year's budget plus an inflation percentage. The division of money between departments is heavily influenced by the Heritage Collections. Departments with Heritage Collections tend to be allocated a larger budget. The budgets for 2008 and 2009 are shown in Figure 1.

Collection	**Number of**	**Budget** ($000)	**Budget** ($000)
Sections	**Heritage collections**	**2008**	**2009**
Architecture	2	120.00	125.00
Art	2	135.00	140.00
Metalwork	1	37.50	39.00
Glass		23.00	24.00
Textiles	1	45.00	47.50
Ceramics		35.00	36.00
Furniture		30.00	31.50
Print & Books		35.00	36.50
Photography		15.00	15.50
Fashion		10.00	10.50
Jewellery	1	50.00	52.50
Sculpture		25.00	26.00
Administration		60.50	63.00
Total		**621.00**	**647.00**

Figure 1: Section budgets; 2008 and 2009

The head of each collection section is an important position and enjoys many privileges, including a large office, a special section heads' dining room and a dedicated personal assistant (PA). The heads of sections which have 'Heritage Collections' also hold the title of professor from the National University.

The departmental structure of the NM (see Figure 2) is largely built around the twelve main sections of the collection. These sections are grouped into three departments, each of which has a Director. The Board of Directors is made up of the three directors of these departments, together with the Director of Administration and the Director General. The museum is a charity run by a Board of Trustees. There are currently eight trustees, two of whom have been recently appointed by the government. The other six trustees are people well-known and respected in academic fields relevant to the museum's collections.

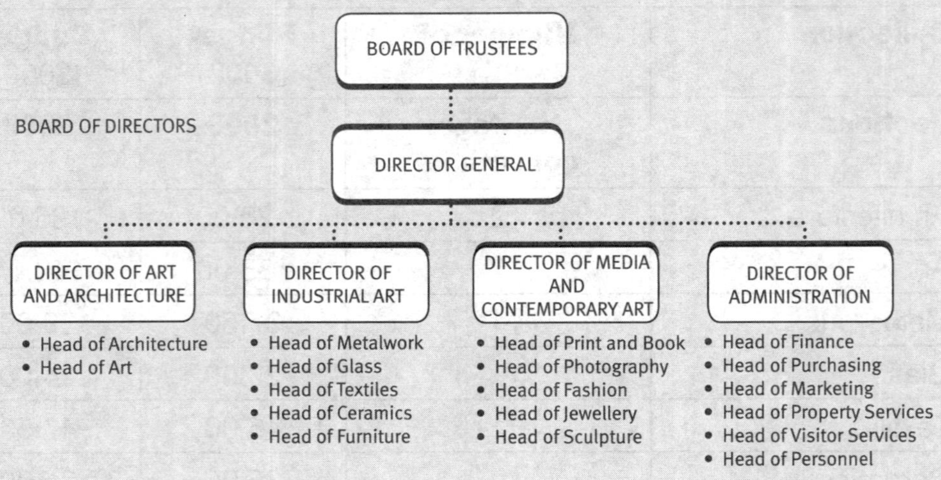

Figure 2: Current Organisational Structure

Government change

One year ago, a new national government was elected. The newly appointed Minister for Culture implemented the government's election manifesto commitment to make museums more self-funding. The minister has declared that in five year's time the museum must cover 60% of its own costs and only 40% will be directly funded by government. This change in funding will gradually be phased in over the next five years. The 40% government grant will be linked to the museum achieving specified targets for disability access, social inclusion and electronic commerce and access. The government is committed to increasing museum attendance by lower socio-economic classes and younger people so that they are more aware of their heritage. Furthermore, it also wishes to give increasing access to museum exhibits to disabled people who cannot physically visit the museum site. The government have asked all museums to produce a strategy document showing how they intend to meet these financial, accessibility and technological objectives. The government's opposition has, since the election, also agreed that the reliance of museums on government funding should be reduced.

Traditionally, the NM has provided administrative support for sections and departments, grouped together beneath a Director of Administration. The role of the Director General has been a part-time post. However, the funding changes introduced by the government and the need to produce a strategy document, has spurred the Board of Trustees to appoint a full-time Director General from the private sector. The trustees felt they needed private industry expertise to develop and implement a strategy to achieve the government's objectives. The new Director General was previously the CEO of a major chain of supermarkets.

Director General's proposal

The new Director General has produced a strategic planning document showing how the NM intends to meet the government's objectives.

Proposals in this document include:

(1) Allocating budgets (from 2010) to sections based on visitor popularity. The most visited collections will receive the most money. The idea is to stimulate sections to come up with innovative ideas that will attract more visitors to the museum. Visitor numbers have been declining (see Figure 3) since 2004.

Visitor numbers (000s)	2007	2006	2005	2004
Age 17 or less	10	12	15	15
Age 18–22	5	8	12	10
Age 23–30	10	15	20	20
Age 31–45	20	20	18	25
Age 46–59	35	35	30	30
Age 60 or over	40	35	35	30
Total	120	125	130	130

Figure 3: Visitor numbers 2004 to 2007

(2) Increasing entrance charges to increase income, but to make entry free to pensioners, students, children and people receiving government benefit payments.

(3) Removing the head of sections' dining room and turning this into a restaurant for visitors. An increase in income from catering is also proposed in the document.

(4) Removing the head of sections' personal assistants and introducing a support staff pool to reduce administrative costs.

(5) Increasing the display of exhibits. Only 10% of the museum's collection is open to the public. The rest is held in storage.

(6) Increasing commercial income from selling posters, postcards and other souvenirs.

The Director General has also suggested a major re-structuring of the organisation as shown in Figure 4.

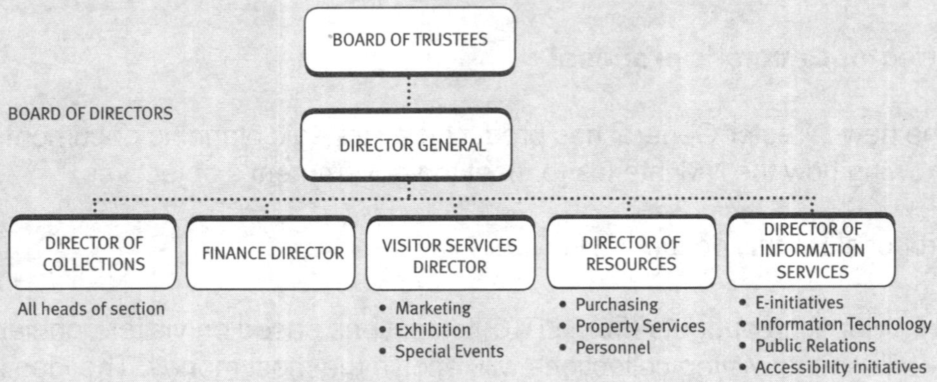

UNSEEN INFORMATION

Reaction to the proposals

Employees have reacted furiously to the Director General's suggestions. The idea of linking budgets to visitor numbers has been greeted with dismay by the Director of Art and Architecture. 'This is a dreadful idea and confuses popularity with historical significance. As previous governments have realised, what is important is the value of the collection. Heritage Collections recognise this significance by putting the nation's interests before those of an undiscerning public. As far as I am concerned, if they want to see fashion, they can look in the high street shops. Unlike fashion, great art and architecture remains.' The Director of Art and Architecture and the two professors who hold the Head of Architecture and Head of Art posts have also lobbied individual members of the Board of Trustees with their concerns about the Director General's proposals.

The Director of Industrial Arts and the Director of Media and Contemporary Art have contacted powerful figures in both television and the press and as a result a number of articles and letters critical of the Director General's proposals have appeared. A recent television programme called 'Strife at the NM' also featured interviews with various heads of collections criticising the proposed changes. They were particularly critical of the lack of consultation; 'these proposals have been produced with no input from museum staff. They have been handed down from on high by an ex-grocer', said one anonymous contributor.

Eventually, the criticism of staff and their lack of cooperation prompted the Director General to ask the Board of Trustees to publicly back him. However, only the two trustees appointed by the government were prepared to do so. Consequently, the Director General resigned. This has prompted an angry response from the government which has now threatened to cut the museum's funding dramatically next year and to change the composition of the Board of Trustees so that the majority of trustees are appointed directly by the government. The Minister of Culture has asked the museum to develop and recommend a new strategy within one month.

Question – National Museum – PESTEL

Analyse the macro-environment of the National Museum using a PESTEL analysis.

(20 marks)

Question – National Museum – Cultural web and change

(a) Using the cultural web model as a framework, explain why the Director General's plans to change the museum have failed.

(20 marks)

(b) Recommend how the Director General could have used the cultural web to implement change successfully.

(10 marks)

Question – National Museum – Methods of strategy development

In the context of the National Museum, evaluate the following different approaches to strategy development:

(a) Strategy is the deliberate positioning of an organisation as the result of some rational, analytical, structured and directive process.

(b) Strategic planning requires an adaptive approach, building on and changing the existing strategy. Changes are incremental as the organisation adapts to new opportunities and threats in the environment.

(c) Strategy should be based on innovation and new ideas, emerging from the variety and diversity in an organisation. It is as likely to come from the bottom of the organisation as from the top.

(10 marks)

3 Lionel Cartwright (Entrepreneurial)

PRESEEN INFORMATION

Lionel Cartwright considers himself to be an entrepreneur. He has been involved in many business ventures, each with minimal planning. He claims that this allows him to respond quickly to changing circumstances. His father had left him a small road haulage firm - three lorries - but he soon sold this to a larger operator when he recognised that operating margins were low and competition was severe. With the money received he bought a fast-food franchise, realising that this was where there was likely to be substantial growth. However, the franchisor required Lionel to limit both his ambitions and ideas for expansion to the development of this single franchise site. Lionel did not like this constraint and sold out and moved on. He then invested his money in an Internet firm, having identified the potential in this market. Unfortunately for Lionel his investment in the company was insufficiently large to permit him to have much say in the management of the company so he again sold out. He demonstrated his opportunism because he managed to sell his investment before the technology shares had fallen on the global stock exchanges. Lionel now has a cash sum of about $12 million seeking a suitable investment.

It is clear from Lionel's track record that he enjoys involvement in the management of businesses and he also prefers some element of control. He appears to have a skill in identifying potential growth markets and he also seems to have an intuitive knowledge of the market place. He is currently showing an interest again in the food/restaurant retailing market and he is looking at organic foods and juices (produce grown without the use of synthetic fertilisers or pesticides). He has noticed a growing trend in the USA for outlets selling fresh vegetable and fruit juices which are squeezed to the customer's demand, either to be consumed on premises or taken away for consumption, as is the case with many fast-food chains. This development is all part of the growing health-conscious climate. Lionel believes that the European market is ready for such a venture and this is his initial objective. He has already opened four outlets in Central London. To acquire the leases, fit out the premises, train labour and buy inventory plus some initial expenditure on marketing has already cost Lionel $3 million. He realises that to become profitable he must open several more outlets so as to gain both from the experience curve and from economies of scale. He estimates that about 30 outlets will provide him with the necessary critical mass. He believes that these outlets could be anywhere in Europe, given the right environment. He is confident that he has identified a transnational segment for a health focused nutritious juice – a segment of the market which is uniform, regardless of nationality. This is based upon the youth market which tends to have common tastes in both entertainment and leisure activities throughout Europe – France, Italy, Germany and the UK appear to be acceptable target areas.

However this segment is believed to be relatively sophisticated and affluent so outlets, therefore, will need to be in expensive city-centre areas or in other similar type areas which this target market group might regularly visit.

One of the problems facing Lionel's new venture and one of the pressures pushing him towards expansion is the need for regular access to suitable organic raw materials. These are in short supply. With large UK supermarkets generating increasing competitive demand for organic produce Lionel is finding it difficult to find reliable, quality suppliers. His current demand is too low and he needs to guarantee his suppliers a larger volume of orders so as to maintain their interest. He can only do this if he can rapidly expand the number of outlets he has or if he increases the volume sold through each outlet. The latter option is not really feasible. The area covered by each outlet is limited and to expand demand might mean either lowering the image which the outlet has developed and/or lowering the price of the products. Given the relative elasticities of demand, although the volumes of sales may rise, the profitability of each outlet may actually fall.

Another problem Lionel faces is obtaining suitable sites for his outlets. It is essential that these are in the appropriate locations. His current ones are in Central London where there is a young and affluent market and also where the tourist trade is high. Future sites need to be acquired if expansion is to be achieved. If he goes into the rest of Europe they will need to be in major city centres or in similar type sophisticated tourist areas. It is inevitable that the availability of these sites will be limited and the cost of acquisition will be expensive. In addition the juice enterprise needs to be marketed in a sympathetic way. The target clientele, being young, mobile and affluent will be easily deterred from buying the product if the marketing lacks subtlety. Consequently any rush towards expansion by using aggressive marketing techniques must be tempered with caution. It will be too easy to downgrade the enterprise's image, so damaging it in the eyes of its potential customers.

Lionel had made an effort to understand his core competences and he hoped that these would match the critical success factors needed for this industry. He believed that he had the necessary market knowledge, his operation was small enough to be flexible and responsive to sudden changes in market circumstances and he felt that he had the level of motivation required to be successful in such a fast-moving, consumer, non-durable industry.

UNSEEN INFORMATION

After one year's operations the results from the four London outlets compared with a chain of similar outlets in the USA seem to demonstrate that Lionel's ambitions may be over-optimistic. Whilst recognising that the enterprise is still young (although there is the novelty attraction and also no near competition) the profits are nowhere near as attractive as those being obtained from a larger chain (20 outlets) in the USA. [See details in Table 1.]

If Lionel is to achieve his ambition of setting up a profitable chain of retail juice outlets he must seek expansion without alienating his customer-base. He can do this gradually and internally by funding any expansion through retained earnings. He could also attempt to acquire another retail/fast food chain and adapt it to this new format. Finally, he could seek some sort of alliance whereby he achieves expansion, using other people's efforts and resources, particularly financial ones. This could involve licensing or franchising agreements. Each of these modes of expansion has its own advantages, but there are also disadvantages associated with each.

Table 1: Details of performance of individual outlets in USA and in the United Kingdom ($000 where appropriate)

All figures refer to the previous calendar year

	UK outlet	*USA outlet*
Sales revenue	600	750
Cost of materials	200	200
Labour costs	125	125
Rental/lease costs	125	85
Inventories held	30	20
Wasted materials as a % of sales	22	9
Varieties of products available for juicing (actual numbers)	14	25
Marketing costs allocated per outlet	60	35
Administration costs allocated per outlet	20	10
Customers per week (actual numbers)	2,000	2,500
Size of store (square metres)	275	250
Numbers of staff	10	15
Number of hours open as a % of total hours available within any given week	40	65
Waiting time (from order to service) in minutes	15	8
Profit	70	295

Question – Lionel Cartwright – Methods of strategy development

It appears that Lionel is a follower of the emergent school of strategy formulation as distinct from the rational model (planning) approach. Discuss the benefits that such an opportunistic approach may bring Lionel and comment on any problems he may experience with such an approach to setting strategy.

(10 marks)

Question – Lionel Cartwright – Critical success factors

Assess the performance of the UK outlets compared with their US equivalents, as indicated in Table 1, and identify from your analysis any critical success factors which may be currently lacking in Lionel's enterprise.

(15 marks)

Question – Lionel Cartwright – Environmental analysis

What external information would you recommend that Lionel should have obtained prior to his decision to enter this market? Consider appropriate academic models Lionel might have utilised to obtain this information.

(10 marks)

Question – Lionel Cartwright – Vehicles for expansion

Discuss both the advantages and disadvantages of:

(a) internal growth

(b) acquisition

(c) franchising

as methods whereby Lionel can achieve the expansion which he believes is necessary for his fresh juice outlets.

(15 marks)

Test your understanding answers

Question – T plc – PEST

T PLC

The following external factors are relevant to T plc:

Political factors

T plc currently dominates its national telecommunications market with an 85% share of the market. The company will be under political pressure from the national government to reduce its dominance by opening up the national telecom market to competition and reducing prices for telecom products charged to consumers.

The government has appointed an industry regulator to be directly involved in the control of the telecom industry and T plc no doubt will be under close scrutiny. Political forces will be a major factor affecting the operations and plan of T plc.

Economic factors

There are three main economic elements that T plc needs to consider. These are:

- Shareholder wealth

  T plc's shareholders are a major stakeholder group who will have economic objectives of profit maximisation and rising share value.

- The contribution of the telecommunications industry to the national economy

  The telecommunications industry plays a major role in contributing towards economic growth and prosperity. T plc has a responsibility to develop new technology and to provide a reliable, value for money service to its users.

- The economies of foreign countries

  The economic conditions in each foreign country T plc operates in should be considered e.g. foreign currency exchange rates and national economic boom and slump cycles.

Social factors

Telecommunication products are social products used by people for many reasons. The company should ensure that it understands the social role of the industry and provides a reliable service. The company should also portray itself as socially responsible, have a set of social objectives and keep in close contact with the consumers e.g. by producing a range of services for elderly citizens who are more dependent on telephones for obtaining help when needed.

Technical factors

The telecommunications industry is a high-tech industry that is currently very dynamic. T plc is the market leader in the industry and must be innovative to maintain its competitive advantage. The company must invest in research and development to ensure it has a constant supply of new products in the years ahead to replace those going into the decline stage of their product life cycle.

Question – T plc – ANSOFF

T PLC

(a) By relating products to markets, Ansoff identified four main strategies for achieving long-term growth. The following diagram shows this:

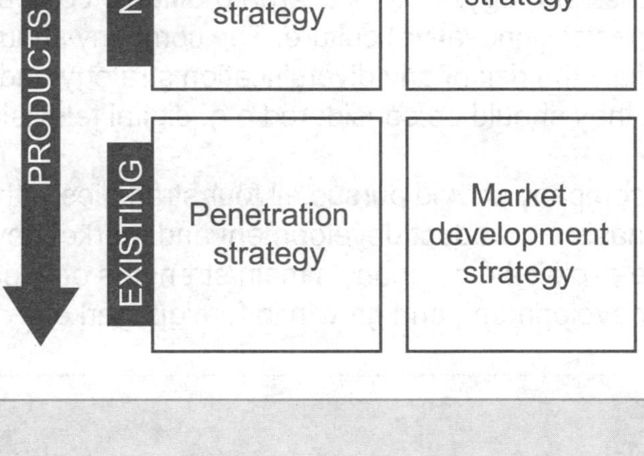

Using this model the potential market opportunities are as follows:

Market penetration strategies

T plc currently has 85% of its national market. There is little scope for obtaining any growth by increasing its market share. Most households and businesses will have a conventional telephone line so some of the company's products will be at the maturity stage of their life cycle offering little prospect of growth. Some market growth might be achieved by getting existing customers to use the telephone more.

A market penetration strategy only offers limited growth prospects.

Product development strategy

This strategy involves introducing new products in existing markets. T plc has already achieved a good track record for new product development and with continued investment in research and development should maintain its momentum. There is a lot of market opportunity in the industry for this strategy, for example further developments in mobile phone and Internet technology.

Market development strategy

T plc has pursued a successful strategy of expanding into foreign markets with existing products. It currently has operations in North America, Europe, India and the Far East. In T plc's latest annual report, the Chairman refers to developing these markets further. Tremendous opportunities exist in additional developing countries such as those in Africa where the company currently has operations.

Diversification strategy

This involves introducing new products to new markets and is a high-risk strategy. T plc is a large profitable company with a prospector (innovative) culture. The company should evaluate carefully the risk of any diversification strategy and if opportunities exist they should be considered e.g. digital television technology.

The company should pursue all four strategies with the main emphasis on product development and market development, as these exploit the company's main strengths of expertise in research and development, and growth in foreign markets.

(b) The planning gap can be defined as the difference between:

- the stakeholder's long-term expectations for the undertaking, and
- results from following existing policies and plans

expressed on a quantified scale such as profit, sale or ROCE.

Ansoff's product/market growth model can be used to show four strategies that can fill the planning gap. It is important to appreciate that all, one or any of the four strategies can fill the gap, depending on the situation. This can be shown by the following illustration:

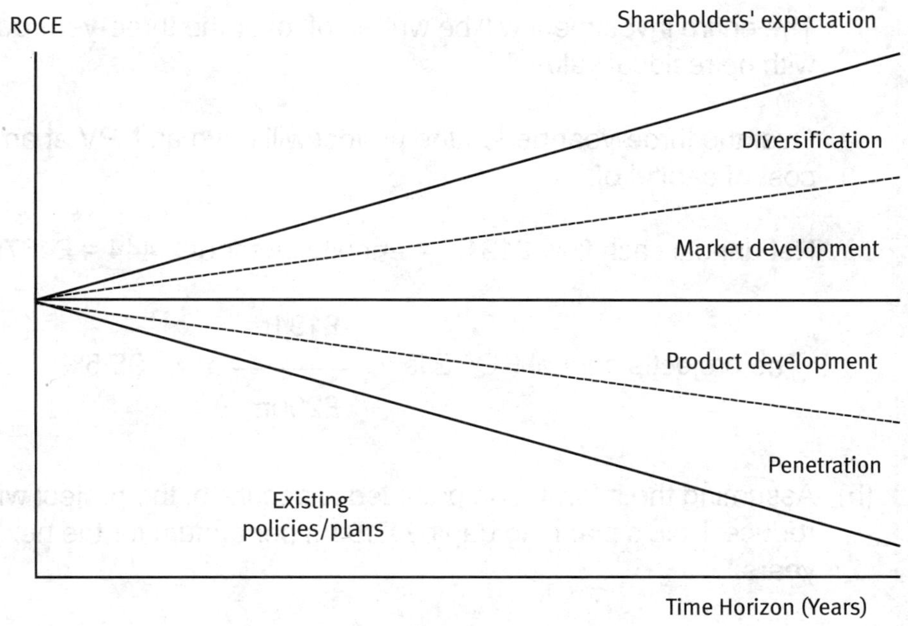

Question – T plc – Closing a planning gap

(a) T plc's planning gap can be calculated as follows:

	£m
Target Return	
Capital employed £22,150m × 20%	4,430
Less Profit before interest and tax	(3,323)
Planning gap (shortfall in profit)	1,107

The planned investment project will increase the company's market share from 85% to 95%, i.e. 10% increase.

This will achieve an increase in sale revenue of:

£16,613m × 10/85 =	£1,954m
Variable costs will be	
£1,954 × 80% =	(£1,563m)
Annual contribution =	£391m
Deduct the annual expenditure on the project of	£200m
Then increase =	£191m

The entire investment will be written off over the three-year period with no residual value.

Over the three-year period the project will have an NPV at an 11% cost of capital of:

Net annual cash flow £191m × annuity factor of 2.444 = £467m

The project's annual ROCE is $\frac{£191m}{£200m}$ = 95.5%

(b) Assuming the information provided is accurate, the project will reduce T plc's planning gap by £191m per annum for the next three years.

This will leave (£1,107m – £191m) = £916m remaining to be filled using other strategies.

The investment project appears to be very attractive as it provides a very high ROCE and will increase T plc's overall performance. Before a final decision is made, T plc's management should consider the potential risks. These appear to be:

- forecasting error
- the possible reaction of the industry regulator if the company's market share rises above its current 85%.

Question – National Museum – PESTEL

The PESTEL framework may be used to explore the macro-environmental influences that might affect an organisation. There are six main influences in the framework: political, economic, social, technological, environmental and legal. However, these influences are inter-linked and so, for example, political developments and environmental requirements are often implemented through enacting legislation.

Political

Monitoring, understanding and adapting to the political environment is absolutely essential for the National Museum. It is currently very reliant on government funding and so is significantly affected by the recently elected government's decision to gradually reduce that funding. The implications of this were recognised by the Board of Trustees and led to the appointment of a new Director General. Unfortunately, senior staff at the museum did not share this perception of the significance of the funding changes. Their opposition to change, which culminated in the Director General's resignation, has led to further political ramifications. The government is now threatening heavier funding cuts and further political trustee appointments. Furthermore, it does appear that the political context has changed for the foreseeable future. The government has only just been elected and the opposition also agrees that the reliance of museums on government funding has to be reduced.

The political appointment of two (and possibly more) trustees is also important to the National Museum. It was significant that it was the two trustees appointed by the government who supported the Director General and his proposed changes. Finally, the continued funding of the government will now largely depend on performance measures – such as accessibility – which have been determined by a political agenda. The museum must strive to meet these objectives even if they are not shared by senior staff. The old ways – built around an assessment of Heritage Collections – appear to have gone forever and senior staff members need to recognise this.

Economic

Up to now the National Museum has been largely sheltered from the economic environment. It has been funded by the government, not the marketplace, and that funding has been largely determined by stable internal factors, such as artefacts in the Heritage Collection. Evidence from the scenario and Figure 1, suggests that this funding is stable, increasing on an annual basis to reflect inflation.

However, the progressive reduction of government funding will mean that the museum will be exposed to economic realities. It will have to set realistic admission charges. Resources will also have to be used effectively and new opportunities identified and exploited for increasing income. The Director General included a number of these ideas in his proposals. However, it will be difficult to set a charge that will attract sufficient customers to cover the museum's costs, particularly as visitors have been used to paying only a nominal entry charge.

Social

The social environment is important to the museum from at least two different perspectives. The first is that social inclusion is an important part of the government's targets. The government is committed to increasing museum attendance by both lower social classes and by younger people who they feel need to be made more aware of their heritage. The visitor information shown in Figure 3 suggests that not only are visitor numbers declining in total, but the average age of these visitors is increasing. The percentage of visitors aged 22 and under visiting the NM has decreased from 19% of the total visitors (in 2004) to just over 12% in 2007. The museum needs to identify what it needs to do to attract such groups to the museum. The Director General had suggested free admission. This could be combined with popular exhibitions (perhaps tied in with television programmes or films) and 'hands-on' opportunities. It appears that the immediate neighbourhood of the museum now houses many of the people the government would like as visitors and so, from this angle, the location of the museum is an advantage. However, the comment of the Director of Art and Architecture about popularity and historical significance hardly bodes well for the future.

The decay of the neighbourhood and the increased crime rate may also deter fee-paying visitors. The museum is becoming increasingly isolated in its environment, with many of its traditional middle-class customers moving away from the area and reluctant to visit. The extensive reporting of a recent assault on a visitor is also likely to deter visitors. The museum needs to react to these issues by ensuring that good and safe transport links are maintained to the museum and by improving security both in the museum and in its immediate vicinity. Visitors need to feel safe and secure. If the museum believes this to be unachievable, then it might consider moving to a new site.

Technological

It is estimated that only 10% of the museum's collection is on view to visitors. Technology provides opportunities for displaying and viewing artefacts on-line. It provides an opportunity for the museum to become a virtual museum – allowing visitors from all over the world access to images and information about its collections. Indeed, such an approach should also help the museum achieve some of its technology and accessibility targets set by the government. Technology can also be used to increase marketing activity, providing on-line access to products and allowing these products to be bought through a secure payment facility. The appropriate use of technology frees the museum from its physical space constraints and also overcomes issues associated with its physical location.

Environmental

It can be argued that all contemporary organisations have to be aware of environmental issues and the impact their activities have on the environment. These are likely to be exacerbated by the museum being located in an old building which itself requires regular maintenance and upgrading to reflect government requirements. It is also very unlikely that such an old building will be energy efficient and so heating costs are likely to be high and to continue to increase. The museum needs to adopt appropriate policies on recycling and energy conservation, but it may be difficult to achieve these targets in the context of an old building. Consequently, environmental issues may combine with social issues to encourage the consideration of the possible relocation of the museum to a modern building in a more appropriate location. However, the museum building is also of architectural importance, and so some acceptable alternative use for the building might also have to be suggested.

Legal

Legal issues affect the museum in at least two ways. Firstly, there is already evidence that the museum has had to adapt to legal requirements for disability access and to reflect health and safety requirements. Some of these requirements appear to have required changes in the building which have been met with disapproval. It is likely that modifications will be expensive and relatively awkward, leading again to unsightly and aesthetically unpleasing modifications to the building. Further tightening of legislation might be expected from a government with a mandate for social inclusion. For example, it might specify that all documentation should be available in Braille or in different languages. Legislation concerning fire safety, heating, cooking and food preparation might also exist or be expected.

Secondly, the museum is run by a Board of Trustees. There are legal requirements about the behaviour of such trustees. The museum must be aware of these and ensure that their work is properly scoped and monitored. Trustees have, and must accept, ultimate responsibility for directing the affairs of the museum, ensuring that it is solvent, well-run, and meeting the needs for which it has been set up. The museum is a charity and it is the responsibility of the trustees to ensure that its operation complies with the charity law of the country.

Question – National Museum – Cultural web and change

(a) **Reasons for failure**

A cultural web for the National Museum is suggested in Figure 1. The cultural web is made up of a set of factors that overlap and reinforce each other. The symbols explore the logos, offices, titles and terminology of the organisation. The large offices, the special dining room and the dedicated personal assistants are clear symbols of hierarchy and power in the museum. Furthermore, the language used by directors in their stories (see below) suggests a certain amount of disdain for both customers and managers. The status of professor conferred on section heads with Heritage Collections also provides relative status within the heads of collection sections themselves. The proposal of the Director General to close the heads' dining room and to remove their dedicated personal assistants would take away two important symbols of status and is likely to be an unpopular suggestion.

Power

The power structures of the organisation are significant. Power can be seen as the ability of certain groups to persuade or coerce others to follow a certain course of action. At present, power is vested in the heads of collection sections, reflected by their dominance on the Board of Directors. Three of the five directors represent collection sections. Similarly the Board of Trustees is dominated by people who are well-known and respected in academic fields relevant to the museum's collections. The power of external stakeholders (such as the government) has, until the election of the new government, been relatively weak. They have merely handed over funding for the trustees to distribute. The Director General of the museum has been a part-time post.

The appointment of an external, full-time Director General with private sector experience threatens this power base and his suggestion for the new organisation structure takes away the dominance of the collection heads. On his proposed board, only one of six directors represents the collection sections.

Organisation

The organisational structure is likely to reflect and reinforce the power structure. This appears to be the case at the museum. However, it is interesting to note that the collections themselves are not evenly represented. Both the Director of Industrial Art and the Director of Media and Contemporary Art represent five collection sections. However, only two collection areas are represented by the Director of Art and Architecture. This imbalance, reinforced by different symbols (professorships) and reflected in stories (see later) might suggest a certain amount of disharmony between the collection heads, which the Director General might have been able to exploit. Management at the museum are largely seen as administrators facilitating the museum's activities. This is reinforced by the title of the director concerned; Director of Administration.

Controls

The controls of the organisation relate to the measurements and reward systems which emphasise what is important to the organisation. At the National Museum the relative budget of each section has been heavily influenced by the Heritage Collections. These collections help determine how much the museum receives as a whole and it appears (from the budget figures) that the Board of Trustees also use this as a guide when allocating the finance internally. Certainly, the sections with the Heritage Collections appear to receive the largest budgets. Once this division has been established the principle of allocating increases based on last year's allocation, plus a percentage, perpetuates the division and indeed accentuates it in real financial terms. Hence, smaller sections remain small and their chance of obtaining artefacts for them to be defined a Heritage Collection becomes slimmer every year. Again, this may suggest a potential conflict between the larger and smaller collection sections of the museum. Finally, up until the election of the new government, there appears to have been no required measures of outputs (visitor numbers, accessibility etc). The museum was given a budget to maintain the collections, not to attract visitors. The proposal of the Director General to allocate budgets on visitor popularity disturbs the well-established way of distributing budgets in a way that reinforced the current power base.

Routines and rituals

The routines and rituals are the way members of the organisation go about their daily work and the special events or particular activities that reinforce the 'way we do things around here'. It is clear from the scenario that it is not thought unacceptable for directors to directly lobby the Board of Trustees and to write letters to the press and appear on television programmes to promote their views. In many organisations issues within the boardroom remain confidential and are resolved there. However, this is clearly not now the case at the National Museum. The scenario suggests that there are certain rites of challenge (exemplified by the new Director General's proposals) but equally there are strong rites of counter-challenge, resistance to the new ways of doing things. Often such rites are limited to grumbling or working-to-rule, but at the National Museum they extend to lobbying powerful external forces in the hope that these forces can be combined to resist the suggested changes.

Stories

Stories are used by members of the organisation to tell people what is important in the organisation. The quotes included in the scenario are illuminating both in content and language. The Director of Art and Architecture believes that Heritage Collections have a value that transcends popularity with the 'undiscerning public'. He also alludes to the relative importance of collections. He suggests that fashion may not be a suitable subject for a collection, unlike art and architecture. Similarly, the anonymous quote about lack of consultation, that includes a reference to the new Director General as 'an ex-grocer', attempts to belittle both management and commerce.

Paradigm

In the centre of the cultural web is the paradigm of the National Museum. This is the set of assumptions that are largely held in common and are taken for granted in the organisation. These might be:

- The museum exists for the good of the nation
- It is a guardian of the continuity of the nation's heritage and culture
- What constitutes heritage and culture is determined by experts
- The government funds the purchase and maintenance of artefacts that represent this heritage and culture

There are two important elements of the Director General's proposals that are missing from this paradigm; visitors and customers. Changing the current paradigm may take considerable time and effort.

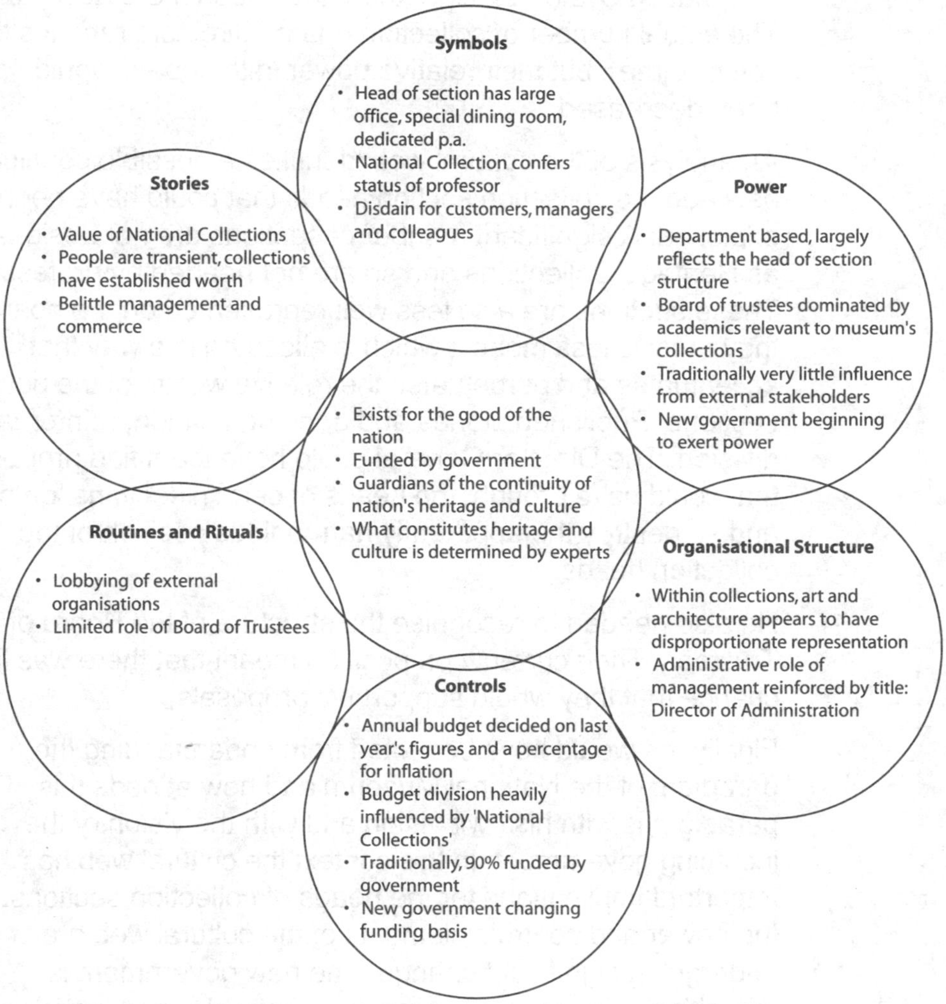

(b) Recommendations on how change could have been managed better

The cultural web might have helped the Director General develop and implement proposals. For example:

– He may have considered deferring one or both of the proposals to remove the head of collection sections' dining room and their dedicated personal assistants. These are important symbols of their status and the financial gains from removing them seem unlikely to outweigh the consequences of their removal.

– He might have considered simply adding directors to the organisational structure, rather than inviting conflict by removing two of the collection directors. For example, replacing the current Director of Administration with the four new directors of his proposed structure (Finance, Visitor Services, Resources, Information Systems) might then have been more acceptable. The actual number of collection related directors remains the same (three), but their relative power in the board would have been decreased.

– An analysis of the cultural web identifies a possible conflict between the collection section heads that could have been exploited. A significant number of sections are not designated as Heritage Collections and so are not headed by professors. These sections are also less well represented on the board and they receive less money, which is allocated in a way that accentuates and perpetuates the relative wealth of the powerful sections. Published stories and deriding fashion, reinforces this division. The Director General could have identified proposals that could have brought the heads of certain sections 'on side' and so destroy the apparently harmonious position of the collection heads.

– He also needed to recognise the structure of the Board of Trustees. Their current composition meant that there was little chance that they would support his proposals.

– Finally, he would have benefited from understanding the paradigm of the National Museum and how at odds this paradigm is with his own vision and with the vision of the incoming government. In this context the cultural web has important implications for the heads of collection sections. Both the power and controls elements of the cultural web are undergoing significant change. The new government is exploiting its position as a major stakeholder and insisting on new controls and measures that reflect their paradigm. Although the heads of collection sections have successfully lobbied for the removal of the Director General, they are very unlikely to change the government's policy. Indeed the sacking of the Director General has strengthened the government's action and resolve. The sacking of the Director General may have been a pyrrhic victory and a much worse defeat now awaits the heads of collection sections.

Question – National Museum – Methods of strategy development

Strategy as the deliberate positioning of an organisation as the result of some 'rational, analytical, structured and directive process'.

In this approach it is usually the responsibility of top management to plan the destiny of the organisation. Lower levels of management carry out the operational actions required by the strategy. The deliberate approach is associated with objective setting and a plan for moving the organisation towards these objectives.

In the context of the scenario, the government is now significantly involved in objective setting and tying funding to those objectives. The Director General has responsibility for defining and delivering a strategy within these objectives. There is evidence that he has gone about this in a 'top-down' way and not sought advice from current employees. On the television programme, employees were particularly critical of a lack of consultation; 'these proposals have been produced with no input from museum staff. They have been handed down from on-high'.

In many ways, this is the approach taken at the National Museum under the new Director General. Such an approach is not unusual in public sector organisations, where elements of strategy are dictated by government manifestos.

A more adaptive approach to strategy, building on and changing the existing strategy.

This approach views strategy development as the combination of individual and collective experience together with the taken-for-granted assumptions of cultural influences. However, it has to be recognised that the assumptions and practices of the organisation may become so ingrained that it is difficult for people to question or change them.

This certainly appears to be true for the heads of collection sections at the National Museum. The museum is now facing a fundamental change in the way it will be funded and the increased influence of the government suggests a change in the paradigm of the organisation. It seems unlikely that people with a vested interest in the current arrangement and perpetuating that current arrangement will come up with the change in strategy that is now required. The 'taken-for-granted' behaviour of people in organisations is one of the major barriers to developing innovative strategies.

The adaptive approach can be innately conservative and can work well when a small incremental change is required within a stable environment. However, this does not appear to be the situation at the National Museum and so developing strategy in increments may not seem a possible way forward and perhaps this is why the Director General explicitly rejected this approach.

Strategy based on innovation and new ideas.

Here the organisation should foster conditions that allow ideas to emerge and to be considered for inclusion in a 'mainstream strategy'. Certain conditions, such as a changing and unpredictable environment foster ideas and innovation.

It could be argued that the macro-environmental conditions for adopting this approach are present at the National Museum. Political, social and environmental influences might lead to new ideas – for example, the relocation of the museum and the exploitation of on-line access to resources creating a virtual museum. The museum is undergoing a fundamental change in priorities and funding and the consequences of these changes is unpredictable.

On the other hand, the museum is a long-established conservative organisation with many symbols of hierarchy and deference. There is no evidence in the scenario of a group of people generating conflicting ideas and encouraged to compete with each other in an open and supportive environment. The National Museum seems to be dominated by powerful individuals protecting their own interests.

Finally, a key factor in the selection of ideas is the marketplace. The National Museum is currently operating in a protected economic environment, although this is set to change.

Conclusions

There is plenty of evidence to suggest that it is difficult to change strategies in a hierarchical structure. At the National Museum the Director General decided to pursue a deliberate, rational approach. In many ways this appeared to be the natural method to adopt given the objectives set by the newly elected government that was beginning to exert its power.

This strategy may have worked if he had been more sensitive to the cultural web and, also, if he had not asked for the backing of the Board of Trustees. This was always unlikely to be forthcoming given its composition.

The paradigm change means that it is unlikely that the adaptive approach would have proved fruitful. However, it may have been possible to exploit an emergent approach based on new ideas if the Director General had carefully selected heads of collection sections who were relative losers under the current system.

Question – Lionel Cartwright – Methods of strategy development

The main focus of this part of the question is on the benefits of **emergent or opportunistic strategy formulation as opposed to the more rational or deliberate approach**.

There are some advantages in Lionel favouring the non-planned approach. The size of Lionel's enterprise and resource commitments is sufficiently small that a disciplined integration of activities is not essential. Furthermore, whereas a deliberate strategy often tends to ignore the human dimension, an emergent strategy is likely to fit into Lionel's philosophical outlook. Lionel has demonstrated that he needs to respond quickly to environmental changes if he is to take advantage of the opportunities available to him. If he had to rely on a formal planned set of procedures this would be an impediment to his 'flexibility'. There is a likelihood of 'paralysis by analysis'. There is also a risk that entrepreneurs such as Lionel may be given a false sense of security by the planning process. It may encourage them to ignore initiative and intuition, believing in the superiority of the planning process. Lionel is known to have a 'feel' for the market and the associated environmental factors. It would be a shame if these skills were to be sacrificed because of an over-confidence in the planning process. It is essential that Lionel should adopt a process that allows him to have the flexibility to respond to changes in the fast moving markets in which he has chosen to do business. One must also recognise that it is not always possible for a small company to finance, or have the skills to acquire the requisite knowledge necessary for, a deliberately planned strategy. Furthermore, as Mintzberg has written, an emergent strategy allows for learning to take place. Ideas develop until 'patterns emerge'. A deliberate strategy would discourage such organisational learning.

However, there are some problems which Lionel might experience as a result of relying on an unplanned approach. It appears that Lionel has **no real sense of direction**. He has moved from road haulage to fast foods, from information technology to health foods. There is no common theme, apart from responding to entrepreneurial instincts. There is **unlikely to be any accumulated learning** from these previous ventures to benefit Lionel in his latest enterprise. Because Lionel only has an intuitive feel for the market, he has **not much expert knowledge of the industry or the relevant environmental factors**. Consequently he will find it difficult to choose between competing alternatives with respect to strategic options. He may also not fully appreciate the resource implications of his decisions, nor may he be able to fully integrate the required activities for strategic implementation. Lionel's track record does not suggest that he has a long-term set of ambitions.

A more **planned approach** might encourage him to be more consistent in his actions and allow the strategies to be more completely fulfilled. Although he seems to have enough financial liquidity at the moment, his past performance might discourage banks or other financial institutions from considering him to be a good risk. In some industries where there are long time frames for decision-making, decisions must be agreed upon and adhered to, otherwise there will be confusion. As *Lynch* has stated, experimentation may be appropriate in the early years but later strategy needs to be more fixed for lengthy projects. It is also easier to control activities if there is a planned scenario. The danger with Lionel's mode of strategy formulation is that it is difficult to assess whether anything is going wrong, because there are no prescribed targets. The rational approach should not be spurned simply because it does not fit in with the entrepreneur's way of working. Evidence and logic can be helpful in formulating a coherent and reliable strategy. Finally if the strategic direction is not clearly specified then it will be difficult for employees to understand their roles and functions within the enterprise. Confusion will reign and there will be a lack of integration of activities.

Question – Lionel Cartwright – Critical success factors

Key answer tips

With many Section A questions you will be required to extract information from a table of data. Here, the comparison is between a UK and comparable US outlet.

In making a comparison, it would seem clear that higher sales revenue/gross profit margin and lower lease costs are significant differences. The key issue, however, is to consider **why**:

- Why are costs better controlled in the US? Compare expenses as well as materials costs.
- Why are sales per outlet higher in the US? The data points to longer opening hours, a larger range of products, and more customers. A higher number of staff per outlet might also affect sales revenue, as well as speed of service to customers.

It is obvious from the financial data that Lionel's stores are not as profitable as those in the USA. He has chosen to operate in a high profile market, focusing on the affluent, trans-national youth segment. This market needs aggressive promotion but Lionel does not have the volume of stores necessary to provide the revenue to fund the necessary level of advertising. Furthermore, although Lionel claims to understand the market, he has no expertise in this line of business. His recent ventures have shown no continuity, so it is unlikely that he will be able to bring much insider knowledge into this operation. Motivation and entrepreneurial activity are no substitutes for operating knowledge.

A number of key pointers can be derived from the table. The two most critical factors differentiating the UK stores from those in the USA are, firstly, the *UK stores sell less than those in the USA*, despite being larger in shop space, and the *rental costs in the USA are much lower*. Labour costs in the two areas are about the same but the US shops are open longer and have more staff, possibly an indication of a *higher level of service*. This might also account for the *longer waiting time within UK stores* – a point not likely to endear itself to the rather selective clientele who would be seeking improved service. If one takes into account the level of sales in the UK it is apparent that the cost of materials is somewhat higher than in the USA. It would also appear that operating efficiency within the UK is lower. *A UK store requires a higher level of inventories and has greater wastage despite offering less choice* than its US counterpart

As one might expect the UK *administrative and marketing costs* are higher but with a larger number of outlets to spread these charges over these would fall substantially. In fact one might argue that marketing expenditure should be increased – a necessity if the image and demand is to be enhanced. These indicators illustrate the poor performance of Lionel's stores compared with those in the USA.

It would appear that Lionel's company does not possess the **critical success factors** required for this type of enterprise. He has over-exaggerated the existence of his core competences. This embryonic company needs a number of competences if it is to survive and prosper in this high profile and competitive market. Firstly it needs a *strong reputation* to attract the affluent youth market, which can be exceptionally fickle and possesses limited brand loyalty. The company has no real reputation in this field. Its *expenditure on advertising* is relatively low and it owns only a few centrally-located sites that are needed to attract the required market. In fact these sites are not only few in number but they are exceptionally expensive to acquire.

They need to be in expensive city centres and Lionel is unlikely to have the *finance* to expand his empire rapidly. It is also critical that the company should have *access to cheap and guaranteed high quality produce*. It appears from the case scenario that these supplies are becoming increasingly difficult to obtain with increased competition from larger and wealthier buyers. Any disruption in, and reduction in the quality of, the supplies will adversely affect the reputation of the juice outlets, so damaging the valuable and critical image of Lionel's outlets. Another important critical success factor, which does not appear to be a core competence of Lionel's young company, is the issue of *operating efficiency*. Compared with US stores (seen as competitors/role models in a global market place) the UK stores are performing poorly. There appears to be less choice of juices, the waiting time (a reflection of customer service) and opening hours are inferior to what is expected within the USA. Unless Lionel can achieve an improvement in these areas, his outlets are unlikely to achieve the profit levels experienced in America.

Question – Lionel Cartwright – Environmental analysis

It is critical that Lionel should obtain as much **external data** concerning the juice market as possible to enable him to 'harmonise' his corporate business strengths with the attractive features of the proposed industry. Lionel could then assess what the attractive features in the market place are and whether they will be helpful to him.

Key questions that need answering include the following:

- What is the annual rate of growth?
- Is the market stable or volatile?
- Is it a seasonal demand or regular throughout the year?
- Is the competition fragmented or dominated by a major player?
- Are customers brand loyal or not?
- Is demand price sensitive or not?

These, with many other features, could help provide Lionel with a picture of the market place and give him an indication as to whether the venture is likely to be successful or not.

To help structure this analysis there are a number of tools and frameworks available.

Michael Porter's five forces model would be a suitable approach for assessing the **competitive environment**. Not only would it assess direct competition, but it would also look at latent competition as well as threats from unanticipated substitutes – other fashion areas which could compete for the spending power of the affluent, sophisticated youth market. This model also would consider the position of the suppliers and examine how they might adversely affect the success of Lionel's enterprise. The model might also help Lionel reflect on his relationships with his prime customers. The benefit of the Porter model is that it provides a comprehensive view over the competitive environment. However, the downside is that it can be too indiscriminate in its approach so it is important that Lionel considers competitive rivalry with respect to the strategies of the most direct competitors – in this case similar companies in the fashionable café markets in Europe and in the USA. In Lionel's case these similar characteristics could include – the extent of product or service diversity, the type of market segment covered, the level of quality and the distribution methods used. This should enable Lionel to know more about his competitive position.

The **PEST environmental model** should enable a scanning and monitoring approach to be used to help Lionel to design an appropriate strategic plan to best attack and capture the target market. Lionel should have been advised to carry out some marketing research to try to uncover the main determinants of demand for the juice drinks – was it health, fashion or convenience that mainly influenced the potential customers? Is the market price-sensitive? Uncovering all of this would be helpful in devising a promotional policy, involving both advertising and sales promotion. It would also be important to have information about 'traffic patterns' so as to know the optimum areas for locating the stores. This would enable Lionel to investigate the availability of potentially suitable outlets. There would also need to be an awareness about food labelling regulations, particularly with reference to promotional activity. It also might be helpful if Lionel and his employees knew about the latest technology and operational techniques. This should help to provide an improved level of service, better inventory control, quicker service, wider choice of products, the need for fewer staff, etc. It would also be useful to know the socio-demographic structure of the population so as to be able to estimate the size of the potential market. An understanding of economic conditions might help Lionel to appreciate whether the economy was buoyant or not. Products such as organic juices are likely to sell better when incomes are growing and the population feels better off, i.e. higher discretionary income and lower income taxes. Equally an understanding of the legal regulations such as employment law and sales taxes would be useful.

Another obvious model is **SWOT analysis**. By examining the external opportunities and threats much of this information should be uncovered and be made available to Lionel.

If Lionel could have a greater understanding as to how the environment might impact upon his operations then he might be able to take remedial action to improve the situation.

Question – Lionel Cartwright – Vehicles for expansion

(a) Lionel would gain a few advantages from **internal growth** but these would be offset by substantial disadvantages. A main advantage of pursuing internal growth is that the company can gain and maintain knowledge of both markets and products. However as this is not a high-tech innovative industry the need to obtain and safeguard proprietary knowledge is not critical. Another benefit of this strategy is that Lionel will not be dependent upon others and he will be able to **maintain control** with no clash in management styles. This will be particularly attractive to Lionel who has already demonstrated that he likes to have control (his IT venture) and that he did not enjoy his experience as a franchisee. There is also a benefit with the internal or organic approach – there would be **minimal disruption to the existing business** as might occur with a strategy of acquisition. However, given the size of Lionel's current enterprise, this is not a critical issue. A major benefit of internal growth is that it is often **cheaper**. While this is certainly true compared with a strategy of acquisitions, the use of strategic alliances involving franchise agreements can be cheaper as partners usually provide much of the finance. The problems of such an approach are, however, important. Lionel desperately needs to expand the number of outlets. This would give him wider exposure and permit him to achieve both operational and purchasing economies of scale.

To attempt this on one's own would be slow, providing **less impetus for growth**. By associating with others, Lionel might overcome barriers to entry by building up networks so getting access to sites and supplies.

(b) While **acquisitions** provide a rapid means of expansion and could provide Lionel's enterprise with the necessary critical mass, there are some disadvantages that need to be understood. First this mode of development can be extremely **expensive**, beyond the means of a smallish entrepreneur such as Lionel. Furthermore there are often **difficulties in integrating** another company or group of companies with the original company. There may be a **lack of cultural fit**. This is very likely with a person like Lionel who appears to have an individualistic, even idiosyncratic, approach to business. Nevertheless the **quick means of expansion** is an attractive proposition in this scenario.

Furthermore an acquisition can often provide a company with **access to product and market knowledge**, often otherwise denied to the acquiring business. **Synergies** can often be obtained, whereby scarce resources can be integrated with other more abundant factors. In this situation Lionel may provide the management and know-how whereas the acquired company could bring to the deal retail sites, finance and even retail skills. It has been suggested that a reason for an acquisition is to buy out a latent competitor. Given the small size of this specialist market segment this does not seem to be a realistic argument in this case.

If both internal/organic development and an acquisition seem to be unattractive modes of corporate growth, another option is a strategic alliance or, as in this case, a franchise operation as the preferred means of development.

(c) The advantage to Lionel of a **franchise operation** is that it can be a quick method of achieving market expansion. One can use the **capital and local market knowledge of the franchisees**. This could be particularly beneficial in developing outlets overseas where expenditure would be high and Lionel possesses no expertise. An additional advantage is that **franchisees are often highly motivated**, having a stake in the enterprise and a share of the profits. This increased commitment from the partners, coupled with the **lower risk and financial exposure** for Lionel might encourage him to consider this form of development. However Lionel, having been a dissatisfied franchisee earlier in his career might not be so enthusiastic. He will recognise the **potential for a conflict of interests**. He may also suspect the **competence of franchise partners**. Will they have access to the necessary prime retail sites and will they understand this new and fashionable business? Another benefit of a franchise operation is that invisible assets (goodwill and brand development) are often at less risk. These assets are often isolated for the purpose of management and with trade-mark/brand protection there should be a reduced threat to Lionel of any asset expropriation.

There is not an easy option for Lionel to choose for market development. Each of the options has fundamental flaws, Lionel must select the one which permits him to have rapid expansion, while maintaining an up-market image. He must protect his existing **investments** and, at the same time, not over-commit himself financially. Other factors should also be taken into consideration but Lionel should not allow personal prejudices to overcome a rational decision. For once this decision needs to be well thought out and argued. It ought not to be intuitively taken.

CIMA

Pillar E

E3 – Enterprise Strategy

Specimen Examination Paper

Instructions to candidates

You are allowed three hours to answer this question paper.
You are allowed 20 minutes reading time **before the examination begins** during which you should read the question paper and, if you wish, highlight and/or make notes on the question paper. However, you will **not** be allowed, **under any circumstances**, to open the answer book and start writing or use your calculator during this reading time.
You are strongly advised to carefully read ALL the question requirements before attempting the question concerned (that is all parts and/or sub-questions). The requirements for all questions are contained in a dotted box.
ALL answers must be written in the answer book. Answers or notes written on the question paper will **not** be submitted for marking.
Answer ALL compulsory questions in Section A on page 9.
Answer TWO of the three questions in Section B on pages 10 to 13.
Maths Tables are provided on pages 14 and 15.
The list of verbs as published in the syllabus is given for reference on the inside back cover of this question paper.
Write your candidate number, the paper number and examination subject title in the spaces provided on the front of the answer book. Also write your contact ID and name in the space provided in the right hand margin and seal to close.
Tick the appropriate boxes on the front of the answer book to indicate the questions you have answered.

E3 – Enterprise Strategy

Power Utilities

Pre-seen Case Study

Background

Power Utilities (PU) is located in a democratic Asian country. Just over 12 months ago, the former nationalised Electricity Generating Corporation (EGC) was privatised and became PU. EGC was established as a nationalised industry many years ago. Its home government at that time had determined that the provision of the utility services of electricity generation production should be managed by boards that were accountable directly to Government. In theory, nationalised industries should be run efficiently, on behalf of the public, without the need to provide any form of risk related return to the funding providers. In other words, EGC, along with other nationalised industries was a non-profit making organisation. This, the Government claimed at the time, would enable prices charged to the final consumer to be kept low.

Privatisation of EGC

The Prime Minister first announced three years ago that the Government intended to pursue the privatisation of the nationalised industries within the country. The first priority was to be the privatisation of the power generating utilities and EGC was selected as the first nationalised industry to be privatised. The main purpose of this strategy was to encourage public subscription for share capital. In addition, the Government's intention was that PU should take a full and active part in commercial activities such as raising capital and earning higher revenue by increasing its share of the power generation and supply market by achieving growth either organically or through making acquisitions. This, of course, also meant that PU was exposed to commercial pressures itself, including satisfying the requirements of shareholders and becoming a potential target for take-over. The major shareholder, with a 51% share, would be the Government. However, the Minister of Energy has recently stated that the Government intends to reduce its shareholding in PU over time after the privatisation takes place.

Industry structure

PU operates 12 coal-fired power stations across the country and transmits electricity through an integrated national grid system which it manages and controls. It is organised into three regions, Northern, Eastern and Western. Each region generates electricity which is sold to 10 private sector electricity distribution companies which are PU's customers.

The three PU regions transmit the electricity they generate into the national grid system. A shortage of electricity generation in one region can be made up by taking from the national grid. This is particularly important when there is a national emergency, such as exceptional weather conditions.

The nationalised utility industries, including the former EGC, were set up in a monopolistic position. As such, no other providers of these particular services were permitted to enter the market within the country. Therefore, when EGC was privatised and became PU it remained the sole generator of electricity in the country. The electricity generating facilities, in the form of the 12 coal-fired power stations, were all built over 15 years ago and some date back to before EGC came into being.

The 10 private sector distribution companies are the suppliers of electricity to final users including households and industry within the country, and are not under the management or control of PU. They are completely independent companies owned by shareholders.

The 10 private sector distribution companies serve a variety of users of electricity. Some, such as AB, mainly serve domestic users whereas others, such as DP, only supply electricity to a few industrial clients. In fact, DP has a limited portfolio of industrial customers and 3 major clients, an industrial conglomerate, a local administrative authority and a supermarket chain. DP finds these clients costly to service.

Structure of PU
The structure of PU is that it has a Board of Directors headed by an independent Chairman and a separate Managing Director. The Chairman of PU was nominated by the Government at the time the announcement that EGC was to be privatised was made. His background is that he is a former Chairman of an industrial conglomerate within the country. There was no previous Chairman of EGC which was managed by a Management Board, headed by the Managing Director. The former EGC Managing Director retired on privatisation and a new Managing Director was appointed.

The structure of PU comprises a hierarchy of many levels of management authority. In addition to the Chairman and Managing Director, the Board consists of the Directors of each of the Northern, Eastern and Western regions, a Technical Director, the Company Secretary and the Finance Director. All of these except the Chairman are the Executive Directors of PU. The Government also appointed seven Non Executive Directors to PU's Board. With the exception of the Company Secretary and Finance Director, all the Executive Directors are qualified electrical engineers. The Chairman and Managing Director of PU have worked hard to overcome some of the inertia which was an attitude that some staff had developed within the former EGC. PU is now operating efficiently as a private sector company. There have been many staff changes at a middle management level within the organisation.

Within the structure of PU's headquarters, there are five support functions; engineering, finance (which includes PU's Internal Audit department), corporate treasury, human resource management (HRM) and administration, each with its own chief officers, apart from HRM. Two Senior HRM Officers and Chief Administrative Officer report to the Company Secretary. The Chief Accountant and Corporate Treasurer each report to the Finance Director. These functions, except Internal Audit, are replicated in each region, each with its own regional officers and support staff. Internal Audit is an organisation wide function and is based at PU headquarters.

Regional Directors of EGC
The Regional Directors all studied in the field of electrical engineering at the country's leading university and have worked together for a long time. Although they did not all attend the university at the same time, they have a strong belief in the quality of their education. After graduation from university, each of the Regional Directors started work at EGC in a junior capacity and then subsequently gained professional electrical engineering qualifications. They believe that the experience of working up through the ranks of EGC has enabled them to have a clear understanding of EGC's culture and the technical aspects of the industry as a whole. Each of the Regional Managers has recognised the changed environment that PU now operates within, compared with the former EGC, and they are now working hard to help PU achieve success as a private sector electricity generator. The Regional Directors are well regarded by both the Chairman and Managing Director, both in terms of their technical skill and managerial competence.

Governance of EGC
Previously, the Managing Director of the Management Board of EGC reported to senior civil servants in the Ministry of Energy. There were no shareholders and ownership of the Corporation rested entirely with the Government. That has now changed. The Government holds 51% of the shares in PU and the Board of Directors is responsible to the shareholders but, inevitably, the Chairman has close links directly with the Minister of Energy, who represents the major shareholder.

The Board meetings are held regularly, normally weekly, and are properly conducted with full minutes being taken. In addition, there is a Remuneration Committee, an Audit Committee and an Appointments Committee, all in accordance with best practice. The model which has been used is the Combined Code on Corporate Governance which applies to companies which have full listing status on the London Stock Exchange. Although PU is not listed on the London Stock Exchange, the principles of the Combined Code were considered by the Government to be appropriate to be applied with regard to the corporate governance of the company.

Currently, PU does not have an effective Executive Information System and this has recently been raised at a Board meeting by one of the non-executive directors because he believes this inhibits the function of the Board and consequently is disadvantageous to the governance of PU.

Remuneration of Executive Directors
In order to provide a financial incentive, the Remuneration Committee of PU has agreed that the Executive Directors be entitled to performance related pay, based on a bonus scheme, in addition to their fixed salary and health benefits.

Capital market
PU exists in a country which has a well developed capital market relating both to equity and loan stock funding. There are well established international institutions which are able to provide funds and corporate entities are free to issue their own loan stock in accordance with internationally recognised principles. PU is listed on the country's main stock exchange.

Strategic opportunity
The Board of PU is considering the possibility of vertical integration into electricity supply and has begun preliminary discussion with DP's Chairman with a view to making an offer for DP. PU's Board is attracted by DP's strong reputation for customer service but is aware, through press comment, that DP has received an increase in complaints regarding its service to customers over the last year. When the former EGC was a nationalised business, break-downs were categorised by the Government as "urgent", when there was a danger to life, and "non-urgent" which was all others. Both the former EGC and DP had a very high success rate in meeting the government's requirements that a service engineer should attend the urgent break-down within 60 minutes. DP's record over this last year in attending urgent break-downs has deteriorated seriously and if PU takes DP over, this situation would need to improve.

Energy consumption within the country and Government drive for increased efficiency and concern for the environment
Energy consumption has doubled in the country over the last 10 years. As PU continues to use coal-fired power stations, it now consumes most of the coal mined within the country.

The Minister of Energy has indicated to the Chairman of PU that the Government wishes to encourage more efficient methods of energy production. This includes the need to reduce production costs. The Government has limited resources for capital investment in energy production and wishes to be sure that future energy production facilities are more efficient and effective than at present.

The Minister of Energy has also expressed the Government's wish to see a reduction in harmful emissions from the country's power stations. (The term harmful emissions in this context, refers to pollution coming out of electricity generating power stations which damage the environment.)

One of PU's non-executive directors is aware that another Asian country is a market leader in coal gasification which is a fuel technology that could be used to replace coal for power generation. In the coal gasification process, coal is mixed with oxygen and water vapour under pressure, normally underground, and then pumped to the surface where the gas can be used in power stations. The process significantly reduces carbon dioxide emissions although it is not widely used at present and not on any significant commercial scale.

Another alternative to coal fired power stations being actively considered by PU's Board is the construction of a dam to generate hydro-electric power. The Board is mindful of the likely adverse response of the public living and working in the area where the dam would be built.

In response to the Government's wishes, PU has established environmental objectives relating to improved efficiency in energy production and reducing harmful emissions such as greenhouse gases. PU has also established an ethical code. Included within the code are sections relating to recycling and reduction in harmful emissions as well as to terms and conditions of employment.

Introduction of commercial accounting practices at EGC
The first financial statements have been produced for PU for 2008. Extracts from the Statement of Financial Position from this are shown in **Appendix A.** Within these financial statements, some of EGC's loans were "notionally" converted by the Government into ordinary shares. Interest is payable on the Government loans as shown in the statement of financial position. Reserves is a sum which was vested in EGC when it was first nationalised. This represents the initial capital stock valued on a historical cost basis from the former electricity generating organisations which became consolidated into EGC when it was first nationalised.

Being previously a nationalised industry and effectively this being the first "commercially based" financial statements, there are no retained earnings brought forward into 2008.

APPENDIX A

EXTRACTS FROM THE PRO FORMA FINANCIAL STATEMENTS OF THE ELECTRICITY GENERATING CORPORATION

Statement of financial position as at 31 December 2008

	P$ million
ASSETS	
Non-current assets	15,837
Current assets	
Inventories	1,529
Receivables	2,679
Cash and Cash equivalents	133
	4,341
Total assets	20,178
EQUITY AND LIABILITIES	
Equity	
Share capital	5,525
Reserves	1,231
Total equity	6,756
Non-current liabilities	
Government loans	9,560
Current liabilities	
Payables	3,862
Total liabilities	13,422
Total equity and liabilities	20,178

End of Pre-seen Material

SECTION A – 50 MARKS

[the indicative time for answering this section is 90 minutes]

ANSWER THIS QUESTION

Question One

Unseen material for Case Study

Background
EGC was privatised just over a year ago and is now Power Utilities (PU). The new Board of Directors of PU is accountable to the shareholders, the major one being the Government which holds 51% of the shares.

In an early move by PU, it has taken over two of the private electricity distribution companies. One of these, DP, located in the Eastern Division of PU, serves a limited portfolio of industrial customers and three major clients. The takeover was not disputed with DP's Board recommending to its shareholders acceptance of the bid. PU now holds 90% of DP's shares.

The Board of Directors of PU has established a Management Board at DP which is independently chaired by a nominee from PU's Board. The previous Executive Directors on DP's board have all retained their posts and their remuneration includes a performance bonus based on DP's overall profitability. The previous Chairman of DP has retired.

Customer service
During the time when EGC was nationalised, customer break-downs had been categorised by the Government as Urgent (when there was a danger to life) and Non-urgent (all other break-downs).

There was a requirement for Urgent break-downs that a service engineer should be with the customer within 60 minutes or less. Before privatisation the electricity distribution industry had a very high success rate in meeting this requirement with 99.9% of customers being attended within 60 minutes and nobody ever waited longer than 90 minutes for attention.

Non-urgent break-downs were attended to in turn but there was no maximum time requirement for an engineer to attend. There were always a significant number of Non-urgent break-downs to attend to and customers might wait as long as six months for attention.

During the last year there have been an increasing number of complaints to DP from its customers regarding the slow attendance of service engineers following a reduction in their numbers. It was often now the case that customers with Urgent break-downs had to wait for up to a day for attention and the situation for customers with Non-urgent break-downs also had got worse.

Options for change
The Technical Director (TD) of DP has been investigating the deteriorating standards of customer service. He believes that there are two possible ways forward which he proposed to put to the Board of Directors of DP.

The first would be to invest a considerable amount of resources to improve the existing in-house customer service carried out by DP's service engineers. The other response would be to outsource customer service. The financial data relating to both these options is given below:

Financial implications
In-house
If the customer service is kept in-house, DP will have to spend money recruiting additional engineers and training and equipping all the engineers to a very high standard. In order to meet the service targets of 100% attendance within 60 minutes for Urgent break-downs (which it is estimated will amount to 6,000 each year) and also that up to 2,000 Non-urgent break-downs are resolved each year, DP will employ 75 engineers. The cost of establishing this new service network together with infrastructure, recruitment, training and equipment set-

up costs in the first year only will amount to P$50,000,000. In addition, there would be an annual running cost of P$8,000,000.

Outsource

DP has had a quote from a reputable service company, RSC. RSC would employ 38 service engineers and would charge DP P$250 for each Urgent break-down which it attended and P$150 for each Non-urgent break-down which it attended. It has enough capacity to attend all the break-downs which DP estimates will occur each year. However, it cannot commit to attending 100% of Urgent break-downs within 60 minutes: RSC estimates it will only be able to attend 99% of Urgent break-downs within 60 minutes. The remainder will take between 2 and 4 hours before RSC can get its engineers to the customer.

As a condition of RSC accepting the contract it will require a 'one off' payment of P$30,000,000 when the contract is signed.

Other information

Industry history shows that there is a probability of fatality or serious injury when the response to an Urgent break-down is delayed. In the case of DP, it is estimated that every urgent break-down not attended by a service engineer within 60 minutes carries a 0.1% chance of a fatality or serious injury.

Investments such as the one proposed by the TD are regarded by DP as having an opportunity cost of capital of 10%.

The TD and the Management Accountant (MA)

In their discussions about the outsourcing of the customer service the MA had asked the TD if it was possible to quantify the financial cost of fatality or serious injury caused by the non-attendance of an engineer within 60 minutes to an Urgent break-down. The TD said it was not worth doing this as the chance was so small and he did not want to distract the Board in its decision making with irrelevant data. The MA agreed that the probability of a fatality or serious injury was low but nevertheless as DP aspired to being a good corporate citizen and in the interests of transparency this information should go before the Board.

The TD stated that these forecasts were his, he took responsibility for them and he would not be placing the information about fatality and serious injury before the Board. The TD stated that he would answer any question put to him by the Board but that the MA should concentrate on his own job and let the TD get on with his.

The requirement for Question One is on page 9

Required

(a)

(i) Compare and contrast the rational planning model with the *Incrementalist* approach to strategic planning.

(6 marks)

(ii) Advise the Board of Directors of DP of another approach to forming strategy which would be most suitable for its organisation's changed circumstances as a privatised company.

(4 marks)

(b) *(i)* Analyse the two alternative methods of servicing DP's customers.
Note: All 10 marks are for calculation in this requirement.

(10 marks)

(ii) Discuss the consequences of the two methods of servicing DP's customers.

(5 marks)

(c) Evaluate the extent to which the views of the Technical Director regarding the disclosure of information about non-attendance at Urgent break-downs within 60 minutes represents an ethical dilemma for the Management Accountant.

(10 marks)

(d) In the light of the changed circumstances of DP, and your findings and evaluation above:

(i) recommend, with reasons, four Critical Success Factors (CSFs) which would be appropriate for DP as a company

(8 marks)

(ii) discuss the main attributes for an effective Information System by which DP would be able to manage the Urgent and Non-urgent breakdowns.

(7 marks)

(Total marks for Question One = 50 marks)

End of Section A

Section B starts on page 10

TURN OVER

SECTION B – 50 MARKS

[the indicative time for answering this section is 90 minutes]

ANSWER *TWO* OF THE THREE QUESTIONS – 25 MARKS EACH

Question Two

ZZM is a multinational company which buys agricultural products for use in its manufacturing process. ZZM has committed to observe all guidelines and codes of conduct for multinationals. This policy was prompted by ZZM's desire to be a good corporate citizen.

ZZM has been trading profitably for ten years with farmers' co-operatives in Agriland, an agricultural country. ZZM's business is an important part of Agriland's economy. ZZM has made efforts to improve both the production techniques of the farmers and the living conditions of farm workers and their families. ZZM has built a number of schools and also a district hospital in Agriland.

The farmers' co-operatives have freedom to trade with anyone but have chosen to deal exclusively with ZZM. ZZM has enjoyed harmonious relationships within Agriland but this now seems threatened by a number of factors.

The Government of Agriland has been under the control of the same political party for the previous 15 years. Recently there have been allegations of corruption made against the Government and its popularity has decreased: some analysts think it might lose the next general election. The main opposition party is very nationalistic and opposed to free trade. It has stated that if it is elected it will nationalise all foreign owned businesses without compensation.

The farm workers' union in Agriland has asked for an immediate 10% pay rise as farm workers' pay has not increased for two years although prices have increased by 20%. The farm workers have never been militant but this is changing. In some areas of Agriland, farm workers have gone on strike.

At a recent meeting between the President of Agriland and ZZM, the President said there was a common interest in preventing the main opposition party from winning the next general election. The President suggested a number of strategies which could be followed:

1. ZZM could give a substantial donation to the President's party for its election funds.
2. ZZM could agree to an extra tax on its Agriland operations. This could be used to increase the national minimum wage for farm workers.
3. ZZM could open an agricultural processes factory within Agriland to assist economic development.

The President stated his strategies were not mutually exclusive. He added that if ZZM was not able to help him, then he would seriously consider nationalising ZZM's operations without any compensation.

The requirement for Question Two is on the opposite page

Required

(a) Advise how stakeholder mapping could assist ZZM in deciding the options to pursue with respect to Agriland.

*Note: You are **not** required to draw Mendelow's matrix*

(4 marks)

(b) Construct a stakeholder analysis for ZZM's business in Agriland.

(9 marks)

(c) Evaluate the options suggested by the President and **one** other option which you have identified.

(8 marks)

(d) Recommend the option which you consider ZZM should follow. Explain the reasons(s) for your recommendation.

(4 marks)

(Total for Question Two = 25 marks)

Section B continues over the page

TURN OVER

Question Three

RTF is an architectural practice owned by 3 partners and employing 20 other staff. Its vision has been stated as: 'Your future designed by RTF: Today!' Its business is focused on designing housing schemes for local governments and also individual houses for wealthy clients. The emphasis in the housing schemes has been to produce high-quality homes to standard designs and ensuring that the schemes were completed on time and within budget. RTF has established a library of designs which it has successfully used and which can be re-used. The relationships which RTF has established with local government employees have been important for the successful completion of its contracts. RTF has a corporate contacts database where every local government employee it has dealt with is recorded. This has proved invaluable to RTF.

RTF's other main income stream comes from the design of individual, 'one-off', houses for wealthy clients. The partners have always enjoyed this work as it gives them the opportunity to express their professional talents. However, the recently appointed Management Accountant has concerns about this business as she believes the partners spend a disproportionate amount of their time on this work. One fundamental control system within a professional practice is the system for recording time which forms the basis for costing work. Unlike most of its industry which uses proprietary software, RTF relies upon a manual system for recording time spent on each project and the results are often inaccurate.

The partners have always believed that a staff development policy is important for success. They have invested in improving the educational and technical background of their staff. RTF has a strong relationship with its local university. One result of this relationship is a computerised design package, '2020Design', which RTF and the university jointly developed and own. The package speeds up the design process and offers the possibility of significant cost savings. If this package is applied within RTF it could result in either a greater throughput of work from the existing staff, staff reductions or some combination of both of these.

RTF has carried out market research regarding the potential demand for 2020Design. This research indicates that 2020Design will be a viable commercial product. In what will be a significant strategic and cultural change for RTF it intends to market 2020Design and has employed a Marketing Manager. The Marketing Manager intends to licence agents to sell 2020Design in RTF's home country and abroad.

RTF does not have any systematic way of relating its operations to its vision or of measuring performance. However, one of the partners has heard of the Balanced Scorecard and has suggested that this might be an appropriate model for RTF to use.

Required

(a) Explain the four different perspectives of the Balanced Scorecard model.

(4 marks)

(b) For each of the four perspectives, discuss and recommend two appropriate measures which would assist RTF.

(8 marks)

(c) Recommend how RTF could introduce and use the Balanced Scorecard to help it achieve the required changes in strategy and culture.

(13 marks)

(Total for Question Three = 25 marks)

Section B continues on the opposite page

Question Four

GHK is a restaurant chain consisting of eight restaurants in an attractive part of a European country which is popular with tourists. GHK has been owned by the same family for the previous15 years and has always traded at a profit. However, a number of factors have meant that GHK is now in danger of making a trading loss. There has been a substantial drop in the number of tourists visiting the region whilst, at the same time, the prices of many of the foodstuffs and drinks used in its restaurants has increased. Added to this, the local economy has shrunk with several large employers reducing the size of their workforce.

The owners of GHK commissioned a restaurant consultant to give them an independent view of their business. The consultant observed that the eight restaurants were all very different in appearance. They also served menus that were very different, for example, one restaurant which was located on a barge in a coastal town specialised in fish dishes, whereas another restaurant 20 miles away had a good reputation as a steak house. The prices varied greatly amongst the restaurants; one restaurant in a historic country house offered 'fine dining' and was extremely expensive; yet another located near a busy railway station served mainly fast food and claimed that its prices were 'the cheapest in town'. Three of GHK's restaurants offered a 'middle of the road' dining experience with conventional menus and average prices. Some of the restaurants had licences which enabled them to serve alcohol with their meals but three restaurants did not have such licences. One restaurant had a good trade in children's birthday parties whereas the restaurant in the historic country house did not admit diners under the age of 18.

The consultant recommended that GHK should examine these differences but did not suggest how. The owners responded that the chain had grown organically over a number of years and that the location, style and pricing decisions made in each restaurant had all been made at different times and depended on trends current at that time.

Required

(a) Advise the owners of GHK how the application of Porter's Three Generic Strategies Model could assist them in maintaining or improving the profitability of their restaurants.

Note: You are not required to suggest individual generic strategies for each of GHK's restaurants.

(10 marks)

(b) Advise how GHK could employ a range of organisational information systems to support whichever generic strategy it chooses to adopt.

(15 marks)

(Total for Question Four = 25 marks)

End of Question Paper

Maths Tables and Formulae are on Pages 14 and 15

MATHS TABLES AND FORMULAE

Present value table

Present value of $1, that is $(1 + r)^{-n}$ where r = interest rate; n = number of periods until payment or receipt.

Periods	Interest rates (*r*)									
(*n*)	1%	2%	3%	4%	5%	6%	7%	8%	9%	10%
1	0.990	0.980	0.971	0.962	0.952	0.943	0.935	0.926	0.917	0.909
2	0.980	0.961	0.943	0.925	0.907	0.890	0.873	0.857	0.842	0.826
3	0.971	0.942	0.915	0.889	0.864	0.840	0.816	0.794	0.772	0.751
4	0.961	0.924	0.888	0.855	0.823	0.792	0.763	0.735	0.708	0.683
5	0.951	0.906	0.863	0.822	0.784	0.747	0.713	0.681	0.650	0.621
6	0.942	0.888	0.837	0.790	0.746	0.705	0.666	0.630	0.596	0.564
7	0.933	0.871	0.813	0.760	0.711	0.665	0.623	0.583	0.547	0.513
8	0.923	0.853	0.789	0.731	0.677	0.627	0.582	0.540	0.502	0.467
9	0.914	0.837	0.766	0.703	0.645	0.592	0.544	0.500	0.460	0.424
10	0.905	0.820	0.744	0.676	0.614	0.558	0.508	0.463	0.422	0.386
11	0.896	0.804	0.722	0.650	0.585	0.527	0.475	0.429	0.388	0.350
12	0.887	0.788	0.701	0.625	0.557	0.497	0.444	0.397	0.356	0.319
13	0.879	0.773	0.681	0.601	0.530	0.469	0.415	0.368	0.326	0.290
14	0.870	0.758	0.661	0.577	0.505	0.442	0.388	0.340	0.299	0.263
15	0.861	0.743	0.642	0.555	0.481	0.417	0.362	0.315	0.275	0.239
16	0.853	0.728	0.623	0.534	0.458	0.394	0.339	0.292	0.252	0.218
17	0.844	0.714	0.605	0.513	0.436	0.371	0.317	0.270	0.231	0.198
18	0.836	0.700	0.587	0.494	0.416	0.350	0.296	0.250	0.212	0.180
19	0.828	0.686	0.570	0.475	0.396	0.331	0.277	0.232	0.194	0.164
20	0.820	0.673	0.554	0.456	0.377	0.312	0.258	0.215	0.178	0.149

Periods	Interest rates (*r*)									
(*n*)	11%	12%	13%	14%	15%	16%	17%	18%	19%	20%
1	0.901	0.893	0.885	0.877	0.870	0.862	0.855	0.847	0.840	0.833
2	0.812	0.797	0.783	0.769	0.756	0.743	0.731	0.718	0.706	0.694
3	0.731	0.712	0.693	0.675	0.658	0.641	0.624	0.609	0.593	0.579
4	0.659	0.636	0.613	0.592	0.572	0.552	0.534	0.516	0.499	0.482
5	0.593	0.567	0.543	0.519	0.497	0.476	0.456	0.437	0.419	0.402
6	0.535	0.507	0.480	0.456	0.432	0.410	0.390	0.370	0.352	0.335
7	0.482	0.452	0.425	0.400	0.376	0.354	0.333	0.314	0.296	0.279
8	0.434	0.404	0.376	0.351	0.327	0.305	0.285	0.266	0.249	0.233
9	0.391	0.361	0.333	0.308	0.284	0.263	0.243	0.225	0.209	0.194
10	0.352	0.322	0.295	0.270	0.247	0.227	0.208	0.191	0.176	0.162
11	0.317	0.287	0.261	0.237	0.215	0.195	0.178	0.162	0.148	0.135
12	0.286	0.257	0.231	0.208	0.187	0.168	0.152	0.137	0.124	0.112
13	0.258	0.229	0.204	0.182	0.163	0.145	0.130	0.116	0.104	0.093
14	0.232	0.205	0.181	0.160	0.141	0.125	0.111	0.099	0.088	0.078
15	0.209	0.183	0.160	0.140	0.123	0.108	0.095	0.084	0.079	0.065
16	0.188	0.163	0.141	0.123	0.107	0.093	0.081	0.071	0.062	0.054
17	0.170	0.146	0.125	0.108	0.093	0.080	0.069	0.060	0.052	0.045
18	0.153	0.130	0.111	0.095	0.081	0.069	0.059	0.051	0.044	0.038
19	0.138	0.116	0.098	0.083	0.070	0.060	0.051	0.043	0.037	0.031
20	0.124	0.104	0.087	0.073	0.061	0.051	0.043	0.037	0.031	0.026

Cumulative present value of $1 per annum, Receivable or Payable at the end of each year for *n* years

$$\frac{1-(1+r)^{-n}}{r}$$

Periods (*n*)	Interest rates (*r*)									
	1%	2%	3%	4%	5%	6%	7%	8%	9%	10%
1	0.990	0.980	0.971	0.962	0.952	0.943	0.935	0.926	0.917	0.909
2	1.970	1.942	1.913	1.886	1.859	1.833	1.808	1.783	1.759	1.736
3	2.941	2.884	2.829	2.775	2.723	2.673	2.624	2.577	2.531	2.487
4	3.902	3.808	3.717	3.630	3.546	3.465	3.387	3.312	3.240	3.170
5	4.853	4.713	4.580	4.452	4.329	4.212	4.100	3.993	3.890	3.791
6	5.795	5.601	5.417	5.242	5.076	4.917	4.767	4.623	4.486	4.355
7	6.728	6.472	6.230	6.002	5.786	5.582	5.389	5.206	5.033	4.868
8	7.652	7.325	7.020	6.733	6.463	6.210	5.971	5.747	5.535	5.335
9	8.566	8.162	7.786	7.435	7.108	6.802	6.515	6.247	5.995	5.759
10	9.471	8.983	8.530	8.111	7.722	7.360	7.024	6.710	6.418	6.145
11	10.368	9.787	9.253	8.760	8.306	7.887	7.499	7.139	6.805	6.495
12	11.255	10.575	9.954	9.385	8.863	8.384	7.943	7.536	7.161	6.814
13	12.134	11.348	10.635	9.986	9.394	8.853	8.358	7.904	7.487	7.103
14	13.004	12.106	11.296	10.563	9.899	9.295	8.745	8.244	7.786	7.367
15	13.865	12.849	11.938	11.118	10.380	9.712	9.108	8.559	8.061	7.606
16	14.718	13.578	12.561	11.652	10.838	10.106	9.447	8.851	8.313	7.824
17	15.562	14.292	13.166	12.166	11.274	10.477	9.763	9.122	8.544	8.022
18	16.398	14.992	13.754	12.659	11.690	10.828	10.059	9.372	8.756	8.201
19	17.226	15.679	14.324	13.134	12.085	11.158	10.336	9.604	8.950	8.365
20	18.046	16.351	14.878	13.590	12.462	11.470	10.594	9.818	9.129	8.514

Periods (*n*)	Interest rates (*r*)									
	11%	12%	13%	14%	15%	16%	17%	18%	19%	20%
1	0.901	0.893	0.885	0.877	0.870	0.862	0.855	0.847	0.840	0.833
2	1.713	1.690	1.668	1.647	1.626	1.605	1.585	1.566	1.547	1.528
3	2.444	2.402	2.361	2.322	2.283	2.246	2.210	2.174	2.140	2.106
4	3.102	3.037	2.974	2.914	2.855	2.798	2.743	2.690	2.639	2.589
5	3.696	3.605	3.517	3.433	3.352	3.274	3.199	3.127	3.058	2.991
6	4.231	4.111	3.998	3.889	3.784	3.685	3.589	3.498	3.410	3.326
7	4.712	4.564	4.423	4.288	4.160	4.039	3.922	3.812	3.706	3.605
8	5.146	4.968	4.799	4.639	4.487	4.344	4.207	4.078	3.954	3.837
9	5.537	5.328	5.132	4.946	4.772	4.607	4.451	4.303	4.163	4.031
10	5.889	5.650	5.426	5.216	5.019	4.833	4.659	4.494	4.339	4.192
11	6.207	5.938	5.687	5.453	5.234	5.029	4.836	4.656	4.486	4.327
12	6.492	6.194	5.918	5.660	5.421	5.197	4.988	7.793	4.611	4.439
13	6.750	6.424	6.122	5.842	5.583	5.342	5.118	4.910	4.715	4.533
14	6.982	6.628	6.302	6.002	5.724	5.468	5.229	5.008	4.802	4.611
15	7.191	6.811	6.462	6.142	5.847	5.575	5.324	5.092	4.876	4.675
16	7.379	6.974	6.604	6.265	5.954	5.668	5.405	5.162	4.938	4.730
17	7.549	7.120	6.729	6.373	6.047	5.749	5.475	5.222	4.990	4.775
18	7.702	7.250	6.840	6.467	6.128	5.818	5.534	5.273	5.033	4.812
19	7.839	7.366	6.938	6.550	6.198	5.877	5.584	5.316	5.070	4.843
20	7.963	7.469	7.025	6.623	6.259	5.929	5.628	5.353	5.101	4.870

Formulae

Annuity

Present value of an annuity of $1 per annum, receivable or payable for *n* years, commencing in one year, discounted at *r*% per annum:

$$PV = \frac{1}{r}\left[1 - \frac{1}{[1+r]^{n}}\right]$$

Perpetuity

Present value of $1 per annum, payable or receivable in perpetuity, commencing in one year, discounted at *r*% per annum:

$$PV = \frac{1}{r}$$

LIST OF VERBS USED IN THE QUESTION REQUIREMENTS

A list of the learning objectives and verbs that appear in the syllabus and in the question requirements for each question in this paper.

It is important that you answer the question according to the definition of the verb.

LEARNING OBJECTIVE	VERBS USED	DEFINITION
Level 1 - KNOWLEDGE What you are expected to know.	List	Make a list of
	State	Express, fully or clearly, the details/facts of
	Define	Give the exact meaning of
Level 2 - COMPREHENSION What you are expected to understand.	Describe	Communicate the key features
	Distinguish	Highlight the differences between
	Explain	Make clear or intelligible/State the meaning or purpose of
	Identify	Recognise, establish or select after consideration
	Illustrate	Use an example to describe or explain something
Level 3 - APPLICATION How you are expected to apply your knowledge.	Apply	Put to practical use
	Calculate/compute	Ascertain or reckon mathematically
	Demonstrate	Prove with certainty or to exhibit by practical means
	Prepare	Make or get ready for use
	Reconcile	Make or prove consistent/compatible
	Solve	Find an answer to
	Tabulate	Arrange in a table
Level 4 - ANALYSIS How are you expected to analyse the detail of what you have learned.	Analyse	Examine in detail the structure of
	Categorise	Place into a defined class or division
	Compare and contrast	Show the similarities and/or differences between
	Construct	Build up or compile
	Discuss	Examine in detail by argument
	Interpret	Translate into intelligible or familiar terms
	Prioritise	Place in order of priority or sequence for action
	Produce	Create or bring into existence
Level 5 - EVALUATION How are you expected to use your learning to evaluate, make decisions or recommendations.	Advise	Counsel, inform or notify
	Evaluate	Appraise or assess the value of
	Recommend	Advise on a course of action

Enterprise Pillar

Strategic Level Paper

E3 – Enterprise Strategy

Specimen Paper

Tuesday Morning Session

The Examiner's Answers – Specimen Paper E3 - Enterprise Strategy

SECTION A

Answer to Question One

Requirement (a)(i)

The rational planning model (RPM) is arguably the model most associated with the formation of strategy. CIMA has defined aspects of this model in the following ways:

'*Planning*: the establishment of objectives and the formulation, evaluation and selection of the policies, strategies, tactics and action required to achieve them. Planning comprises long-term strategic planning, and short-term/operational planning.'

'*Strategy*: a course of action, including the specification of resources required, to achieve a specific objective.'

'*Strategic plan*: a statement of long-term goals along with a definition of the strategies and policies which will ensure achievement of these goals.'

RPM has the advantage of being well-known and it offers a procedure to enable organisations to construct their strategies which articulate the organisation's desired relationships with its external environments. Added to this, the rational planning model when viewed at its short-term perspective has an obvious interface with accounting constructs such as annual accounts and budgets.

The use of RPM is often a requirement for organisations receiving funds from central government such as hospitals and universities who are asked to produce, for example, one year and five year plans.

RPM has as an underlying tenet the concept of maximization derived from classical economic theory. In contrast, H Simon suggested that managers were more likely to pursue satisfactory goals: that they were 'satisficers'. This is associated with the idea of incrementalism: making small and slow changes to strategy rather than radical changes, 'Evolution not Revolution'. Quinn described the process of logical incrementalism whereby strategy is made not by planning but rather by gradual discrete changes allied to an underlying logic.

The two approaches represent different philosophies regarding the formation of strategy. Arguably, there is no right way of formulating strategy; what is most suitable for an organisation is contingent upon its individual circumstances.

Other approaches which have been observed in practice include, Mintzberg's 'crafting' strategy and the antithesis of planning, 'freewheeling opportunism'.

Requirement (a)(ii)

In the circumstances of DP having newly emerged from state control it is most likely that RPM is the most familiar approach for them. If the contention that there is no right way of approaching strategy is valid DP could continue with its RPM but adapt it and make it more flexible by admitting the emergent. Thus, for example, it might shorten its planning period and be willing to continuously monitor and change its strategy, if that should prove beneficial.

Requirement (b)(i)

Option 1 *In-house*		**P$'000s**	**Option 2** *Outsource*		**P$'000s**	
Capital cost		**50,000**	Capital cost		**30,000**	
Yearly running cost		**8,000**	Yearly running cost			
Urgent visits	6,000		Urgent visits	6,000	1,500	P$250 a visit
Non-urgent visits	2,000		Non-urgent visits	2,000	300	P$150 a visit
			Yearly running cost		**1,800**	
No. of engineers	75		No. of engineers	38		
Service standard			**Service standard**			
Urgent	100%		Urgent	99%		
Non-urgent	Within 1 month		Non-urgent	ASAP		
10 year period			10 year period			
Year	**P$'000s**	**P$'000s**	**Year**	**P$'000s**	**P$'000s**	
0		-50,000	0		-30,000	
1 to 10	8,000		1 to 10	1,800		
Annuity factor 10 years/10%	6.145	-49,160		6.145	-11,061	
Total		**-99,160**			**-41,061**	

Requirement (b)(ii)

The financial aspect of this decision indicates the adoption of outsourcing which is only 41% of the cost of the in-house operation. However, the service attainment projected for this option is inferior to that of the in-house: only 99% of the Urgent break-downs are attended to within 60 minutes and it is not clear when the Non-urgent break-downs will be attended to. This lower standard of customer service is, presumably, a result of employing only half the number of service engineers as compared to the in-house option.

The lower customer service standard also carries a small but arguably significant risk of a fatality or serious injury due to non-attendance within 60 minutes:

6,000 break-downs x 1% = 60 breakdowns not attended to within 60 minutes
60 break-downs x 0.1% = 0.6 fatalities or serious injury.

The consequence in terms of human life of this lower service standard is that 0.6 or 1 person could die each year. This could have serious financial consequences for DP and the image of the company would be dámaged if it was known that it had implemented a service policy with this attendant risk of fatality and serious injury.

It is also possible that this risk may conflict with corporate values and it would certainly conflict with the personal values of some of the employees of DP, for example, its service engineers.

Requirement (c)

The Chartered Institute of Management Accountants (CIMA) has adopted a Code of Ethics (hereafter the Code) to give guidance to its members with regard to their behaviour.

CIMA has established fundamental principles of professional ethics for professional accountants which include:

Integrity 'A professional accountant should be straightforward and honest in all professional and business relationships'.

CIMA further state that 'A professional accountant should not be associated with reports etc. where they believe that the information:

Omits or obscures information required to be included where such omission or obscurity would be misleading'.

It is arguable that not telling the Board of Directors of DP about all the consequences of the out-sourcing service option, namely the likelihood of a fatality or serious injury conflicts with corporate and ethical values and is not behaviour that is 'straightforward and honest'.

Objectivity 'A professional accountant should not allow bias, conflict of interest or undue influence of others to override professional or business judgements'.

The principle of objectivity imposes an obligation on all professional accountants not to compromise their professional or business judgement because of bias, conflict of interest or the undue influence of others.'

It is arguable that the Technical Director is using his position and personality to keep the Management Accountant silent, on the aspect of safety, which is a conflict under the Code.

The situation in which the Management Accountant is in with regards to the non-disclosure of the information about a potential fatality or serious injury should the out-sourcing service option be followed is potentially in conflict with two of the fundamental principles of the Code.

As such the Management Accountant has an ethical dilemma to resolve and should seek further guidance from the Code as to how to proceed.

All the quotations in this section are from the CIMA Code of Ethics for Professional Accountants, October 2007.

Requirement (d)(i)

CIMA defines Critical Success Factors (CSFs) as: 'CSFs are elements of the organisational activity which are central to its future success. CSFs may change over time and may include items such as product quality, employee attitudes, manufacturing flexibility and brand awareness'.

Product quality
DP's product is electricity and its supply should be fit for purpose. This implies continuity of supply and that means that DP must work to ensure that power fluctuations and interruptions are kept to a minimum. DP would need to specify CSFs to monitor these aspects which would be amenable to ratio analysis and also variance analysis. Examples would be :

- % number of minutes supply was interrupted
- Cost of interruptions in penalty payments

Employee attitudes
DP's employees have undergone a significant change in their working lives due to change in ownership structure. This change from nationalised industry to private sector company has many cultural implications. These changes will have impacted upon employee morale and DP would be concerned whether the changes have had beneficial or detrimental effects.

Examples of CSFs in this area would include:

- Employee turnover
- Absenteeism

Manufacturing flexibility
Not discussed as it would require specialist knowledge of the electricity distribution industry.

Brand awareness
In a free market environment and given that electricity is an homogenous product, from the point of view of the customer, it is comparatively easy for customers to change their suppliers. Suppliers will try to reduce the rate at which customers move between them, the churn rate, by offering loyalty incentives and by competing on price.

A further competitive option which is available to producers of homogenous products is to try to establish some form of brand identity. An example of this in the UK is the energy company E.ON which sponsors a major English sporting competition, the FA Cup.

DP could establish CSFs such as:

- % of market aware of the DP brand
- Number of customers moving to DP in the previous period
- Number of customers moving from DP in the previous period

Note: The CSFs given in this section are examples and not an exhaustive list. Candidates would also be rewarded for other appropriate examples.

Requirement (d)(ii)

DP needs to manage breakdowns which have important implications for customer service and safety. Whatever system it employs it must have the characteristics of being robust, flexible and comprehensive.

An essential element of such a system is a database with its allied database management system. The database should hold, and allow access to, for example, details of all of DP's customers including their service histories, geographic and contact details. The database should also include, for bigger/industrial customers, layout plans of their electrical equipment and have the ability to access and transmit to the service engineers fault-finding information and manufacturers' drawings and information.

The service engineers would need to be equipped with wireless computers which could communicate with the database whilst the service engineer is attending a break-down and provision should be made for alternate communication in areas of poor wireless reception. They will also require a suitable GPS device to assist in locating the break-downs.

The information system should also incorporate software to identify where each service engineer is located and their current status. The software should also incorporate algorithms to optimise the responses of the service engineers to break-downs.

SECTION B

Answer to Question Two

Requirement (a)

A stakeholder analysis for ZZM's operations within Agriland would enable ZZM to identify the degree of interest and power possessed by each group or stakeholder. As an example, consider both the President of Agriland and a farm worker in one of the co-operatives. Both have an interest in ZZM's business but that of the President is very great whilst the farm workers' is much smaller. Similarly, the power to affect ZZM's business is very high in the case of the President but would be negligible in the case of the farm workers.

Having identified the stakeholders, it would be clear to ZZM whose support it will need in order to be successful. It will also identify any stakeholders who may have the power or potential power to disrupt its business.

Having categorised the stakeholders, ZZM then has guidance as to how it should manage these and their expectations in the future. Mendelow's suggested stances are:

- Minimal effort
- Keep informed
- Keep satisfied
- Must secure agreement

Requirement (b)

Using Mendelow's model the following stakeholders are present for ZZM's operations within Agriland:

High power/High interest
These would include the President of Agriland and also the Government of the country. The main opposition party has the potential to also be included in this category. However, unless and until it wins the general election it does not possess high power. The farmworkers' union is in a similar position to the main opposition party as its power seems low at present but could grow with increased militancy.

High power/low interest
ZZM's shareholders have ultimate power over the company should they choose to exercise it. However, as Agriland represents only one of the many countries where ZZM does business the shareholders are unlikely to have a high level of interest in it.

Low power/High interest
The main opposition party and the farmworkers' union both have high levels of interest in ZZM's business but, at present, have little power.

Other groups
The farmers' co-operatives, the farmers and the farmworkers and their families would all probably have interests ranging from medium to high. The amount of power which they possess is not clear. It could range at its highest for the co-operatives if they were to take combined action with respect to ZZM, to low to non-existent in the case of an individual member of a farmworker's family.

Low power/low interest
There are no groups mentioned in the scenario which fall into this category.

Requirement (c)

ZZM could give a substantial donation to the President's party for its election funds.

Given the concerns about corruption this option seems questionable and it may conflict with the codes of conduct which ZZM supports. It would create a definite association between ZZM and the President so that, if the President did not win the election, it could prove very difficult for ZZM to carry on business within Agriland. However, if the main opposition party wins the election ZZM will be nationalised without compensation.

ZZM could agree to an extra tax on its Agriland operations. This could be used to increase the national minimum wage for farmworkers.

The effect of this tax may make ZZM's business in Agriland uneconomic. Although ZZM is an important part of Agriland's economy, it does not directly employ the agricultural workers. ZZM may consider that this proposal is unreasonable and, if agreed to, may create a bad precedent both within Agriland and also in other countries where ZZM trades.

ZZM should open an agricultural processes factory within Agriland to assist economic development.

The economic viability of this proposal needs to be examined. It could prove to be a realistic option and the contribution which it makes to the development of the economy of Agriland is important.

The President stated that his strategies were not mutually exclusive. He added that if ZZM was not able to help him then he would seriously consider nationalising ZZM operations without any compensation.

Of the three options proposed by the President only the last one seems to be potentially acceptable. The President's further comments suggest that he may be requiring that ZZM agrees to all three proposals and he has also threatened ZZM with nationalisation without compensation.

Taken as a whole, the President's views could lead ZZM to a strategy of its own; withdrawal from Agriland. This would have the disadvantages of the loss of profits from the business in Agriland and the effects upon the economy and people of Agriland. However, depending upon the results of the next general election, or even earlier depending upon the President's actions, ZZM may lose its business anyway.

Requirement (d)

It is not obvious which option ZZM should follow. It will depend upon a number of factors, including an assessment of the likely results of the next general election and also how much the President's suggestions represent a bargaining stance and how much they are definite plans. ZZM also needs to evaluate changes in social conditions; the rise in militancy within the farmworkers and the climate of corruption within Agriland. ZZM should also always have the interests of its shareholders in mind. Against these factors must be set the damage which will be incurred to ZZM's profits and also to the people and economy of Agriland should ZZM withdraw. Based on current information it is recommended that ZZM prepares to withdraw from doing business in Agriland.

Answer to Question Three

Requirement (a)

The Balanced Scorecard model was developed by Kaplan and Norton (1992, 1996) as a means to integrate an organisation's vision, strategy and operations. It is a multi-dimensional model which contains four perspectives which embrace both financial and non-financial control measures.

The four perspectives are:

Financial: where the question posed is 'To succeed financially how should we appear to our shareholders?'

Customer: similarly asks, 'To achieve our vision how should we appear to our customers?'

Learning and growth: demands, 'To achieve our vision, how will we sustain our ability to change and improve?'

Internal business process: asks, 'To satisfy our shareholders and customers, what business processes must we excel at?'

The inclusion of the organisation's vision is central to the model.

Requirement (b)

The following are sample measures which would be appropriate for RTF to use within the Balanced Scorecard model.

Financial measures:
Gross profit: it is expected that RTF already calculates this but it is an important measure which should be reported upon regularly.

Net profit: the same comment applies as for gross profit.

Profit per contract: as RTF undertakes a variety of work it should be able to identify the profitability of each of these aspects.

Return on Capital employed: an important and well-known measure which captures the totality of the business.

Customer measures:
Number of new customers in period: it is important for RTF, as with any company, that it continues to attract new business.

Number of customer complaints: this measure gives an indication of the quality of the work produced by RTF.

Amount of repeat business: RTF has built up relationships with local government and also spends time and money maintaining its corporate contacts database. This measure will give an indication if this effort is worthwhile.

Market share: RTF operates in a competitive market and needs to know the size of its market share and the trend in its growth or decline.

Learning and growth measures:
Number of academic and professional qualifications possessed by staff: in what is essentially a knowledge and craft industry, it is important that RTF maintains a high level of academic and professional ability within its personnel.

Number of technical qualifications possessed by staff: this measure demonstrates the level of technical expertise possessed by the business.

Number of new designs added to library: this measure indicates directly one aspect of RTF's creativity.

Number of 'one-off' houses designed in period: these houses give opportunity for RTF to express their creativity. This measure indicates the degree of innovation within the business.

Internal business process measures:
Average design time spent per contract: it is important that the time of the business's staff is used efficiently. This measure gives an indication of staff efficiency.

Time spent each week by partner on design work: it is important to utilise the design skills of the partners to best advantage.

Number of contacts in corporate database: relationships are important in this business and this measure shows how extensive these relationships are.

Number of contacts added to database in period: this measure supplements the one immediately above and it shows the rate at which the corporate contracts are growing.

Requirement (c)

The use of the Balanced Scorecard is a departure from RTF's previous practice. It will now have a systematic way of reporting on its performance from four different perspectives which are linked to the achievement of its vision. It is also going to be transformed from a purely architectural practice to one that has a valuable commercial computerised design package to market and sell. Furthermore, it will be bringing people into the business that may not necessarily have a background in architecture.

Although there is not a single right way to help RTF successfully make the transition, a number of elements can be identified which are important:

Translating the vision
Vision is at the centre of the Balanced Scorecard. With the developments that are taking place within the company it may be that the vision, 'Your future designed by RTF: Today!' should be re-negotiated. There needs to be an opportunity for this to be discussed and for a consensus to be formed within RTF about what their vision should be. The implications of the (new) vision need to be understood by all the participants in the business.

Communication and linkage
An important part of the cultural change introduced by the Balance Scorecard is the system of performance management which has not existed within RTF previously. The essence of the Balanced Scorecard is one of integration of vision with strategy and operations. Therefore, the aspirations of the vision should find expression in both departmental and individual objectives. Some organisations have associated the achievement of these objectivises with reward systems and introduced performance related pay. RTF would have to evaluate if performance related pay is appropriate for the type of work carried out by its staff.

Business planning
RTF now has the opportunity to develop a business plan, or plans, which should be integrated with the staffs' individual plans as well as the departmental ones. The Marketing Manager will have an important role in identifying the potential sales for the 2020Design package

Change and learning
There is going to be a period of change and learning for RTF as it adjusts to the development and implementation of the Balanced Scorecard and also to its new commercial venture the 2020Design package. RTF should actively encourage its staff to embrace this opportunity for learning. There may also be an opportunity to involve stakeholders outside the business, such as customers and suppliers, who are in a good position to offer feedback.

Answer to Question Four

Requirement (a)

Porter's 'Three Generic Strategies Model' was developed in 1980 and since then has gained international dissemination. The model analyses how firms can achieve competitive advantage which Porter suggests can come about by adopting one of the following policies:

Overall cost leadership: the firm is the lowest cost producer relative to its competitors.

Differentiation: the firm can create something which is unique and for which consumers will pay a premium.

Focus: the firm serves a narrow strategic target more effectively than its competitors who are competing more broadly.

Porter asserts that each generic strategy requires different attributes and, therefore, it is unlikely that any firm can pursue more than one generic strategy simultaneously and be successful. He cautions against firms becoming 'stuck in the middle'.

As well as Porter's model being used analytically, it can also be used pro-actively to help a firm design its competitive strategy. In the case of GHK no coherent strategy has been followed with respect to its eight restaurants. A preliminary analysis suggests that the following strategies are being followed:

Overall cost leadership: (the firm is the lowest cost producer relative to its competitors), at the restaurant near the busy railway station.

Differentiation: (the firm can create something which is unique and for which consumers will pay a premium) at the 'fine dining' restaurant in the historic country house.

Focus: (the firm serves a narrow strategic target more effectively than its competitors who are competing more broadly) at the fish restaurant, the steak restaurant, the restaurant offering children's birthday parties.

Stuck in the middle: three 'middle of the road' restaurants with conventional menus and average prices.

The generic strategy which GHK decides to follow will be linked to a marketing strategy. It is not necessarily the case that GHK is wrong to follow a number of generic strategies because if each restaurant is taken as a strategic business unit it will have a particular catchment area from which it draws its customers and looked at in isolation that strategy might be the optimal one for that restaurant. However, a systematic examination of each restaurant using the logic of Porter's model and examining the basis by which that restaurant competes and whether this will yield a long-term competitive advantage will be invaluable.

With respect to the restaurant near the busy railway station, if this is attempting to compete on the basis of being the lowest cost producer and, therefore, charging its customers the lowest prices, it is doubtful that this can give a long-term competitive advantage. The prices of a restaurant's inputs, mainly food and labour, are set within their local markets and available to any competitor. The technology and processes of restaurants are mature ones and it is unlikely that GHK could innovate in this area to secure competitive advantage.

The three restaurants which are 'stuck in the middle' should be given immediate attention as Porter's model suggests they are unlikely to be successful.

If the owners of GHK use Porter's 'Three Generic Strategies Model' it will give them an appreciation of the basis upon which their various restaurants compete and should prompt them to make modifications to their strategy and attempt to secure long-term competitive advantage.

It may be the case that GHK treat each of its restaurants as a strategic business unit and, therefore, employ a number of different generic competitive strategies. Alternatively, GHK may wish to trade as a homogenous entity which would imply it would use only one of the three generic competitive strategies to avoid being 'stuck in the middle'.

Requirement (b)

Information systems could support GHK's chosen strategy in the following ways:

Strategic
In order to decide which of the generic strategies would be appropriate, GHK will require information to construct a PEST analysis. It will need detailed market and demographic information, for example, to decide whether a particular restaurant has access to a hinterland of customers who are willing to pay a premium price. This would then indicate the suitability of a differentiation strategy. Marketing research could then indicate the type of differentiation for which these customers are willing to pay a premium. It could be the case that the differentiation strategy would be suitable not only for the restaurant in the historic country house but also for the fish and the steak restaurants. Statistics of market share would demonstrate GHK comparative position. The degree of success of the strategy it was following would be monitored by periodic reporting of market share.

GHK owners could utilise an executive information system to help them in their decision-making. Inputs to this system would include both their own researches and data and also data from specialist external databases.

If GHK wanted to pursue a strategy of overall cost leadership (although the answer in *(a)* suggests that this is unlikely to be successful) an information system which tracked market prices for restaurant supplies would be required.

GHK could use information systems to help it determine the most appropriate generic competitive strategy for its business. However, it should also recognise that the information systems which it chooses to deploy can, of itself, be a source of competitive advantage for its business. An example of this could be that GHK, through its PEST and market research, may identify profitable groups of customers whose needs are not being met at present, such as vegans. GHK may be able to construct a website offering a booking service for restaurants in its regions and link this with an affinity or loyalty card. This would then generate valuable current data about the restaurant which GHK could incorporate in its strategic review processes.

Operational
At the operational level there is much that good information systems and management accountancy can contribute to a successful generic strategy for GHK. Porter's 'Three Generic strategies model' is essentially about achieving and maintaining competitive advantage: that is out-performing its rivals. For its basic requirements GHK would require a comprehensive database, allied to a system for capturing real-time operational data, and a reporting package.

Given these requirements, GHK could address such important parameters as its capacity utilisation. The management accountant using real-time information could provide timely information about the number of customers served each day. This information could be further analysed to reveal variations in demand by both day and time: Which day are we busiest? What time of day is the quietest? Such analysis could be presented in management accounting reports and would assist in decisions such as: At what times should the restaurants be open? Is it worth opening every day of the week?

The restaurants could also equip its waiters with PDA's (Personal Digital Assistants)to record orders and 'Smart-tills' to record and analyse its sales receipts. At the operational level GHK could use proprietary industry software to cost and plan its menus. These functions could be integrated to order ingredients and monitor stock levels. This information allied to the real-time information about orders and sales would enable real-time profitability information to be generated by the management accountant.

The results emanating from the operational level would indicate the degree of success of the generic strategy. It would also indicate either the continuance of that strategy or could suggest that it was time for a strategic review and a possible change of strategy.

Index

Index

Index

Index

barclays membership no - 201070084292